ADVANCE PRAISE FOR

Seven Going on Seventeen

"Just when we thought everything had been written about tween girls, Claudia Mitchell and Jacqueline Reid-Walsh prove us wrong with a stunning collection brimming with accessible and original interpretations of early puberty, popularity, hair, girls' magazines, Hello Kitty, and more. Not all is pink and perky in the globalized network of tween markets and discourses, according to the international contributors. The chapters also offer a useful range of methodological approaches to studying and analyzing tween girls."

Nancy Lesko, Teachers College, Columbia University

Seven Going on Seventeen

Studies in the
Postmodern Theory of Education

Joe L. Kincheloe and Shirley R. Steinberg
General Editors

Vol. 245

PETER LANG
New York • Washington, D.C./Baltimore • Bern
Frankfurt am Main • Berlin • Brussels • Vienna • Oxford

Seven Going on Seventeen

Tween Studies
in the Culture of Girlhood

Claudia Mitchell &
Jacqueline Reid-Walsh, EDITORS

PETER LANG
New York • Washington, D.C./Baltimore • Bern
Frankfurt am Main • Berlin • Brussels • Vienna • Oxford

Library of Congress Cataloging-in-Publication Data

Seven going on seventeen: tween studies in the culture of girlhood /
edited by Claudia Mitchell, Jacqueline Reid-Walsh.
p. cm. — (Counterpoints; v. 245)
Includes bibliographical references and index.
1. Girls—Social conditions. I. Mitchell, Claudia. II. Reid-Walsh, Jacqueline.
III. Series: Counterpoints (New York, N.Y.); v. 245.
HQ777.S43   305.23'082—dc22   2004022766
ISBN 978-0-8204-6771-9
ISSN 1058-1634

Bibliographic information published by **Die Deutsche Bibliothek**.
Die Deutsche Bibliothek lists this publication in the "Deutsche
Nationalbibliografie"; detailed bibliographic data is available
on the Internet at http://dnb.ddb.de/.

Cover design by Lisa Barfield
Cover photo by Guillaume Simoneau (www.7578.com)

The paper in this book meets the guidelines for permanence and durability
of the Committee on Production Guidelines for Book Longevity
of the Council of Library Resources.

Claudia Mitchell: To Ann, for your love, support, and commitment to asking questions and finding answers.

Jacqueline Reid-Walsh: To my daughter Krista, a former tween, and both a girl and a young woman.

CONTENTS

ILLUSTRATIONS

TABLES

ACKNOWLEDGMENTS

We start with acknowledging the support of the Research Grants Office of the University of KwaZulu-Natal in Durban, South Africa, and funds from two grants within the Social Sciences and Humanities Research Council of Canada: 'Digital Girls: From Play to Policy' and 'Sick of AIDS' for assistance in completing this book.

Beyond financial support, there are many people to acknowledge in a book that has so many contributors and from so many different locations, both geographic and academic. The diverse perspectives presented here offer a unique look into the 'new girl on the block' of Girlhood Studies, the tween girl, and we thank each of the contributors for their commitment to this project.

We particularly wish to thank Noreen Marshall, Curator of Dress and Nursery Collection Museum of Childhood, London, England, for her most illuminating tour of three-dimensional and paper dolls.

For inspiration, we would also like to acknowledge Sandra Weber of Concordia University for her on-going interest in the study of girlhood, and in particular, her enthusiastic support for working with tween girls as co-researchers. While the book is about the study of young girls—with Rebecca, Sarah, and Dorian Mitchell, and Krista Walsh as 'forever girls' in our lives, we would like to acknowledge the inspiration of some 'new boys on the block', too, whose presence offers new insights within gender studies more generally: Jakob and Devon Peterli, and Kieran and Dylan Smith.

We wish to acknowledge the work of Kathleen Pithouse of the University of KwaZulu-Natal for her editorial assistance. Her conscientious care and dedication, her skills as an editor, and her commitment to following up with authors across four continents have been remarkable and without her this book would still be somewhere in cyber space! Finally thanks to Shannon Walsh for assistance in the final editing and indexing.

CHAPTER ONE

Theorizing Tween Culture Within Girlhood Studies

Claudia Mitchell
Jacqueline Reid-Walsh

New Girl on the Block

A few years ago we published an article called "And I Want to Thank You Barbie" (Mitchell and Reid-Walsh 1997), where we acknowledge Barbie's contribution to theorizing girlhood. We examined Barbie as a cultural site in her own right, one that allows an interrogation of the social positioning of girls and former girls in western popular culture. Our approach consisted of conceptualizing her as a cumulative cultural text in order to refer to both the intergenerational and intertextual features of the extended text of Barbie. We examined various manifestations in addition to the three-dimensional artifacts such as trading cards, comic books, and a board game called "We Girls Can Do Anything." In so doing, we explored issues ranging from the history of devaluing of girls' pleasures, to the covering over of girlhood play, to moral panics around girls and sexuality, to highlighting the need for ethnographies of girls' play. Since Barbie is a site of changing and accumulating contradictory meanings, we argued, she is a perfect vehicle with which to interrogate the basic premises underlying societal assumptions about girls and women. She is a contradictory emblem of plenitude yet absence, ironically, an icon of excess to the degree she almost becomes an empty container to be filled at will by the player or commentator. Barbie, we contended not only 'has it all' but does it all—and for this we thanked Mattel!

In this volume, we present a range of chapters demonstrating that constructions of pre-adolescent girls as a niche market called 'tweens' function in a similar way. Thanks to the appearance of the 'new girl on the block' of niche marketing, young girls (as opposed to female children or adolescent girls) suddenly have a currency all of their own, and there is now no shortage of public data on the dollar figure attached to the purchasing power of nine- to thirteen-year-old girls to consume clothing, hair products, CDs, tickets to rock concerts, and so on. For our purposes, though, the media coverage around girls of this age has helped to draw attention to the specificity of pre-adolescent girls within the emerging area of girlhood studies and to create a way to break down the amorphousness of a conception of girlhood that now seems to stretch from birth to the late 20s. Much research within the burgeoning area of girlhood studies though has tended to focus on adolescent girls and even on the 'grrrrrrrrrrrrrrrls' on the other edge of adolescence (17/18 to 25) but has had relatively little to say about the ways so many of the texts analyzed within adolescent culture are in fact marketed covertly as well as quite blatantly towards the under-tens.

Where and who are pre-adolescent girls? Marketers know where they are, but when we sent out a call for proposals about this age group, many scholars who we knew to be studying girlhood admitted that they hadn't actually looked at this category. Ironically, there appears to be almost an invisibility of younger girls in girl studies, something we also observed when we have attended conferences that have been specifically on girlhood![1]

Tween Artifacts

When we first thought of a book, about tween girls, our intention was to focus primarily on the media texts that are targeted to eight-, nine-, and ten-year-old girls, with the idea that not that much is known about how contemporary girls consume teen fashion magazines, *Nancy Drew* mysteries, *Babysitter's Club* fiction, *Archie* comics, Britney Spears CDs, music videos, and so on. However, in the interval between the call for papers and the submissions, tween culture has been growing at a rapid pace, almost exponentially it seems, in terms of tween artifacts. New dolls, such as My Scene, Flava, Bratz, clothing (Bratz clothes; Hilary Duff fashion, thong underwear for girls), films about young adolescent girl culture such as those featuring the Olsen twins, and novels that could be called 'junior chick lit' such as those by Meg Cabot, but particularly by British authors such as Cathy Hopkins, and Louise Rennison appear on almost a monthly basis. To keep pace, some long-lived popular culture icons are reinventing themselves. Notably there is a new series of Nancy Drew mysteries called *Nancy Drew…Girl Detective* narrated in the first person by Nancy herself. Defending yet another "updating of Nancy," Ellen Kreiger, the vice-president of Simon and Schuster observes: "The kids who read Nancy Drew also listen to Britney Spears. That's one reason we wanted to make Nancy cooler and more contemporary....But don't expect anything racy. Middle school readers—ages eight to twelve— are 'schizoid', wanting to grow up but wanting the security of childhood." (*The Star.* May 18, 2004). As we have observed in our own field-site visits to teen and tween doll sections of toy stores, similarly there is a fascinating interplay of "wanting to grown up" teen culture and "wanting the security of childhood" play to be found in these artifacts. The Bratz dolls are a good example. The male and female versions of the doll are all of the same mould: short, with a big head and feet (conveniently detachable above the ankle for different platform shoes and boots). The trunk is quite compressed with a small chest or breasts with big hips. They appear to be a three- dimensional cartoon or stylized caricature of a young teen, or even tween, body. They have large eyes, slightly slanted upwards, with long eyelashes, and the eyes appear slightly closed. The gaze is direct and indeed almost feline. The lips are oversized as well. The expression is slightly pouting and no teeth are visible. Because the dolls are obviously caricatures or cartoons, they could not be construed as models for children to imitate. This non-modeling aspect could lend to their play appeal. These dolls as a type could indicate a move of material tween culture into the parody mode of burlesque (a strategy which has been popular in children's media with *The Simpsons* cartoon show) from what was formerly a representational form that has been largely construed as realistic. The dolls are anti- or counter- Barbie physically and representationally. The colors on the boxes tend to be dark—for the boys orange and dark blue, for the girls purple/fuchsia and dark blue. The activities are located inside and outside—for example, skateboarding, dancing at clubs, attending slumber parties and so on.

The type of play that is implied is not 'playing at' growing up (as with Barbie) but instead 'playing with' teen culture. This is present in multiple ways such as making fun of, or deliberately masquerading in the style or dress as in a parody of playing 'dress up' when a small child. Since the implied invitation is not to enact a teen role but self-consciously to pretend to be a teen also, this suggests that the player may assume a different stance towards the subject of play, namely one of critical distance as opposed to one of imitation. It could be argued that by enjoining small children to play at or masquerade at being a teen when much younger, this activity could set up a space for interrogation at the age when child theorists from the medievalists onwards have considered that the young person's stance to adult life is supposed to be one of imitation or repetition.

By contrast, the My Scene dolls and accessories by Mattel are representational, which unintentionally projects a tone of seriousness or at least imitation. The genre of the dolls and artifacts of the My Scene sets suggest they are three-dimensional renderings of characters and activities associated with 'teen' TV shows such as *Dawson's Creek* or *One Tree Hill*. As well, the implied heterosexual partnering (explicit in the My Scene website) reinforces this impression. The figures are all lean, clean-cut, middle-class, and Barbie and Ken size. The main difference is the head. All the dolls have a bigger head with exaggerated eyes and lips but although these features are individually similar to the Bratz dolls, the difference in scale neutralizes the effect. They are simply fashion dolls with a larger head and features; indeed, a modified Barbie is one of the characters of the three female dolls in the series.

All of these dolls portray aspects of an active and either middle class or slightly counterculture world. This is a material teen world, not an adult world of work and responsibility (as Barbie belongs to) but rather one located in artifacts of music, dance, fashion, skateboarding, and shopping for urban clothes. It is a censored world—no drugs or violence—and (hetero) sexuality is only implied. The focus is on social and cultural aspects located both within and without the domestic sphere and the figures portray girls and boys. Each type of doll has an intended edge to them—on a scale of 1–10 with the implied age seeming to be the youngest for Bratz. Indeed, the Bratz doll most resembles an undeveloped body similar to that of the intended players. The other two by contrast are fashion doll shapes and have an older implied age due to their body shape. In some ways, the genre of tween dolls resemble that of the new 'junior chick lit' books that are directed toward an audience of girl readers (e.g., Louise Rennison, Cathy Hopkins) the covers of which are clearly identified by teen material culture on a girl's body.

Why the Title Seven Going on Seventeen?

The title of this collection of essays carries with it a number of underlying ideas. First, it is meant both as a nod to *Seventeen,* the popular North America magazine for girls, and to the fact that the term tween is derived from the mediated culture of marketing in North America in the first place. *Seventeen* magazine is the perfect emblem for this simply because it is one of the most popular teen magazines, the longest lasting in that it has been around since 1944, and 'is' unabashedly about fashion, hair, music—what Angela McRobbie earlier described in relation to comparable British magazines as the codes of fashion, beauty, and romance (1991) and what Linda Christian-Smith has called "texts of desire" (1993). At least conceptually, *Seventeen* in North American culture (and now Russian and South African) still seems to symbolize the end of innocence, coming of age, growing up, the prom, sexuality, and so on. Our initial formulation in thinking about young girls was actually 'nine going on seventeen' and comes out of an observation in our field work that it was often nine- and ten-year-old girls who were reading *Seventeen* magazines, little sisters getting their hands on their older sisters' (13 and 14) copies of the magazine. Indeed, when we examined the fashion layouts and ads in *Seventeen* we were struck by how 'little girl' the magazine had become between the 1980s and the late 1990s. The ads for example in the 1980s for china and cutlery and hints of preparing for weddings had been replaced by competitions to design a prom dress to fit a Barbie doll and paper dolls. Textually the magazine had become younger as had its readership! (Mitchell and Reid-Walsh 1999).

Accordingly, in recognition of the downward shift in age of much of girls' consumer culture (Barbie originally played with by 10-year-olds is now played with by 3-year-olds; *Nancy Drew* which used to be read by 14-year-olds is now read by 9-year-olds) our actual, and conceptual 'nine' itself experienced a downward shift itself to become a 'seven.'

In a contrasting vein and very different contexts, our title also alludes to a much more complex relationship to experience and to knowing with regard not only to many girls in parts of Africa and India but also in relation to a whole range of girls in North America who are located outside of mainstream popular culture: refugee girls, girls who do not subscribe to a dominant heterosexual culture, and so on. As we argue in an article "Visualizing the Politics of Innocence in the Age of AIDS" (Mitchell, Walsh, and Larkin 2004), the notion of protection (protection from knowledge about sex or protection from ignorance about safe sex) may be a newly contested one within the arena of girls growing up. In that article we are speaking specifically about South Africa, but the heightened awareness of the vulnerability of girls more generally (sexual stalking and predators on the Net) suggests that a girl's preadolescence years are significantly shaped by new cultural contexts.[2]

From Teens to Tweens: Historicizing Tween as 'the Seventh Age of Woman'

The term 'teenager' (girls as well as boys) is commonly understood to be a post-World War II construction associated with western societies. The OED defines this stage as such: "teenager (post / during WWII) One who is in his or her teens; *loosely*, an adolescent." This identity connects to the commodity culture of the post-war period where magazines, books, films, movie stars, and an emerging popular music all addressed this new audience. Significantly, females were considered 'teens' as equally as males, for before the emergence of the teen girl in this epoch, adolescence was a stage normally understood to be a male characteristic.[3] By comparison, although the word is not (yet) listed in the *OED* the word 'tween' is commonly understood to be a construction of the present day pertaining to a younger pre-adolescent and young adolescent age group exclusively or almost exclusively female, possessing, or as critics express it, defined by a distinct commodity culture.

In terms of historicizing girlhood, the idea of tween needs to be understood within a longer conceptual range such as one perhaps analogous to the old idea of the 'seven stages of mankind.' This medieval idea was a commonplace by Shakespeare's time, and today the most familiar expression of it remains Shakespeare's *As You Like It* (c. 1600). The first four stages are outlined in a famous speech by Jacques, which begins as follows:

> All the world's a stage,
> And all the men and women merely players;
> They have their exits and their entrances;
> And one man in his time plays many parts,
> His acts being seven ages. At first the infant,
> Mewling and puking in the nurse's arms;
> Then the whining school-boy, with his satchel
> And shining morning face, creeping like snail
> Unwillingly to school. And then the lover,
> Sighing like furnace, with a woeful ballad
> Made to his mistress' eyebrow. Then a soldier,
> Full of strange oaths, sudden and quick in quarrel,
> Seeking the bubble reputation
> Even in the cannon's mouth....
> (II. vii)

In Shakespeare's version, interestingly, the (male) child seems to have no adolescence but leaps from boyhood to young manhood. By contrast, women are scarcely mentioned, except as the object of the lover's attentions. Shake-speare's rendition is unusual in some ways for in the Renaissance there was a sophisticated and nuanced representation of the ages of man and woman oc-curring in visual and print culture.[4]

Accordingly, in his school text (a precursor of the picture book) *Orbis Sensualism Pictus*, translated from Latin into English by Charles Hoole in 1659, Johan Amos Comenius could draw upon a long pictorial tradition in his enumeration of the sets of stages. The first four are as follows: "A man is first an Infant, then a Boy, then a Youth, then a Young-Man, than a man...." "So also in the other Sex there are, a Girl, A Damosel, A maid, a woman...." (cited in Demers 2004: 40). In the accompanying illustration the infant is set apart in its cradle, while the other ages, in balanced pairs, move up and down the stairs of life stages. Males and females are represented equally. It is inter-esting to note that the infant who is set off by itself can be interpreted two ways: either as sexless and genderless or by the lack of repetition in the fe-male list perhaps male. Also the imprecision or ambiguity of the English translation becomes apparent when the terms for different ages of girls are investigated more closely. As will be seen, the impression is given that there are six ages for woman and seven for man. Hoole's English translations for the stages of young female are as follows: girl, damosel, and maid for the latin *pupa*, *puella*, and *virgo*. If the *OED* is consulted, it will be seen that damsel, damosel is defined as follows:

> **1. a.** A virgin; *spec.* the Virgin Mary = MAIDEN *n.* 2a
> **1.** A young unmarried lady; originally one of noble or gentle birth, but gradually extended as a respectful appellation to those of lower rank. Now merged in sense 2; but modern poets and romantic writers (led by Sir W. Scott) have recalled the 16-17th c. *damosel, damozel*, to express a more stately notion than is now conveyed by *damsel*.
> **2.** A young unmarried woman (without any connotation of rank or respect-sometimes even slightingly); a maid, maiden, girl, country lass.
> Since 17th c., archaic and literary or playful; not in ordinary spoken use.
> **2. a.** A girl; a young (unmarried) woman; = MAIDEN

The conflation of the term damosel (damsel) with the maiden state suggests that the stage is defined by the presumed absence of (hetero) sexual activity, not age.

Medievalists who study childhood, such as Shulamith Shahar (1990) and Nicholas Orme (2001), elaborate the three stages of childhood in such a manner that they introduce ambiguity into the definitions in different ways. Shahar introduces her discussion of medieval ideas of age and stage by quoting the work of child developmental psychologists Jean Piaget and Erik Erikson (1990: 21–22) and considering them as continuing the medieval approach. She notes that in medieval thought the upper end of the second stage of childhood "pueritia" was 7–12 for girls or 7–14 for boys (22) whereupon they entered the third stage. The second stage was defined in terms of ability to articulate oneself. Before this, in infancy, *infans,* the child was considered incapable of true comprehension, only speaking in imitation of adults. Some authors even believed there was a sub-stage in this second phase of childhood that began around the age of 10 or 12. By the second half of the 12th century, while a child could be betrothed at the age of 7, it was not considered binding. By the end of the second stage, though (12 for girls and 14 for boys) a marriage betrothal or contact was considered binding, and they also began to bear criminal responsibility. The upper age limit of this stage was determined by puberty (Shahar 1990: 24–26). The entry into the third stage (*adolescentia*) was connected with the ability to sin and to receive the sacrament. Depending on gender and class the activities associated with this stage differed: for a peasant boy it might be tending one's own flocks; for a noble boy it might be entering training to become a knight or for girls marriage.

Significant for our purposes, Shahar notes in her comments about the first stage of childhood that girls and boys were usually treated the same and that in analyses of the second stage girls and boys were discussed separately, although the focus was on the education of boys. In commentaries on the third stage, which started earlier for girls than boys, girls were almost overlooked. The change from childhood to married life seemed to occur "without the transitional stage undergone by young men from the nobility and urban class before they married and settled down." Even Dante was interested in only the "rational soul" of boys. She states, "it was no accident that authors felt no need to attend at length to girls when discussing adolescentia and the transition to full adulthood" (1990: 29–30).

For his part, in his discussion of ideas of childhood in the Middle Ages, Nicholas Orme (2001) focuses on refuting the work of Philippe Aries, Lloyd de Mause, and Lawrence Stone, who argued that childhood was not a distinct cultural period until the 16–17th centuries. Orme argues that since the medieval period childhood has been understood as a separate stage with attendant cultural activities and possessions. To support this contention, he examines, for example, a famous 1495 edition of Bartholomew's *Encyclopeidia* depicting the Ages of Man that shows certain material possessions being associated with different ages—a boy on a hobbyhorse and a youth with a bow (illustration 3.7). In his discussion of the terms denoting stages of childhood, Orme focuses on childhood as a unified conceptual category so does not explore sex and gender differences (2001: 3–10).[5]

From the Middle Ages on, it appears that in western societies young females were understood to exist in a binary process of aging, for as Shahar notes, girls became women with little or no transitional period. In the course of the 18th century it would appear that a state comparable to the latter end of the continuum of boys' *adolescentia* emerged in practice and within strict social-cultural limits: 'young lady hood.'

…Going on Seventeen: The Construction of Female Late 'Adolescentia'

In the 18th–19th century, girls of a certain class (middle and higher) at a certain time in the late middle teen years 'came out' and 'entered the world' (hence the subtitle of Frances Burney's novel *Evelina: or, The History of a Young Lady's Entrance in to the World* (1778)). Girls moved from the private sphere of the home to the public sphere of polite society, attending a round of social events that included assemblies, balls and musical events. If a girl possessed a high enough social status, this might include a coming out, ball held in her honor. This served as a rite of passage for 'entering society' and was a trial by public opinion, which women writers such as Frances Burney, Maria Edgeworth, and Jane Austen interrogated in depth. Since a lady did not usually work, marriage was the main career option. Based on the family's financial capital, on a young woman's accomplishments (the ability to display knowledge of dancing, singing, drawing, and so on—but never at an exceptional level) and on her physical 'assets' she became a commodity on a 'marriage market.' Every aspect of the girl's appearance, deportment, and conduct was intensely scrutinized by self-interested and even predatory onlookers. Conduct book manuals for girls and mothers proliferated, such as that by Dr. Gregory in his *Father's Legacy to His Daughters* (1774) (see Reid-Walsh 1994).

In this system, there appears to have been a binary state of 'not being out' or 'being out.' In *Northanger Abbey,* Austen in a tongue-in-cheek manner depicts this shift from the first stage to readiness for the second through the enumeration of opposing sets of activities that the heroine Catherine engages in at different ages of her childhood and adolescence. At ten she is a tomboy: "...noisy and wild, hated confinement and cleanliness, and loved nothing so well in the world as rolling down the green slope at the back of the house." At fourteen, she is an older version of ten, for she preferred "cricket, base ball, riding on horseback, and running about the country." But by the next year Catherine has changed completely; she has been transformed into a young lady: "...appearances were mending; she began to curl her hair and long for balls; her complexion improved; her features were softened by plumpness and colour, her eyes gained more animation, and her figure more consequence. Her love of dirt gave way to an inclination for finery, and she grew clean as she grew smart" (1985a: 38–39). The shift from the active world of late 18th century girlhood to the adolescent one focusing on appearance is economically presented by Austen (Reid-Walsh 1998).

The girl's debut into society usually occurred around 17 years of age, although it could be younger, for in *Pride and Prejudice*, Lydia, Elizabeth's sister of 15 is also out and so is the occasional heroine in Austen's juvenilia (e.g., *A Collection of Letters*).

Jumping forward some 200 years to the present day, it is interesting to note that remnants of the initiation ball into 'society' are still in evidence. The most obvious examples are the 'Debutante Balls' that still occur in major cities such as Montreal, New York and London, but there is a more playful version that extends across a wider class spectrum in North America—the prom. The usual age when finishing high school corresponds to the time when a young lady 'entered society'—and hence the prom can be seen as both a vestigial trace of the coming-out ball as well as a democratization of a rite of passage (Mitchell and Reid-Walsh 1999).

In the novel, *Mansfield Park*, Jane Austen explores the differences manifest in the attire and the actions of girls who have 'entered society' and those who have not. One of the male characters, the unobservant Tom Bertram, cannot distinguish between girls who are 'out' and those who are 'not out.' The sophisticated Mary Crawford explicates the fashion and conduct shift for him:

> And yet in general, nothing can be more easily ascertained. The distinction is so broad. Manners as well as appearance are, generally speaking, so totally different. Till now, I could not have supposed it possible to be mistaken as to a girl's being out or not. A girl not out has always the same sort of dress: a close bonnet, for instance;

looks very demure, and never says a word. You may smile—but it is so, I assure you—and except that it is sometimes carried a little too far, it is all very proper. Girls should be quiet and modest. The most objectionable part is, that the alteration of manners on being introduced into company is frequently too sudden. They sometimes pass in such very little time from reserve to quite the opposite — to confidence! *That* is the faulty part of the present system. One does not like to see a girl of eighteen or nineteen so immediately up to every thing — and perhaps when one has seen her hardly able to speak the year before. Mr. Bertram [Tom], I dare say *you* have sometimes met with such changes. (1985b: 81)

Part of the satire in *Mansfield Park* concerns the constructed nature of this apparently 'natural' switch (Reid-Walsh 1995: 132). As Mary Crawford points out though, knowledgeable observers could distinguish girls who were 'not out' from those who were by reading their apparel.

This distinction of dress was even reproduced in the details of clothing of the occasional fashion doll. There is an unusual fashion doll with a yellow dress c. 1740-50 on display at the Bethnal Green Museum of Childhood in London and available on the images website of the Victoria and Albert Museum: http://images.vam.ac.uk.[6] The website description is as follows:

Although this 18th century doll looks as if she represents an adult woman, her clothing presents clues which demonstrate very clearly that she is not an adult. In the 18th century, dresses fastening at the back like this were for children, not women. Long streamers of matching fabric called 'leading strings' at the back of the dress indicate that she represents a teenage girl. Leading strings originated in the clothing of very young children, where they helped adults to assist the child who was learning to walk. In the 18th century they also became customary for unmarried teenage girls, perhaps to symbolise the fact that they were still under parental control. (Information given by R. M. Gregory) (REF)

As can be seen, this shapely doll is most unusual in that the dress suggests this doll is not depicting a woman but rather a teenage girl. This doll then may be an example of a very early teen fashion doll—a "Barbie"!

Seven Going on... The Construction of Female Pre-'adolescentia': A Field Trip to the Bethnal Green Museum of Childhood

In the 18th and 19th centuries, it seems that ideas about girls and girlhood were generic categories. Girls of the lower classes still existed in a binary system of child and adult, while girls of the middling class and higher had a third stage of 'young lady' as discussed above. While the transition into adulthood was a focal point, the transition into adolescence was not important to address publicly. Indeed, it took another 200 years for the present day notion of tween to be developed and to fill the conceptual category of a time of transition between childhood and adolescence. The idea of tweens could be seen to link to current discussions of early puberty and or sexuality in girls and to ideas stemming from the medieval period. As mentioned above, some medieval authors believed there was a sub-stage in this second phase of childhood, which began around the age of 10 or 12 (depending on circumstances) (Shahar 1990: 24). We would like to propose that the concept of tween is a way to differentiate between these two stages/ages of girlhood that were conflated in medieval times and have not been separated afterwards. If teenager corresponds to "maid" or "*virgo*" (and at the upper age end of adolescence and includes 18th and 19th century girls entering the commodified marriage market), tween can be understood as corresponding to "damosel"— the first age after girlhood.

Modern definitions of teen and tween have concerned contestations about sexuality. Ironically, much of the discourse of concern around teen culture in the 1950's and 60's now seems to the baby boomers who helped define the generation to eerily be re-playing. Now, though, the attribute has been 'down shifted' or 'down sized' as it were to a younger group still categorized as children. A couple of years ago when we first visited the Bethnal Green Museum of Childhood in London, we were struck by how the exhibits of clothes and accessories on one floor and the toys on the other floors seemed gendered or even sexualized in different ways, evocative of gender distinctions in contemporary toys and fashion. On the toy floors the toys 'for boys'—hoops, hobby horses, optical toys—seemed neutral or sexless when compared with the shapely three-dimensional dolls and paper fashion dolls for girls that were based on a idealized woman's body. On the clothing floor, the fashion for boys similarly seemed sexless or androgynous, while that for girls, which adopted women's dresses to the unformed girl's body, appeared to be sexed not in terms of the body shape but in the implied lack of mobility in the constraining garments—both undergarments and clothes for wearing outside the home. The girls' clothing exhibit was provocatively entitled "a girl's childhood." We found the wording and the questions implied by the ambiguous phrasing to be intriguing. For instance, by using the phrase as a label, were the curators intending somehow to highlight age, stage, and physiological development? Were they contrasting the differences between a gender neutral or boys' childhood and a sexualized girls' one? Were they suggesting that girls are sexualized differently at different ages? Looking at tween fashion today, which similarly adapts clothing associated with a woman's developed body—bustiers or particularly the notorious example of thong underwear—to a unformed shape we asked ourselves: what are the similarities and differences in the ideas of childhood being implied or contained in these garments? What is different and similar in each era's sexualizing of young girls?

In most commentary about tween girls, there is the recognition and concern about the category being one constructed by marketers to target and exploit a vulnerable age group as opposed to a 'natural' or developmental category. It is ironic that these present-day concerns about inability to resist marketing wiles are in some ways an unknowing expansion of medieval ideas of childhood competence, when it was believed that at the ages of 7–12 children are unable to reason and only able to mimic adults' ideas with no comprehension (Shahar 1990: 24).

The idea of tween may be a way to fill the conceptual category of the time of transition between a girl's childhood and her adolescence. It is not a stable category, though, but one that seems to be shifting ever so slightly downward. There is a downward limit obviously—as with Barbie dolls (where warnings stipulate there are small parts that may be swallowed by very small children) or with clothing and music style. There is, always, as David Buckingham observes regarding research in childhood studies, a developmental aspect that has to be acknowledged and explored (1993). Below a certain age, there is no interest or even physical ability on a child's part to engage in any form of youth culture.

As in other constructions around youth, there is also a physiological dimension. For instance, although the idea of teenager is a post World War II invention, the stage seems linked with physiological puberty and entering adolescence. Regarding tweens as well, there is often made mention of an earlier outset of puberty occurring more commonly in girls. This may concern breast development and the menarche, or stories about girls giving birth, and we think of a news story in the January 23, 2004, *St. Petersburg Times* about an 11-year-old girl in Kiev, Ukraine, giving birth, or the recurring stories of alarm about early puberty.[7] Here we think of the coverage of nine-year-old girl's early onset of puberty on CNN March 31, 2000, and its possible causes, which range from shampoo to insecticides.[8] It appears that a market construction has somehow anticipated or is at least paralleling a physiological one. In some cases, western concerns about 'death of childhood' and 'hurried childhood' seem to be coming true for some western and westernized girls, as they have always been for the majority of girls in developing countries throughout the world.[9]

Tween and Tween Studies—'Under Construction'

The idea of tween is beginning to appear in popular discourse in an apparently uninflected way simply as an age-demarcated category. An early example may be seen in Pigeon's "Packaging Up Coolness" *Marketing Magazine* 20–27 July 1998: 21: "We need to make a concerted effort to listen to the underground culture. If we want to successfully package our products for teens and tweens we have to scrounge around in their world to find what's important to them..." (cited in Kline, Dyer-Witheford, and de Peuter 2003: 233, note 49). It is interesting to see how by referring to the music industry as a model, this marketer uses the term as an adjunct of teen with no reference to gender but to boys and girls generally. A more recent example occurred in the *Montreal Gazette,* March 12, 2004, where in a piece entitled "Tweens Can Bank on Spy Caper," Kathryn Greenaway reviews a film called *Agent Cody Banks 2: Destination London.* The review (addressed to parents) discusses the film in terms of age and stage using tween simply as an age category (7–12) to describe a demographic age group and its supposed taste (D 3).

These two examples demonstrate how a term that began as a marketing ploy has become naturalized to the degree that it can be used in the popular press as a developmental term and one that can apply to boys as well as to girls. A similar shift in meaning is apparently beginning to occur in the talk by the young themselves. One young British boy of the 7–12 age group, after learning of the concept from an adult researcher, began to use it as well as a age category (R. Willett, pers. comm.). What are the implications of this (apparently) gender equal or neutral application of the term tween? Is there potential self-awareness of even agency in its use? Can a boy be a tween?

A number of paradoxes are emerging: on the one hand, tween culture seems to be moving progressively downward in age to touch upon even the lower age limits of girlhood and expanding outward to include boys. Perhaps the word 'tween' itself as suggested by the insertion of the diminutive consonant 'w,' will come to mean simply a variation or miniaturization of teen culture. On the other hand, teen culture and girl culture is elongating as a category at the upper end—until 25 or 30—so potentially a youth culture encompasses much of childhood, all of adolescence, and all of young adulthood. What is one to make of this? Are we trying to construct a simplified process of aging composed of two negligible stages (infancy and old age are insignificant due to lack of physical autonomy or stigma) and one viable one: youth or at least youth culture? Boomers shop at the Gap, struggle to keep fit; females of all ages dye their hair to the degree it becomes a norm; makeover shows abound on cable television including one about extreme makeovers that involve plastic surgery. All these activities and popular culture center on a construction of youth (Mitchell and Reid-Walsh 2002). Since women are living longer, a female, then, can be a girl by participating in girl culture for almost a third of her life! What is the larger significance of this? In some ways, this can be seen as a logical outcome of a process that started hundreds of years ago in the west. Is it a moral tale or lesson in the constructedness of young femininity highlighting the artificiality and fabricated nature of youth?

About the Organization of *Seven Going on Seventeen*

A volume such as this could be organized in several ways—including a developmental or chronological ordering that would focus on age, say, at either 'edge' of the tween-age, or the emphasis could be on the cross-cultural dimension of our contributors and field sites wherein we could have used a geographical map as our organizing principle, stressing the global nature of tween culture. Instead, although these aspects are present, we decided to use a network or constellation of related concepts that provide a critical perspective on the subject of tween girls as our organizing principle. In so doing, we have divided the book into three main sections—*Girl-method, Knowing Girls*, and *Marketing Girlhood/Consuming Girlhood*—categories that also contain the two previous categories within them. As is apparent, a number of our contributors, offering up an interesting 'take' on girlhood, have written about the lower edge of adolescence—11 and 12 year olds. This is something that we have found provocative in that we realized that one way to construct parts of the book might have been to follow age categories: *Just Eleven, Turning Twelve* and so on, something that the controversial photographer, Sally Mann uses with her photography series *At Twelve*, and complementary to the rite of passage ages of sixteen ('sweet sixteen') and seventeen (including the magazines *Seventeen* and *Just Seventeen).*

And while many authors did submit abstracts that addressed tween marketing culture—shopping, fashion, magazines, series literature, and very specific girl-focused popular culture texts such as *Hello Kitty* and *Sailor Moon* (along with Britney Spears, the Spice Girls)—we also found that there were other submissions that focused more on cultural constructions of age and the idea of 'growing older sooner' in the context of biology and physicality, proposals that dealt with sexual violence and the vulnerability of young girls, and clear indications that work with this age group is far from 'little girl innocence.' Others offered research on cultural contexts beyond both mainstream popular culture and beyond the *geopolitical* spaces of industrialized countries. In so doing, they highlight the ways that pre-adolescent girls are represented in literary studies, film, photography, and art and how these representations can inform the whole area of girlhood studies as well as how girlhoods in developing contexts such as in India and South Africa can provide still other views of the space between being a little girl and a big girl. For example, the number of child-headed (girl-headed) households due to the high incidence of HIV and AIDS in southern Africa repositions the idea of a girl's childhood as one not of free play but of being burdened with responsibility. The high incidence of sexual abuse in South Africa reframes notions of childhood sexuality. At the same time, as Berry Mayall and others have pointed out, romantic notions of childhood are also out of place in industrialized countries. She discusses in her edited volume *Children's Childhoods Observed and Experienced* how children as young as seven or eight who are terminally ill may try to protect their parents from the fact that they know they are dying.

In the first grouping, which we label *Girl-method*, we focus on various approaches to studying girlhood. Drawing from the emerging body of 'method work' that attests to new field sites for knowing—using one's self in studying professional practices (Mitchell, Weber, and O'Reilly-Scanlon 2004) for example, or clothing-as-method (Weber and Mitchell 2004), we acknowledge that within feminist discourses there has been heretofore an absence of a framework to name the kind of method work that adult women might engage in *with* girls, *for* girls, and *about* girlhood, even though there has been a rich body of work and a long history of research that speaks to the nuances of women researching women (see for example Anne Oakley's now-classic article "Interviewing Women: A Contradiction in Terms").[10] In this section, we include investigations that take a range of methodological and theoretical approaches singly or in tandem and adapt them to study girls and girlhood. This section starts with the work of Elizabeth Seaton, who uses postmodern theory and cultural studies to interrogate the phenomenon of early puberty. Both Marnina Gonick and Kristina Hackmann in their respective chapters use aspects of video construction as a participatory research tool, the former having girls construct video scripts and the latter analyzing girls' video production. The chapter by Meredith Cherland and the chapter by Kathleen O'Reilly-Scanlon and Sonya Dwyer both adapt feminist memory-work methods to a self-study and to comparative age studies. Finally, Miki Flockemann uses literary textual analysis to investigate the use of the tween voice in South African literature.

In the second grouping called *Knowing Girls*, the contributors explore the limits of presumed (hetero) sexuality in tween discourse and explode the safe binaries of innocence and knowing with respect to girls' experience and knowledge. Here we place the following contributions: a chapter by the Balkishori Team of VACHA Women's Resource Center (with Jackie Kirk), which seeks to understand girlhood in Mumbai, India. Relebohile Moletsane investigates the autobiographical writing of girls in a South African township in relation to gender-based violence. Deevia Bhana explores schoolyard rhymes in a South African school, focusing in particular on how sexuality permeates the primary school. Yasmin Jiwani combines focus groups with individual interviews of refugee girls in Canada. Finally, Shannon Walsh analyzes film and photography about (and appropriated by) tween girls.

In the third and largest category labeled *Marketing Girlhood/Consuming Girlhood*, we situate papers that explore the 'bedrock' of tween culture but in unusual theoretical and methodological ways. Anita Harris critiques Australian tween magazines, Catherine Driscoll deconstructs girls and Barbie dolls, Amy Lai works within cross-cultural media studies to study *Hello Kitty*. Farah Malik combines a girl-centered ethnography of collective shopping field trips with magazine analysis; Rebekah Willett examines tween girl websites and interviews girls about web page construction; Hoi Cheu employs cross-cultural film theory to examine *Sailor Moon*; Peggy Tally examines the emergence of a mainstream tween film culture. Natalie Coulter uses interviews of former tweens to provide a contemporary historical context for the tween girl phenomenon.

We consider that our contributors have pushed the boundaries of tween studies in various ways. They often combine a focus on a certain set of tween girls or texts intended for or produced by tween girls with a nuanced consideration of class, race, and location. Significantly, the contributors have analyzed tweens and tween culture in a wide range of geographical locations: Hong Kong (Amy Lai); Japan (Hoi Cheu); India (Balkishori Team); South Africa (Deevia Bhana, Relebohile Moletsane, Miki Flockemann); Australia (Anita Harris, Catherine Driscoll); Germany (Kristina Hackmann); England (Rebekah Willett); United States (Farah Malik, Meredith Cherland); and Canada (Yasmin Jiwani, Kathleen O'Reilly-Scanlon, Sonya Corbin Dwyer).

Throughout the volume, there is a range of disciplinary interests and contrasting theoretical perspectives that work to question received assumptions about girls, girlhood, and girl culture. By using the idea of tween and tween culture as a springboard for thoughtful and provocative discussion and analysis, the contributors in this volume have shown how elastic the term can be. Similar to the many websites created by tween girls themselves, the term is still 'under construction.'

The study of tween life may have derived from a particular marketing orientation but is not limited by it. On the contrary, this collection of essays shows that tween is not a simple or unified concept, nor is it limited to a certain class of girls in a few countries. *Seven Going on Seventeen: Tween Studies in the Culture of Girlhood* offers a reading on three or four years of a girl's life that suggests that this period is at least as fascinating as the teen years and at least as generative in its implications for further research in girlhood studies as either studies of younger girls or adolescent girls. We want to thank you tween marketers!

Notes

[1] See, for example, the conference programs for "New Girl Order: Young Women and the Future of Feminist Inquiry" sponsored by Monash University, at King's College London, November 14–16, 2001, and "Transforming Spaces: Girlhood, Agency, and Power" at Concordia University Montreal, November 21–23, 2003.

[2] This point is also taken up in a paper, "Mapping a Southern African Girlhood in the Age of AIDS" (Mitchell 2004, Gender Equality and Education Conference, Cape Town, May 15–18).

[3] In the *OED* online the word "teens" is defined as follows with examples dating from 1673:

1. a. *pl.* The years of the life of any person (*rarely*, of the age of anything) of which the numbers end in *-teen*, i.e. from thirteen to nineteen; chiefly in phrases *in*, *out of one's teens*. **1673** WYCHERLEY *Gentl. Dancing Master* IV. i, Your poor young things, when they are once in the teens, think they shall never be married. **1693** *Humours Town* 98 A young Girl in the Teens. **1709** E. W. *Life Donna Rosina* 10 Her Daughter, who was by this time come into the Teens. **1763** CHURCHILL *Proph. Famine* 3 The stripling raw, just enter'd in his teens. In Latin, the word 'youth' is a translation for 'Adolescens' (while young man is 'uvenis') (Comenius, cited in Demers 2004: 37). Even the modern definition has a differential age span. In the OED online, adolescence is defined as:

A. *n.* A person in the age of adolescence; a youth between childhood and manhood. **1482** *Monk of Evesham* (1869) 103 A certen adolescente a yonge man. **1495** CAXTON *Vitas Patr.* (W. de Worde) I. li. 104bb, He admonested..the adolescentes as his chyldren. **1815** W. TAYLOR in *Monthly Rev.* LXXVI. 498 Conveying, without indecency, to adolescents many facts concerning the human frame. **B.** *adj.* Growing towards maturity; advancing from childhood to maturity. **1785** COWPER *Tirocin.* 219 Schools, unless discipline were doubly strong, Detain their adolescent charge too long. **1809** J. BARLOW *Columb.* VIII. 149 Unfold each day some adolescent grace. **1878** B. TAYLOR *Pr. Deukal.* III. i. 100, I see Near manhood in thy adolescent limbs. The entry for adolescence in the *OED* online is as follows: The process or condition of growing up; the growing age of human beings; the period which extends from childhood to manhood or womanhood; youth; ordinarily considered as extending from 14 to 25 in males, and from 12 to 21 in females. Also *fig*

[4] Some commentators consider the Renaissance representation in images to be more sophisticated than provided in words. For instance, Nicholas Pioch of the web museum Paris gives as an example, "The Seven Ages of Women" by the Dutch artist Hans Baldung Grien (b. 1484/85) in the Museum der Bildenden Künste, Leipzig. Nicholas Pioch, Museum der Bildenden Künste, "The Seven Ages of Women". http://sunsite.tus.ac.jp/wm/paint/auth/baldung/ages/seven-ages-woman.jpg
Christiane Andersson in the *Grove Dictionary of Art* Online notes that here Baldung Grien continues to work in the late medieval image traditions of vanitas, the Ages of Man and the Dance of Death to explore the transitory nature of female beauty.

[5] Orme discusses aristocratic girls and their education in an earlier book, *From Childhood to Chivalry: The Education of English Kings and Aristocracy 1066-1530.* London: Methuen, 1984. Building on the work of Shahar and Orme, Barbara A. Hanawalt (2002: 447–448) notes that the term puella was the most popular Latin term for girls, and it was applied to newborns up to girls of 16 years. Virgo was used mostly to refer to girls of 8-16 years.

[6] The address for the Access to images site at the Victoria & Albert Museum is: V& A Museum http://images.vam.ac.uk/ixbin/hixclient.exe?_IXSESSION_=&submit-button=search&search-form=main/index.html.
The doll in a yellow dress is of English manufacture, c. 1740–50, of wood, with gesso, paint, and varnish and is 40.6 cm. high. The item number is MISC.271-1981.

In the credit line is stated that the doll is given by R. M. Gregory. We are grateful to Noreen Marshall, Curator of Dress and Nursery Collections at the Museum of Childhood, a branch of the Victoria and Albert Museum for providing further documentation for us on this early 18th century teen doll during her tour of the doll collections at the museum.

[7] http://customwire.ap.org/dynamic/stories/U/UKRAINE_YOUNGMOTHER?SITE= FLPET&SECTION=HOME.

[8] Jennifer Haupt, "More girls experience early puberty," CNN, March 31, 2000, http://www.cnn.com/2000/HEALTH/children/03/31/early.puberty.wmd/.

[9] Here, for example, we are thinking of a group of 12-year-old girls in rural Swaziland who, when asked to photograph 'safe' and 'not so safe' spaces in their schools pictured themselves engaged in rape scenes in the bushes with one girl on top of the other. While their choice of a scene clearly pointed out that they recognized the realities of the dangers around them, the grins on their faces also spoke to the feature of play in which they found themselves in carrying out this photo-event. (Mitchell, C. and Larkin, J. "Disrupting the Silences: Photo-voice in Addressing Gender-based Violence." Paper presented to the Pleasures & Dangers Conference, Cardiff, Wales, June, 29–July 2 2004).

[10] Here we acknowledge a conversation with Helen Berman at the Transforming Spaces conference, held in Montreal, November 19–21, 2003 about the need for a term within feminist research to refer to intergenerational work involving girls and women. Enter the term 'girl-method.'

References

Andersson, C. "Hans Baldung Grien.'" *The Grove Dictionary of Art* Online, Oxford University Press. Also available online at http://www.groveart.com.

Austen, J. *Northanger Abbey*. Edited by H. Ehrenpreis. London: Penguin, 1985a.

———. *Mansfield Park*. Edited by T. Tanner. London: Penguin, 1985b.

Buckingham, D. *Reading Audiences: Young People and the Media.* Manchester: Manchester UP, 1993.

Christian-Smith, L. *Texts of Desire: Essays on Fiction, Femininity, and Schooling.* London: Falmer, 1993.

Demers, P., ed *From Instruction to Delight: An Anthology of Children's Literature to 1850,* 2nd edition. Toronto: Oxford UP, 2004.

Greenaway, K. "Tweens Can Bank on Spy Caper." *Montreal Gazette* Friday March 12 2004, D3.

Hanawalt, B. A. "Medievalists and the Study of Childhood." *Speculum* 77 (2002): 440–460.

Kline, S., Dyer-Witheford, D., and de Peuter, G. *Digital Play: The Interaction of Technology, Culture and Marketing.* Montreal: McGill-Queens, UP, 2003.

McRobbie, A. *Feminism and Youth Culture: From Jackie to Just Seventeen.* Basingstoke: Macmillan, 1991.

Mann, S. *At Twelve: Portraits of Young Women.* Turin, Italy: Aperture, 1988.

Mayall, B. *Children's Childhoods Observed and Experienced.* London: Falmer Press, 1994.

Mitchell, C. "Mapping a Southern African Girlhood in the Age of AIDS." Paper presented at the Gender Equality and Education Conference, Cape Town, May 15–18, 2004.

Mitchell, C. and Larkin, J. "Disrupting the Silences: Photo-voice in Addressing Gender-based Violence." Paper presented to the Pleasures & Dangers Conference, Cardiff, Wales, June 29–July, 2 2004

Mitchell, C. and Reid-Walsh, J. "And I Want to Thank You Barbie: Barbie as a Site of Cultural Interrogation." In *Education and Cultural Studies: Toward a Performative Practice*, edited by H. Giroux and P. Shannon, 103-116. New York: Routledge, 1997.

———. "Nine Going on Seventeen: Boundary Crises in the Cultural Map of Childhood/Adolescence." Paper presented at the AERA Montreal Canada April 19–24, 1999.

———. *Researching Children's Popular Culture: The Cultural Spaces of Childhood.* London and New York: Routledge, 2002.

Mitchell, C., Walsh, S., and Larkin, J. "Visualizing the Politics of Innocence in the Age of AIDS." *Sex Education* 3, no. 2 (2004): 159–172.

Mitchell, C., Weber, S., and O'Reilly-Scanlon, K. *Just Who Do We Think We Are? Methodologies for Autobiography and Self-study in Teaching.* London: RoutledgeFalmer, 2004.

Orme, N. *From Childhood to Chivalry: The Education of English Kings and Aristocracy 1066-1530.* London: Methuen, 1984.

———. *Medieval Children.* New York: Yale UP, 2001.

Reid-Walsh, J. "'Entering the World' of Regency Society: The Ballroom Scenes in *Northanger Abbey*, "The Watsons," and *Mansfield Park*." *Persuasions* 16 (1994): 115–124.

———. "Pray is She Out, is She Not?—I am Puzzled: Decoding Fanny's Position at Mansfield Park." *Persuasions* 17 (1995): 130–136.

———. "'Born to be a Heroine': The Early Education of Catherine Morland." Jane Austen Society of North America. Quebec City, Quebec. October 9–11 1998.

Shahar, S. *Childhood in the Middle Ages.* London: Routledge, 1990.

The Star. "The Case of Nancy Drew." May 18, 2004.

Weber, S. and Mitchell, C. "Theorizing Dress Stories." In *Not Just Any Dress: Narratives of Memory, Body, and Identity*, edited by S. Weber and C. Mitchell, 251–272. New York: Peter Lang, 2004.

PART I

Girl-method

CHAPTER TWO

Tween Social and Biological Reproduction: Early Puberty in Girls

Elizabeth Seaton

In 1997, the publication of a major study in the journal, *Pediatrics,* caused a nationwide media storm in Canada and the United States. The research offered compelling evidence that North American girls were experiencing the onset of puberty one or two years earlier than their counterparts had 30 years ago (Hermann-Giddens et al. 1997). This phenomenon of early puberty—termed "precocious sexual development" by the medical establishment—became the causal underpinning for a new generation of media panics and normative social representations of girls. With varying degrees of scientific fact and inflammatory rhetoric, *Time Magazine*, *Newsweek*, *The New York Times*, countless other dailies, talk shows and web-magazines described "a generation in fast forward"…of girls who are "8 going on 25" and "becoming sexually active at an alarmingly early age" (*Newsweek* 1999: 17). For all those parents and teachers who had long suspected that young girls were becoming more mature overnight, there was now scientific 'proof' that the age of puberty was plummeting. More fortuitously for target marketers, ad types and the media, it could now be claimed that there was a biological veracity to what remains an invention of marketing and cultural representation: the 'tween' girl.

'Precocious sexual development' provides an especially rich ground for inquiry into the discursive embodiment of social identity. Having captured the imaginations of both 'legitimate' (medical and social scientific) sources and unauthorized (popular) audiences, it lends important insights into the discursive frameworks which construct notions of a body, its sex, gender and age, and the assumptions of value and causality which support these. But perhaps more intriguing is the way in which 'precocious sexual development' appears to move in fidelity with our radically shifting social, cultural and natural environments. And in this respect, it begs the question, "Does discourse simply stop at flesh and bone? Or does the social interact reciprocally with the physical in ways both contrived and accidental? What manner of fluid interchanges—discursive, material and physical—exists among social, cultural, and natural environments?

"Childhood," as James, Jenks, and Prout describe it, "is less a fact of nature than an interpretation of it" (1998: 62). Certainly, these changing bodies tell us much about the changing conceptions and social values attached to the identities of children. Children act as important symbolic and mediating figures for society: they serve as both the nostalgic reserves of 'fond childhood memories' and as the corporeal agents of society's future; they delineate both the maturity and rationality of 'adulthood' and the irrational and asexual 'nature' of childhood. Girls may be even more sensitive to such discursive shaping, for they are held within doubled dualisms which posit children as 'animalistic' or 'primitive' and females, by virtue of their physiology, as 'closer to nature' than men. Yet, the phenomenon of 'precocious sexual development' raises the possibility that not all is what it is *meant* to be: that even while we may refute the naturalization of arbitrary social identities upon a body, we are also constantly faced with its residual, morphological, 'nature'. These changing bodies thus strongly gesture to the oblique and dialectical interplay of biological and social reproduction.

The past three decades have seen dramatic changes to the economic, political, and social structures of North American society, many of which directly affect the present and future of young people. The 'liberalizations' of global trade laws and the digitalized speed and efficiencies of 'fictive' finance capital have resulted in the massive exportation of manufacturing jobs to countries believed to have more compliant and cheap labor pools.[1] With jobless futures (Aronowitz and DiFazio 1995) have also come deteriorating social benefits—from pensions to quality health care to welfare and social security—which were once viewed as immutable and sacrosanct (in Canada at least) but now are increasingly under attack. In this respect, the prospects for employment, and the progressive forms of citizenship and value offered to young people in North America have become far more limited.[2]

The abstractions of a 'fictive' finance capitalism, which amasses wealth through exchange and replication, are matched by the ascension of a pervasive consumer culture fashioned within the mantra of synergy, duplication, and disposability (Baudrillard 1988; Rifkin 2000). We are no longer enticed but rather swarmed by commercial culture. Desire has become unhinged, replaced by the more "unfastened and licentious" 'wish' as the motivating force of consumption (Bauman 2001: 14). Zygmunt Bauman (ibid.) argues that 'the wish' perfectly corresponds to a time in which nothing of consequence transpires beyond the immediate moment: nothing of lasting duration, nothing contextualized by history.

These times, too, are marked by high anxiety. Not too long ago, the constant fear of an unknown danger was the purlieu of the self-important or the self-delusional. Today this fear is dispersed, democratized, and commodified (Seaton 2001). No doubt, the demise of social protections under a 'liberalized' economy has added to the prevalence of social insecurities. So too do the new commodities of fear—the police forces, both private and public, the monstrous Hummers, the armed and alarmed houses, gated communities and surveillance cameras, the War on Terror, the new identity documents, and the smug visage of G.W. Bush—which, like all media, impart particular messages about the state of the world and how we should live in it.

Something too has gone terribly amiss in the relationship between humanity and nature. We are now in the midst of a full-blown environmental crisis, which, even for the cosseted occupants of a 'society of abundance', is impossible to ignore. And as the natural environment mutates, changes texture and temperature and finally vanishes under the weight of human excess, its only remaining value is as a spectacle or experience for consumption. Nature is no longer itself. Even those ontological certainties once supported by the blueprint of natural history are rendered null and void, as genomic maps are re-written, sheep are cloned, human fetuses are 'resourced,' and the food we eat is genetically engineered. We seem to be witnessing the dramatic alteration of life itself.

'Precocious sexual development' may thus act as a touchstone for more distant and impersonal forces. The ambivalence and discomfort with which we may experience these changes—whose effects are as intimate as they are remote—speak to a more subtle perception that life, labor, and language are becoming undone, realigned, and re-made by forces beyond our control. What happens to young bodies when their future becomes uncertain?

There are thus two broad focal points to this investigation into 'precocious sexual development.' The first concerns the discursive premises and powers that shape its representation. *How* is the problem of precocious sexual development socially produced within regimes of power and knowledge?

What epistemological and ontological premises guide the various hypotheses of its scientific investigation, and from what historical conditions do these premises arise? And how are its different referential components—childhood, puberty, adolescent girls, etc.—held within networks of control that are at once both disciplinary and pleasurable? The second part of this investigation seeks to understand precocious sexual development as the result of a mutually generative relationship between human beings and their social and cultural environments. A common sentiment forwarded (either implicitly or explicitly) in much of the writing on early puberty is that it is the physiological effect, or incorporation, of culture. If this is so, how is it so? And if it is so, may not early puberty affect the world as much as it is affected? Can it be seen as a strategic reaction to the social environment?

Competing Hypotheses

The research project on precocious sexual development was principally authored by Dr. Marcia Hermann-Giddens, who, in collaboration with the American Academy of Pediatrics, undertook a major study of 17,077 girls aged 3–10 across the United States (Hermann-Giddens et al. 1997).[3] Six percent of the girls were African-American, and 90.4% were white. The results of the study were surprisingly consistent. For white girls, the mean age of the on-set of puberty was 9.96 years. For African-American girls, that age was 8.87 years. At every age, African-American girls were shown to be more advanced in puberty than white girls were. At age eight, 48.3% of African-American girls and 14.7% of white girls showed pubertal maturation. At age seven, 27.2% of African-American girls, and 6.7% of white girls had begun development. Close to one-third of the African-American girls showed pubertal characteristics by their seventh birthday (puberty here measured by appearance of breast-buds or pubic hair). These girls are in their second-grade of grammar school.

Since 1969, medical textbooks and pediatricians have commonly cited the expected normative age for the start of puberty in young girls as 11 and by these standards, pubescent girls younger than eight would be considered 'precocious' sexual developers.[4]

It is important to note that the incidence of early onset of puberty does not necessarily mean the early onset of menstruation. In fact, the majority of girls who begin puberty early progress through this stage slowly and tend to reach first menstruation at the same age (13 years) as their cohorts. In this respect, puberty is not so much accelerated as it is elongated (from 18 months to 3 years).

On its own, the development of puberty for girls stands as a significant event, as it signals the onset of profound changes in a girl's life and impacts the give and take of family control. Yet, such changes also resonate within more expansive social parameters. This is because puberty involves not just the physiological modifications taking place within an adolescent body but the ways in which these changes are socially understood and the changing social contexts in which these understandings are formed. As child-centered ethnographies have shown (e.g., James 1993), bodies are of great importance to children in the creation of self and social identity. A child's size, shape, gender, sex, and any number of other visible characteristics (spectacles and skin, hair or eye color) are all crucial markers of social distinction. And as her own body constantly changes through on-going and varying forms of development—of which puberty is only one instance—a child's sense of self and her perception of others are re-created as well.

In a like manner, so too does a child's changing body affect, as it is affected by, social perception. Children, more than any other age group, are held to strict normative limits and controls. A great deal of attention is paid to a child's 'proper' development—as the archival documents of growth charts, school records, vaccination histories and family photo albums attest. As Kovarik (1994) has argued, childhood is temporally and spatially structured into 'stages and scripts': a child's given age, from infant to toddler to preschooler to school-ager to adolescent and teenager, involves different expectations about the capabilities of different bodies and their different types of independent movement and access to different social spaces. Puberty is obviously perceived as a most important marker within this genealogy. It signals a girl's imminent entrance into the social and temporal spaces of adult life—and therefore her entry into the complex social, political, and economic relations of gender and sexuality.

Girls come of age in a patriarchal culture. The concessions paid as the price of this admission can be seen in the behavioral changes from childhood to adolescence. Girls begin to learn that their lives will always be shaped by the constraints of gendered power relations. These lessons are made concrete in instances of economic inequality or dependence, in shared peer group assumptions about appropriate gendered behavior, and in the simple, and sometimes violent, day-to-day affirmation of the subordinate values males place upon females as sexual beings (McRobbie 1991; Friedman 1994; Pipher 1994). Yet, such determinations are not without their contradictions. Girls are also portrayed as impertinent and powerful (e.g., Lolita or Grrrrl culture)—an image which bolsters, as it ostensibly belies, a sexualized and commodified image of adolescent girls as precocious, delinquent and deviant.

Puberty is therefore shaped by a whole concatenation of personal, physical, and political forces. Deviations from such markers of normal development—such as early puberty—can cause a great deal of social anxiety. Early maturing girls are not sticking to the temporal and spatial script.

Such societal concerns have undoubtedly contributed to the popular and professional interest that Hermann-Giddens' study has provoked. The research not only appears to show an increase in sexual maturation in young girls in the United States but a quite dramatic racial distinction in the rate of maturation. Underlying these findings is the provocative question of why these changes are taking place *now*. While much is known of the varying consequences which early puberty may have for a girl, relatively little has been concretely determined about the social, psychological, and physiological antecedents of these consequences. Instead, there are competing hypotheses that attempt to account for the accelerated maturation of young girls.

Body weight is crucial for the timing of sexual development. It is commonly accepted that overweight girls tend to menstruate early, while for severely underweight girls the onset of menses begins late if at all. This is because menstruation is triggered by body weight—it starts when a girl is heavy enough (has enough body fat) to support a pregnancy—which is virtually always at 105 lbs or 17% body fat. Eighty years ago, menstruation began at age 16 and now, because of the substantive increase in the quality of nutrition, it begins on average at age 13.

Hermann-Giddens' research compared the weight and height of study girls against a national sample of race-specific data from the first and second national Health and Nutrition Examination Surveys (HANES). The girls in Hermann-Giddens study were found in general to be larger than in the HANES sample, especially as age increased. Moreover, "[study] girls who had one or more secondary sexual characteristics [evidence of breast development or pubic hair] were larger and heavier than sexually immature girls" (Hermann-Giddens et al. 1997: 508). Hermann-Giddens et al. proposed two factors that may have bearing on these findings. Because the HANES data are approximately 20 years old, girls in general today may be taller and heavier. Moreover, the report cites several studies undertaken in the United States in the 1970s and 1980s that found African-American girls to be taller, heavier, and maturing earlier than white girls of the same age. Nonetheless, Hermann-Giddens et al. were unable to offer an "explanation for the discrepancy in timing sequence between the African-American and white girls for either the on-set of puberty and subsequent menses or appearance and spacing of the secondary sexual characteristics. Neither [could they] explain the earlier development among African-American girls in general" (ibid.: 510).

Still, the association of early puberty with heaviness has grown apace with recent concerns regarding the weight and health of children in the United States and Canada.[5] Twenty-five percent of children under the age of 19 in the U.S. are obese or overweight. Twenty-five percent of children in the U.S. also live in poverty (in Canada, 1 in 5 children lives in poverty). Obesity is crosscut with the politics of class and race. It is the urban working poor and their increasing need for cheap and fast meals as they run from home to job, from job to job, or from school to home, that has fuelled the growth of fast-food empires such as McDonalds or Wendy's (Townsend et al. 2001).

Food is also a culprit in another popular theory, which argues that the presence of growth hormone additives in dairy products (or even the nutritional make-up of cow's milk itself) causes 'precocious sexual development.' Today, there is many a mother who will not allow her daughter to consume industrial dairy products, in the fear that "she will have the body of a grown woman by the time she is ten" (Belkin 2000: 41). While there has yet to be any strong epidemiological evidence pointing to milk as the cause of accelerated maturation, nonetheless, this theory remains perhaps the most compelling to a popular audience.

Hormones have long been associated with puberty and its rages, as puberty begins when estrogen levels are at a peak. Hormones are 'chemical messengers'—the natural secreting products of endocrine glands found in plants, animals, and humans. In higher vertebrates, they travel through the blood stream, where they affect the tissues and organs they come into contact with. In binding with cells, hormones influence the regulation, growth, and equilibrium of body function. Key endocrine glands are the hypothalamus, pituitary, thyroid, parathyroid, pancreas, adrenal, ovary, and testes.

The fears associated with hormone-ridden cattle are also connected to the more dispersed, and increasingly more deadly, consequences of our degraded environment. In 1997, the U.S. Environmental Protection Agency reported, "evidence has been accumulating that humans and domestic and wild species have suffered adverse health consequences resulting from exposure to environmental chemicals that interact with the endocrine system "(EPA 1997: vii)." These chemicals are believed to mimic the effects of the body's own natural hormones, such as estrogen, and thus produce a cascade of developmental problems, including hormone-sensitive cancers such as breast, ovarian, cervical and testicular cancers and, potentially, early puberty. At least fifty chemicals have been identified as possible hormone disruptors, the majority of which are found in pesticides, fungicides, herbicides, insecticides, and nematocides. They can also be found in solvents, sunscreen lotions, plastic bottles, hair straighteners, nail polish and in the lining of food cans— in short, the everyday ingredients of our Chemical Age. Billions of pounds of these chemicals are released into the environment every year—exposing plants, humans, and animals to any number of chemical compounds at every point of the globe.

While there are, as yet, no hard evidentiary claims linking endocrine disruptors to early puberty, those studies investigating the linkage have strengthened the possibility. A research team of pediatric endocrinologists led by Jean-Pierre Bourguignon of Belgium found that girls who immigrated to Belgium from countries such as India or Colombia were 80 times more likely to begin puberty before the age of eight. The researchers found high levels of DDE (a derivative of DDT and a well-known estrogenic pesticide) in the blood of these children (M. Krstevska-Konstaninova et al. 2001). In the U.S., an on-going study at Emory University has found that girls born to women exposed to the chemical polybrominated biphenyl (PBB) in 1973— inadvertently mixed with cattle feed in one of the largest food contamination accidents in U.S. history—started menstruating one-half to a full year earlier than others (Blanck et al. 2000). Research published in 1994 suggests that hair products containing estrogen may be related to the increasing prevalence of early puberty amongst African-American girls (Tiwary 1994: 135, 108A). These studies that investigate endocrine disruptors are especially compelling because they forward notions of an 'unseen' yet prevalent danger preying upon children while they are fetuses in utereo or while they work or play in agricultural fields.

Not surprisingly, social scientific studies have also contributed to the causal hypotheses regarding 'precocious sexual development.' One of these is "the absent-father hypothesis" proposed by developmental psychologists (Ellis et al. 1999). Expanding from evolutionary psychology's contention that early family environment has the capacity to shape reproductive behavior; the absent-father hypothesis suggests that the quality of a father-daughter relationship has important consequences for a daughter's age of puberty and that the greater the level of supportive and positive interactions between father and daughter, the later the onset of puberty. However, if the biological father is absent in a daughter's early life, then the earlier the puberty (cf. Jones et al. 1972; Moffitt et al 1992; Wierson et al. 1993). Moreover, if there is an unrelated male in the household, this maturation is further accelerated. One of the principal researchers of this study has proposed that this may be due to the influence of pheromones from the unrelated male (Ellis and Garber 2000).

The Attractions of Vulnerability

My interest lies less in the veracity of each of these competing explanations, than the way in which they are folded within and are articulated to both each other and to other locations of societal concern. Explanations of 'precocious sexual development,' as with most scientific claims, are based upon the strength of association among variables rather than upon a direct causal relationship. And it is the degree of concern with which we attend to such variables—the ways in which we respond to and regard the relations of poverty, television, fast food, endocrine additives, or the break-up of marriages and absent fathers, especially as these are culled through the sieve of North American class, gender and racial ideologies—that builds the strength of these associations. This acknowledgment of the historical and social construction of epistemic value guides us to expand the question of 'precocious sexual development' onto a multi-layered milieu of substances, qualities, forces and events, rather than one of origins. If we accept that causal hypotheses are the product of social conditions, then we may also begin approaching this question (hopefully somewhat) free from reductionist traps. As feminist sociologist Christine Delphi once argued:

> When we connect gender and sex, are we comparing something social to something natural or are we connecting something social with something which is also social (in this case, the way that a given society represents biology to itself)? (1993: 5)

How now does society represent the biology, the bodies, of its children to itself? What is being made meaningful in the stories told about 'precocious sexual development'?

In his 1967 work, *Coldness and Cruelty*, Gilles Deleuze notes that medicine is comprised of three different activities: "symptomatology," which is the study of signs of illness and the grouping of these "signs" into "symptoms"; etiology, which is the search for causes; and therapy, which is the development and application of treatment. Deleuze argues that etiology, "which is the scientific or experimental side of medicine, must be subordinated to symptomatology, which is its literary, artistic aspect" (1989: 133). Thus, it is the signifying capacity of 'precocious sexual development' that takes precedence over and guides the search for antecedent causal factors. The narrative told by this syndrome is far more compelling than the 'scientific proof.'

A recurring figure in the majority of hypotheses concerning early puberty is the 'vulnerable' child, impoverished or assailed by unseen outside forces. This premise of vulnerability offers a most compelling narrative. Something is changing the bodies of children. (Although, it is not one thing, but many things: a number of multi-causal factors.) Regardless of what *it* is, there is the consistent and implicit assumption that it comes not from within but from without. It is a foreign body acting upon the bodies of the innocent.

Representations of modern childhood are heavily reliant upon the idea of 'innocence'; a term which rose from the Industrial Revolutions of the 18th and 19th centuries, and today gains its efficacy from a number of complex material, economic, and semiotic registers (Aries 1962; James, Jenks and Prout 1998; Giroux 2000). Childhood is commonly represented as a 'natural' state, a kind of 'never-land' temporally and spatially removed from the 'real' world of adults. Ideally, children should be shielded from the instrumental relations of economics and the productive sphere. Their social worth then lies not in the ability to generate surplus value as workers but in being objects of expressive or "sentimental value" (Zelizer 1994). As those who are 'innocent' of the exigencies of economics, history and politics, children are posited as pre-social beings who act upon instinct and unreason and are not yet reined to, or ruined by, the conventions or corruptions of the social. In this respect, the modern child is closely linked to historical conceptions of 'the primitive Other,' that "creature without speech" (Soper 1995: 76) who inhabits a pristine natural state.

Innocence, however, is a gilded cage. The non-economic appeal of children allows for its own exploitations, and it is a conceptual apparatus that excludes some children as it captures others within its grasp. With its signifiers of nostalgia, comfort and stasis, the concept of 'innocence' tends to halo white upper-middle class children, whilst leaving poor children and children of color in another, less pure and thus less worthy state. Moreover, the obligations of a protected and 'priceless' childhood safely removed from the corruptions of labor ironically remove children from their own experiences of autonomy and agency (Giroux 2000). Children are to be the real, everyday equivalent of Anne Geddes' perverse photographs of children guised as vegetables: immobile, mute and something to be picked up at the market. Economically worthless, but symbolically priceless, the child becomes wholly dependent upon the adult for any designation of value. As James Kincaid puts it, "[innocence] makes you vulnerable—badly in need of protection" (1998: 54).

Threats to the state of innocence are dealt a swift paternal hand. Children are kept in custody, locked indoors and entertained by the commercial predations of television perhaps, but away from the predatory reach of child molesters. And children themselves are carefully watched for any infractions of 'purity.' A child's non-economic appeal is dependent upon his or her ability to remain attractive as an emotional object—an often-difficult task, given the difficulties of child development in general. A child should always be pleasant, playful, and compliant, and transgressions of this code are often strictly enforced. No doubt, the violence meted out to children on a weekly (if not daily) basis is a result of the frustrations experienced by those stifled within the confines of domesticity and childhood innocence.[6] The structural passivity and powerlessness of school and home lend themselves to practices of discipline and enforcement, often to the level of abuse.

There is a great deal of ideological work performed under the auspices of this historically recent, and Western concept, of childhood. It aids the legitimation of the sexual and spatial separation of work from home—thus normalizing wage labor and the sequestering of women and children into the emotional, domestic sphere. It defines adulthood in so far as it is the innocence of childhood that constructs its antithesis. It universalizes childhood. Childhood innocence is constituted as an innate, essential part of *all* children, an ontological trick which renders the lives of children homogenous despite their social-economic, racial and cultural differences and thus excludes those who have 'fallen from innocence' by virtue of these differences. Lastly, childhood innocence allows for the conceptualization of children as passive, commodified, and sexualized objects. It is a short distance from adoration to exploitation.

Michel Foucault spoke of the ways in which inhibition also always circulates back upon a pleasurable incitement. The productivities of discourse, especially as they "trace around bodies and sexes," revolve in "perpetual spirals of pleasure and power" (1990: 45). As that which is free from the corruptions of adult society, innocence is also *always potentially corruptible*, and so it is constantly shadowed and shaped by its future debasement. What begins as a negation ultimately begins again as an enticement. In this respect, it is interesting that the term 'precocious sexual development' turns so readily to its eroticized twin: 'the sexually promiscuous child.' The vulnerable is not only to be protected but also promoted.

In his acerbic analysis of the culture of child molesting—the media spectacles, the endless and ongoing talk on talk shows, the hypocrisies— James Kincaid writes:

> Few stories in our culture right now are as popular as those of child molesting....Why do we generate these stories and not others? What rewards do they offer? Who profits from their circulation and who pays the price? (1998:3)

The United States has long been besotted with the matter of child abuse. Its global cultural industries are vehicles in which girl children are frequently trafficked—the Olsen twins, the 5-year old 'beauty queen' JonBenet Ramsey, or the more 'intermediate' Britney Spears (she who is 'not a girl, not yet a woman') are only a few of its more recent commodities. However, it is also a place that regards an erotic response to children as a heinous crime. In other words, it professes to prohibit that which it also perpetrates. Its denunciations are always and only just further deployments of desire. As Kincaid puts it (in a manner which evokes Foucault's "repressive hypothesis"): "When we speak of the unspeakable, we keep the speaking going" (ibid.: 21).

Both the representations of precocious sexual development and the cultural industry of child molestation are premised upon an image of the vulnerable child: an innocent whose protection has failed. In this provocative story of the violation of innocence, the character of the violating agent is always foreign. And yet, harm is perpetrated within the more familiar limits of nation and home. It results from those social policies and political economies that allow for the continuation of childhood poverty, junk food, chemicals in the environment, hormones in cow's milk, and little girls dressed up as Joan Collins. 'Innocence' is a fetishistic tale serving to deflect attention away from the harm that a society *systemically* inflects upon its children. As Henry Giroux has argued, "innocence…makes children invisible except as projections of adult fantasies—fantasies that allow adults to believe that children do not suffer from their greed, recklessness, perversions of will and spirit and that adults are, in the final analysis, unaccountable for their actions" (2000: 40).

The attractions of vulnerability speak to the paradoxical times we inhabit. The economic restructuring of the past twenty years has indeed made us more susceptible. The replacement of long-term and binding agreements of employment with short-term, tendered services has got us used to the idea that mutual obligations are no longer to be expected and that only an uncertain future lies ahead. At the same time, the ideologies of self-interest and individualism accompanying the 'structural adjustments' of neo-liberalism cast us as so many autonomous competitors: each one fighting for our own piece of propertied enrichment, each one "utterly, unqualifiedly responsible for [our]selves" and yet at the same time, "dependent upon conditions which completely elude [our] grasp" (Beck 1992: 137). We are left with the paradoxical situation of a society experiencing an 'enforced' vulnerability, and those people and things which purport to protect us—tax cuts, downsizing, privatization of social services, ethnic profiling, pre-emptive strikes and regime change—are also those which perpetuate harm. Vulnerability no longer has to refer to any real referent of injury or actual suffering. It has become a heuristic device for social control.

A Habitus of Some Uncertainty

Surely, a nation's political and social landscape becomes a child's experience, as she must travel through it in so many various ways. Following the work of Pierre Bourdieu, it may be argued that this contemporary landscape constitutes an entirely different "field" of objective social conditions, within which children variously occupy different "structuring structures" or "habitus." In a dialectic of internal and external relations, the 'field' supplies those objective conditions which structure the 'habitus', while the 'habitus'— through the embodiment of meaningful social action—is constitutive of the 'field' (Bourdieu 1977: 72). Habitus describes that generative location, system, and time whereby the social—ingrained, taken-for-granted time whereby the social—ingrained, taken-for-granted assumptions and so-cial inequalities—is incorporated into the corporeal and psychological dispo-sitions of individuals. In this respect, 'habitus' importantly involves the reproduction of class and gender relations. Yet, this is more of a generative, than strictly determinative process. Bourdieu places a temporal accent upon 'habitus,' opening up its accepted practices to contingency and historical change. As Lois McNay describes it, the embodied responses of habitus are not just repetitive acts of social reproduction but "a creative anticipation of future uncertainty on the part of social actors" or a "practical reference to the future" (1999:102).

Habitus is realized in *le sens pratique* ('feel for the game'), a mode of knowledge that involves the habitual or 'instinctual' responses of a body without conscious thought, a form of behavior which is automatic because it is engrained in bodily practice (Bourdieu 1990: 52). For instance, a primary distinction of small child from adult is the latter's internalized performance of bodily practices in a socially prescribed manner, such as eating or defe-cating in the right way and at the right time. But, while such learned social behavior may be 'automatic,' it is also strategic, as it involves the manipula-tion of the tempo (the pace of time unfolding) of the habitual response of a body. What implications, then, may the current objective structures of society hold for girls in Canada and the U.S.—not only in terms of their life condi-tions (which have already been found to suffer[7])—but also for the manner and *the pace* with which they now conduct themselves? Does early puberty involve a habituated and strategic response to the uncertain terrain of neo-liberalism?

Lately, a number of cultural analysts have focused their attention upon the recent changes wrought by neo-liberal society in the conceptualization, evaluation, and treatment of children in North American society (e.g., Giroux 2000; Lee 2001; Grossberg 2001). In varying ways, each of these writers finds that recent shifts towards less stable economic and political arrange-ments, and the free-run of a consumer ethos, have been deleterious for chil-dren. In an essay that convincingly argues that the United States is engaged in a "war on children," Larry Grossberg links neoliberalism's "radical de-valuation of labor" to a diminished appraisal of children. Labor and the social inclusion and citizenship that accrue from it are crucial components of mod-ernity and as such are also articulated to its key concepts of progress, the dy-namic movement of time, and the investment in the future. Grossberg argues that, "by placing finance capital at the centre, [neoliberalism] is attempting...to negate—or at least amend and partially retreat from—the assumption of labor as the source of value" (2001: 131). Children and youth have long acted as privileged signifiers for the continuation and progress of society into the future. Yet, in the shift from industrial commodity capital to a 'fictive' finance capital, youth is no longer of value (to put it in Althusserian terms) for the reproduction of the conditions of production. Or, as Grossberg puts it, youth have lost their value as "the trope of the universal faith in futurity" (ibid.: 133). In fact, they have become so de-valued to the point of being erased. They have become adults before their time.

The telescoping of childhood into adulthood neatly parallels concern paid to the synchronic position of contemporary children. A popular nostalgic representation portrays childhood as a time of idleness; an 'endless summer' of slowly moving bodies and hours. Today, the rhythms of childhood are believed to have sped up dramatically, keeping pace with the tempo of contemporary life in which time is a precious commodity. Recent ethnographic research commissioned by the Girl Scouts of the U.S.A. finds that girls of "middle childhood" (ages 8–12) "seem to be pressured to deal with typically 'teenage' issues years before they reach their teens" (2000: 5). The research supports parents' beliefs that child development is becoming "hurried" or "compressed" (ibid.). Similarly, Allan Mirabelli, executive director of the Vanier Institute of the Family in Ottawa, comments that, "Our children do suffer from what Daniel Elkind characterizes as the "hurried child syndrome," as they rush, at younger and younger ages, to emulate and imitate adults and their behaviors. It is more convenient to us if our children grow up quickly so that they become less dependent upon us" (Fulsang 2002: L1). Given the economic necessity of working parents and government cutbacks to funding of schools, most children's lives today are far more shaped by regimen and discipline than those of a previous generation were. School time now segues onto structured (and paid for) after-school activity, and family evenings have become a tyranny of school-assigned duties. School-aged children are given the appearance of miniature flight attendants as they wheel suitcases, instead of knapsacks, to carry home their heavy burdens. The rigid structure and stressful obligations of the parent have become shared by the child.

Are girls not only addressed by society's synchronic rhythms, social policies, and ideological reproductions as adult females but also responding to these mediations in embodied ways? If discourse (pace Foucault) creates its own productivities, what new bodies are produced by advanced capitalism? Here's one deterministic and rather crude answer: Perhaps young girls are becoming the only thing of value in this new world of de-valued laboring bodies—the value of commodified sexual objects? This is a response, which is evocative of Henry Giroux's contention that "corporate culture's promotion of the sexualization of children has shortened the distance between childhood and adulthood" (2000: 16). Similarly, this response echoes the parental panics ensuing from the current 'pop-tart' look of bared midriffs, 'junior thong' underwear, and hip-hugger jeans cut down to the pubis favored by pre-teen girls (Fulsang 2002). However, such answers are too expedient and not explanatory enough. They do not go far enough in attempting to deal with the multi-faceted milieu that revolves around this troublesome subject.

Despite the fact that young people now occupy a social order in which employment or social services can no longer be taken for granted, their responses to such uncertainty cannot be generalized as reactionary or pessimistic. In fact, in the midst of a widespread attenuation of security and life choices, young people are found to adopt a highly individualist approach to life that emphasizes choice and agency. As Johanna Wyn and Rob White have recently discovered, there is a growing gap "between the structural position of young people, in terms of schooling, employment and income, and the experiences and perceptions of young people as they attempt to deal with new social constraints and opportunities" (2000: 165). This makes some sense too. Young people today have little or no experience with an expansionary welfare state, life-long employment, and collective society. They have come to know a completely different world, which prioritizes a 'rationalized economy' and 'the entrepreneurial self' as ideological 'commonsense.' 'Self-possession' and 'self-confidence' have become the panacea for the intense competition that occupies society today. While it may seem contradictory to acquire a highly individualistic perspective about one's life circumstances when such circumstances would be better understood in terms of the structural conditions of neo-liberalism, such an "epistemological fallacy" (Furlong and Cartmel 1997) may also be read as a strategic response. The dispositions of habitus emerge from a "practical evaluation of the likelihood of success of a given action in a given situation…" (Bourdieu 1977: 77).

Precociousness may be read as a type of strategic reaction—a 'becoming adult,' becoming self-possessed—for a society that no longer has time for children. Perhaps precocious sexual development can be understood in a similar way. The class and gender-specific conditions of socialization that girls occupy today are fraught with contradiction: stressing both conventional, if not reactionary, gender roles and the necessity of accumulating economic capital. Why not grow up quickly? But something, again, interrupts this smooth equation.

Recall that precocious sexual development involves less an accelerated maturation than the *elongation of the time* of puberty. Girls are not becoming women earlier—in terms of reaching menses—but rather become pubescent earlier and remain that way for extended durations. The distinction is important—as one signifies an attainment of adulthood (at least in a physiological respect) while the other signifies an anticipation of adulthood. If we are to read early puberty as an 'embodied social practice,' then this important temporal dimension to the encounter of habitus and field cannot be overlooked. For again, it is the tempo or pace of a social action that lends it its strategic qualities: the brushing up against ambiguity and contradiction as it moves through space and time.

Jacques Deleuze and Felix Guatarri once wrote, "We are not *in* the world, we *become with* the world" (1994: 169). The ways in which a child grows into and occupies the world are dependent upon the ways in which the world grows into and occupies her. Not only are these through the signs and languages of an external world but also the manner in which these signs and languages *sound* to her, the means by which they resonate against her body with different degrees of intensity, or what Greg Seigworth (1999) describes as "the slow, steady and continual accumulation of seeming insignificances." How a body is affected is also how a body is connected—to moments of space and time and the composition and conjunction of these moments. The images and languages of our social world are influential beyond the signifying productions of ideology—they entail *affect*, in addition to effects. May not precocious sexual development be the result (as one part of a multiple) of affects—a body affected by the different shifting resonances and tempo of this new social terrain?

Notes

I acknowledge financial and course-release support from the Social Sciences and Humanities Research Council (SSHRC), the Faculty of Arts at York University, and the York University Research Development Fellowship towards the researching and writing of this project.

[1]   Wal-Mart, which, as the world's largest corporation, makes $220 billion a year in revenues, is also the largest importer of Chinese-made products in the world, buying $10 billion worth of merchandise from several Chinese factories annually (Hightower, *The CCPA Monitor*, November 2002, 10–11).

[2]   The gap between rich and poor in Canada is now dramatic. Statistics Canada's most recent survey (1994) shows that while Canadians hold $2.4 trillion in personal wealth (averaging an impressive $199,664 for each family unit), the actual distribution of this wealth is anything but equitable. "The wealthiest 10% of family units in Canada held 53% of the personal wealth, and the top 50% controlled an almost unbelievable 94.4% of the wealth. That left only 5.6% to be shared amongst the bottom 50%" (Kerstetter, *The CCPA Monitor*, November 2002, 1).

[3]   This study was conducted via the American Academy of Pediatrics (AAP) Pediatric Research in Office Settings (PROS) network. The goal of the study was to describe the prevalence of secondary sexual characteristics and occurrences in U.S. girls aged 3–12 as seen in pediatric office practice. Data were collected from July 1992 to Sept. 1993 from 17,077 girls who were seen for a health supervision (well-child) visit, or a problem (e.g., abdominal pain, fatigue) that according to office routine would require a complete physical examination. Although it was recognized that a study drawn from office practice would not represent a population-based sample, it was believed that findings from such a study would provide more relevant norms for U.S. girls than currently exist. Of the 17,077 girls, 9.6% were African-American and 90.4% were Caucasian.

[4]   Because nationally representative data on the subject were lacking up until the publication of Hermann-Giddens et al. 1997 (see below), clinicians largely relied on Marshall and Tanner's classic study on pubertal changes in girls, published in 1969. See Marshall and Tanner 1969.

[5]   There has been a dramatic increase in overweight and obese children in the United States over the past 20 years, and a concurrent rise in incidence of Type 2 diabetes in youth. See Shinha et al. 2002.

[6]   Despite widespread awareness and condemnation of child abuse, a 1995 study (Giles-Stiles et al 1995: 170-176), offers evidence that a majority of parents in the U.S. physically punish their children. Interviews with mothers showed that 61% had spanked their pre-schooler in the past week. Twenty-six percent had spanked their pre-schooler three or more times over the past week. It is estimated that a pre-schooler receives over 150 spankings a year. The physical punishment of children also continues to enjoy state and institutional sanction: 22 states in the U.S. still allow corporeal punishment in schools.

[7]   In 1989, when the Parliament of Canada vowed to eliminate child poverty by the year 2000, 15% of the nation's children (or one in seven) were living in poverty. Since then, 400,000 more Canadian children have become poor, increasing Canada's child poverty

rate by 39%. One in five, or 20% of all children in Canada now live in poverty. Food bank use has also increased in Canada since 1989. The largest group of people served by food banks is single-mother-headed families (Canadian Association of Food Banks, *2001 Hunger Count Survey*, March 2001).

References

Ariés, P. *Centuries of Childhood: A Social History of Family Life.* Translated by R. Baldick. New York: Alfred A. Knopf, 1962.

Aronowitz, S., and W. DiFazio. *The Jobless Future: Sci-Tech and the Dogma of Work.* Minneapolis: University of Minnesota Press, 1995.

Baudrillard, J. *The Ecstasy of Communication.* Translated by B. Schutz and C. Schutz. New York: Semiotexte, 1988.

Bauman, Z. "Consuming Life." *Journal of Consumer Culture* 1, no.1 (2001): 9–29.

Beck, U. *Risk Society Toward a New Modernity.* Translated by M. Ritter. London: Sage, 1992.

Belkin, L. "The Making of an 8 Year Old Woman." *New York Times Magazine,* December 24, 2000, 38–43.

Blanck, H. M., M. Marcus, P. E. Tolbert, C. Rubin, A. K. Henderson, V. S. Hertzberg, R. H. Zhang, and L. Cameron. "Age at Menarche and Tanner Stage in Girls Exposed in Utero and Postnatally to Polybrominated Biphenyl." *Epidemiology* 6 (November 11 2000): 641–647.

Bourdieu, P. *The Logic of Practice.* Cambridge: Polity Press, 1990.

———. *Outline of a Theory of Practice.* Cambridge: Cambridge University Press, 1977.

Butler, J. *Bodies That Matter: On the Discursive Limits of Sex.* London: Routledge, 1993.

———. *Gender Trouble: Feminism and the Subversion of Identity.* London: Routledge, 1990.

Canadian Association of Food Banks. *2001 Hunger Count Survey*, March 2001.

Caspi. A., and T. E. Moffitt. "Individual Differences are Accentuated During Periods of Social Change: The Sample Case of Girls at Puberty." *Journal of Personality and Social Psychology* 61 (1991): 157–168.

Deleuze, G. *Coldness and Cruelty. A Discussion of 'Venus in Furs' by Leopold von Sacher-Masoch.* New York: Zone Press, 1989.

———. *Essays Critical and Clinical.* Translated by D. Smith and M. Greco. Minneapolis: University of Minnesota Press, 1997.

Deleuze, G., and F. Guattari. *A Thousand Plateaus: Capitalism and Schizophrenia.* Translated by B. Massumi. Minneapolis: University of Minnesota Press, 1987.

Delphi, C. "Rethinking Sex and Gender." *Women's Studies International Forum.*16, no. 1 (1993): 1–9.

Ellis, B. J., S. McFayden-Ketchum, K. Dodge, G. Pettit, and J. Bates. "Quality of Early Family Relationships and Individual Differences in the Timing of Pubertal Maturation in Girls: A Longitudinal Test of an Evolutionary Model." *Journal of Personality and Social Psychology* 77, no. 2 (1999): 387–401.

Ellis, B. J., and J. Garber. "Psychological Antecedents of Pubertal Maturation in Girls: Parental Psychopathology, Stepfather Presence, and Family and Marital Stress." *Child Development* 71 (2000): 485–501.

Environmental Protection Agency (EPA). *Special Report on Environmental Endrocrine Disruption: An Effects Assessment and Analysis.* Washington, D.C.: U.S. EPA, 1997.

Foucault, M. *The History of Sexuality, Vol. 1: An Introduction.* New York: Vintage Books, 1990.

Friedman, S. *Girls in the 90's.* Vancouver, Canada: Salal, 1994.

Fulsang, D. "Mom, I'm Ready for School." *The Globe and Mail*, Saturday September 28, 2002, L1.

Furlong, A., and F. Cartmel. *Young People and Social Change.* Buckingham: Open University Press, 1997.

Fuss, D. *Essentially Speaking: Feminism, Nature, Difference.* New York: Routledge, 1989.

Giles-Sims, J., M. A. Straus, and D. B. Sugerman. "Child, Maternal and Family Characteristics Associated with Spanking." *Family Relations* 44, no.2 (1995): 170–176.

Girl Scout Research Institute, (2000) *Girls Speak Out: Teens Before Their Time.* New York: Girl Scouts of the USA, 2000.

Giroux, H. *Stealing Innocence: Youth, Corporate Power and the Politics of Culture.* New York: St. Martin's Press, 2000.

Grossberg, L. "Why Does Neo-Liberalism Hate Kids?: The War on Youth and the Culture of Politics." *The Review of Education/Pedagogy/Cultural Studies* 23, no.2 (2001): 111–136.

Grosz, E. *Volatile Bodies: Towards a Corporeal Feminism.* London and New York: Routledge, 1994.

Hermann-Giddens, M., E. Slora, R. Wasserman, C. J. Bourdony, M. V. Bhapkar, G. Koch, and C. M. Hasemeier. "Secondary Sexual Characteristics and Menses in Young Girls Seen in Office Practice: A Study from the Pediatric Research in Office Settings Network." *Pediatrics* 99, no. 4 (1997): 505–512.

Hightower, J. "How Wal-Mart Is Re-Making the World." *The CCPA Monitor* 9, no. 6 (2002): 10–12.

James, A. *Childhood Identities: Self and Social Relationships in the Experience of a Child.* Edinburgh: Edinburgh University Press, 1993.

James, A., C. Jenks, and A. Prout. *Theorizing Childhood.* Cambridge: Polity Press, 1998.

Jones, B., J. Leeton, L. McLeod, and C. Wood. "Factors Influencing the Age of Menarche in a Lower Socio-Economic Group in Melbourne." *Medical Journal of Australia* 2 (1972): 533–535.

Kampert, J. B., A. S. Whittemore, and R. S. Paffenbarger. "Combined Effects of Childbearing, Menstrual Effects and Body Size on Age-Specific Breast Cancer Risk." *American Journal of Epidemiology* 128 (1988): 962–979.

Kerstetter, S. "Rags and Riches." *The CCPA Monitor* 9, no.6 (2002): 1,7.

Kincaid, J. R. *Erotic Innocence: The Culture of Child Molesting.* Durham and London: Duke University Press, 1998.

Kovarik, J. "The Space and Time of Children at the Interface of Psychology and Sociology." In *Childhood Matters: Social Theory, Practice and Politics*, edited by J. Qvortrup, M. Bandy, G. Sgritta and H. Wintersbeger. Aldershot: Avebury, 1994.

Krstevska-Konstantinova, M., C. Charlier, M. Craen, M. DuCaju, C. Heinrichs, C. deBeaufort, G. Plomteux, and J. P. Bourguigon. "Sexual Precocity after Immigration from Developing Countries to Belgium: Evidence of Previous Exposure to Organochlorine Pesticides." *Human Reproduction* 16, no. 5 (2001): 1020–1026.

Lee, N. *Childhood and Society: Growing Up in an Age of Uncertainty.* Buckingham: Open University Press, 2001.

Lukacs, G. *History and Class Consciousness: Studies in Marxist Dialectics.* Translated by R. Livingstone. Cambridge, Mass.: MIT Press, 1971.

Manlove, J. "Early Motherhood in an Intergenerational Perspective: The Experiences of a British Cohort." *Journal of Marriage and the Family* 59 (1997): 263–279.

Marshall, W. A., and J. M. Tanner. "Variations in the Pattern of Pubertal Changes in Girls." *Archives of Diseased Child* 44 (1969): 291–303.

McNay, L. "Gender, Habitus and the Field: Pierre Bourdieu and the Limits of Reflexivity." *Theory, Culture and* Society 16, no.1 (1999): 95–117.

McRobbie, A. *Feminism and Youth Culture.* Boston: Unwin Hyman, 1991.

Moffitt, T. E., A. Caspi, J. Belsky, and P. A. Silva. "Childhood Experience and the On-set of Menarche: A Test of a Sociobiological Method." *Child Development* 63 (1992): 47–58.

Ness, R. "Adiposity and Age of Menarche in Hispanic Women." *American Journal of Human Biology* 3 (1991): 41–48.

Pipher, M. *Reviving Ophelia: Saving the Selves of Adolescent Girls.* New York: Ballentine, 1994.

Rifkin, J. *The Age of Access: The New Culture of Hypercapitalism Where All of Life Is a Paid-For Experience.* New York: Putnam Books, 2000.

Seaton, E. "The Commodification of Fear." *Topia* no. 5 (2001): 1–15.

Seigworth, G. "Sound Affects." CultStud-L List, September 5 1999. Available from www.cas.usf.edu/communication/rodman/cultstud/columns.

Shinha, R., G. Fisch, B. Teague, W. Tamborlane, B. Banyas, K. Allen, M. Savoye, V. Rieger, S. Taksali, G. Barbetta, R. Sherwin, and S. Caprio. "Prevalence of Impaired Glucose Tolerance Among Children and Adolescents with Marked Obesity." *The New England Journal of Medicine* 346, no. 2 (2002): 802–810.

Soper, K. *What Is Nature?: Culture, Politics and the Non-human.* Oxford: Blackwell, 1995.

Tiwary, C. M. "Premature Sexual Development in Children Following the Use of Placenta and/or Estrogen Containing Hair Products." *Pediatric Research* 135 (1994): 108A (abstract).

Townsend, M. S., J. Person, B. Love, C. Achetenberg, and S. Murphy. "Food Insecurity Is Positively Related to Overweight in Women." *Journal of Nutrition* 131 (2001): 1738–1745.

Wierson, M., P. J. Long, and R. L. Forehand. "Toward a New Understanding of Early Menarche: The Role of Environmental Stress in Pubertal Timing." *Adolescence* 28 (1993): 913–924.

Wyn, J., and R. White. "Negotiating Social Change: The Paradox of Youth." *Youth and Society* 32, issue 2 (2000): 165–183.

Zelizer, V. *Pricing the Priceless Child: The Changing Social Value of Children.* Princeton, New Jersey: Princeton University Press, 1994.

CHAPTER THREE

From Nerd to Popular?
Re-figuring School Identities
and Transformation Stories

Marnina Gonick

The bell rings. Two girls sit around a table, eating. It's lunchtime. They are engaged in an animated conversation. A third girl joins them—looking gloomy. Walking slowly, Tori makes her entrance.

Girl 1:	*So what's up?*
Tori:	*Nothing really.*
Girl 2:	*Something wrong?*
Tori:	*I don't want to talk about it.*
Girl 1:	*You can tell us.*
Tori:	*Okay, I have a problem. It's a school problem. Not about homework or anything, right? It's just that I feel like a nerd. I'm so ugly.*

FAST FORWARD. Tile floor, blue stalls— it's the girls' washroom. Dance music can be heard, coming from some distance away. Tori's feet are visible from underneath one of the stalls, surrounded by articles of clothing. She addresses the two girls waiting on the other side of the stall.

Tori:	*I feel so uncomfortable in these clothes!*
Girl 1:	*Come on!*
Girl 2:	*Don't be chicken!*
Tori:	*Promise not to laugh?*
Girl 1:	*Okay.*

THE DOOR OPENS AND TORI CAUTIOUSLY EXITS THE STALL.

Tori's story is one of a series of fictional narratives about girls' lives written, performed, and videotaped by a group of middle school girls, living in Toronto. The girls, ages 12–14, are of racially diverse backgrounds and came with their families as immigrants and refugees from Vietnam, Cambodia, Hong Kong, Grenada, and Portugal. The video stories were created as part of a school-community project that I facilitated for two and half years. Out of the experience, I eventually produced a book-length ethnography (Gonick 2003). In this chapter, I want to use the story the girls wrote for their character, Tori, as an entry into a broader discussion of the cultural and meaning-making practices of these young women. In particular, the story offers some important insights into how the female versions of the seemingly ubiquitous social categories 'nerd' and 'popular' operate in girl culture.

Schools and Transformation Stories

The predicament of the nerd, as Tori defines it for her friends, is a "school problem." The nerd-popular categorization is something of a cultural signature of North American schools. It pervades many popular culture exposés of adolescent life in film, television, and books, and it has also been the subject of academic studies documenting life in schools (Canaan 1990; Eckert 1989; Eder 1985, 1995; Kinney 1993). At one time, the question of popularity was also a serious topic of debate by teachers, parents, and school administrators. Thompson argues that in the 1920s and 1930s parents and teachers encouraged the proliferation of adolescent social and extracurricular life with the underlying assumption that sociability prepared middle-class girls to be social assets in their futures as wives of businessmen and professionals (Thompson 1995: 48). Social and political scientists considered the economic and political implications of the popular\unpopular split as early as the 1920s. According to Thompson, the apparatus of clubs, proms, and student government was thought to confer schools' institutional power on popular students, creating an elite and undermining what some believed should be the equality-building projects of schools. Seen by some as a function of class, it was argued that either popularity had to be abolished or its skills taught to all, as part of an education in the ways of middle-class life (Thompson 1995: 50).

This historical debate about popularity highlights the relationship between youth culture and schools and the way they share jointly in the constitution of the identities, nerd and popular. The debate also illustrates how schools seem to be expected to perform a number of contradictory tasks: to both confirm and challenge social divisions, to control, regulate and emancipate, and to be sites for maintaining the social order and for producing social change. However, perhaps the most interesting aspect of this debate is the way both positions in it pivot around a valuing of middle- class over working-class norms. Making a shift into a position of popularity may therefore be viewed as a move out of and into a series of related discursive and social relations, involving a complex of gendered, classed—and I will add heterosexual and racialized—positionings.

More recently, the question of popularity and its opposite is usually analyzed in the media and by education experts as an individual and psychologized phenomena produced by an out-of-control youth culture. However, the terms on which the girls work with these categories in the telling of Tori's story harkens back to the historical terms of the debate. I suggest that the girls' interest in these categories to tell their story is, at least in part, what they represent as an embodiment of the power/knowledge nexus through which social difference is produced. The story investigates the ways in which social meanings and systems of valuation work to make difference recognizable. And it explores how these differences, in their contradictions and multiplicity, are lived and their meanings struggled over. In this fusion of themes, Tori's story serves as a vehicle through which to inquire into difficult questions about the assignment of recognition, vulnerabilities to misrecognition and the cultural practices girls use in the intricate and on-going project of becoming certain kinds of feminine subjects.

In creating a story about a nerd who wants to be popular, the girls turned to one of the genres most commonly used to tell the stories of women's lives, that of transformation. Closely related to the genre of romance, the rags-to-riches formula of these stories usually unfolds around a physical, moral, or linguistic transformation for the female protagonist. Its successful accomplishment is followed by women's traditional reward: the love of an eligible man. Cameron suggests that transformation stories are also what is being promised in the lengthy tradition of self-improvement literature specifically addressed to women as well as in the perennially popular 'make-over' feature in women's magazines (1995: 172). Playing on both desire and guilt, the seductiveness of this formula, Cameron argues, goes to the heart of a powerful fantasy for women in consumer cultures. Transformation, however, figures in an even older tradition of stories that significantly pre-dates modern capitalism. In these stories, rather than a professional army of fashion consultants, hair stylists and make-up artists, ugly ducklings become beautiful swans with only a wave of a magic wand. I am, of course referring to the fairy-tale. The structure of Tori's story also draws on the fairy tale that perhaps most epito-mizes the transformation genre: Cinderella.

As summarized by Jo Spence, the sequence of the tale of the kitchen maid turned princess may be characterized as a perceived lack on the part of the female protagonist, the intervention of an outside agent, and a resolution to the lack (Spence 1995: 63). Likewise, the structure of Tori's story is or-ganized into three distinct video segments arranged around the anticipation of, preparation for, and participation in a school dance. Each segment fea-tures Tori and her two friends in different school settings: the lunchroom, the girls' washroom, and the gym. Supported by the dialogue between characters and a visual vocabulary of props, wardrobe and hairstyle, these shifts in lo-cation propel the narrative's forward movement and signal the various stages of Tori's transformation. As a result, the transformation appears to take place in a logical and 'natural' sequencing order, making it possible to interpret it in particular (social) ways (Gilbert, 1992). The actuality of a school dance scheduled to take place around the time the videotaping was planned prompted the group to incorporate it into Tori's story—a decision which served to perhaps inadvertently further strengthen the resemblance of our protagonist's tale to that of her prototype, Cinderella. But, just as relevant, school dances may also have served the girls many of the same purposes they designed this particular one to perform for Tori.

Famous Movie Star or Garbage Picker?: Identification, Class, and the Popular Girl

As I have already suggested, one of the factors compelling the creation of a video character whose story revolved around the themes of popularity was the opportunity for the girls to use Tori's story as a relay point to engage with what was going on in the social world of their own school. I want to suggest that the writing of the story afforded the girls an opportunity to work through their own positionings within this valuation system as well as to fantasize alternative positions and what these might promise for something else. How-ever, although they neither considered themselves popular nor thought others did, it is too simple to suggest that the girls' identification(s) with their char-acter was a completely straightforward one.

1 Lan: Why does she want to be popular?
2 Fanny: Cause she's a nerd.
3 Mai: Don't you want to be in the popular crowd?

4 Fanny:	I'm a nerd and I don't care.
5 LeLy:	Don't you want to be popular?
6 Kenisha:	No.
7 Lan:	I just want to be normal.

There is a suggestion here of an ambivalent identification in the way the girls' responses, clearly articulated from an outside position, move from acceptance to resistance and refusal. Fanny's initial response to Lan's question (2) rehearses what Corrigan understands as the privileging of preferred forms: "a desire to be in 'those places' so designated so approved" (Corrigan 1987: 139). The only explanation required for why Tori wants to be popular is that she is a nerd (2). On her own behalf, however, she refuses this 'desired place' and Kenisha does the same (4, 6). Perhaps, as Lan seems to be suggesting, the struggle for even meeting the criteria of hegemonic definitions of 'normality' takes on particular force when one is, like these girls are, denied full access to dominant forms of cultural and social power (7).

However, as the discussion continues, this identificatory relationship with the idealized 'popular girl' becomes significantly more complex when LeLy forcefully insists that the other girls and Lan in particular, confront the privileges, power, pleasure, and excitement promised by inhabiting this 'desired place.' Perhaps what is most important about the insights that are offered here is what they have to suggest about the workings of a hunger for positive identification within a history of experienced rejection (Wexler 1992).

8 LeLy:	Don't tell me no one in here want to be popular!
9 Kenisha:	What do you mean popular? Popular sucks a lot.
10 LeLy:	In your heart, people!
11 Kenisha:	[mimicking] In your heart. You want to be popular. Popular sucks.
12 LeLy:	Okay, if you're taking Lidia and taking Fanny who do you want to be? Lidia or Fanny?
13 Kenisha:	[laughing] Fanny.
14 LeLy:	YOUR FACE! Who don't want to be Lidia? She's smart, she's popular, she's pretty, who don't?
15 Maria:	[inaudible]…she's popular, she's smart, she's pretty.
16 Fanny:	I don't care. I don't want to be her, even if she's smart.
17 LeLy:	They're not being honest, why bother? Who don't? Right Maria?
18 Lan:	I want to be rich and famous [inaudible].
19 Kenisha:	What's so nice about Lidia?
20 Maria:	Exactly, popular.
21 Kenisha:	[teasing] popular, she's pretty, she's a brainer, ahhhh.

22 Lan:	There, LeLy says she's a bitch.
23 Maria:	She is a bitch.
24 Fanny:	Horny, slut.
25 Lan:	Whoaa!
26 Mai:	But I don't think Lan's being honest here, she doesn't want to be Lidia. I'd rather be Lidia than Fanny too.
27 ?:	Of course you would!
28 LeLy:	Okay, let's put it this way. Lan, would you rather be a famous singer star or be a garbage picker?
29 Lan:	Famous movie star!
30 LeLy:	There, IN YOUR FACE! Who wouldn't want to be popular? Just putting another looking, another angle, thing.
31 Lan:	I don't want to be garbage picker, yuck. Garbage picker smells, you know.
32 LeLy:	I'm not talking about how they smell.
33 Mai:	Movie star has more respect than garbage picker.
34 LeLy:	You don't admit it one way, if you put it another way, you'll admit it!

While there is much to analyze in this exchange, I want to focus on the ways in which the famous movie star and garbage picker are suggestive of the classed dimensions of femininity embedded within the nerd-popular divide. Within the context of a discussion about popularity, the split pair establishes popularity as not only as the route to forms of recognition, visibility, and respect within the school but also as intimately connected with, and perhaps a symbolic analogy for, differential positions of power within class relations in a wider social context.

In the story, like others within the rags-to-riches genre (e.g., *Cinderella*, *My Fair Lady*) class is seen as something to be overcome, through a trajectory of education, leading to respectability, glamour, romance, and marriage. With the advice of her friends Tori discards her old outfit: the badly fitting jeans with cartoon character decals which hang well above her ankles; the scuffed running shoes; the blouse with the collar choked up around her neck, leaving her wrists as exposed as her ankles; her hair, brushed off her face and tightly fastened into two short braids. Her friends assure her that with the proper clothes and hairstyle she will attract the attention she desires from a boy named Scott at the school dance. However, as the friends discuss the plan the prospects for transformation are significantly complicated by a series of seemingly insurmountable obstacles:

Girl 2:   *If you like, get some new clothes*

Tori: *Yeah, I don't know. I'm so shy to go shopping by myself. I don't know which clothes match me and which not. And my mother always buys my clothes.*

Girl 2:   *Well, you have to tell her—*

Tori: *I'm spending their money, so I have to do whatever they say.*

Girl 1:   *Yeah, you have to stand up for your rights here.*

Tori: *I don't have that much confidence. You guys are strong, I'm not.*

Girl 2:   *How you felt like, you can do it. You know that, you know who you are.*

Tori: *But what can a geek do?*

Girl 1:   *You're not a geek! How many times do we have to tell you?*

Tori: *Yes, I am a geek! Not two people make a difference, when thousands of people call you a geek!*

Girl 1:   *Fine, we going to change your appearance.*

Tori: *I'll still be a geek.*

Girl 1:   *No you won't! Meet us after school today and we're going shopping. Tomorrow you'll be a whole new self!*

Class position is the contributing factor in Tori's skepticism about the success of the shopping expedition in winning her a position within popularity. Not only does she claim to lack the required skills and experience to select the right clothes, but she also argues that her spending options are fully defined by her position within the family: "*I'm spending their money, so I have to do whatever they say.*" Mai outlines what it is Tori may be being told to do and how this may be both impeding the shopping trip and contributing to her lowly status:

> Well, cause she sees other people, like the girls go shopping, just for them, and like she's got to stay home and they're asking her, "Oh, what did you buy?" and stuff like that, it's like "oh, I stayed home, washed the dishes." And they're like this, "Oh, what a geek!" and stuff like that.

In Spence's interpretation of the story of Cinderella, it is predominantly a story about class (1995: 64). Central to this claim is the way in which family and economic conflict, manifested through Cinderella's household labor, is resolved by a magical transformation that allows her true worth to be recognized and her successful taking up of a higher-class position through marriage. Cinderella motifs circulate in popular consciousness, Hey suggests, precisely because they connect to working-class girls' immersion in household labor (1997: 98). Tori's responsibilities at home obstruct her inclusion in the sociality of group shopping trips, one of the means by which girls both learn and participate in constructing gendered norms and meanings (Chapkis 1986; Chua 1992; Ganetz 1995).

Tori's friends respond to her protestations about family constraints by introducing a new discourse into the discussion: *"You have to stand up for yourself"* and *"You're old enough to go and get your own clothes."* Shopping for oneself becomes a claim to the right to self-definition through the construction of one's own appearance and a marker of adult status (Skeggs 1997: 103). This discourse of rights within the family is offered as a means to counter that of Cinderella-the-family-drudge. Thus, part of the intervening role Tori's friends play in her initiation into popularity is teaching her about another way to name and think about relations in families. However, this new discourse also seems to be one that is based on a voluntarism, which assumes that change can follow from subjects' recognizing and choosing to stand outside the conditions of their own regulation. Intensely individualist, it is a discourse embedded within a bourgeois order that has little place for an understanding of regulation that is the product of scarcity of money with which to keep up with fashion trends and surviving harsh living conditions, in part by relying on daughters' household labor.

Race, Gender, and Popularity

In negotiating the interplay of race and popularity in Tori's story, the girls were interested in representing the dynamic discussed above—the obstacles they felt particular collective identities may pose as a factor limiting access to positions of power within popularity. But, they were clearly also highly invested in being able to portray the 'just people' argument. That is, they assert the right to be seen and treated as individuals with complex facets, abilities, and potential. Indeed, the premise of transformation at the heart of Tori's story would seem to insist on this possibility. Juggling these two axioms, the girls produce an "(ambiguously) non-hegemonic" racial positioning for Tori, to use Rachel Blau DuPlessis's (1985) phrase for contradictory subject positions. Her mother being Vietnamese and her father English, Tori is of mixed race. This ambiguous positioning, a means of addressing contradictory axiomatic narrative dictates, becomes a threshold place where social boundaries may be questioned, (re)configured, and (re)articulated. The mixed-race girl throws flagrantly into question the purity of binary raced categories—white and Asian, black and white, Asian and black—and the bounded communities from which they might be expected to emerge. Tori's mixed-race embodiment may therefore mark an uncertainty about identity and play on the girls' own multiple and competing identifications with the 'popular girl.'

The girls articulate their own interest in this ambiguous position, using an entirely different framework. For them the significance of Tori's mixed-race position seems to lie within the moral and ethical considerations the prospect of her transformation might precipitate. To illustrate some of the features of these considerations, the girls use one of the trials those existing as 'other' within schools encounter daily. Tori explains:

Tori:	*But you guys don't understand.*
Girl 1:	*What do you mean? We're trying to understand.*
Tori:	*You guys are popular; no one makes fun of you. I'm not popular. I'm a geek. Every second, every minute people make fun of me.*
Girl 2:	*They make fun of you; you don't bother. You laugh about it after.*
Tori:	*I try to laugh, after a while, it really hurts my feelings you know.*

This teasing which, as we will see shortly, is highly racialized, is clearly one of the social practices that regulates identities and signifies relations of power between groups of students in the school. As a person whose racial position is ambiguous, who is interested in and for whom it might be possible to cross the nerd-popular boundary, this practice poses an ethical and moral dilemma for Tori's successful transformation. Within the politics of the group dynamics, the discussion of this dilemma unleashes something of a crisis.

1 LeLy:	I was wondering, which way [inaudible] like sometimes they were trying to make fun of Chinese or Vietnamese people, right? Like what I'm talking about Tori is like you're in the middle. Like Portuguese people are talking about your own culture, and if you argue with them, they start picking on you. If you go on with them, you feel inside like you're making fun of your own country. So, she have to decide—
2 Lan:	But if she's half English and half Vietnamese and people can't tell you're real Vietnamese and they wouldn't make fun of you—
3 LeLy:	Cause the way she look, she look more like Vietnamese people, so in this community is Portuguese—don't look at me like that—so she don't fit in with them, so like you or not is depending on the way you look.
4 Fanny:	How do you say people mixed in English?
5 Mai:	I guess mixed.
6 Fanny:	No, there's a politer way.

7 LeLy:	Yeah, there's some word to it.
8 Fanny:	My mom got the word in her English notebook—
9 Marnina:	So for Tori, what do you think she should do?
10 Mai:	Or let me give you an example. Let's say LeLy and Kenisha is popular and Lan is and Fanny is in it. You're gonna say, Fanny is so short, so brainless, so lazy because she's Chinese and she's so ugly cause she's Chinese.
11 Fanny:	Yeah, sure!
12 LeLy:	You Chinese people are so short, there!
13 Fanny:	Oh, my god!
14 LeLy:	If she argue, she get picked on.
15 Mai:	I'm not saying Portuguese is rude or anything, right?
16 LeLy:	Yeah, I'm not saying—
17 Mai:	But around here there's Portuguese people, even little kids, even little kids even make fun of Oriental people.
18 Fanny:	I know.
19 Mai:	Even little kids—
20 Mai:	Or another example, her and Fanny—
21 Fanny:	DON'T TALK ABOUT ME!

Attempting and failing to find the 'truth' of racialized identity within official texts (4, 5, 6, 7, 8), telling the story of the mixed-race girl complicates any notion of narrating identity as something that is cohesive and coherent. At first glance, however, their discussion seems to revolve precisely around the issue of how to identify the signifiers of 'English' or 'Vietnamese' as if their meaning could be exactly guaranteed. Only they soon find that this 'guarantee' and the difficulty of the question of identity are exacerbated by a lack of proper language that threatens to implicate them in a contravening of the rules of politeness (6, 15). The complications of race seem to produce here a very uncomfortable in-between-ness that on the one hand the body tries to master, but any fixed meaning is continually undone through the social interaction the mixed-race setting of this conversation occasions. For, although almost silent until the very end of the day's session both Maria (who is Portuguese) and Kenisha (who is Grenadian) were present for this discussion. Their silence as much as their participation is expressive of the on-going challenges the group faced in conversing across our racialized differences and of the on-going work the group undertook to investigate the various ways in which sex, race, and social difference may be imagined.

| 23 Marnina: | Before we end, I just want to hear from Maria, because she hasn't said much today. Are you okay? |

24 Maria:	I don't want to defend, like [inaudible] like you guys are more right to defend, like [inaudible].
25 LeLy:	We're not telling you to defend them. We're just trying to make a point. If you think that's wrong, say it out.
26 Mai:	It's your culture, you can defend them. We could be wrong.
27 Marnina:	Well, if she doesn't—
28 Maria:	And I don't want to. That's why I'm quiet. So, forget me today. I don't want to defend anyone right now, so—
29 LeLy:	My point is—
30 Mai:	We're just making a statement—
31 Maria:	They might be Portuguese, but I hate them. Doesn't mean I have to like them, just because they're Portuguese.
32 LeLy:	There! There, can we bring this situation in here? She's Portuguese, but she doesn't fit in with those Portuguese.
33 Maria:	I'm not saying that.
34 Marnina:	Some Portuguese, just like you might say some Vietnamese—
35 LeLy:	[indicating Mai] like this person, so ugly.

The moral and ethical dilemma around which this anxious exchange takes place is also the query that is at the center of Tori's story: the layered effects of difference, social power, recognition, and the fantasies that both constitute social identities and constantly undo them. More intriguingly, perhaps, both are also interested in exploring how the cultural and social resources available—in terms of the identities that can be inhabited and the forms of identification enabled or disavowed—allow for greater or less ease in living through the contradiction and complexity of racialized positions.

Above, the girls suggest that the metamorphosis Tori dreams of is achievable by way of what Butler calls the "trick of passing" (1993: 178). Her ambiguous racial positioning means that the popular Portuguese girls may accept her as one of their own. However, while the mobility afforded by this 'passing' is certainly seductive for the power and privileges it confers, it seems to also come with an enormous cost. To be recognizable as popular in the terms the girls lay out also entails participating in the perverse exclusionary practices of using racist insults against Vietnamese girls. For Tori, doing so would mean having to disavow her own 'self' and community. Or in the terms LeLy uses, having to 'make fun of your own country' (1). Maria, who acknowledges the difference in the structural dominance of her position (23) through a language of "dis-identification with racism" (Mercer 1992), suggests that for her such a position also entails a certain dis-identification with community (30).

To become acceptable to a racist society, Wong suggests, the marginalized outsider is presented with a cruel bind: one must reject an integral part of oneself (Wong 1993: 77). Cast in a position of ambivalence, the price of accepting the bait of social promotion and acceptance within this arrangement becomes, for Tori, first having to admit her own 'inferiority' (Bauman 1991: 73).

It is no wonder that the girls seem to simultaneously long for and distrust the recognition, attention, and power of the popular girl. In developing Tori's story, the girls return to analyze the splitting required of them in making the identification with the 'popular girl' over and over. Significantly, such a splitting is also performed in the process of discussing these very exigencies. Ostensibly providing examples to illustrate their point, LeLy and Mai (re)stage the comparison of themselves to the ideal through a voicing of the racist criticisms of their peers. Alternately taking turns, they project these critical self-appraisals onto Fanny (2, 4, 20), who is positioned as the repository of the group's ambivalence. Fanny's response seems to first protest the way in which these criticisms are used against Asians collectively (11, 13). Only later does she object to the way in which she is singled out as the personification of this critique and refuse to go along with the pretence of innocence assumed by the others (21).

The Blue Stall Opens/Reconfiguring Transformation

Like Cinderella's ball, the school dance becomes the culminating moment of Tori's transformation. At once social, heterosexual, and highly visible, the space of the dance offers more than the mere promise of romance. Rather, by using it in some quite specific ways, it offers Tori a means with which to attempt to distinguish herself as a popular girl and not a nerd. Heterosexual display becomes one of the distinctive signs that seem to promise full access to this space and to public recognition as a 'normal' girl.

However, as the dialogue above makes clear, while Tori's invested desire to be approved continues to retain its power, the question of the likelihood she will be able to make the criteria is constantly re-opened. In Cinderella's story, along with some magical help, the ball and the events leading up to it facilitate the smooth path of 'justice' and the restoration of moral and social order (Spence 1995: 67). In Tori's case however, the restoration that Spence suggests ends a 'proper' fairy tale appears to be perpetually postponed. Instead, the girls' story interrogates the moral and social order of the school.

Before actually appearing at the dance, a series of necessary preparatory tasks were collectively accomplished. This preparation takes place in a prefatory space to that of the actual dance—the girls' bathroom. Congregating in the large outer vestibule to await Tori's dramatic exit from the stall, here her friends collaborate to provide Tori with both the fashion assistance she requires and some instructions on how to make proper use of the space of the dance so that she may be recognizable as popular.

In the first of two sequences in the washroom, Maria, playing the role of fairy god-mother, pulls the instruments of magic from her large shoulder bag: hair brush and comb, hairspray, eyeliner, eye shadow, mascara, lipstick, blush, sponges, Q-tips, and when her work is done, a long-handled mirror so that Tori can appraise her new 'self.' Replicating a scene familiar not only for its widespread representation in teen-girl movies, but also for the regularity with which the girls gave each other this kind of sensuous attention—climbing into each other's laps, brushing each other's hair, hanging onto each others arms, hands and necks—Maria sets out with much apparent pleasure to 'fix up' her friend.

Girl 1:	*You look great!*
Tori:	*You sure?*
Girl 1:	*Positive. No one will recognize you. Sit down. I'm going to do this hair of yours and it's going to be wonderful!*
	[Maria starts brushing out her hair]
Tori:	*How am I supposed to act at the dance?*
Girl 1:	*Just go up to him and go "do you want to dance?"*
Tori:	*But I've never asked a guy to dance with me before.*
Girl 1:	*Want me to ask him for you?*
Tori:	*No, no, no! I'm embarrassed.*
Girl 1:	*You shouldn't be, you going to look wonderful! Oh, that looks good (she finishes with the hair). Here now get ready for this! You're not going to know who you are! Hair spray, so that it holds. See doesn't that look wonderful? [hands her the mirror]*

The washroom, often considered something of a private and/or marginal space is, for the purposes of Tori''s transformation converted into a semi-public one. There the girls produce useful (gendered) knowledge and spend time together in one of the few places in the school where they might do so, away from boys and teachers. Capturing the way in which marginalized girls may be discursively productive in marginalized spaces (Hey 1997: 20), this video segment seems to emphasize the opportunities of this space rather than its limitations.

Just as Maria's work is completed, Kenisha swaggers into the washroom and introduces Tori to one of the other material practices that could support her attempts to meet the conditions of recognizability as a popular girl. The marginal space of the washroom engenders in this second segment an opportunity for the production of important sources of information and counter-information. It becomes a place in which to express affiliation with and opposition to certain collective identities, interests, values, and knowledge.

Girl 2:	*Hey what's up? Hey! You look so cool, man! Just the way you look, not those ponytails! Want to smoke, man?*
Girl 1:	*Sure.*
Tori:	*Okay. [takes a puff and coughs]*
Girl 2:	*What's wrong? You okay? Don't you know how to smoke?*
Tori:	*Of course I know how to smoke!*
	[Two other girls walk into the washroom look over at Tori, do a double take, and whisper loudly: The geeky girl!]
Girl 1:	*They're going to take a little time getting used to it.*

Kenisha's intervention shifts the tone of things significantly. As we have already seen, in contrast to Maria's use of a gentle motherly discourse with which to assist Tori with her problem, Kenisha has all along presented something of a tougher stance. Here this is accentuated even further through her choice of language and the introduction of the quasi-illicit properties of cigarettes, smoked secretly in the washroom, contravening school rules. Cigarettes are commonly interpreted as a symbol of adulthood, sophistication, rebellion, or 'coolness' (Eckert 1989). Like new clothes, hairstyles, and heterosexuality, they are also displayable, and therein lays their value for Tori. Participation in the ritualized practices of smoking is an expression of category affiliation. Moreover, the risk factor, the collective strategizing to secure a place in which to do it, as well as the practice of sharing cigarettes solidifies this alliance, making it visible both to other group members and to outsiders.

If instruction in smoking was not part of Cinderella's preparation for the ball, neither was her fairy godmother's transformative work met with quite the same response as the one that Tori received in the washroom. Whereas Cinderella spends the entire evening at the ball so completely unrecognizable that even her family cannot guess at her identify, Tori's transformation is not so thorough. "It's the geeky girl," the two other girls say, almost the minute they enter the washroom. Still identifiably a nerd, this contrast suggests a complicating of the girls' investment in the transformation story. But, it also surfaces a structural difference in Cinderella and Tori's positions, demonstrating that 'passing' involves the re-staging of a fractured history of identifications that constitutes the limits to a given subject's mobility (Ahmed 1999: 93). It suggests that the process of fixation where identities are adopted through dress and manner also involves the threatening potential of its own un-fixability. The crisis of 'not belonging' for the passing subject then becomes a crisis of knowledge, of knowing there is always a danger of being found out (Ahmed 1999: 100).

As the location in which these activities transpire, the washroom becomes a threshold space, mediating the transition from nerd to popular girl. It is here that the signs and symbols of class, race, sexuality, and gender (the new clothes, make-up, hair, the nerd, the popular girl, the boy, and the cigarettes) and that of recognition (the mirror), are brought together to signify the re-configuration of identity boundaries which are, with the metaphor that Maria supplies, secured with the holding power of hairspray. However, whereas the visual matrix of this video segment may suggest the potential for transformation, the narrative structure, particularly in the first washroom segment, works against the normalizing authority of the transformation genre, creating a turbulence, a site of impossible irresolution. That is, despite the fixity promised by the metaphor of hairspray (or perhaps because of it), the play between identity and difference does not elude the mirror. For, as Walkerdine warns, projects for wished-for transformation are "shaky and highly likely to produce forms of anxiety, overt conflict and other modes of defence" (Walkerdine 1990: 44).

"No one will recognize you," Maria tells Tori, early on in their discussion. Later she adds, "You're not going to know who you are." Intended to reassure, the words capture both the promise and terror of transformation. On the one hand, Tori's efforts to position herself as a subject within the discursive and social practices of popularity guarantee that others will be unable to continue to identify her as a nerd. And on the other, as we have already seen, the high price to be paid for inhabiting this 'desired place' is the repudiation of certain identifications, so that even she may no longer recognize herself. Tori's transformation threatens to separate her from her own knowledge of self.

Successfully producing oneself as a 'popular girl' within the space of the school depends on the negotiation of an impossible array of identifications. These slip between sameness and difference, desire and aversion, recognition and mis-recognition, and are variously invested in the certainty of fixity and the possibilities for choice. In attending to the repetitions of these conflicts and contradictions, Tori's story shows how they are lived as paradoxical moments of comedy and pain, complexity and crudeness. In troubling the smooth transition of the nerd into the popular girl, the story opens up the possibility for thinking about representations of gender and racial identities as sites of identification where our fantasmatic ideals might be called into question, assessed, reconfigured, and perhaps even refused.

References

Ahmed, S. ""She'll Wake up One of These Days and Find She's Turned in to a Nigger": Passing through Hybridity." *Theory, Culture and Society* 1, no. 2 (1999): 87–106.

Bauman, Z. *Modernity and Ambivalence*. Cambridge: Polity Press, 1991.

Butler, J. *Bodies That Matter: On the Discursive Limits of "Sex."* New York: Routledge, 1993.

Cameron, D. *Verbal Hygiene*. New York: Routledge, 1995.

Canaan, J. "Passing Notes and Telling Jokes: Strategies of Gendering Among American Suburban Middle Class Teenagers." In *Uncertain Terms: Negotiating Gender in America*, Faye Ginsburg and Anna Tsing, eds., Boston: Beacon Press, 1990.

Chapkis, W. *Beauty Secrets: Women and the Politics of Appearance*. London: The Women's Press, 1986.

Chua, B. H. "Shopping for Women's Fashion in Singapore." In *Lifestyle Shopping: The Subject of Consumption*, edited by R. Shields, 114–135. New York: Routledge, 1992.

Corrigan, P. "The Making of the Boy: Meditations on what Grammar School Did with, to, and for My Body." *Journal of Education* 170, no. 3 (1988): 142–61.

DuPlessis, R. B. *Writing Beyond the Ending: Narrative Strategies of 20th Century Women Writers*. Bloomington: Indiana University Press, 1985.

Eckert, P. *From Jocks to Burnouts: Social Identities in the High School*. New York: Teachers College Press, 1989.

Eder, D. "The Cycle of Popularity: Interpersonal Relations among Female Adolescents." *Sociology of Education* 58 (1985): 154–65.

Eder, D. *School Talk: Gender and Adolescent Culture*. New Brunswick, N.J.: Rutgers University Press, 1995.

Ganetz, H. "The Shop, the Home and Femininity as a Masquerade." In *Youth Culture in Late Modernity*, edited by J. Fornas and G. Bolin, 72–99. Thousand Oaks: Sage, 1995.

Gilbert, P. "The Story so Far: Gender, Literacy and Social Regulation." *Gender and Education* 4, no. 3 (1992): 185–199.

Gonick, M. *Between Femininities: Ambivalence, Identity and the Education of Girls*. Albany: State University of New York Press, 2003.

Hey, V. *The Company She Keeps: An Ethnography of Girls' Friendship*. Buckingham: Open University Press, 1997.

Kinney, D. A. "From Nerds to Normals: The Recovery of Identity among Adolescents from Middle School to High School." *Sociology of Education* 66 (January 1993): 21–40.

Mercer, K. "'1968'": Periodising Postmodern Politics and Identity." In *Cultural Studies*, edited by L. Grossberg, C. Nelson, and P. Treichler, 424–438. London: Routledge, 1992.

Skeggs, B. *Formations of Class and Gender*. London: Sage Publications, 1997.

Spence, J. *Cultural Sniping: The Art of Transgression*. New York: Routledge, 1995.

Thompson, S. *Going All the Way: Teenage Girls' Tales of Sex, Romance and Pregnancy*. New York: Hill and Wang, 1995.

Walkerdine, V. *Schoolgirl Fictions*. London: Verso, 1990.

Wexler, P. *Becoming Somebody: Toward a Social Psychology of School*. London: Falmer Press, 1992.

Wong, S. C. *Reading Asian American Literature: From Necessity to Extravagance*. Princeton: Princeton University Press, 1993.

CHAPTER FOUR

Video Girls: Between Changing Exploratory Behavior and Self-authorization

Kristina Hackmann

Material and Objective

This chapter focuses on central issues that arose in the process of a girls' video production project, which centered on the role of fan culture as part of youth culture. In this project (which I facilitated in 2003), a group of seven sixth grade girls, ages 11–12, produced their own video called *Girl Power*. The video was based on a script they had devised collectively.

The objective of my investigation into the video production project is to develop parameters for analyzing interactions and communication patterns of girls within their female peer group. In the process, special consideration is given to the social concepts of gender, femininity, masculinity, and homo- and heterosexuality that the girls refer to as well as to the ideas and conceptions they develop in the course of their discussions of these issues and in the video they produced. Analysis focuses on the implications that gender and the prevailing norm of heterosexuality related to it have on individual processes of socialization and on the development of a gendered self-image in girls. Both the interaction among the girls and the socializing effect that their interaction with the group's instructor had on them are of interest in this context. Theoretical referents of the study are current sociological discussions of the cultural/symbolic system of gender (sexual bimorphism), which explicitly includes the prevailing norm of heterosexuality (heterocentrism).

From an ethnomethodological perspective, heterocentrism and commonplace theories about gender are useful instruments for constructing reality and for the production of social reality. They are perceived as instruments of everyday action and interaction because they enable both an allocation of people to one sex or the other and the construction of heterosexuality as an unquestionable and self-evident reality. Referring to the ethnomethodological view of doing gender does not mean that the authenticity of emotions and bodily experiences is disregarded. It means, however, that a sociological perspective of 'affection' should take into account that expressions of authentic feelings make use of cultural codes. Those codes allow people to experience these feelings as real sensations.

Methodological and Analytical Procedure

Empirical studies on youths only rarely focus on the issue that is to be analyzed: the everyday life of young people and the collective practices that dominate it. At least for many of the widely known German studies it can be stated that they are based on a specific methodology: everyday practices are reconstructed on the basis of interviews, filled-out questionnaires or ethnographical data. This means that these studies do not analyze the everyday practices themselves. Most studies concentrate on the 'contents' of adolescent lives and disregard the formal and functional organization of young peoples' everyday practices although it is well known that communication and interactive practices constitute and reproduce youth cultures. Goodwin's study of 1990 is a good example of what can be gained for sociological perception by detailed linguistic research. Therefore, it seems to be advisable to use conversation analysis as a main tool for conducting ethnography and for extending the classical conversation analysis by aspects of content as has been done in Lorenzer's *Tiefenhermeneutik* (depth hermeneutics). Depth hermeneutics is designed to analyze unconscious subtexts in conversations or other data.

The girls' activities within the group were documented on videotape; then they were transcribed and subsequently they were analyzed, using an ethnomethodological/conversation analytical approach to the construction of social reality. Following this perspective, I will analyze the regularities in the girls´ use of instruments for the construction of reality. Among the questions I will address are:

- What patterns of social relationships do the girls establish?
- Which topics do they choose and how are these embedded in their interaction?
- Which styles of speech do they use?
- What kind of interactive patterns are noticeable?

Since it lies in the nature of commonplace phenomena and everyday self-evidences that these are not referred to explicitly, this analysis will give special attention to such self-evidences in everyday life, e.g., to what is left *un*-spoken and to the absence of action in situations of social interaction.

Conversation analysis is a suitable method of dealing with the question of how girls reproduce gender and the norm of heterosexuality in their interactions. But in order to describe the social concepts girls refer to and the ideas, fantasies, and wishes they develop, I decided to adopt a psychoanalytical approach to analyze the unconscious 'subtext' of expressions used and interactions.

Tiefenhermeneutik refers to the critical rereading of Freud's *Psychoanalysis*, as done by Alfred Lorenzer (1986) for German-language contexts. *Tiefenhermeneutik* is based on the concept of cultural systems of sense. Those systems provide frameworks for the perception and construction of subjective and social reality. *Tiefenhermeneutik* differentiates between the surface of experience and behavior, which is comprehensible to individuals and such structures of sense that are not immediately open to everyday individual reflection.

As a method of analysis, *Tiefenhermeneutik* follows certain procedures. The method is based on the understanding that the text-reader-relationship is an interaction. This means that we do not have access to an 'original' text but only to its reception. The work performed by an analyst is comparable to the work done by an archaeologist who also looks beneath the surface of soils: the analyst not only focuses on the 'surface' of a text but tries to find meaning beneath the first level of perception: the subtext of a text. The central category for the subtext of a text is the unconscious, which Lorenzer defines as the forbidden, the wishes which are in conflict with social norms and values of the current culture. The aim of the *Tiefenhermeneutik* is to reveal the hidden structures of meaning. Of course, there is not just one subtext; there are many. The analysis will focus on the construction of probable, arguable interpretations of the text.

The analytical method of *Tiefenhermeneutik* can be outlined in four steps:

1. Constant attentiveness and free association of ideas: Every reading of a text is meaningful. Its aim is to remove the censorship of every

day consciousness in order to uncover innermost fantasies, ideas and wishes.

2. Note confusions: Initial access to the subtext can be gained by looking at parts that seem illogical or irritating to the analyst. This approach uses the subjectivity and the feelings of the analyst, a proceeding that was adapted from the original psychoanalytic method of counter-transference in therapeutic relationships.

3. Scenic understanding: Associations and confusions that occur in the discussion of a text can be described as tracks. Tracks per se do not explain anything; they have to be linked with other tracks so that the analyst can develop a realistic scene or picture. There may be alternative pictures or readings, which are acceptable as long as they can be verified by the text. To control the subjectivity of the analyst, the tools used are documented self-reflection and theoretical knowledge. Group-validation: Discussing readings in a group of analysts is an other way of controlling and/or changing the analysts' subjectivity and of making interpretations more probable.

It can be shown that a relationship exists between what is said, what subtext is involved, and how the speaker's intention is understood by the hearers. In my analysis, I will therefore switch between conversation analysis and the search for culturally determined subtexts. As mentioned before, the analysts' own constructions and re-constructions of social meaning must be taken into account in this context.

In my research, Goffman's method of frame analysis (1977) has been very helpful. In earlier studies, I have been able to show how the conversational construction of the 'elder brother' by girls can be interpreted as a means to establish their understanding of gender and the norm of heterosexuality.

Girl Power

The plot of the video film *Girl Power* focuses on two rival girl-gangs: the Black Outs and the Modern Girls. Especially in the first part of the film, the Black Outs exhibit what is commonly called 'masculine' behavior: they talk about 'Gangsta Rap' (a music style) and play basketball; they wear caps, sweatshirts and trousers that are much too big. The Modern Girls display what is commonly called 'female' behavior: they use make-up, wear feminine clothes, they talk about boys they have a crush on, and they are enthusiastic about the Backstreet Boys. One of the Modern Girls is kidnapped at a Backstreet Boys concert, and the Black Outs offer their help. Adults are not involved in solving the problem. The two gangs join efforts and successfully free the kidnapped girl from a mysterious Black man.[1] In the end, they become friends, and we can see all of them sitting together, talking about boys in general and the Backstreet Boys in particular.

The video film has been discussed in several student groups. All of the students agreed that the way in which the two gangs freed the kidnapped girl is not logical. The fact that in the end the Black Outs also take part in discussions about boys and Backstreet Boys was viewed as a paradox. These comments of the students are indications of subtexts of the film. The kidnapping and the rescue of the girl are not the only stories told: The film also documents the wide range of fantasies about sexuality the girls have—heterosexual as well as homoerotic ones.

The topic of heterosexuality is discussed on the basis of the cultural ideal of beauty. The Modern Girls are presented as objects of desire (here: objects of the kidnappers' desire). But the girls refer to the youth-cultural trend of 'girlism,' which deals ironically with the ideal of beauty and makes it possible to view the Modern Girls as active members of society and as subjects of their own desire. The topic of heterosexuality is extended to the issue of romanticism: the Modern Girls are fans of the Backstreet Boys.

As regards the music preferred by the Black Outs, Gangsta Rap, it can be viewed as the girls' construction of a connection between heterosexuality and violence. At the same time, the Black Outs are associated with ideas of male-identified lesbianism.

Overall, it can be stated that the girls, referring to different cultural meanings and interpretations of these meanings, develop their own system of meanings that symbolize different aspects of fantasies surrounding the issue of sexuality. These different aspects are organized as interaction of the different film characters, which serve as symbolic representations of different aspects and which are also reflected in the interactions occurring at the group level.

During the making of the video, the girls only once discussed the gender of the kidnapper. One girl asked why the kidnapper had to be conceptualized as a male person, when the person who played the role was actually a woman (the instructor of the group and author of this text). I wrote a transcript of this sequence, which was not longer than 45 seconds. Using the method of conversation analysis, I looked at the introduction to the topic 'gender' by considering the following question of one of the girls: "Why does the kidnapper have to be a man?" The introduction was followed by a co-operative non-establishment of the topic by the rest of the group. The girl who had put the question about the kidnapper's gender accepted the reply that this question could not be answered. If we take the sexualized, or, to be more precise, the heterosexualized subtext of the film into account, we can see why the girls refused to discuss this question: Since it lies in the nature of subtexts that they do not have to be and sometimes cannot be explicitly alluded to, the subtext was simply not suitable for discussion. The logic of the subtext seems to be that the 'Black' man symbolizes the girls' fantasies about heterosexuality in a threatening manner. For this reason, there was no need to discuss the question about the kidnapper's gender: it had to be a man.

One major result of my investigation was that the range of fantasies of girls exceeds the range of social pictures available to the girls to act these fantasies out. For the girls this means that social pictures have to be reinterpreted to meet their individual needs. The complexity of adolescent development becomes apparent: on the one hand the girls fall back on social pictures, e.g., the prevailing norm of heterosexuality; on the other hand, the girls reinterpret these pictures and use them for living out norm-deviating fantasies. A correlation has emerged which can be dissolved neither to the one nor to the other side.

Dimensions of Fan Culture

The following excerpt from a transcript is part of the video recording taken by the girls. The scene takes place in the bathroom of one of the Modern Girls, where the girls get ready for the upcoming concert of the Backstreet Boys (at which one of the girls will be kidnapped). The camera shows the reflections of the girls in the mirror: They put on make-up and brush their hair throughout the entire scene. It will become clear that putting on make-up jointly in an intimate location like the bathroom is not only a way of expressing female connectedness but also that the intimate location is also a suitable place for experiencing erotic fantasies together. The context in which this occurs—celebrity fan culture—is of great importance in the scene.

Nicky: *Ohoh, your make-up is absolutely stonking; [looks at Cindy]*
Cindy: *Mmh, that's normal; ⌈oh I'm so jittery;*

Nancy:	Maybe one of us is⌐/asked to come on stage,
Cindy:	Oh I bet not; there are so many ... but the nicest, well, me; [poses in front of the mirror and moves her hips] nay, no, rubbish;
Nina:	Oh sorry
Cindy:	But it will be real cool=I'm really looking forward to it
Nancy:	Me too
Nina:	And me too
Cindy:	⌐Okay, afterwards, at your place; [looks at Nina]
Nina:	[Drops hairbrush]⌐/
Nicky:	[Laughs] Oh, I am so: excited; [looks at Nina]
Cindy:	Okay, if we get lost, we'll meet at your place [A song of the Backstreet Boys is played]
Nancy:	Okay
Nina:	Okay
Nicky:	Good
Cindy:	Okay
??:	⌐)
Nancy:	(Okay, let's go) or else we won't get any seats;
Cindy:	Yes, exactly, cause we have to get real close (); (1 sec) okay
Nancy:	Okay, come on, let's go ()
Nina:	Exactly [The Modern Girls leave the bathroom]

Looking at Cindy, Nicky remarks, "Ohoh, your make-up is absolutely stonking," which Cindy dismisses with "Mmh, that's normal." Nicky's comment might also be interpreted as criticism, meaning, 'you've overdone it.' On the one hand, this might be an attempt to correct a friend's behavior—an attitude that is typical among girls—but to which Cindy does not respond in this scene. On the other hand, this (possibly critical) remark may also be interpreted against the background of rivalry among women, i.e., Nicky reproaches Cindy for trying to gain an advantage over the other girls by using too much make-up in order to attract the attention of the stars on stage as well as the attention of potential romantic partners. Hence, friendships among girls are not exclusively about cooperation but also about competition. This is not necessarily a contradiction but rather points to ambivalent and conflicting negotiating processes in friendships among girls.

In her next comment, Cindy changes to the topic of her own feelings, "Oh I'm so jittery," whereas Nancy expresses the hope that "Maybe one of us is asked to come on stage." This comment clearly shows that the main reason for going to the concert is to get close to the stars on stage; this 'getting close to the boys' symbolizes their wish for a heterosexual relationship. This wishful thinking makes it possible for the girls to experience their fantasies and let them run free without having to fear real consequences. Cindy's next remark implies that the notion of being asked to come on stage is a conscious wish, "Oh I bet not; there are so many." The argument she brings up, i.e., that this will not happen because there are so many fans that it is highly unlikely that one of them is singled out, shows that although the girls associate their individual fantasies with Backstreet Boys, they have not lost sight of reality. The Boys will probably never come within reach—and the fans are aware of this—but despite the pop group's inaccessibility, the girls toy with the idea of overcoming this distance, "but the nicest, well, me, [poses in front of the mirror and moves her hips] nay, no, rubbish." And, precisely this challenge seems to hold the pleasurable potential that appeals to the girls. Within this framework each girl can imagine herself to be the nicest of all the fans present, to be the one whose beauty attracts the Boys' attention and who is eventually singled out. It appears that in this context seducing others and being seduced are close to one another and despite the competition that this causes among the girls—which Cindy refers to in her tag clause, "nay, no, rubbish"—these opposing concepts can be expressed and acted out within their group of friends. It is precisely the knowledge that the pop group is unattainable which provides the 'space of grace' the girls need to bear with each other and act out the competition among them. Jointly acting out their seduction fantasies and their individual desires seem to be sources of lust. Cindy, for instance, expresses her pleasant anticipation twice, "But it will be real cool=I'm really looking forward to it," and this anticipation cannot even be marred by the realization that their wish to join the group on stage will probably not come true. This anticipation is shared by Nancy and Nina, "Me too," "And me too".

Cindy's hint, "Okay, afterwards, at your place; [looks at Nina]" not only implies that viewers do not have all the information but also suggests that the shared experience of attending the pop concert is of great importance. This experience not only includes getting ready for the concert and attending it but also spending the rest of the night in the same house.

It is at this moment that Nina drops the hairbrush, which Nicky views as evidence of her overwhelming excitement, "[laughs] Oh, I am so: excited; [looks at Nina]," which fits in perfectly with what was said before. While a song by the Backstreet Boys is played, the girls agree to meet at Nina's place after the concert in case anyone gets lost during the show. After this has been settled, Nancy suggests that they go to the concert or else they might not get seats; Cindy enforces this statement this by saying, "Yes, exactly, cause we have to get real close ()."

In this sequence, it becomes clear that the girls believe that good looks provide them with access to the heterosexual world. By looking at their reflection in the mirror, the girls design a physical image of themselves as beautiful women; in the process, the feedback from their peers is of the utmost importance. The attractive appearance that the girls try to create to appeal to members of the other sex first has to be approved by members of their own sex; hence, initially, heteroerotic desires take the second place behind homoerotic desires. As part of these 'negotiations', evaluation criteria for good looks and sexual attractiveness are set and tested. These criteria not only relate to girls but also to potential (in this case virtual) romantic partners.

Celebrity fan culture has turned out to be a suitable setting for playfully dealing with one's own desires and sexual arousal. It provides support and protection and makes it possible for groups of girl friends to reassure each other and to share experiences in a group. Heterosexual advances that are made to discover one's individual style are not only shaped by co-operation between the girls but also by competition. Working on the knowledge that the pop stars are unattainable, the adolescents can let their fantasies about seducing and being seduced run free; this experience, which is preferably shared with peers, is not perceived as threatening because there are no real consequences involved.

Fans of Boy Groups and their Exploratory Behavior in the Field of Heterosexual Love

Which lifestyle do the Backstreet Boys stand for? Which symbolic world do young adolescents, predominantly girls, who adore this boy group, create? The Backstreet Boys are viewed as a typical boy group; they can be called one of the most successful ones. Fritzsche (2003) summarized the typical features of boy groups as follows: In general, boy groups are comprised of several young men who are not older than 25. They are chosen by placing want ads and holding casting sessions, and they are prepared systematically for their career. They receive singing and choreography lessons; they are given image counseling and the songs composed—most of them about romantic heterosexual love—are specifically tailored to them. As soon as their style of music has become established in the music charts, the group goes on professionally prepared tours, in the course of which posters, t-shirts and other fan articles are traded extensively. This additional trade, which is just as profitable as the sale of their music, is another typical feature of boy groups. The most important aspects of a boy group's image are their public refusal of drugs, their love for their parents, and particularly their presentation of themselves as single young men in search of a romantic partner. This is the image portrayed of them in the youth media (radio stations, music channels and youth magazines) that are read/viewed by potential fans. These marketing strategies are aimed at creating an active fan culture, particularly among girls. So far, this phenomenon has only been treated marginally by German-language social scientists.

Fritzsche relates the term 'culture' to the concept of 'popular culture,' which forms part of British cultural studies (2003). Popular culture describes the use of mass culture as a self-directed cultural act that underlines the correlation between the use of media and everyday culture. Huyssen (1986) and Thornton (1996) discovered that frequently mass culture and those who use it are referred to in a disparaging manner in the relevant literature that coincides with a feminization of the mainstream trend. Fritzsche also identified this kind of derogatory presentation when she re-read German-language sociological literature on pop fans: Most of these texts contain derogatory, sexualizing and sexist descriptions of—mostly female—adolescents and focus on their bodies, which are described as immature and unattractive.[2] However, the author also points to the fact that the relevant German-language research regards media reception by youths as an active and creative process, and she ties this approach to the one pursued in British cultural studies. Hence, from a scientific angle the activities of pop fans are placed in the context of a youth-specific popular culture which not only takes up forms of culture that have been predetermined by the media and commerce but also enables youths to creatively deal with age-specific needs.

In interviews and group discussions, which she analyzed using the documentary method (cf. e.g., Bohnsack 1999), Fritzsche identified different functions of celebrity fan culture and varying interpretations by fans. These are strikingly similar to the linguistic processes and latent meanings I discovered in my study. One possible method to analyze latent meanings is the documentary method, which, however, is not explicitly focused on identifying latent meanings but on the reconstruction of experiences reflected in texts. The extent to which the interpretations obtained through different methods complement one another highlights the importance of analyzing the same phenomenon from different angles.

Fritzsche's analysis of the interviews conducted also reveals that the consumption of pop music rather serves the function of maintaining relationships within the peer group than satisfying the aesthetic needs of individual adolescents. Being a fan means, above all, to adopt certain practices (e.g., collecting devotional objects). Hence, one is only accepted as a fan if certain actions are performed. According to Fritzsche, girls associate being a fan with reaching a certain developmental stage at which one's position within the peer group and relationships to members of the other sex are negotiated.

In the respondents' descriptions of concert visits Fritzsche identified an erotic, romantic element, which manifests itself in their wish to be close to the stars on stage. However, the actual concert situation must rather be viewed as a would-be fulfillment of the youths' wish because it is in fact impossible for most of the fans to get close to the stars. Despite this, the respondents describe the concert visit as a positive experience because of the sense of community that is found there and because of the physical closeness to other fans. But, they admit that feelings of hatred and competition may also occur.

The interviews conducted reveal that being a fan is viewed as an age-related phenomenon. Particularly, girls ages 10–14 use the opportunities which 'being a fan' provides: i.e., to practice, approaching members of the other sex while at the same time keeping a real relationship to a boy at a certain distance. Accordingly, Fritzsche defines 'being a fan' as the virtual negotiation of a heterosexual relationship in which the fact that the person targeted is male is of major importance: Being a fan provides the opportunity to fall in love from a distance and thus to avoid the risks involved in a real relationship. Because of its repetitive and process-like nature, fan culture must be considered a performative and exploratory form of behavior, which makes it possible for adolescents to experience the state of being in love without having to fear real heterosexual contacts. In the process, the individual youth does not interpret her desires as being naturally heterosexual but rather as a cautious approach, which may still turn to the 'wrong side' of homosexuality.

Fritzsche demonstrated that fan culture might serve as a platform for performative approaches to the practice of heterosexual relations, which the girls experience as pleasurable because their desires and wishes are met but which are also viewed as a norm that has to be achieved. To substantiate her point Fritzsche referred to Judith Butler (1991; 1995), who states that a coherent sexual identity always includes sexual desires; it is not only a cultural construct but has to be re-established again and again through performative acts. According to Butler, constant recurrence to the same sexual norms at the discursive and performing level has a naturalizing effect, which disguises the actual hypothetical nature of these norms. In accordance with Butler, the following theory can be evolved: the fragility of a coherent sexual identity, which cannot be detected by adults because of the already mentioned naturalization effects, may be much more distinct at the age of twelve. The relevant research findings suggest that 'being a fan' provides girls with the opportunity to grapple intensively with their relationship to members of their own sex and to members of the male sex.

Fritzsche summarized her findings by stating that fans are well-informed media users who are experienced in distinguishing between different levels of reality. They are well aware that their relationship to the star(s) on stage is imaginary and helps them to develop certain fantasies and let them run free in a playful manner. Initially the girls do not take into account or explicitly rule out any other levels—a finding which sheds new light on a strikingly paradoxical aspect of 'being a fan'—the desire for closeness to an unattainable person.

Reflections on Educational Work with Girls in Schools

The principal objective of educational work with girls is to help them find 'their own voice' and to empower them to overcome the notion that females are subordinated to men and are only complementary (to males). In U.S. feminist research on female adolescence, the term 'desire' is used to describe a girl's ability to choose friends and companions independently, to shape her own life and to create new patterns of living, thus refusing to adopt a heterocentric lifestyle and the norm of heterosexuality. In *Mother Daughter Revolution* Elizabeth Debold et al. (1993) state:

> *Desire—wanting, lusting, craving, longing, needing in all and every way—is critical to women's integrity and power. The power of desire is the root of women's power. Desire gives force to what she can and will do. It empowers her life and liveliness. Forbidding or compromising desire cuts off a girl's life force. (202)*

The overall development of the girls' working group over a period of one and a half years has shown that the factor of *time* plays a decisive role in the educational work with girls. Thus, creating time frames serves two educational purposes: setting structural frameworks, e.g., for participation in a regularly convening working group even beyond a school year and allowing the girls to take the time they need to develop their own dynamics within these time frames. For instance, dwelling on the characterization of the two sets of girls who recorded the video that started the work on the film was necessary because this extended time frame made it possible for the girls to develop a thematic framework and to establish interactions between themselves (in the film scenes as well as in their team work on the film). As part of these interactions, issues that particularly concerned the girls continued to be at work at the latent level until—after some time—they were brought to the level of awareness by the girls themselves. This process became apparent during the—initially implicit and later on explicit— discussion of the topic of being lesbian. From the perspective of the teacher—who also has to consider the educational objectives of teaching units—the lengthy discussion at the beginning of this teaching phase had negative implications. By allowing the girls' lengthy deviations from concentrated work on the script, the girls did not have enough time at the end of the teaching unit to edit the video, a task that is of major importance for productive media work. The reason why I took over the 'final editing' of the video was to give the girls a feeling of success at the end of the school year, to make them feel 'we've done it.' It turned out that the girls' non-participation in the final editing—which had not been planned—opened up the opportunity for them to work out their own dynamics. If I had developed and followed a detailed educational schedule, I probably would have urged the girls from the very beginning to focus on the script and 'for reasons of time' I would have cut off any deviations to other issues. Yet, if I had proceeded in that way it would not have been in line with my teaching objectives since the working team was set up to focus on the girls and their concerns rather than on media.

If activities like this are offered at school, the question of the educational objectives pursued through these measures always arises because frequently these are not laid down in the curriculum. Such measures can only be implemented at schools where an atmosphere of openness and flexibility prevails.

The girls' development during the video production has shown that girls who are given the opportunity to participate in social activities at school—

i.e., those who are provided with a suitable platform—are actually able to concern themselves with issues of gender and sexuality. However, the findings of this empirical study also suggest that the presence of a grown-up supportive supervisor of the same sex is particularly important for the girls and their emotional balance. Due to her age, the team leader also represents the girls' visions of their future role in society and hence is viewed as 'deputy' negotiator of inter-gender relationships. The female supervisor can be 'used' to try out what is acceptable and what is not. And, she can be given assignments that the girls themselves consider too 'hot', e.g., playing the role of the kidnapper.

Flaake (1996) pointed out that school might serve as a location that, at least potentially, provides new opportunities for becoming aware of one's body and for defining it. Given this context, a female team leader may serve an important function for a group of girls. Daughters frequently have ambivalent feelings towards their mother: they are torn between the wish for closeness and the wish to differentiate themselves from her. By contrast, female teachers or team leaders can take over the function of an attachment figure that raises fewer ambivalent feelings and therefore is important to the girls. However, this role can only be assumed, and the interplay between inter-group processes and the actions and interventions of the team leader can only occur if the grown-up supervisor succeeds in considering herself part of the group but not equal to the girls. If these conditions are given, the creative potential of such an inter-group process can thrive.

In her analysis of therapeutic situations, Köhncke (1997; 2001) found that in groups there is a general readiness to transfer fantasies, emotions, and action impulses to other group members or the leader(s) of the group. This stimulates the creative potential within groups. Time and space provide the framework that is needed for acting out latent feelings. Within this framework, each girl can fill her world with fantasies and her own language. The team leader has an important supportive function in this. Time and space provide the fixed framework that is needed to act out issues that are at work at the latent level. Within this framework, the girls can fill their own worlds with fantasies and use their own language. In the process, the group leader provides the protective support the girls need.

The female group leader is faced with the challenge of accepting the girls' ambivalent wishes—their wish for differentiation from others on the one hand and their wish for closeness on the other hand—and not to mix these wishes with her own desires. Moreover, she is faced with the challenge of striking a happy medium between imposing her own concepts of a 'good, successful' life on the girls and concealing these concepts from them. Hence, the main task to be met by an educator working with girls is to open up room for and together with the girls in which they not only concern themselves with gender-related issues and conflicts but also with their desires and yearnings. And, as an adult, an educator should provide support and be available as a companion who is ready to discuss relevant issues with them.

Ethnomethodology, conversation analysis, and the methods applied in depth hermeneutics may be very helpful in reflecting on one's own involvement in constructions and reconstructions of social reality and in opening up new prospects for the educational work with girls.

Notes

[1] The girls are referring to the black clothes the man is wearing. Nevertheless it is most probable that this term originates from colonial discourse.

[2] For critical remarks on English-language scientific studies of fan culture, cf. Lewis 1992: 1–64.

Symbols

⌐	start of simultaneous talk
⌐	end of simultaneous talk
=	quick connexion of a next contribution or speedy talking
(2 sec)	length of a pause
(-)	short pause (ca. ¼ sec.)
:::	lengthening of a vowel
°ja°	low voice
°°ja°°	very low
ja	accented
JA	loud
. ;	strong or slight fall of intonation
? ,	strong or slight rise of intonation
viellei-	break off
(ach)	unsure transcription
( )	unintelligible
[lacht]	description of mimicry and gestures
.	
.	letting outs in transcript

References

Bohnsack, R. *Rekonstruktive Sozialforschung. Einführung in Methodologie und Praxis qualitativer Forschung.* Opladen: Leske & Budrich, 1999.

Butler, J. *Das Unbehagen der Geschlechter*. Frankfurt a.M.: Suhrkamp, 1991.

———. *Körper von Gewicht. Die diskursiven Grenzen des Geschlechts*. Frankfurt a.M.: Suhrkamp, 1995.

Debold, E., I. Malavé, and M. Wilson. *Mother Daughter Revolution: From Good Girls to Great Women*. New York: Bantam Books, 1993.

Flaake, K. "Ein eigenes Begehren?—Weibliche Adoleszenz und das Verhältnis zu Körperlichkeit und Sexualität." In *Frauen Stärken—Ändern Schule. 10. Bundeskongreß Frauen und Schule*, edited by A. Kaiser, 146–152. Bielefeld: Kleine Verlag, 1996.

———. *Körper, Sexualität und Geschlecht*. Studien zur Adoleszenz junger Frauen- Gießen: Psychosozial Verlag, 2001.

Fritzsche, B. *Pop-Fans. Studie einer Mädchenkultur*. Opladen: Leske & Budrich, 2003.

Goffman, E. *Rahmen-Analyse. Ein Versuch über die Organisation von Alltagserfahrungen*. Frankfurt a.M.: Suhrkamp, 1977.

Goodwin, M. H. *He Said—She Said. Talk as Social Organization among Black Children*. Bloomington: Indiana University Press, 1990.

Hackmann, K. *Adoleszenz, Geschlecht und sexuelle Orientierungen. Eine Empirische Studie mit Schülerinnen*. Opladen: Leske & Budrich, 2003.

Huyssen, A. *After the Great Divide. Modernism, Mass Culture, Postmodernism*. Bloomington: Indiana University Press, 1986.

Köhncke, D. "Die Gruppe als Möglichkeitsraum. Gedanken zur Kreativität des therapeutischen Prozesses." *Gruppenanalyse* 7, no. 2 (1997): 103–127.

———. "Schrecken und Zauber des offenen Raumes—das kreative Potenzial der Gruppe." *Gruppenanalyse* 11, no. 1 (2001): 11–29.

Lewis, L. A. (editor) *The Adoring Audience. Fan Culture and Popular Media*. London/New York: Routledge, 1992.

Lorenzer, A. "Tiefenhermeneutische Kulturanalyse." In *Kultur-Analysen. Psychoanalytische Analysen zur Kultur,* edited by H.-D. König and A. Lorenzer et al. 11–98. Frankfurt a.M.: Suhrkamp, 1986.

Thornton, S. *Club Cultures*. Hanover: Wesleyan University Press, 1996.

CHAPTER FIVE

Memory-work as a (be)Tween Research Method: The Beauty, the Splendor, the Wonder of My Hair

Kathleen O'Reilly-Scanlon
Sonya Corbin Dwyer

Give me a head of hair, long beautiful hair, shining, gleaming, steaming, flaxen, waxen…let it fly in the breeze…I want it long, straight, curly, fuzzy, snaggy, shaggy…

> —As sung by the freedom-loving Claude in the musical, *Hair*

While the popular musical of 1968, *Hair*, provided insights into the philosophy of the flower children of the 1960s, hair continues to provide insights into the identities of other groups including tweens—both their group identity and their own sense of self. This transformation of self (McCracken 1995) is particularly evident in tweens' relationship with hair and related "aspirational products" (George 2003: SP7), products specifically designed to fulfill tweens' desired persona. In this chapter, we explore the socializing role of hair (Haug 1992) in the development of girlhood.

In this chapter, we begin with a discussion of hair as it relates to female identity. Next, we use the research method of memory-work to interrogate our identities and self-concepts as they relate to our tween experiences of hair. We then go on to examine how advertisements aimed at tweens may influence their sense of self in their search for identity fulfillment. We find that tweens are told whom and what to look like, what to strive for, and are provided with step-by-step instructions of how to reach this goal. Advertising and fashion photography continue to influence the perceptions that tweens (and most women) have of themselves and continue to give "form to the longing for glamour, sexuality, beauty and class" (Ewen 1979: 45). As

McLuhan proposed, "[t]he continuous pressure is to create ads more and more in the image of audience motives and desires. The product matters less as the audience participation increases" (1964: 201).

Hair and Identity

At first glance, tweens' relationship with hair may appear to be a frivolous topic. However, we illustrate how hair plays an important role in identity development. As Baker Miller notes (1986), a person's sense of identity is linked very early with the person's sense of being female or male. By the age of a year and a half to three years, a child already 'thinks' as a sexed, rather than as a generic, person. And, the meanings we give femaleness and maleness are culturally imposed. This extends to the cultural meanings of hairstyles and of what it means to be a female tween. We show how tween magazines actually create anxiety about one's (female) identity because as Faludi (1991) points out, "personal insecurity is the great motivator to shop" (174).

We were interested in exploring how the development of physical identity, with particular emphasis on hair, may be manifested in the lives of tweens. Faludi (1991) supports our exploration of the role of hairstyles in identity development:

> The beauty industry may seem the most superficial of the cultural institutions participating in the backlash, but its impact on women was, in many respects, the most intimately destructive—to both female bodies and minds…And the beauty industry helped to deepen the psychic isolation that so many women felt…by reinforcing the representation of women's problems as purely personal ills, unrelated to social pressures and curable only to the degree that the individual woman succeeded in fitting the universal standard—by physically changing herself. (203)

The search for identity has been widely acknowledged as one of the earmarks of early development, setting the stage for peer pressure. In other words, identity as the total concept of self "is personal because it is a sense of 'I-ness,' but it is also social, for it includes 'we-ness,' or one's collective identity" (Rice 1992: 78). By extension, one wonders how this collective identity—social "we-ness"—is played out in the media.

In her study of female appearance and "the beauty ritual," Ewen (1979) argues that sameness helps us feel less exposed and therefore more confident. She proposes that:

… being different makes one isolated and vulnerable. Rather, we dress and wear our hair like our friends and those with whom we identify. Within these limits, we select our images from a[n increasingly narrow] range of options. (45)

Similarly, the Gender Intensification Hypothesis, proposed by John Hill and Mary Ellen Lynch, explains that psychological and behavioral differences between males and females become more pronounced at adolescence due to intensified socialization pressures to conform to culturally prescribed gender roles (Arnett 2001). In particular, girls become notably more self-conscious about physical appearance than boys do because physical attractiveness is an especially important part of the female gender role.

After considering female identity development, and how girls are *shaped* by hair and hair is *shaped* by girls, we began to wonder about our own tween hair experiences. In turn, we questioned how our own tween identities and self-concepts could help us understand contemporary tweens. Would our experiences resonate with those of today's tweens?

Back to our Roots: Doing Memory-work

Following Adrienne Rich's (1986) lead, we wish to situate ourselves for the reader. We are two women academics with backgrounds in education, language arts, and psychology. We are white, Canadian, and middle class. We grew up in different eras: Kathleen in the 60s and Sonya in the 70s. One of us has naturally curly and highlighted blonde hair and the other has naturally straight and dyed reddish-brown hair. We cut, curl, straighten, shape, blow-dry, color, shampoo, condition, gel, lacquer, spray, tease, brush, tie-back, put-up, comb, wax, putty, highlight, and cover grey hair. In short, we, too, attempt to transform ourselves through the manipulation of our hair. As teacher-educators in the same institution, we have worked and socialized together for the past three years. We looked forward to writing with each other. In short, we trust one another, which is a critical component of the memory-work process. As Ingleton (1995) notes, memory-work requires a climate of openness and trust where participants feel comfortable and safe about sharing experiences. This supports Finch's argument (1984) that "the only morally defensible way for a feminist to conduct research with women is through a non-hierarchical relationship in which she is prepared to invest some of her own identity" (81).

Memory work methodology promotes self-reflection and discovery. It originates and continues to evolve within a feminist context (Haug 1992;

Crawford et al. 1992; Ingleton 1995). It also resonates with feminist approaches to therapy (Worell and Remer 1996) that help women become aware of the unwritten rules or messages they use to guide their lives. The majority of these rules are not within active awareness for most women. One technique, called sex-role analysis, encourages women to examine the gender rules that guide their thoughts, feelings, and behavior. Women can explore how the rules were learned, how well the rules function for them now, and decide which of these rules they would like to revise.

Memory-work is described here to inform the reader of our process, but is also offered as a way for others to gain insights into how the past has shaped the present and in this case, how we might try to understand contemporary girlhood and tween culture by exploring our own girlhoods.

Memory-work: A (be)Tween Research Method

German sociologist and scholar, Frigga Haug, developed memory-work, a research method that originated and continues to evolve within a feminist context (Haug 1992; Crawford et al. 1992; Ingleton 1995). The process of memory-work—of "working backwards into the future"—is made up of a number of stages, which at first glance may appear distinct and separate but which in practice are both recursive and reciprocating. These stages include the:

- collection of written memories according to particular specifications;
- collective analysis of the memories; and
- appraisal and eventual theorizing of the memories within the context of a number of disciplines including, but not limited to, political science, history, psychology, education, sociology, and feminism.

Since Haug (1992) maintains that the self is socially constructed through reflection, one of the major goals of memory-work is to uncover the ways in which individuals build their own identity. It appears that this symbiotic relationship of what we remember, how we construct our memories, and how we *re-member and re-construct* our pasts can provide us with clues as to the formation of our identities. This leads to one of the most important aspects of memory-work: experience itself is a resource and ought to be acknowledged as a basis for theory and research. Thus, the initial data in memory-work are the memories themselves (O'Reilly-Scanlon 2001).

Mirrors to the Past

Memory-work practitioners (Crawford et al. 1992; Haug 1992) believe that the actual writing down of the memories is integral to memory-work. In addition to providing a permanent record, the act of writing makes the everyday experience of our lives and all that may appear on the surface, at least, seem mundane and ubiquitous, a special significance worth exploring (Crawford et al.; Haug 1992).

Photographs as Memory Prompts

A number of studies (Aron 1979; Collier; 1979; Wagner 1979, Mitchell and Weber 1999; O'Reilly-Scanlon 2001) have used photographs successfully to help viewers recall specific events, information, and places. Kosonen (1993a) acknowledges the power of photographs as memory prompts in her self-study and describes how, when looking at photographs of herself as a child, the photographs transgressed time and space as they "brought it all back so vividly, our courtyard and all the things we used to do there" (52).

Similarly, Martin (1986) and Spence (1995) argue that a photograph is an excellent tool for asking questions because it can serve as both a memory prompt and a point of departure for interrogating the (often contradicting and conflicting) emotions and experiences that have formed and shaped us. Walker (1993), noting the interplay and interconnectedness of photograph and memory, argues:

> [Voice], memory and biography are inextricably interrelated. The reading of a photograph is a cultural act and one that allows the observer some glimpse of ways in which individuals create meaning in their lives...We can use the photograph in the context of memory-work, as an instrument for the recovery of meaning, in a way that we all recognize when we think of how we view collections of photographs in the drawer at home. What is important is not the image in itself so much as the relationship between the image and the ways we make sense of it and the ways in which we value it. (82, 83)

Reflecting on Our Images:
Highlights of the Past, Coloring the Present

Some of the guiding questions we used to interrogate memories of girlhood and hairstyles included: What were the motivations behind our wanting this particular hairstyle? Who or what influenced us? Why was this particular hairstyle desirable? What meanings did these hairstyles have for us? What did they represent? What were the reactions of peers, parents, others? How did our hairstyles 'shape' our identities, that is, what did we think our hairstyles said about us? By extension, in what ways are we continuing to live out these same motivations?

Letting Our Hair Down

To begin, we chose photographs that signified our definition of self through hair. In Sonya's case, she immediately recalled her grade seven school picture. The mere reminder of it immediately brought back many memories of a particular hairstyle , time, and event—even though it would be a couple of weeks before she actually had it in her hands because it was at her parents' house. Kathleen was spontaneous in her reaction too. Kathleen's photograph, like Sonya's, was one in which hair featured prominently as a marker of identity.

Kathleen's Memory: Fitting In. *This particular photograph with the too-short bangs (see figure 5.1.) encapsulates the identity that I was trying to forge for myself—a ten-year-old girl, specifically a ten-year-old Canadian girl, wanting to be like the other girls who went to my school and who lived in my neighborhood. I longed to have bangs—what my mother called a fringe—like my friends and my idol, Hayley Mills, who had starred in the film,* Pollyanna. *Bangs or fringe, it didn't matter what one called them, the answer was always no. Any suggestions about cutting any part of my hair would be met with a chorus of protests: Why would I want to do such a thing? My hair was lovely as it was—pulled back and off my face. It showed off my high forehead. Why did I need to look like everyone else? Didn't I like being different?*

And so, taking the matter into my own hands, I remember standing in front of the bureau mirror in my bedroom with a pair of small nail scissors. I pulled the front section of my hair forward, and then slowly and carefully, I began to cut. I recall the difficulty I had trying to get the bangs even and straight. Even after several failed attempts, I was undaunted. I kept cutting until the bangs were as even as I could make them. I remember thinking that they were perhaps a little short, but I recall being terribly pleased with the result. When my mother saw what I had done, she was furious, of course. I caught hell for ruining the pictures, but the next day when the photographer came, I was ready with my new bangs and my new identity.

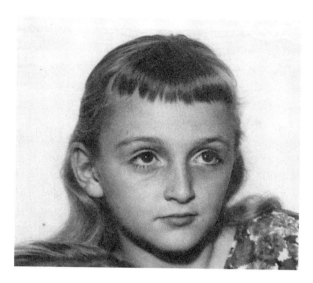

Figure 5.1 Kathleen's Bangs

Figure 5.2 Sonya's Mushroom

What did hair mean to me as I was growing up? I recall hair as a central focus from as long as I can remember. When I was very young, I had very light—almost white—blonde hair, which by the time I was seven, fell down my back almost to my waist. This long, very fair hair always seemed to garner a lot of positive attention from both my parents and friends. Even strangers would frequently compliment me on my hair. These compliments pleased my parents, which in turn, pleased me. But when I wanted to get my hair cut—I wanted a pixie cut like some of my friends—these compliments worked against me, since my parents would offer them up as the very reasons not to cut my hair. Why did I want to 'ruin' one of my best features? Besides, if I were to cut my hair, it would darken, and I understood that this would not be desirable. When my mother washed my hair in the spring and summer, she would comb it out so there wouldn't be tangles and then send me outside to let it dry in the sun to help keep it blonde. Thus, I learned from an early age that blonde was preferable to 'mousy' brown. While my hair defined me from the outset—from very early on—because of all the attention it garnered, the attention was not always pleasant.

When I was in the second grade, I attended an all-girls' boarding school in Toronto. I slept in a dorm with about twenty other girls. I was one of the youngest boarders. At the end of the row of beds, and next to mine, was where the supervising nun— 'Sister'—slept. Sister's sleeping quarters were curtained off from the rest of us. It was her job to wake us in the morning, lead us in morning prayers, and ensure that we were properly washed and dressed for breakfast. In the evening, she monitored our bedtime routines, including evening prayers and the eventual order of 'lights out.' Because of my hair, Sister had an additional task.

The nuns in charge said that my hair could not be worn loose down my back. It needed to be kept neat and orderly. Braids were the answer. Sister would wake me up ten minutes earlier than the other girls and braid my hair, as I sat on a wooden chair next to my bed. The dorm would still be dark, and the pulling and jostling would be done in silence or muted whispers. If Sister happened to be in a bad mood— and it seemed that she often was—my braids would be very tightly done and would rest quite high up on my head. This pulling of my hair would make my scalp ache, but as the day wore on, the braids would eventually loosen and I would get some relief. I recall one day when Sister bitterly complained to me in hoarse whispers and jerky pulls of my hair that if I'd just get my hair cut like the other girls, she wouldn't have to get up ten minutes earlier and waste her precious time. Although I wanted shorter hair, I didn't want her to know that it was my parents' wishes to have my hair long. Somehow, I felt that I'd be letting them down if I commiserated with her and told her that I, too, wanted short hair. In the evening, the ritual would be reversed. The braids would be undone and my hair would be brushed out, along with any residual achiness from the too-tightly wound braids.

Sonya's Memory: The Magic Mushroom. *Hair has always been a huge aspect of my life—mainly because my mother is a hairdresser, which is a relevant part of my experience of being 11 years old and entering junior high. My grade seven school picture (see figure 5.2.) was taken in September...I'm wearing a burgundy v-neck long-sleeve top and burgundy pants, purchased the month before at K-Mart. I thought my new school clothes were mature and very fitting for junior high. But the hair! Wow! It was my first perm. That in itself was a rite of passage, a 'coming of age' ritual of sorts. You see, my mother's career was a big part of my growing up, of my everyday experience. I would sit, albeit for various lengths of time (usually short but frequent) and watch my mother cut, color, shampoo, blow dry, curl, tease or perm hair. The most desirable of all treatments for me was the perm. My hair is naturally 'straight as a whip.' And, as fate would have it, 1979 saw the popularity of 'the mushroom' (one look at the picture and no explanation is required). I had longed for a perm but my requests were always met with the reply that I was too young. But I was told I would be able to get a perm before going to junior high. I was thrilled. I felt so grown up. And I had curly hair. That was my first of many perms but it was the most significant for me. I also got a 'pick' to use on my hair, and only people with certain hairstyles could use a pick and not a comb or brush. So, I started grade 7 with a very stylish perm, which marked that I was growing up.*

Looking at the picture, I remember how I felt when I received the picture—I had combed out my curls too much (in primping for the photo sitting). I remember feeling, "this is not how my hair looks," that it wasn't an accurate representation of my hair. I had wanted those curls so much and then I combed them out! Did I try too hard? What did hair mean to me growing up? Perhaps the first thing that comes to mind is my Chrissie dolls. Every Christmas (for a few years) there would be a Chrissie doll under the stocking among my other toys. My sister would get a different one as would my three female cousins who visited Christmas day. We would spend hours braiding and combing, lengthening and shortening their hair. They were blonde, brunette, and various shades in between (there must have been a redhead but I don't recall). I remember 'Brandy'—so named because of her hair color. While we dressed them up, the big focus was their hair. I longed to be like her—press my belly button and my hair would immediately grow.

So, what did hair mean? It was fun, something to play with (on my dolls and even on each other); it was a sociable event, getting one's hair done (I could hear the laughter, the talking—and they would often drink tea and have biscuits)—a time when secrets and fears were shared. It was a job—at Christmas and on some Saturdays, my sister and I earned extra money being 'shampoo girls.' I think I learned a lot about people through their reactions to hairstyles, their 'wants' regarding hair, but above all, I realized how personal it all is—in style and taste but also the role of the hairdresser. It's quite intimate because of the touching. I've gone to physicians many, many times who never came within 2 feet of me. You can't ever go to a hairdresser and not have this initial 'stranger' touch your head. I first realized it as a shampoo girl and felt very uncomfortable about it. Some people have sensitive heads and others the opposite. How do you know? I knew then I didn't want to be a hairdresser. My mom didn't want me to because she said standing on your feet all day was hard. And I think it's hard pleasing people, especially people who want things from their hair that their hair can't provide.

Our Hair-Raising Consciousness

As a number of memory-work scholars have noted (Crawford et al. 1992; Haug 1992), our personal memories may not be so personal and individual after all. Because we are not isolated from the influence of the larger society of which we are a part, our memories, while assuredly an integral part of who we are, may also represent a number of people's experiences and be a reflection of who we *all* are. As Leibowitz (1989), in his discussion of autobiography, notes the "story of a single life is always *entangled* in the complex folds of a culture" (xix). These *entanglements* remind us that our memories need to be interrogated in the light of existing social structures since the aim of memory-work analyses is to uncover the social meanings embodied by the actions described in the written accounts and to uncover the processes whereby the meanings—both then and now—are arrived at (Crawford et al. 1992: 49).

When we look at our memories and think of them as identity shaping, we both acknowledge that our memories focused on the power of hair and how we used hair to try to become who we wanted to be. In Kathleen's case, having bangs would help her enter the world of the everyday and provide a stamp of acceptance. The bangs were a way to disentangle herself from her family. For Sonya, a perm represented coming of age, maturity, increased freedom, and, of course, the curls she longed for. Our hair was an identity marker, a signifier for tween independence, yet at the same time, manipulated to allow us to gain entry into 'the group' that we had chosen. It was evident that we both strongly believed in the transformative power of hair, as in "if I had hair like that, then I would be...."

Popular Couture—Hair Today

Today's tweens, more than any generation of kids before them, have the media savvy and the financial resources to outfit themselves (George 2003: SP1). When we read about the recent marketing demographic of tweens with their "unique emotional needs and impressive purchasing power" (George 2003: SP1), we wondered how this was manifested in the popular culture. To investigate further, we reviewed recent issues (2002 and 2003) of widely read North American magazines including *Teen People*, *YM*, *Seventeen*, and *Teen*, all designed for girls in this age group and found at the public library. As part of our analysis, we developed an organizational framework to help us gauge the numbers of advertisements and articles on hair and hair-related products. We considered the personality influences (for example, models' ethnicity and age), product purpose or intent, and the manifestation of the idealized girl, including the overt messages, as well as the clichés, metaphors, contradictions, absences, gaps and silences embodied within the hair-related ads and articles.

One of our first observations was that the notion of hair was difficult to avoid as hair was such an entangled theme; in fact, hair featured prominently in most ads and pictures, even when it was not the intended focus, such as those ads highlighting jeans, perfume, boys, and make-up tips. The number of advertisements featuring hair products far outnumbered the articles on hair. Even some of the articles were thinly disguised advertisements since they, too, promoted particular brands of hair products.

The majority of models, including those pictured in the articles, were white females with blonde hair or highlights. Hairstyles were predominately long—beyond shoulder length—and mainly straight or slightly wavy and flowing. On the rare occasion when women of color were included, they also tended to have straight hair. The female models in the advertisements appeared to be adults—far older than the expected reading audience of these magazines is.

One of the strongest messages throughout the advertisements was that certain hairstyles could make young girls look older. Articles often echoed this message. As Charlene (18 years old) complained in *YM,* "Make Me Over," November 2002: 62): "I'm not a baby…everyone always thinks I'm 12."

The notion of what the idealized girl looked like was clearly stated along with the 'fact' that hair could help create the perfect image of this perfect girl. On the cover of *YM* (November 2002) the presentation of straight hair as ideal is stated clearly: "Get perfectly straight hair (not that there's anything wrong with curly)." This rather limp lip service to there nothing being 'wrong' with curly hair merely highlights the 'perfection' of straight hair. This emphasis on the desirability of the current vogue of straight hair certainly has huge implications for women of color. Not only does it teach tweens to devalue certain hair types, it elevates the white ideal, thereby promoting and maintaining white dominance, particularly in the fashion world.[1] In another *YM* "Make Me Over" (December 2002: 66), racial implications are apparent: "Don't make me a poodle—messing with curls is a delicate operation," promoting the acceptability of a certain type of curl, only achieved with a certain type of hair. An article in *Teen* (May 2002: 34–35), "Mission Makeover," gave instructions on "how to get your hair from slick and straight to cute and curly," once again emphasizing the desirability of the 'right look.'

The overriding message is that hair can change a young girl's image from boring to sexy, as was declared on the cover of *Seventeen* (January 2003): "hair news: why short, blond & sexy can work for you." As one reader in *YM*'s article "Out of Control Crushes" (September 2002: 140–141) was quoted as saying: "I thought of dyeing my hair blond to match his profile of the 'perfect woman.'" On the cover of the same magazine was the enticement "Be a sexy blond (in 10 minutes)." The messages go well beyond what makes a perfect girl and how to achieve a certain look. They present the ultimate motivation as that of doing it *for* a man, to get and keep a man, to please a man, and to make manifest *his* version of perfect womanhood. The message is that girls' quest for sexiness is well entrenched in heterosexuality. In other words, while it is considered 'healthy,' 'normal,' and 'natural' to strive to be 'sexy,' this look is clearly designed for one purpose only—to attract *men*. We believe magazines, mirroring these imposed gender roles, play a significant part in tween girls' socialization of self.

Sitting in the Hairdresser's Chair

A beauty salon is, as Ewen (1979) demonstrates, a visually rich site for research. In our work on tweens' beauty rituals, we asked Mary Corbin, a hairstylist for over 40 years (and Sonya's mother), whether she had noticed a difference in tween clients over the years (personal communication, 24 July 2003). Without hesitating, she exclaimed, "Yes, big time!" Mary went on to explain:

> Now they want 'grown up' hairstyles, they want what women in their twenties are wearing. Kids are getting their hair dyed at younger and younger ages. I've seen little girls as young as 5 with their hair dyed. It used to be that women didn't color their hair until after they left high school. Parents are encouraging it. I don't think it's healthy for young girls' scalps and I try to talk them out of it. It's only my personal opinion but I don't feel a young child should have chemicals on her scalp, perms or colors.

When asked about the proliferation of hair repair products in teen magazines and whether they were necessary for such a young age group, Mary said:

> Definitely because they're using more chemicals on their hair than most adults. They experiment with products and buy everything they see in the drugstore. They wash their hair twice a day, blow-dry it, curl it, and straighten it. They even put their hair on ironing boards and iron it.

When asked why tweens are so focused on hair, she explained, "Because of advertising and television and movies. They want their hair done like singers, movie stars. Some make video tapes to bring me to show me the hairstyle they want." She concluded by saying, "They're worried about their physical appearance at younger and younger ages. But they're also physically developing at younger ages."

Mary's experiences certainly resonate with the current marketing demographic information on tweens (George 2003) and our own findings of our magazine analysis.

The Hair Is the Message

In the section called "The Hair Project" (Haug 1992), a participant's girlhood experience of hair highlights its transformative power:

> At the age of 10 or 11, I found myself observing trends in my class with increasing anxiety. One girl after another came to school with newly-shorn hair. Whereas it had previously been possible to divide the class—at least superficially—into two groups, one grown up, one more childlike. I was left in the end, at the age of 12, as the only one in plaits, clearly viewed by the whole class as the only remaining child. (97)

The findings of our meta-analysis of today's tween magazines echo this experience: one of the strongest messages throughout the advertisements was that certain hairstyles could make young girls look older.[2] Like clothing, hair is a means of defining the self socially (McLuhan 1964). It, too, has transformative powers, as we found out when we interrogated our girlhood memories of hair. "Quietly and unexpectedly, hair has become our court of deliberation, the place where we contemplate who and what we are" (McCracken: 2). As we analyzed our pasts through the process of memory-work, we began to see differences and similarities (be)tween our experiences of hair and those of young girls today. Unlike today's tweens, we were not the deliberate targets of such extensive corporate advertising and consumer products aimed to help in the achievement of our goals of looking older and fitting in. We were not bombarded with "[n]ew lines of teen-inspired cosmetics…and personal-hygiene products…through which tweens can vicariously experience a 'teen' lifestyle" (George 2003: S7). Like them, however, we were enamored with "the mythology of teendom" (George 2003: S7) and manipulated our hair to fit in and to grow up faster. We too were socialized by celebrities, television, and older peers. Hair was, and continues to be, a site of possibilities for tweens searching for their sense of envisioned idealized selves.

Notes

[1] For an analysis of hair-straightening products that regularly appear in advertisements that target women of color, see also Mayes (1997).

² For a more extensive discussion within popularized work on women's lives, see Wolf (1991) and Faludi (1991).

References

A-bite-of-Broadway.org. *A Bite of Broadway.* http://www.a-bite-of-broadway.org/Synopsis. htm.

Arnett, J. J. *Adolescence and Emerging Adulthood: A Cultural Approach.Upper Saddle River* New Jersey: Prentice Hall, 2001.

Aron, B. "A Disappearing Community." In *Images of Information,* edited by J. Wagner, 59–67. Beverly Hills/London: Sage, 1979.

Baker Miller, J. *Toward a New Psychology of Women,* 2ⁿᵈ edition. Boston: Beacon Press, 1986.

Baca Zinn, M., P. Hondagneu-Sotelo, and M. Messner. *Gender Through the Prism of Difference,* 2ⁿᵈ edition. Toronto: Allyn & Bacon, 2000.

Collier, J. "Visual Anthropology: Images of Information." In *Images of Information,* edited by J. Wagner, 271–282. Beverly Hills/London: Sage, 1979.

Crawford, J., S. Kippax, J. Onyx, U. Gault, and P. Benton. *Emotion and Gender: Constructing Meaning from Memory.* London: Sage, 1992.

Ewen, P. "The Beauty Ritual." In *Images of Information,* edited by J. Wagner, 43–57. Beverly Hills/London: Sage, 1979.

Faludi, S. *Backlash: The Undeclared War against American Women.* Toronto: Doubleday, 1991.

Finch, J. "'It's Great to have Someone to Talk to': The Ethics and Politics of Interviewing Women." In *Social Researching: Politics, Problems, Practice,* edited by C. Bell and H. Roberts, 70–87. London: Routledge, 1984.

George, L. "This ain't OshKosh B'Gosh." *Saturday Post,* April 19 2003, SP1, SP7–SP8.

Haug, F., ed. *Female Sexualization: A Collective Work of Memory.* London: Verso, 1992.

Ingleton, C. "Gender and Learning: Does Emotion Make a Difference?" *Higher Education* 30 (1995): 323–335.

Kosonen, U. "Personal Is Scientific!" In *On the Fringes of Sport,* edited by L. Laine , 49–57. Germany: Academia Verlag, 1993a.

_____. "Running Girl: Fragments of My Body History." In *On the Fringes of Sport,* edited by L. Laine , 16–25. Germany: Academia Verlag, 1993b.

Leibowitz, H. *Fabricating Lives: Explorations in American Autobiography.* New York: New Directions Books, 1989.

Martin, R. "Phototherapy: The School Photograph (Happy Days are Here again)." In *Photography/Politics: Two*, edited by P. Holland, J. Spence and S. Watney, 40–42. London: Comedia/Photography Workshop, 1986.

Mayes, E. M. "As Soft as Straight Gets: African American Women and Mainstream Beauty Standards in Haircare Advertising." In *Undressing the Ad: Reading Culture in Advertising*, edited by K. T. Frith, 85–108. New York: Peter Lang, 1997.

McCracken, G. *Big Hair: A Journey into the Transformation of Self.* Middlesex: Viking, 1995.

McLuhan, M. *Understanding Media: The Extensions of Man.* New York: Signet, 1964.

Mitchell, C., and Weber, S. *Reinventing Ourselves as Teachers: Beyond Nostalgia* . London: Falmer, 1999.

O'Reilly-Scanlon, K. *She's Still on my Mind: Teachers' Memories, Memory-work and Self-study*. PhD dissertation. McGill University, Montreal, Quebec, 2001.

Rice, P. *The Adolescent: Development, Relationships, and Culture,* 7th edition. Toronto: Allyn & Bacon, 1992.

Rich, A. "Notes Towards a Politics of Location." In *Blood, Red, and Poetry: Selected Prose 1979-1985*, edited by A. Rich, 210–231. New York: W.W. Norton & Co, 1986.

Spence, J. *Cultural Sniping: The Art of Transgression.* New York: Routledge, 1995.

Tams-Witmark Music Library, Inc. "Highlights of Hair" In Tams-Witmark Music Library, Inc., 2000 -2002. http://www.tamswitmark.com/musicals/hair.html#synopsis.

van Manen, M. *Researching Lived Experience: Human Science for an Action Sensitive Pedagogy.* London, ON: The Althouse Press, 1990.

Wagner, J. "Photography and Social Science Process." In *Images of Information: Still Photography in the Human Sciences*, edited by J. Wagner, 283–298. Beverly Hills and London: Sage, 1979.

Walker, R. "Finding a Silent Voice for the Researcher: Using Photographs in Evaluation and Research." In *Qualitative Voices in Educational Research*, edited by M. Schratz, 74-92. London, Falmer, 1993.

Wolf, N. *The Beauty Myth: How Images of Beauty Are Used against Women.* New York: William Morrow and Company, 1991.

Worell, J., and P. Remer. *Feminist Perspectives in Therapy*. John Wiley & Sons, 1996.

CHAPTER SIX

Reading Elisabeth's Girlhood: History and Popular Culture at Work in the Subjectivity of a Tween

Meredith Cherland

It is easier to find the cultural markers of solidarity and resistance than to engage with the complex and painful intersection of the psychic and the social.

—Valerie Walkerdine 1997: 14

Introduction

Like most of us, I have changed in the past ten years. I not only look older, I also see the world differently. Ten years ago, I used critical theory and feminist theory to explain the ways in which society and culture shape the phenomenon of preteen girls reading fiction. Today, I work from a sociological and a psychological perspective at the same time. I follow Walkerdine (1997) in believing that neither a psychology that focuses on the individual mind, nor a sociology that focuses solely on the workings of society will be adequate to the task of explaining how human beings interact with the artifacts of popular culture and how they live in the world.

By way of introduction, let me make three theoretical points. First, in this chapter I am going to make use of Walkerdine's concept of a "psychology of survival" that allows human subjects to think and endure. Pointing out that classed femininity is always achieved through both social and psychic struggle (49), Walkerdine uses her own feelings, fantasies, and memories as part of her research process, and psychoanalysis as a "useful toolkit" for explaining the ways in which popular culture and contemporary society can factor in the subjectivity of the little girl.[1] I will do the same.

Second, I will also look at girlhood as situated in history, because pointing out that a concept like 'girlhood' is produced in history is a way to highlight its constructedness and to take account of the poststructural idea that meaning shifts as its context changes. It also brings power into the discussion, because power exists in relations. Power is a situation, and situations occur in history (Foucault 1997).

Third, I am going to use the concept of 'subjectivity' (and not 'identity' or 'psyche') in this chapter in order to avoid the pitfalls of a narrowly humanistic conception of the individual as a rational, coherent, pre-existing self. Subjectivity is "the conscious and unconscious thoughts and emotions of the individual, her sense of herself and her ways of understanding her relation to the world" (Weedon 1998: 32). Subjectivity is produced as the human subject interacts with the cultural discourses and the social practices that surround her. It is constantly changing.

The individual subjects of this research are my daughter Elisabeth and me. I was born in 1947 in Providence, Rhode Island, to working-class parents who prospered during the post-World War II economic boom, and I grew up to be a good, white, middle-class girl. I became a teacher in the United States, and then a teacher educator at a university in Western Canada.[2]

Elisabeth Cherland was born in 1978 to my husband and me—white Americans living in Regina, Saskatchewan. Raised in Canada, she spent thirteen months of her childhood (June 1987–June 1988) living in Tempe, Arizona, where her parents were enrolled as doctoral students at Arizona State University. She spent that year in third grade at the Early School (a private elementary school for children aged three to nine).[3]

This chapter is an auto-ethnography (Ellis and Bochner 2000; Brodkey 2000) of our family's life in 1988. This was the year that Elisabeth read every available book from *The Babysitters Club* series—which sold 150 million copies for Scholastic Books Services between 1986 and 2000. Scholastic hired the series author (Ann M. Martin) to produce a four-part series about a group of friends who form a babysitting cooperative. Elisabeth bought the first four volumes of the series in Arizona in 1987 as a prepackaged set. She had purchased the first 69 books in the series by the time her interest waned in 1991.[4]

In this chapter, I will be analyzing data from interviews with my adult daughter and from my own memories of our family's life in 1988. I will attempt to answer this question: What can I learn about girlhood today from this consideration of sociology, psychology, and history at work in my daughter's girlhood?

Memory and Method

Frigga Haug (1987) has written at length about a research method she calls "memory-work." Briefly, memory-work is collective work that calls for members of a research group to write down and talk about their memories of the past that focus upon a certain theme. It is work done by women, for the purpose of "unraveling gender socialization." Memory work, says Haug, follows from Marx's idea that society is organized and evolves through the life processes of particular individuals. Through memory-work, women try to understand how individuals construct themselves into (and are positioned into) existing social relations, and how the individual woman becomes part of society. It is a research method that has great potential to connect the psychic and the social. Using our memories of the year 1988, and using the *Babysitters Club* books as our theme, my daughter, Elisabeth Cherland, and I have attempted to do memory-work, following procedures outlined by Haug and her colleagues.[5]

To summarize, I remember 1988 as a bittersweet year in our family's life. My memories are full of the stresses of living in unfamiliar Arizona, of working to accomplish as much as I possibly could in my doctoral program within a short period, of caring for two small children and keeping house, of moving back to Canada, of finding childcare, of returning to a demanding job, and more. I remember feeling overweight and unkempt (I lost over 30 pounds that year and changed my hairstyle when I returned to Canada). I also remember the physical beauty of my two small children and the satisfactions and pleasures of reading *The Chronicles of Narnia* and the Laura Ingalls Wilder books aloud to them in the car, while my husband drove the half-hour to their school in the mornings and home again in the evenings. I remember our enjoyment of the Arizona sun and heat, and also the joy of returning later that year to our home in Canada.

Elisabeth too has bittersweet memories of 1988. She remembers many things that brought her happiness and satisfaction, but she also remembers the terrors of childhood and the confusion and stress of trying to understand the world and her place in it. What follows provides an overview of Elisabeth's memories of 1988. I have organized it around these five themes:

- Theme 1: Anxiety
- Theme 2: Performing Capable Adult
- Theme 3: Performing Whiteness

- Theme 4: Performing Middle Class
- Theme 5: Performing Femininity

Theme 1: Anxiety

Elisabeth recalls that as a nine-year-old in 1988 she was "watching what went on in the world." So much was frightening for her:

> *I remember reading* Sadako and the Thousand Paper Cranes,[6] *and how that sort of started the anxiety stuff that I had for just a few months, I guess it was, but just being really scared and worried about stuf, and not completely understanding. I remember (that in the book) Sadako starts getting cancer and she's dizzy, and so I kind of had this self-induced dizziness thing going on. I mean not really understanding.*
>
> *And I remember at school I was playing on the swings, and I touched the metal on the chain, you know on the swing? And I remember a minute later, I touched my hand to my mouth and I could taste that metal. And I had a panic attack! And just, I was like, "I'm gonna die! I can taste this metal! There's disease!" I was just freaking out, and Marie (my teacher) having to reassure me.*

Elisabeth's memories and the transcription of our discussion of them are full of her awareness of the environmental concerns that were in the newspapers in 1988. She remembers that one of her classmates brought to school an article about the greenhouse effect and damage to the ozone layer, and that this frightened her. She remembers the prediction that Arizona would be running out of water in the year 2001 and her own relief that we would be moving back to Canada before that could happen. She remembers playing a game with the other children at school that they called "Poison Sun."

Elisabeth remembers believing that there were unseen, unpredictable forces around her that could cause her death. Unseen radiation had caused Sadako's cancer, and the greenhouse effect was making the Arizona sun even more dangerous. When nine-year-old Elisabeth experienced the discomfort of breast buds, she became very frightened, thinking they were cancerous and suffered with anxiety until we could visit a doctor who reassured her.

Elisabeth remembers that her world—which seemed stable and predictable enough most of the time—sometimes seemed "freaky," mysterious, and malignant. She remembers the plane crash of 1988 in which her friend Nicole's aunt died, and where only one small child, of all the passengers, survived. Elisabeth's anxiety was a significant and painful part of her life in 1988. She remembers that when anxiety struck she had shortness of breath and suffered physical distress. She says, "The anxiety and the worry were significant. I will always remember them."

Theme 2: Performing Capable Adult

You know what I remember is the little kids' class, like the three-year-olds' class, and one particular kid, Jared. He was three, and he had behavioral problems. But he loved me, and I felt really honored...so we would do things with the whole school, and I would walk with him and hold his hand. Yeah. And I loved having that role, and playing with little kids. You know, not so much with Ben [her own little brother]. [She laughs.] But with other kids. Ben was a little too much reality. [She laughs.] Yeah.

At the age of nine, Elisabeth was not yet a babysitter, but she remembers that she desperately wanted to be. She loved playing Big Sister to her little brother's friends. She recalls her brother's birthday party in January of 1988 and her pride in helping her parents manage a large group of five-year-olds for several hours. She looked forward to the Reading Buddies program at school, where she could be responsible for a kindergarten student for an hour or more.

Elisabeth enjoyed every opportunity to be in the position of 'older.' She remembers how much she enjoyed going out in the car with our neighbor Nancy, Nancy's five-year-old son, and Elisabeth's little brother Ben. Nancy would strap the little boys into the back seat, and Elisabeth would ride up front with Nancy. Elisabeth says, "She talked to me as if I were a grown up, and she treated the boys like babies. I *loved* that!"

As a member of the Grade 3/4 class, then the oldest class at the Early School, Elisabeth enjoyed all the structures of school that recognized her age and maturity. She enjoyed calling her teachers by their first names; she enjoyed choosing her own books for Readers' Workshop, and working through the math book at her own pace. She loved not having to ask permission to go to the bathroom. She remembers her pride at being included in the fourth graders' trip to Disneyland, because, like them, she would be leaving the Early School at the end of the year.

Ten years ago, I would have looked at this data and thought about desire for agency and about hidden resistance in the production of gendered subjectivity. I still see those things. But now, I also see a "psychology of survival" (Walkerdine 1997) that allowed Elisabeth to think and endure. Growing up in a culture that (in 1988 at least) positioned white middle-class girls as innocent, helpless and vulnerable, Elisabeth longed to be knowledgeable, capable, and strong.[7] Reading the *Babysitters Club* books allowed her to fantasize a stronger and more capable social position, perhaps the only one available to girls her age. In her desire to be responsible for younger children, I see the ways in which race, class, and gender come together in the subjectivity of this child. It is *white* girls the society works to position as helpless (Lesko 2001). It is *middle-class* girls who are positioned as innocent (Walkerdine 1998; Fine 1992). It is *girls* (and not boys) who are positioned as vulnerable (Fine 1992; Cherland 1994; Pecora 1998). In Elisabeth's desire to care for younger children, I see her reading the culture and constructing her subjectivity to perform her race, class, and gender.

Theme 3: Performing Whiteness

I wasn't a babysitter yet. But I desperately wanted to be.

Carol Schick (2000) says that the successful production of white domination requires demonstrations of ability, of hierarchies, of devotion to duty. It requires the creation of moral rectitude. It requires that you position yourself as one who matters and create a positive self-identity. In Elisabeth's memories and in her talk about them, I can see her doing these things. Part of wanting to be seen as a capable adult has to do performing femininity, with positioning yourself as one who serves others competently and well, but part of wanting to be seen as a capable adult has to do with performing whiteness (see Note 2), which requires one to desire legitimacy, authority, and power (91). Fantasy and desire came into play, as Elisabeth played the role of adult and good girl.

Schick (2000) recalls that as a child she was told to "act like a lady." Now she sees that "being a lady" embodied what it meant to be white: straight, able-bodied, gendered, a Christian, and therefore capable of acting in the world. Schick was made to know, unconsciously at least, that through a particular production of whiteness, she could have middle-class respectability (101). I would add that she could also achieve femininity. Race, class, and gender are bound up together and are performed together. Elisabeth desperately wanted to be a nine-year-old who performed well and met the expectations of her parents, her teachers, and the society. To this day, when Elisabeth looks at the family videos of our life in Arizona and Regina in 1988, she is embarrassed by what she calls her "rambunctiousness" and the "mean" way she treated her little brother. She believes these ways of behaving were and are inappropriate for what she meant to be, for what she should have been at the age of nine.

There is some explicit discussion of race in Elisabeth's transcript. When asked, she talks about Julie (an Arizona classmate) and about Mindy (a Regina classmate). Mindy in Regina was Elisabeth's only dark-skinned classmate, a recent immigrant from the Caribbean who wore ski pants when it did not seem cold enough to Canadian children and whose mother accompanied her everywhere. Elisabeth and the other girls kept their distance. She says, "We weren't mean. We were nice to her. But none of us were really friends with her." Elisabeth also recalls that with Julie, her only African American classmate in Arizona, who was much lighter skinned and who was from a family that had been American for many generations, things were different. Julie wore the same kinds of clothes as Elisabeth and was able to attend the same private school. She was clearly a member of the same socioeconomic group. Even as she remembers the racial difference, Elisabeth says, "Julie was one of us."

There is much more in Elisabeth's memories that does *not* speak explicitly of race but that I am able to interpret as the production of whiteness. Many of Elisabeth's memories have to do with white privilege. She expected to be invited to birthday parties. She expected to have a teacher of her own race. She expected the books she read to be about white girls. Others (like Mindy) were different, but Elisabeth belonged.

And, many of Elisabeth's memories have to do with the ways in which she positioned and produced herself as well behaved, as helpful as smart and capable, as responsible, as productive, as middle-class, as *white*. She remembers the satisfactions of working her way independently through her math book without difficulty, of reading the guidebook aloud at the Botanical Gardens when Nana and Grampa came to visit, of being the one to push the shopping cart around at the grocery store. In positioning herself as capable, helpful, and productive, Elisabeth was reading cultural discourses that told her how she was inscribed by the dominant culture and responding by demonstrating her position as a white, middle-class girl. This was not a choice. She did it because it was necessary for her psychic survival (Schick 2000).[8] She had internalized the disciplining codes for whiteness and the social expectations for living out those codes, and she did not resist them, because enacting them gave her pleasure.

Theme 4: Performing Middle Class

> *Things were consistent at home, and at school things were pretty consistent too, so that was nice, and I think having that routine, you know going to the ice cream restaurant for supper once a week, and the swimming pool, that was really helpful to me too...I remember having my favorite bathing suit.*

When I look at Elisabeth's memories of the year that she was nine, I can see the class differences between her childhood and my own. I was aware of money as a child and knew that it was sometimes in short supply. But Elisabeth did not have to think about money. She could take it for granted without worry. She did not think about the money that bought her clothes, that allowed her to have more than one bathing suit, that allowed her to buy books, to fly to Disneyland, and to have supper at the ice cream restaurant every Tuesday night. What Elisabeth calls "consistency" has to do with the predictability that two comfortable and regular salaries make possible. Her parents had job security (and I notice this because mine did not). Knowing that our move to Arizona was not permanent also added to her security. She had not left the past behind. She knew she would be returning to it. Sabbatical years, of course, are a class privilege.

Many things in Elisabeth's life were, to her, simply facts of life (having her own room, the swimming pool she enjoyed every day, her private school). But, these are markers of social class, and class is more than a fact of life. It is also an identity performance. All the accoutrements of twentieth-century middle-class Canadian-American life are there in Elisabeth's interview transcript: swimming, restaurants, violin lessons, French at school, awards, clothes, library books, and attendance at a Protestant church. Beneath these, we can see her performance of middle class. When she presented her excellent report card to her parents, when she attended a performance of *The Nutcracker* at the invitation of a school friend that Christmas, when she played the board game *Go to the Head of the Class* with Kara, she was performing and 'doing' middle class. When she played violin in the intergenerational orchestra at church and when she brought me a leather-bound book of original poems produced at school as a Mother's Day project, Elisabeth was participating in group enactments of 'middle class,' arranged and sanctioned by the adults around her.

Walkerdine (1997) says that while working-class girls struggle to be somebody, middle-class girls know they already are (154). Elisabeth's memories are full of struggle, but she knew that her middle-class parents had a place in the world and that she did too. Elisabeth grew up in a home with parents who had resources, who knew where to go for help (like a child psychiatrist) when they needed it, who could find a private school when they moved to a new community, who had education and mobility. I grew up in a home where my grandmother lived with us because she had nowhere else to go and where income was not always secure. My father worked for sales commissions, and when I was in elementary school, my mother struggled to get enough hours on her part-time job as a store detective. Being middle class feels good. I know this, because I have not always been middle class. I live 'middle class' now as a position of stability, which gives me the comfort of knowing I *am* someone and can expect to *be* someone. (Conscious of this construction, I still find it difficult to do anything that might jeopardize my status as middle class.) I think that at the age of nine, performing middle class, bound up with performing whiteness and performing femininity, felt good to Elisabeth and offered her pleasure, both material and psychic, rather than pain.

Theme 5: Performing Femininity

I remember... We've watched (family) video tapes of that year, so it's funny for me to separate what I remember about watching the videotape, and what I remember from actually experiencing it. I have a lot of retrospect from watching those videotapes and seeing myself... remember that whole pink outfit Nana gave me for Christmas ...gotta love pink...and the pink high top basketball shoes I got at Smitty's! Aunt Joyce loved them so much, she bought some too.

In Elisabeth's interview transcript, I see our family watching her, and I see Elisabeth watching herself. I am reminded of Foucault's (1979) concept of the panopticon, which comes from the design of a prison where there is one guard in the center who watches the prisoners in cells in a circle around him, all day and all night. Foucault points out that one effect of the constant watching is that the prisoners begin to keep watch upon themselves. Those who become conditioned to being watched and evaluated come to self-surveillance. Their subjectivities are affected, and they are controlled through normalization.

Ten years ago (Cherland 1994) I used film criticism to explain that as young girls become aware that they are the objects of a male gaze (Kaplan

1983), they begin to watch themselves and each other as they perform femininity. Foucault's panopticon provides another, slightly richer, metaphor for explaining femininity as a performance. Elsewhere I have reviewed fifty years of research that explains the ways in which femininity is created and sustained through social performances (Cherland 1994). Now Foucault's metaphor helps me understand the ways in which women also gaze upon themselves and each other and come to internalize the strictures of femininity.

Gender is (like race) a performance. That Elisabeth was enacting the culture by wearing pink and by playing with the cultural role of 'nurturing mother' is one way of explaining her actions in 1988. 'Pretty girl' and 'capable feminine adult' are performances she watched herself playing, and she realized others were watching her playing. These performances were culturally approved and culturally *required* for children like Elisabeth who were white, middle class, and female. (We see the requirement in the fact that children who made mistakes in these areas were punished—see Note 8.)

I still see in memories like Elisabeth's the enactments of gender that I saw in 1994. I still see her using books, for example, to solidify relationships with other girls and with me. But now, I also see her watching herself, evaluating her own performances of gender, and watching the responses of the adults around her. Once her friend Kara's divorced father and his girlfriend took Kara and Elisabeth bowling. A self-surveilling prisoner of gender at the age of nine, Elisabeth remembers that when she came home and told us that the girlfriend was 19 years old and pregnant, we (her parents) communicated our shock and disapproval without actually saying anything about it, and she knew that the girlfriend had done something wrong, something she herself must never do.

Ten years later, I still see resistance in what tweens have to say about girlhood. I see Elisabeth reading to escape the stresses in her life. I see her resistance to violin practice and to what she experienced as the oppression of forced 'creativity' in Writing Workshop. But now I also see her mind at work in a psychology of survival that is a response to the cultural discourses that were constructing her girlhood and positioning her as a certain kind of white, middle class, feminine subject: innocent, vulnerable, and helpless. And I now see Elisabeth's psychological responses as produced in historically specific regimes of meaning and truth (Walkerdine 1997:260)

History in the Positioning of the Subject

In the first part of this chapter, I have looked at five themes I found in Elisabeth's interview transcripts and in my own memories of 1988, explaining the "psychology of survival" through which she produced her subjectivity in interaction with the society in which she lived. In order to situate psychology and sociology in history, I will go on to look at how each of these themes (and Elisabeth's psychology of survival) is historically contingent. I do this in order to highlight their constructedness, to show how meanings shift as context changes, and to show power at work in the situations of daily life.

History shows us that childhood is very much a social invention, one redefined by every society in every age. The next generation is always subjected to the dictates and desires of an adult society that seeks to shape and mold young people (Inness 1998). Categories of identity are constructed in time. Whiteness, for example, is a political category constructed historically to unify European colonialists, to rationalize their difference from and domination of Aboriginal others (Kelly 1997). Gender, too, is an identity tenuously constituted in time, created and sustained through social performances (Butler 1990).

Taking Haug's (1987) suggestion, I went to the newspapers to review the history of 1988 (see Orlofsky 1989). There I saw the well-established political conservativism of the United States. George Bush (the elder) defeated Michael Dukakis in the presidential election in November 1988 as Ronald Reagan was finishing his eight-year term as president. The stock market had crashed in 1987, and homelessness was a growing phenomenon as the economy faltered and the gap between rich and poor Americans widened. In Arizona in 1988, Elisabeth could look out the windows of our station wagon in Phoenix and see families in rags camping under freeway overpasses. Her Sunday School class collected money and canned goods for the homeless, and our church organized a Thanksgiving dinner for poor and homeless people that year.

In 1988, Conservative Brian Mulroney was prime minister in Canada, and the Conservative Party had been in power in Saskatchewan for six years. Canadian newspapers were full of the fact that 10,000 people in Canada had the AIDS virus (as did 5 to 10 million people worldwide). In Iran, the Ayatollah Khomeini was still in power. Iran and Iraq were at war, and there had been a deadlock in the Persian Gulf peace talks. In the United States and Canada, there were many anti-abortion demonstrations in 1988. Elisabeth remembers that one of her classmates brought a newspaper article to school about environmental damage to the ozone layer and its consequences. She came home from school one day to tell me that the 13-year-old actor Drew Barrymore had been released from a rehab center for alcohol abuse. These news items were part of the historical moment that framed the production of the meanings we gave our lives.

Theme 1: Anxiety

When I look back at what I have written about Elisabeth's memories of anxiety in 1988, I do see meanings that were produced in that historical moment. Anxiety-provoking news items can be found in any historical age, but the large number of news items about dangers in the environment was something new in 1988. The increase in homelessness was something new in 1988. And the kind of marketing research that led to the production of the *Babysitters Club* series was a new phenomenon.

The *Babysitters Club* books were produced to target a large and specific market — white middle-class preteen girls — and they were wildly successful. Elisabeth recalls that the books met her need for reassurance and her need for escape. Scholastic Books made money by meeting her psychological need for predictability. However, it is important to note that at nine years old, Elisabeth appropriated an artifact of popular culture for her own psychic purposes.

Elisabeth's love of routine in daily life was in all likelihood a response to the threatening unpredictability of events in the world around her and a response to the culturally constructed helplessness of childhood. She remembers enjoying the formulaic structure of the *Babysitters Club* books and feeling comforted by their utter predictability. The plot structure was always the same. The characters were always the same, and Elisabeth relied on that predictability. She says, "I could count on it that none of the characters would die."

Ten years ago, I saw fear and anxiety in the psychic lives of preteen girls (Cherland 1994). I traced discourses of horror and female victimization in popular culture. Now I also look to history (the larger context of world events) for the sources of Elisabeth's fears and anxieties in 1988. As I write this, fifteen years later, we are living in a society that *markets* fear. President George W. Bush and the men around him have justified their invasion of Iraq in March 2003 by demonizing Saddam Hussein, and by selling the American people the idea that Hussein would eventually attack and harm them if they did not strike at him first. This idea was easier to sell after the events of 11 September 2001. Terrorist alerts at US airports and borders have fostered this fear as have the incursions on American civil liberties debated in Congress as 'security measures' proposed by the Bush administration. It seems to me that persuading people to fear is serving the purposes of America's conservative government by diverting Americans' attention away from the ways in which their freedoms are being limited and their lives controlled.

Today people are being encouraged to fear not only terrorists and 'the enemy' but other forces as well. Television programs about environmental disasters still seem to flood the airways, and scholars from a number of different disciplines are explaining how conservative discourses generate fear of the poor and the racialized (Thobani 2002), fear of the working class (Walkerdine 1997), and fear of teachers and of unscripted, unpackaged curriculum (Edelsky in press). People are being encouraged to fear each other. (I regularly receive advertisements over the Internet that encourage me to use electronic 'detective' services to spy on my husband and other people I love in order to uncover their betrayals of me and expose the evils they are probably perpetrating.) Girls and women are still portrayed as victims in popular fiction (Pecora 1998), in popular music and music videos (Lemish 1998), and in films (Hausknecht 1998). Anxiety is still a common form of mental illness in children.

Fear and anxiety are produced in historically contingent ways. I believe that their effects on children may be worse today than they were in 1988. Elisabeth recalls suffering for only a few months. She used the *Baby-sitters Club* series and anything else that came to hand to reassure herself and grew up to feel stable and healthy. Today's nine-year-old girls may have to struggle harder against fear and anxiety at an historical moment when fear is being sold by the government and used as a means for controlling the masses.

Theme 2: Performing Capable Adult

As a nine-year-old in 1988, Elisabeth was trying to position herself as competent and capable. Fantasy allowed her to see herself this way. Ten years ago, I wrote about how the culture positions little girls as helpless and denies them power and agency. I explained how this has psychological consequences and suggested instructional strategies within a progressive language arts curriculum that might help girls cope (Cherland 1994; Cherland and Edelsky 1993). Today, I have a different view of curriculum.

In 1988, the progressive literacy curriculum that has dominated Language Arts Curriculum Guides and teacher education programs in Canada and the United States for the past fifteen years was in regular use at the Early School. For the first six months of 1988, Elisabeth engaged in Reading Workshop and Writing Workshop every day at school. Reading Workshop, Elisabeth recalls, did give her a feeling of independence and did support her desire to be a capable adult. But she experienced Writing Workshop as coercive. She found it difficult to be a 'creative' writer, and the constant demand for original stories oppressed her. She was probably not alone. Peg Finders (1997) has written about other girls who have found the demands and the routines of Writing Workshop oppressive and worked to subvert the system.

Walkerdine (1984) has also shown how progressive pedagogies, which are grounded in humanist conceptions of an active, natural, expressive (and male) child, can be oppressive for little girls. Ursula Kelly (1997), in a discussion of curriculum as politics, has pointed out that progressive pedagogies like Writing Workshop are often informed by discourses of individualism and personal growth.[9] Fifteen years after 1988, educators are much more aware that human subjects relate to curriculum within relations of power. Today the progressive literacy curriculum has been challenged, and critical literacy instruction, which teaches children to question the social order and use literacy to transform it, allows for active resistance to government efforts to control literacy instruction (and teachers) through scripted curriculum, mandatory phonics instruction, and standardized testing. Critical literacy curriculum is a sign of hope.

Theme 3: Performing Whiteness

Ten years ago, I thought that when I studied white girls, there was not much to say about race (Cherland 1994). I wrote about gender and class without explaining their intersections with race. I wrote as if white subjects had no race and as if white people could not be racist without coming into contact with racialized people. Now I think differently.

This is a time in history when scholars are turning to the study of whiteness in an effort to explain the origins of racism and the construction of the racialized Other. In Ursula Kelly's (1997) explanation of whiteness as a political category, she points out that difference is a signifying necessity. White people cannot be white unless they position themselves as different from those who are not white. Social identities are constructed to sustain difference and dominance.

Elisabeth's racial privilege and her desire to perform whiteness are things I could not see in 1988. But today, race is being deconstructed, denaturalized, and understood as a social category maintained by discursive power. I see race in the fact that in her memories of 1988 she never mentions race or racism unless I ask about them. I see race in her desire to be a good reading buddy, to be a capable babysitter, to get all her homework done and done well. Now I believe that series books like *The Babysitters Club* contribute to the discourses that sustain racial oppression. The fact that not every character in *The Babysitters Club* is white (one character is a Japanese American) does not disguise that fact that the books offer white girls fantasies through which they can perform white (middle-class and female) identity.

Theme 4: Performing Middle Class

When Elisabeth sat on her bed, adjusted the special backrest pillow we had bought her to use while reading, and picked up a book from the *Babysitters Club* series, she was also enacting 'middle class.' All the Babysitters Club girls were of the same socioeconomic group and played by the same rules. The *BabySitters Club* books, marketed to the middle class, helped to convince Elisabeth that, under the skin, all girls were like her, and that her middle-class privileges were universal and natural.

But, Elisabeth's middle-class privileges were not natural. They were produced in history. Four to six *Babysitters Club* books were published each year in the series, at a cost of $3.50 Canadian (each) in 1988. Elisabeth could afford to be part of the preteen market, but many little girls in American and Canadian elementary schools could not. Girls did use series books as social currency to establish friendships and maintain relationships, but although girls' books are sometimes lent and borrowed, they are more commonly collected and displayed (Cherland 1994). Those who could not afford to buy the books were often excluded, and economic social divisions were maintained.

Today there is greater and growing child poverty in Canada and the United States. A global economy that did not exist in 1988 provides the context for a children's publishing industry that now, more than ever, positions children as consumers and divides those who have money from those who do not. Middle-class girls today are buried in the discourses of consumerism and distracted from an awareness of world poverty and suffering.

But there are signs of awareness and resistance in the current popularity of 'zines,' some produced by young girls as projects of social activism and rebellion against social norms (Guzzetti 2002). Zines are made possible by computers and inexpensive home publishing software packages. They are often distributed over the Internet. These technologies, now available to the middle class, did not exist in 1988. I find hope in young girls' appropriations of middle-class technologies for their own subversive purposes and in their reconstruction of 'middle-class' subjectivity as 'socially responsible.'

Theme 5: Performing Femininity

The cultural discourses that shape girlhood are always situated in history, existing at one historical moment. Today, in an age of global capitalism, of technological advancements, of AIDS and SARS and other pandemics, of nuclear armaments and constant war and threat of war, cultural myths position white middle-class girls as innocent, vulnerable, and helpless. Nancy Lesko (2001) would call these discourses our contemporary culture's "confident characterizations" of girlhood. What purposes do they serve?

Innocent. The 'nature of the child' is not discovered. Rather, it is something produced within regimes of truth (Walkerdine 1997). Childhood innocence was created during the Enlightenment (Foucault 1979; Lesko 2001) as part of a grand narrative of human development (and human progress) over time. European cultures began to tell themselves stories of how the child develops from primitive to civilized, from ignorant to knowledgeable, from innocent to wise (Lesko 2001; Walkerdine 1997).

But, in a patriarchal society, the story of childhood innocence cannot be true for all children. In a patriarchal society, characterizations of innocence position little girls differently from little boys. Our culture eroticizes little girls *and* declares them innocent, finding pleasure in the image of the innocent little girl who entices the predatory practices of male desire. Yet the culture pathologizes sexuality in little girls, because it threatens the stories we tell ourselves about a rational social order.

This dynamic works differently for girls of different races and classes. Patriarchy exists as "practices of sexuality and eroticism which operate differently for different social groups with differing degrees of privilege"

(Walkerdine 1997:183). We maintain innocence in girlhood as a cultural ideal by allowing *some* little girls to remain innocent while we eroticize others. The culture divides by class and race, positioning working class and racialized little girls as more corrupt and as the targets of sexual violence (Lemish uses the Spice Girls phenomenon of 1998 as an example of this dynamic at work, pointing out that only the black girl was connected with rape in the publicity that surrounded the rock group). At the same time, we maintain the cultural ideal by keeping middle-class girls innocent.

However, even for middle-class girls, fictions of innocence are impossible to live. While the culture insists that middle-class girls must be innocent, and allows for claims of innocence to contribute to the performance of whiteness (Schick 2000), it also directs discourses of sexuality, danger, and victimization at little girls (of all social classes) through popular culture and the media. (Remember the December 1996 newspaper pictures of murdered six-year-old JonBenet Ramsay in makeup and sexualized adult poses.) We teach middle-class girls especially to fear and defend against desire (Fine 1992) in an effort to preserve their innocence within a sexualized culture. Girls must live with *both* positions. This leads to the phenomenon of sexually active teenage girls refusing to use birth control in an effort to maintain their innocence (Lesko 2001). The girl herself is made to bear the psychic and material consequences of the conflict.

Helpless. Innocence can only be maintained through processes of protection and control. Keeping white middle-class girls innocent and asexual requires that they be carefully watched and policed (Lesko 2001). The culture employs mechanisms of subordination which teach girls to watch and discipline themselves and which ensure the automatic functioning of power (Lesko 2001). Girls are taught to see themselves as helpless, and to wait passively for the future (Cherland 1994).

But, fictions of helplessness are painful and impossible to live. Through a psychology of survival, the little middle-class white girl works to position herself as one who does not need to be helped. Fantasy offers her a space to reinvent that hostile and dangerous world in which she is helpless, to make the world into something different. Popular texts allow little girls to dream, understand, and face their conflicts over what is happening to them. Popular reading provides one way in which a girl can re-imagine herself as capable and active. Elisabeth remembers wanting to be capable and wanting to be adored, and I hear this as a counter-cultural story. She remembers loving the

Babysitters Club books because in reading them she could fantasize about being able to act without her parents' permission, about being able to organize her own schedule, about remembering to do what she had said she would do. Those babysitters were not helpless. Through fantasy, motivated by her desire for the legitimacy, authority, and power that the culture denied her, Elisabeth found psychic relief.

Vulnerable. Helpless people are vulnerable. Pipher (1994) reminds us that today's little girls are coming of age in a dangerous, sexualized, media-saturated culture in which the beauty/body obsession starts at a younger and younger age. Helpless, girls read the media for discourses of sexuality as violence and victimization (Cherland and Edelsky 1993). The implied subject of these discourses is positioned as passive and dependent (Fine 1992).

Elisabeth remembers that at the age of nine she felt vulnerable in a number of ways. She felt vulnerable around boys and enjoyed the *Babysitters Club* books because boys were rarely present in them. Fiction provided her with a space for fantasies of strength and protection from men. But, it is important that Elisabeth also felt vulnerable in relation to other girls. She remembers that the girls at school were never great friends like the girls in the *Baby-sitters Club*, who trusted each other. In the real world, relationships with other girls were uncomfortable. "You had to be on your guard around them." You were vulnerable to betrayal.

It is painful to be vulnerable, and girls have to survive. Self-production is therefore imbued with fantasy (Walkerdine 1997). Girls fantasize to find a space that is free of anxiety and provides respite from a dangerous world. Popular culture still teaches the old social codes that center on the value of obedience, appearance, modesty, and thoughtfulness of others (Saxton 1998). But, fifteen years after Elisabeth's experiences with the *Babysitters Club* books, there are other stories circulating as the culture begins to rewrite the girl. Popular culture carries stories of Girl Power, girl bands, zines, and films that rewrite the girl as a speaking, acting subject who is strong and powerful. Through a psychology of survival, the girl can use these new stories to defend herself, to position herself, and perform as one who does not need to be helped and in the process make herself less vulnerable.

Girlhood Today

This chapter considers social context in the production of girlhood and in doing so highlights the discourses and features of this historical moment that did not exist in the same way in 1988. The *Babysitters Club* series is no longer published, and today different artifacts of popular culture are making money for their creators. Today fear is marketed; globalization makes events like the bombing of the World Trade Towers possible, and the availability of the Internet and computer technology to the middle class has changed the way many people think and live their lives. All of these new phenomena contribute to the construction of the subjectivity of today's tween in ways that are different from what could have happened in 1988. Some of today's more privileged tweens have begun to question, analyze, and deconstruct their world and themselves through the publication of 'zines' and through social action (Finders 1996; Guzzetti 2002).[10]

But, this chapter also looks at the "psychology of survival," which is still at work in the production of tween subjectivity today. While historical and social contexts for girlhood have changed since 1988, the social and psychological processes at work in the production of a tween's subjectivity have not. Revealing the ways in which the psychic and the social intersect is still important work, because it shows us that girlhood is a fiction. The culture still *produces* girlhood through practices and discourses that subjugate and regulate (Walkerdine 1997).

Studies like this one demonstrate that the production of subjectivity is an ongoing activity. They also make the construction of gender, race, and class visible (Lesko 2001). They open up the category 'girl' (or 'tween') and help us to imagine the possibility that things might be different. They teach us to believe that although it is difficult to transform the self-constructed prisons of everyday life, it can perhaps be done (Haug 1987: 42). Deconstructing the experience and the psyche of the subject of privilege and dominance is important work, for it is in the realm of pleasure and longing that social change meets its greatest obstacle, hegemonic desire (Kelly 1997). If we understand our desires as factors in our dominance, we can perhaps give up our privileges so that the world can change. That is the hope I find in this consideration of my daughter Elisabeth's girlhood.

Notes

I thank the Department of Language Education at the University of Georgia for welcoming me as a Visiting Scholar during the 2002–2003 academic year.

I also thank Elisabeth Cherland for her cooperation, and for the joy she adds to my life.

[1] The psychoanalytic toolkit Walkerdine uses includes many of these concepts: fantasies, defenses, myths, transference, dangerous desires, and projections. In this chapter, I have focused on fantasies and desire.

[2] Identity is performative. Butler (1990) explains that the reality of gender is created through sustained social performances. Gender, race, and class are all identities tenuously constituted in time, created and sustained through a person's social performances. I believe that I became a teacher in 1970 in order to perform (unconsciously) my identity as white, middle class, and feminine. 'Whiteness' (like gender) is produced and becomes effective within socially constructed "regimes of truth" (Foucault 1979). The social construction of the category 'whiteness' occurs through the citation of difference in the actions and attitudes that a human subject uses to distinguish itself from those who are 'Other'.

[3] 'The Early School' is a pseudonym. We realize that Elisabeth's memories may differ from those of others who were there with us fifteen years ago.

[4] Fast capitalism provides the backdrop for this phenomenon. During the 1980s and 1990s, Scholastic (and many other publishers) began to engage in market research and as a result created several wildly successful series of books for a particular market, the female teen-aged reader. Characterized by formulaic plots and stock characters, series like *Sweet Valley High* were immensely profitable. When market research suggested that preteen girls were another potential market, Scholastic approached Ann M. Martin about doing a series for preteen girls. Like the series books for older girls, the *Baby-sitters Club* books reflect life in predominantly white, middle-class American suburbs.

Because series books are formulaic (produced quickly) and specifically designed for the consumer child, they are enormously lucrative. Successful series books become part of multimedia merchandising programs in which books, movies, television programs, lunch boxes, calendars, and more are coordinated, packaged, and marketed aggressively. Trademark characters are registered and licensed. The demand for series books is socially created and regulated. (See Taxel 2002 for a full discussion of the political economy of the children's publishing industry today.)

[5] I also acknowledge my debt to Linda Brodkey (2000), who gives a brilliant demonstration of how to write autoethnography as she tells a story of her family's life in the 1950s and connects it to social categories, history, and societal themes.

[6] *Sadako and the Thousand Paper Cranes* by Eleanor Coerr tells the story of a young Japanese girl who has survived the bombing of Hiroshima, is diagnosed with 'radiation sickness' (leukemia) shortly after the war, and dies. Elisabeth read this novel in Arizona in 1988 and again in her Regina school that fall.

[7] See Lesko (2001) for a demonstration of how cultural discourses, created in history, construct, characterize, and position young people in ways that serve the society's purposes.

[8] West and Zimmerman (1987) have explained that "doing gender" is not optional behavior, because there are disruptive social consequences for performing gender incorrectly. Failing to comply with the culture's expectations and norms for doing gender brings suspicion, humiliation, and rejection. In the same way, performing race and class are not optional either.

[9] But not always. Progressive pedagogies can also be informed by discourses of critical theory and social justice. See Edelsky (1999), for example.

[10] 'Zines' refers here to self-published magazines through which teen girls resist social norms.

References

Brodkey, L. "Writing on the Bias." In *Construction Sites: Excavating Race, Class, and Gender Among Urban Youth,* edited by L. Weis and M. Fine, 5–25. New York: Teachers College Press, 2000.

Butler, J. *Gender Trouble: Feminism and the Subversion of Identity.* New York: Routledge, 1990.

Cherland, M. *Private Practices: Girls Reading Fiction and Constructing Identity.* London: Taylor and Francis, 1994.

Cherland, M., and C. Edelsky. "Girls and Reading: The Desire for Agency and the Horror of Helplessness in Fictional Encounters." In *Texts of Desire: Essays on Fiction, Femininity and Schooling*, edited by L. Christian-Smith, 28–44. London: Falmer Press, 1993.

Coerr, E. *Sadako and the Thousand Paper Cranes.* Paintings by Ronald Himler. New York: Putnam, 1977.

Edelsky, C., ed. *Making Justice Our Project: Teachers Working Toward Critical Whole Language Practice.* Urbana, IL: National Council of Teachers of English, 1999.

———. "Relatively Speaking: McCarthyism and Teacher-Resisters" in *Marketing Fear in America's Public Schools*, edited by L. Poynor and P. Wolfe. New York: Lawrence Erlbaum, in press.

Ellis, C., and A. Bochner. "Autoethnography, Personal Narrative, Reflexivity: Researcher as Subject" In *Handbook of Qualitative Research in Education*, edited by N. K. Denzin and Y. S. Lincoln, 733–768. Thousand Oaks, CA: Sage Publications Inc. 2000.

Finders, M. J. *Just Girls: Hidden Literacies and Life in Junior High.* New York: Teachers College Press, 1997.

———. "Queens and Teen Zines: Early Adolescent Females Reading Their Way Toward Adulthood." *Anthropology and Education Quarterly* 27, no. 1 (1996): 236–253.

Fine, M. *Disruptive Voices: The Possibilities of Feminist Research.* Ann Arbor: University of Michigan, 1992.

Foucault, M. *Discipline and Punish: The Birth of the Prison.* Translated by A. Sheridan. New York: Vintage Books, 1979.

———. *Ethics: Subjectivity and Truth.* Edited by P. Rabinow. New York: New Press, 1997.

Guzzetti, B. J. "Zines." In *Literacy in America: An Encyclopedia of History, Theory, and Practice, Volume Two*, edited by B. J. Guzzetti., 669. Santa Barbara, California: ABC-Clio, 2002.

Haug, F. *Female Sexualization: A Collective Work of Memory.* London: Verso, 1987.

Hausknecht, G. "Self-Possession, Dolls, Beatlemania, Loss: Telling the Girl's Own Story." In *The Girl: Constructions of the Girl in Contemporary Fiction by Women*, edited by R. O. Saxton., 21–42. New York: St. Martin's Press, 1998.

Inness, S. "Introduction." In *Millennium Girls: Today's Girls Around the World*, edited by S. Inness, 2–9. Lanham, MD: Rowman and Littlefield Publishers, Inc. 1998.

Kaplan, E. Ann. *Women and film: both sides of the camera.* New York: Methuen, 1983.

Kelly, U. *Schooling Desire: Literacy, Cultural Politics, and Pedagogy.* New York: Routledge, 1997.

Lemish, D. "Spice Girls Talk: A Case Study in the Development of Gendered Identity." In *Millennium Girls: Today's Girls Around the World*, edited by S. Inness, 45–167. Lanham, MD: Rowman and Littlefield Publishers, Inc. 1998.

Lesko, N. (2001) *Act Your Age! A Cultural Construction of Adolescence.* New York: Routledge Falmer, 2001.

Orlofsky, S., ed. *Facts on File Yearbook 1988, Volume XLVIII.* New York: Facts on File, Inc. 1989.

Pecora, N. "Identity by Design: The Corporate Construction of Teen Romance Novels." In *Growing Up Girls: Popular Culture and the Construction of Identity*, edited by S. R. Mazzarella, and N. O. Pecora, 49–77. New York: Peter Lang, 1998.

Pipher, M. *Reviving Ophelia: Saving the Selves of Adolescent Girls.* New York: Putnam, 1994.

Saxton, R. O. ed *The Girl: Constructions of the Girl in Contemporary Fiction by Women.* New York: St. Martin's Press, 1998.

Schick, C. "'By Virtue of Being White': Resistance in Anti-Racist Pedagogy." *Race, Ethnicity and Education* 3, no. 1 (2000): 83–102.

Taxel, J. "Children's Literature at the Turn of the Century: Toward a Political Economy of the Publishing Industry." *Research in the Teaching of English* 37, no. 2 (2002): 145–197.

Thobani, S. "The Speech That Shook the Country." *Herizons* 15, no. 3 (2002): 18–21.

Walkerdine, V. "Someday My Prince Will Come: Young Girls and the Preparation for Adult Sexuality." In *Gender and Generation*, edited by A. McRobbie and M. Niva, 162–184. Houndmills, England: Macmillan, 1984.

———. *Daddy's Girl: Young Girls and Popular Culture.* Cambridge, MA: Harvard University Press, 1997.

———. "Popular Culture and the Eroticization of Little Girls." In *The Children's Culture Reader*, edited by H. Jenkins, 254–264. New York: New York University Press, 1998.

Weedon, C. *Feminist Practice and Poststructuralist Theory, Second Edition.* Oxford: Basil Blackwell, 1998.

West, C., and D. Zimmerman. "Doing Gender." *Gender and Society* 1, no. 2 (1987): 125–151.

CHAPTER SEVEN

Mirrors and Windows: Re-reading South African Girlhoods as Strategies of Selfhood

Marika Flockemann

Not all of us are like that.

—Jeanne Goosen, *Not All of Us*

In life there is no escape from history.

—Mark Behr, *The Smell of Apples*

It is striking how many contributions in recent anthologies of writings by young South Africans are characterized by images of entrapment, helplessness, isolation, and betrayal.[1] However, a different picture of childhood is evoked in texts by adult writers who use pre-adolescent voices as a means of recollection, reinvention, and even reconstitution. Why is it that in these representations of 'tweenness,' a sense of potentiality commonly transcends the focus on lost innocence? In some texts, the young narrator acts as a 'spy' or 'looter' of language and social codes, as a playful or potentially subversive agent who actively engages with or negotiates her way through adult realities. In other texts, the child narrator serves as a passive "forgotten camera in the corner" (LeSeur 1995: 10), recording, observing, reacting to the adult world and offering an apparently unconscious critique of it in the process. Then there are also instances where the child serves as the repository of social trauma, as victim or survivor—and here the girlchild carries the familiar trope of woman as embodiment of social conflict.

In his aptly titled piece, "Home Is Where the Hurt Is," Matthew Krouse comments on the prevalence of the concept of 'home' currently hovering over South African cultural production. This, he claims, could be read as a cause for either alarm or celebration, since this interrogation of home indicates a shift from dealing prescriptively with familiar themes like race, democracy, and reconciliation, to "beginning to look deep within" (2003: 11). At the same time, the South African home is a contested site with the world's highest child abuse, crime and HIV rates—"all centered in the home." (2003: 11). Home is thus also a place of alienation, and as Carle Boyce Davies points out, for black women in particular, "the complicated notion of home mirrors the problematizing of the interrelatedness of community, nation and identity"; she notes how a focus on domesticity in turn "results in a shutting down of possibilities for the girlchild" (1994: 21). However, for some, this focus on the inner life, on the domestic space, and more especially on childhood, is cause for alarm. For instance, Nadine Gordimer and Achmat Dangor have expressed concern about the number of people who are currently writing about their childhood under apartheid—black, white or Indian, "as if that's the only experience we've had," and this suggests that, "[p]eople shy away from contemporary issues because they are difficult to deal with" (Dangor 2002: 55). Despite the reservations expressed by Dangor and Gordimer, I will argue that fictionalizing childhood does not simply trap the writers in the past but in some cases can be reconstitutive or even transformative. Memory has an important function in a society undergoing rapid transformation, since, through an exploration of the past writers can attempt to investigate both origins and determining forces which have shaped the present (Du Plooy 2002: 128). Another reason that narratives that reconstruct childhood have become increasingly popular is the focus on the processes of subjectivity or coming to personhood.

The distinctions between mirrors and windows point to the acts of representation, reflection, and mimicry but also the boundaries to, or thresholds into, other states of being. This involves either the mother-daughter dyad referred to by psychoanalytic theorists like Nancy Chodorow, where the mother as central focus is initially idolized and idealized, and the girlchild must undergo a period of rejection to split the subject/self away from the object/mother (Timothy 1990: 234). One should also consider the role played by a girlhood peer (close friend or relative) who acts as either mirror or window in the psychosocial processes of subjectivity—this is, of course, also a powerful feature of popular youth culture. It will be useful to compare the intimacy of this often-narcissistic bond with a similar peer relationship in representations of boyhood, where the relationship is often less a case of 'split selves' than of oppositional ones; in turn, this raises questions about the way subjecthood is (en)gendered.

One important aspect of these fictions of childhood is the extent to which the child is able to resist the overt or covert mechanisms of silencing and self-censorship and sustain the ability to question given ideas and realities. Clearly, this ability to ask questions is crucial to the development of consciousness, and Gordon Stevenson speculates that there is a point in the child's development when "answers to questions cannot be taught—but can only be learned" (1980: 107). In describing her girlhood in East Germany during the Second World War, acclaimed German novelist Christa Wolf in *Kindheitsmuster* or *Patterns of Childhood* (1984) uses the voice of a child to explore self-reflexively some of the issues touched on in the epigraphs above—such as the connection between asking questions and being able to resist, or simply survive under an oppressive system. Recalling how she was prohibited from sharing soup with a group of fellow women field workers from the Ukraine, the remembering adult enquires of her former self, the child, whether it would have "occurred to her to get up and walk the thirty steps across the separating abyss, over to the foreigners?" She asks, "Had her curiosity meanwhile diminished? Does curiosity diminish if it remains unsatisfied for a long time? Is it possible to numb a child's curiosity completely?" (Levine 1997: 115). Referring to Wolf's use of the figure of the child to, as it were, 'penetrate' the web of secrecy woven by family ideology, Michael Levine claims that:

> One might say that writing between family lines involves an attempt to gain access to aspects of one's own child by indirectly approaching her through the mediation of another, through the irreducible *otherness* of one's own childhood. (My emphasis, Levine 1997: 113)

In other words, the memory of childhood is itself a kind of fiction through which one attempts to make sense of one's adult experience, and in Wolf's case, this 'otherness' of childhood is manifested in the avoidance of the 'I' as narrating voice in recollecting the experience of her own childhood.

There are, of course, obvious parallels between the questions posed by Christa Wolf and the issues raised in the texts to be discussed here, namely, why some children growing up in an oppressive regime "lose the ability to differentiate between dangerous and nondangerous subjects" and eventually "cease asking questions altogether?" (Levine: 115). Further, how do others manage to develop and sustain the ability to distinguish between dangerous and nondangerous subjects and continue to ask questions and in the process achieve a sense of control over their environment? In addition, how does the use of liminal childhood voices, as 'speakerly' rather than 'writerly' texts, oppose, rupture, or re-write master discourses? The speakerly text being a narrative, which as it were gathers many voices into it, and in the process, approximates a communal ethos (see Holloway 1992: 11). This raises another question: what alternatives, if any, are offered in readings of and through girlhood?

The choice of a youthful narrator of between six to eleven years is particularly apposite for representing the kind of 'speakerly texts' referred to, which subvert the traditionally individualistic novel of development to present a communal experience. The child presents an unmediated account, often repeating the voices and social registers, colloquial idioms, and values articulated by grown-ups. However, when the child narrator in Jeanne Goosen's *Not All of Us* repeats her mother's claim that "not all of us are like that," she indicates a resistance to mirroring or conforming unequivocally to dominant expectations. One can ask why the experiences of two white Afrikaner children growing up in the 50s and 70s, respectively, differ so vastly. The boychild in Behr's *The Smell of Apples* (1995) and *Embrace* (2000) feels trapped by history, whereas Gertie in Goosen's *Not All of Us* can to some extent resist these pressures by sustaining the ability to distinguish between "dangerous and nondangerous subjects."

In *Not All of Us*, Gertie establishes herself as an astute observer who, as a species of "forgotten camera," records the platitudes, banal fatalism, and prejudices of the popular social and political discourse she is exposed to in her Afrikaner working-class suburban environment in Goodwood, Cape Town, during the 1950s. She is provided with an array of social registers when she overhears conversations between her parents, neighbors, and especially the daily kitchen conversations when Mavis and her communist boyfriend, Tank, drop in for glasses of sherry and Cavallas while Gertie's father is at work. Gertie, who mimics her mother's behavior in the way she holds and smokes her sweet cigarettes, is described admiringly by her mother, as "clever one" (48), a "real little shrewdie" (39), and "already a little chancer" (96). This helps to situate her as an engaging narrative consciousness, and the frequent slippage into the present tense contributes to the immediacy of her insider's perspective. In fact, much of the comedy of the novel comes from the unconscious ironies of her reported conversation, with its code switching between colloquial Afrikaans and English, suggestive of the fluidity of the social discourse of urban experience. On the other hand, her asthmatic and embittered father who works for The Railways believes in only mixing with people who want to 'improve themselves' and generally addresses her sternly in injunctions. Concerned that she's "seeing things she's not supposed to see" (87), he attempts to censor her interactions with other children in the neighborhood. These contrasting parental attitudes contribute to Gertie's growing awareness of the performativity of subjectivity when she notes how Doris, her fun-loving and bioscope-obsessed mother, literally adopts various voices for different people and situations. For instance, when Gertie's strictly Calvinist grandpa comes to visit, Doris hides her ashtrays and Cavallas, uses Sen-Sen for her breath, and indeed, "changes all the way. She speaks with a thin slit of a mouth" (46), and inducts her daughter into keeping certain secrets from her menfolk in order "not to hurt their feelings" (48). The skillful way in which the narrative strategy exposes both the deliberate manipulation of different subject positions as well as the interrelatedness of class, race and gender stratifications within the contested site of home is graphically illustrated when, for instance, Gertie witnesses a domestic argument between her parents.

The argument starts harmlessly when Doris announces at supper that she intends to work as an usherette again, When her husband pronounces his disapproval of both this and her friendship with Mavis and Tank, who he claims are "bad examples" to Gertie, this unleashes a sudden torrent of rage from Doris: "My mom looks quite ugly now. Her lips are drawn tight and thin. She speaks in a voice I don't know and that scares me" (42), and the argument quickly deteriorates into a shouting match between them:

My mom sits down again, lighting another Cavalla. Her hands are trembling and she's breathing fast.

Now *you* shut up, Piet, and let me talk,' says my mom and her voice sounds all right again. 'I've seen right through you. It's not Tank or Mavis that's the problem. The problem is you. You just can't stand seeing me have a bit of fun.'

'Ha!' says my dad. (43)

Just as Doris regains her 'normal' voice, the asthmatic father loses his breath, and comically, while still haranguing Piet, who is now turning blue, Doris nevertheless interrupts her tirade to order Gertie to fetch his asthma pump. The rest of the argument turns into a completely one-sided affair with the father's only responses being the "scrrreech-scrrreech" of the pump which he presses faster and faster while Doris appropriates his voice in savage mimicry: asking, "Who's the blarry fool in this house?…And why?" and proceeds to answers her own question: "Yes, Piet, no Piet,' my mom says in that kind of squeaky voice" (44). Gertie is thus exposed to the way her mother both directly challenges the father by saying 'she can see through him' (to the extent that she even erases his face from the photograph of him in the passage directly after the argument). She also manages to silence him by—though not deliberately—inducing the asthma attack, which is not helped by her smoking. The Cavallas, used almost as a dramatic prop in the argument, also signify her secret rebellion against the grandfather's prohibitions: Doris tells Gertie that if Grandpa were to find out about her mother's bioscope-going and smoking, "His heart will give in" (46). Moreover, the child witnesses the contradictions in the mother's response. On the one hand she accuses her husband of hypocrisy when he tries to invoke the grandpa's disapproval however, at the end of the argument Doris's parting shot is to invoke the grandpa's opinion herself when she says that she should have listened when he warned her against "that Van Greunen chap" and his "bad streak" (45). This is further interesting in that earlier Doris had permitted herself to be shouted at in what appears a demeaning way by her employer Byrd, while here she articulates a liberating anger that is inconsistent with her generally conventional behavior and reveals her ability to manipulate various subject positions in the domestic, if not the public, sphere.

But more importantly for this discussion, the incident also throws light on the child's ability to ask questions, and this, I argue, has significant implications for her developing consciousness. It is noteworthy that Gertie is not just a passive observer but also an actor in the little domestic drama. After she has gone to fetch the pump, it is she who interrupts the proceedings when, witnessing the silencing of the father, "I feel so sorry for him I start crying" (45), thus reclaiming her mother's attention away from the husband. Throughout, the relationship between Gertie and her mother is clearly of the mother-daughter dyad referred to earlier, as the child is herself intensely identified with the mother but also idealizes and identifies the mother with the fictional and resourceful, much admired "Spider Lady" of popular culture. This bond causes the child some trauma when the marriage disintegrates and Doris finds herself gradually replacing her obsession with images in the movies with a flesh and blood lover. Gertie responds to this threat of replacement physically, by throwing up, and attempts to refuse this separation from her mother:

> I look at my mom. Her eyes are a real see-through blue. I've never seen her looking quite so beautiful before. I feel like leaning against her so that she can hold me tight. I don't want anybody else to be near us, not even my dad. As far as I'm concerned he can stay in that blarry Touws River for ever. (128)

Here it is Gertie who appropriates her mother's voice in the last sentence. However, what is striking is that despite the fact that Gertie identifies so closely with the mother, both Gertie and her mother possess what can be termed as a kind of 'saving empathy,' which enables them to recognize the needs of 'others' even in the moment of claiming their own needs. This is demonstrated in Gertie's compassion towards her father's physical distress under Doris' tongue-lashing. This empathy, it seems to me, plays a crucial role in the processes of subjectivity and distinguishes Doris and Gertie from others in their community. It acts as the 'window' or wedge that ruptures prevailing discourses and enables them to see and potentially to think, beyond the narrow race, class, and gender prejudices to which they are exposed.

For instance, while Doris both articulates the stereotypical and blatantly racist values of her class and community, she simultaneously challenges them, even if at an unconscious level, by an expression of empathy that undercuts these expressed views. When her parents discuss the newspaper account of "some kaffirs who got on a train at Langa station" and entered carriages designated White as part of the defiance campaign, Gertie asks, "Why can't the kaffirs ride in our part of the train any more, Mom?" To this her father answers absurdly, "Because they cut the throats of white kids," but her mother, who had referred to their arrest at Cape Town station as "actually a disgrace," responds, "'Your dad's talking nonsense!' says my mom. 'I can't help feeling sorry for them'" (57). When Gertie's colored friend Gregory and his family are forced to move because of the newly implemented Group Areas Act of 1950, Doris attempts to show some sense of neighborliness. However, it is far too late, and when she is politely rebuffed by Gregory's mother, she runs after their departing car holding the cake she had baked them, shouting, "Not all of us are like that" (30). This ridiculous scene nevertheless characterizes how an underlying human empathy cuts across the mirroring of dominant attitudes, even while Doris mouths the racist terminology of the time. In addition, Doris has a powerful imagination, and her sister describes her as "a seeker" (154). Here she is very different from her husband who models himself on heroes of the newly appointed Apartheid regime: he's "a Ben Schoeman man," he claims. For Gertie, this empathy and openness to new experiences also play an important role in her ability to survive her mother's breakdown after the father's death. In the course of the novel, the focal point gradually shifts from Gertie to her mother. And the choice of child as narrating consciousness can thus also be read as an attempt at reconstitution. The child appears to signify the potential the mother feels she has failed to realize in her adult life: "My mom laughed, pressed me tight against her and said, "I wish I could have been more like you, my little Gertie" (96).

Though largely ignored by the literary establishment, texts like Goosen's *Not All of Us* and Diane Case's *92 Queen's Road* offer an important corrective to discourses focusing on public struggles.[2] These discourses tend to devalue the contested domestic site of home or fail to read the potential for critique offered by the "paradoxical space" opened up through these narratives of childhood, in which the child is, to re-phrase Gillian Rose's terms, "both within and without" (in Mahlis 1998: 165). While there are similarities here with another novel set in 1950s Cape Town, Rayda Jacobs' *Sachs Street* (2001), which explores Muslim and mixed race experience, Jacobs' narration of childhood is interspersed with adult retrospection which dilutes the coherence of the strategy used so successfully by Goosen and Case. Despite the cultural and linguistic specificity of the South African texts, interesting reciprocities are established when comparing these with other narratives of girlhood such as *The Bear from the North* (1989) by Yvonne du Fresne, and *Hand-me-downs* (1985) by Liz Barnes. *The Bear from the North* is set in New Zealand and explores how the child of Danish immigrants takes on the challenges of living as a minor of minority status in a colonial context. *Hand-me-downs*, set in 1930s East Tennessee, tracks the coming to consciousness of the child trying to resist the pressures of impending womanhood as manifested in sexual assaults masked by the avowed parental concern that "what they don't know won't hurt them" (41).

Common to all these texts is the way the child narrator is situated as simultaneously insider and outsider. Astrid Westergaard in *Bear from the*

North immediately foregrounds her awareness of a dual heritage; she claims that as soon as she could walk, "I lifted my eyes from my feet and started watching. I watched and listened for the rest of my life. Astrid the spy" (1). Astrid sees herself as a "discoverer," and her quest to find New Zealand and her place in it, is strongly informed by a cohesive family tradition of cultural connectedness to Norse mythic lore and the cultural practices of South Jutland from where the family originates. Throughout, this serves as a refracting lens through which she responds to her environment. These cohesive familial and cultural bonds which stem from their immigrant status provide the framework for Astrid's precocious and confident sense of agency as seen in the military language in which her discoveries are described: she "penetrated her first English house," and once inside, "I never once blinked, in case I missed the smallest sign" (3). She deliberately mimics what she assumes the values of Englishness (and Empire) require: "I made my spine a ramrod of steel, I rehearsed in my mind my new, light, cool voice" (3). In the same way, her Fader and Onkels raucously mimic the class inflections, typical expressions and voices of their English neighbors as well as the social discourses of English novels they read voraciously. In fact, Astrid too sees herself as a subversive "looter" like her Fader and Onkels, who bring home prizes they have taken from the English language: "Astrid the spy, watching other spies, much more skilful than me" (20). However, no sooner has she begun to take in the pictures of "the descendants of those who had died for the Empire" (3) inside the gloomy English house (so different from the lightness of her Danish home), than she instinctively rejects the values she appears to be mimicking. In a violent reaction, she unexpectedly vomits on the varnished floor at the sight of the unappetizing spread she is offered to eat, shockingly unlike the creamy wholesomeness of the food of home.

This kind of pathological reaction where the child rejects what to her represent coercive, threatening, or traumatic experiences in non-verbal ways is another common trend in representations of 'tweenness.' For instance, in Rayda Jacobs' *Sachs Street*, in response to a teacher's unfair treatment of her, the child Khadiya finds that her anger seems to translate itself into the full bladder she struggles to control: "I hated her, and was ready to say something." Instead, she finds herself tearing down her bloomers, and 'letting go' in full sight of the teacher: "I was peeing on the grounds. No words would save me, and I didn't try. And my pee was noisy, rushing out of me like an angry little stream" (35). This is followed by the familiar stomach

cramps she experiences every time she witnesses a stressful encounter between her parents. As in other texts, there is a kind of transference of the
emotion to the body, and this recalls Gertie's somatic response when, in a
typical primal Oedipal moment, she witnesses her mother having sex with
her lover while her father is away. Instinctively she senses something is
amiss; as she moves towards the bedroom we are invited to share her experience through use of the present tense, "I want to call out to my mom, but
something doesn't feel right. I'm getting hot. My heart is throbbing very hard
and loud and I'm beginning to feel a bit sick" (135). Interestingly as Gertie
moves through the house, she does so secretly, and when she does enter the
parental bedroom, she does so unnoticed, which, of course, exacerbates her
trauma. The child's response is located in the body because, as yet, there are
no words to express the confusion of emotions aroused by what she is experiencing—in this case betrayal and fear of separation as well as the unnerving
strangeness of adult sexuality.

A similar incident occurs in Liz Barnes's *Hand-me-downs*, where the
child Cassie is caught up in a sexually abusive relationship with her older
brother, who exhorts her "to exercise his peejabber" regularly so that it will
grow to his knees one day. "He also told me of my calling. It was to get married to the likes of him and carry babies in my stomach…He said that men
have all the seeds and women are the dirt" (1). Like the other children described here, the naïve Cassie is inquisitive, "I knew lots of things and
thought about them all the time" (1). She claims that the most important
thing she knows is the difference between herself and her brother, Til: "It
was his peejabber" (1). Cassie is repulsed by the penis of her brother, his
friend Ralph, and the lecherous Mr. Simpson (a family acquaintance), who
all try to penetrate her. But at the same time, she unconsciously recognizes
that her lack of the despised peejabber makes her the "dirt": this explains
why she also attempts to mimic the boys' behavior and resist the overdetermined 'calling' of girlhood and impending motherhood. When Ralph after
several attempts finally penetrates her with the aid of her brother in a boastful
competition of manliness, Til tells her to stop crying and "quit acting like a
baby" (177), since, "it's like a vaccination, something you have to get to
grow up" (177). After the rape she is speechless, and in response to Til's
"Did you feel anything" she responds only in sobs and whimpers. However,
once she is alone in the bathroom, she does speak:

I couldn't take my eyes off the blurred face in the mirror.

"I hate you, Cassandra Blevins," I whimpered. "Ugly thing you. I wish you were dead." I rubbed my eyes with the cold washrag and then rubbed it between my legs. It was streaked with blood.

"I wish you were dead," I whimpered again, and wondered how long the hurting would last. And the blood. The vaccination scab still clung to my leg. I washed out my bloomers and crept into the bedroom to get a clean pair. When I opened the dresser drawer, I heard Til laugh. They were looking in the window.

"Don't worry," he said to Ralph. "She ain't gonna tell. She's all right. She's tough." (178)

Cassie here both watches herself and is aware of others watching her. Significantly, she, like Gertie, keeps this encounter with sex secret from the grown-ups, as she appears to accept that this is one of the questions she cannot ask—just as she does not tell her parents about Mr. Wilson's sexual assault, since 'who would believe her?' Her parents, on the other hand, see sexuality as a something to be physically 'tamed,' and her mother insists that Til be circumcised to prevent him from 'abusing himself' and otherwise getting out of control yet allows him to share a room with his younger sister. Like Gertie's father, the general view here is that "the less they know, the better off they are" (41); similarly, in response to Cassie's question about why the colored boy Woody goes to a different school, the mother avoids the question: "What they don't know won't hurt them" (41). It is telling how Cassie transfers her anger at her brother and Ralph to herself as she looks at the "blurred face in the mirror," which represents a disassociated image of the potential womanhood into which she has been initiated.

This introduces yet another common thematic trend in these texts, where the social induction into gender roles is associated with a process of 'self-othering' or 'split selves' which can be destructively self-alienating as in Cassie's case here or potentially liberating in foregrounding the performativity of identity as in the case of *Not All of Us*. This is demonstrated when Astrid in *Bear from the North* attempts to "beat the system" that is English colonial education by deliberately taking on a second persona, when she adopts "my other self that grew up at school" (18). When patronizingly rebuffed by the teacher who refuses to acknowledge the validity of Astrid's Danish cultural practices, Astrid's response is not physically located in the body as with the other children, nor does this result in a sense of internalized inferiority; instead, she retains agency: "I shut her out of my life forever" (29). At the same time, this also needs to be read in terms of the novel's somewhat strained utopian project, which is to recollect a "sweet buried childhood" (131) and to claim a shared past with her Maori friend Rangi Katani's warrior ancestors.

Apart from the mother-daughter dyad where, as in *Not All of Us*, Gertie as self/subject must separate herself from her mother/object in order to achieve some sense of autonomy, there is also the role of the girlhood peer, someone who is "not quite the same, not quite the other" (Minh-ha 1988: 76). It has been noted how there is often an almost 'narcissistic' relationship between two girls who see themselves mirrored in each other. Psychoanalytic theories of subjectivity point to the way in which many girls 'regress' during adolescence and long for a pre-oedipal fusion with the mother. However, as Daniel, Ross points out, "a close friend is often the key to helping them out of this regression." The narcissistic friend thus acts as "the initiator of activities as well as the provider of a value system which the patient embraces as germinating ego ideal" (Hymer, in Ross 1988: 75). For Cassie in *Hand-me-downs*, this role is played by the much older girl, Jimmy Lou, herself an outsider to the community, who gives Cassie advice, affirmation, and more importantly, tenderness—which has a similar effect to empathy in *Not All of Us*. She also offers alternative scenarios of womanhood. Significantly, however, these visits to Jimmy Lou are kept secret from her family, since Jimmy Lou is seen as a pariah figure or 'white trash.' As they sit together before Jimmy Lou's mirror, "I reached up and put my arms around her neck, but when our eyes met, I looked away and stuffed my hands into my pockets" (116). By stuffing her hands into her pockets, Cassie the tomboy still resists the female bond mirrored in Jimmy Lou. However, the older girl responds maternally: "She held me tight against her and dropped her cheek against the top of my head. 'Has anybody but me ever told you how perty your hair is, Miss Cassandra?'" (116). Later that night, Cass is able to draw on Jimmy Lou's action when for the first time she is able to respond caringly to her own young sister.

This thematic concern with 'split selves,' however, often manifests as 'oppositional selves' in novels of white South African boyhood. According to Mark Behr, one of his aims in writing his controversial novel, *The Smell of Apples*—which gives an insider's account of growing up in the heart of the

Apartheid regime—was to reveal the coercions of family love. These forces 'trap' the narrator, the eleven-year-old Marnus, the son of a general in the SA defense force, into replicating the patriarchal structures underpinning the oppressive political regime. In this, the novel offers a far more restrictive and monolithic account of subjectivity than the potentialities offered by the 'paradoxical space' explored in fictions of girlhood. In his second, ambitiously framed novel, *Embrace* (2000), Behr again explores Afrikaaner boyhood against the political background of the mid-1970s.[3] He juxtaposes the experiences of the eleven- to fourteen-year-old narrator, Karl de Man, at the elite Drakensberg Boys' Choir School, with early childhood memories. Behr focuses on Karl's attempts to deal with the consequences of his own intellectual and sexual appetite, as well as the familial, institutional, and religious prohibitions on that appetite.[4] Of interest here is the way the child is represented, not as an innocent but rather as a desiring subject. The novel attempts to explore questions of betrayal and forgiveness and the existence of a "moral imagination" (See Crocker 2000: 1). In this Behr attempts to articulate the often-silenced experiences and processes of psychosexual, and more particularly, homosexual identity in childhood and to 'explain' the apparently causal relationship between betrayal and betraying.

It is interesting to compare Behr's texts with Michiel Heyns' *The Children's Day* (2002). Again, we have an eleven-year-old narrator, Simon, giving another apparently naïve insider's account of growing up as white Afrikaner during the 1960s.[5] However, the differences are telling: while in Behr's texts there is the pervasive emphasis on the child's overdetermined identity, in Heyns' text, the child is presented as actively making meaning. And he appears able to question parental and other social attitudes, partly because the parents themselves discuss and disagree with some of the prevailing ideas; moreover, theirs is a bilingual household, which offers further scope for differing views.

In comparing depictions of girlhood with boyhood, one notes significant differences resulting from the way the girlchild is situated as simultaneously inside and outside the adult values through which she has to negotiate her way. This is evident in the way these narratives track the contradictions exposed by the apparently unconscious judgments made by the naïve narrator. It is striking how narratives of girlhood illustrate the girlchild's growing awareness of the instability of given or fixed identities through her exposure to, and even adoption of, different 'voices'; this focus on a multiplicity of voices, as feminist theorists point out, is characteristic of writing by minority women and, by extension seems apposite to these narratives of tweenness. Girlhood can thus be described as a period for creatively making symbolic meaning (Willis 1990) or for rehearsing identity (Whitlock 1995) as well as for negotiating apparently given realities—either accepting them as inescapable aspects of history or claiming that we are 'not all like that.'

As represented in these texts, one can identify a number of strategies available to the girlchild for sustaining the ability to question or to refuse given 'callings.' Apart from the child narrator's apparently innate inquisitiveness and resourcefulness, these include an awareness (conscious or otherwise) of the performativity of identity and the ability to articulate, through various modes of expression, some form of resistance to given realities or to formulate alternatives, even fictional ones. For instance, at the end of Barnes' *Hand-me-downs*, Cassie, who previously felt unable to resist her brother or Mr. Simpson's coercions and assaults, finds that through artistic expression, by literally 'painting herself in to the picture,' she is able to resist. When her brother threatens to tie her onto the kite he is making, she instead paints him strung up on the kite, "*his* hands and feet tied down" (203) while she holds up the string ready to run across the field. She then decides that she is never going to show her pictures to Mr. Simpson again, since it was on that pretext that he had previously got her into his bedroom. Cassie thus uses a fiction to act out alternative realities in which she achieves some sense of control over her world. Although she has not told anyone about her abuse yet, she says, "I'd have to wait until I could write it myself" (189).

It has been claimed that in post-apartheid South Africa, a significant aspect of reconstruction is the process of telling our own stories in an attempt to understand the past, the role played by social structures in shaping our identities as well as our own complicity in this (Govinden 1995: 182). As indicated here, narrations of girlhood enact scenarios for exploring, retrospectively, the processes of coming of age, since the girlchild appears more acutely aware of living within several mental realities (Stevenson 1980: 110). It is, therefore, not surprising that the focus on girlhood has become a dominant trend in literature focusing on transitional states. Here, the adoption of the pre-adolescent child as narrating consciousness can be seen as a useful strategy to re-vision hegemonic discourses in ways that affirm, challenge, or subvert through the creative inversion achieved by the limited, yet limitless, perspectives of tweenness.

Notes

See Kwela Books' Young South African Writing Series, which presents a selection of writings from the senior grades from all over South Africa, rural as well as urban areas (*I a Living Arrow* 1998).

[1] Case's novel, set in Woodstock, Cape Town, has the naïve narrator recount growing up as Colored child in the 1960s and in the process providing a graphically intimate insider's account of the period through the speakerly text referred to earlier. (See Flockemann 1999.)

[2] For a fuller discussion of *Embrace* from which these comments are drawn, see the Internet review, "Appetite and Confession in Mark Behr's *Embrace*." *Litnet Internet Review.*

[3] David Medalie in an interesting comparative discussion of Marguerite Poland's *Iron Love*, Behr's *The Smell of Apples*, and J.M. Coetzee's *Boyhood* explores how these present the boy protagonists as assenting, agnostic, or atheist participants in dominant belief systems and how this in turn affects the way the protagonists are able to resist prevailing discourses of masculinity

[4] Heyns says that he withheld publication of his novel because of the similarity in narrative devices to Behr's *Smell of Apples* (which are of course strongly similar to Goosen's *Not All of Us* and Case's *92 Queen's Road*).

References

Barnes, L. *Hand-me-downs*. San Francisco: Spinster's Ink, 1985.

Behr, M. *The Smell of Apples*. London: Abacus, 1995.

Behr, M. *Embrace*. London: Penguin, 2000.

Behr, M. "Speaking the Unspeakable." Sunday Analysis, *Sunday Times*, April 9, 2000, 32.

Boyce Davies, C. 1994. *Black Women, Writing and Identity*. London and New York: Routledge, 1994.

Crocker, J. "From the Heart *Embrace* Addresses Betrayal and Life." Books Supplement, *Cape Times*, Friday June 2, 2000, 1.

Dangor, A. "Achmat Dangor in Interview with Elaine Young." *Kunapipi* XXIV, no. 1&2 (2002): 52–60.

Du Fresne, Y. *The Bear from the North*. London: The Women's Press, 1989.

Du Plooy, H. "Traces of Identity in the Mirror of the Past." *Kunapipi* XXIV, no. 1&2 (2002): 126–139.

Flockemann, M. "'If I were her'—Fictions of Development from Cape Town, Canada and the Caribbean: A Relational Reading." *Journal of Literary Studies* 15, no.1&2 (1999): 176–194.

Goosen, J. *Not All of U.*, Translated by André Brink. Strand: Queillerire Publishers, 1990.

Govinden, B. "Learning Myself Anew." *Alternation* 2, no. 2 (1995): 170–83.

Heyns, M. *The Children's Day*. Johannesburg and Cape Town: Jonathan Ball Publishers, 2002.

Holloway, K. F. C. *Moorings and Metaphors: Figures of Culture and Gender in Black Women's Literature*. New Jersey; Rutgers: University Press, 1992.

Jacobs, R. *Sachs Street*. Cape Town: Kwela Books, 2001.

Krouse, M. "Home Is Where the Hurt Is." Friday Supplement, *Mail & Guardian*, July 4–10 2003, 11.

LeSeur, G. *Ten Is the Age of Darkness: The Black Bildungsroman*. Columbia, Missouri: University of Missouri Press, 1995.

Levine, M. "Writing Anxiety: Christa Wolf's Kindheidsmuster." *Writing Between the Lines* (Summer 1997): 106–122.

Mahlis, K. "Gender and Exile in Jamaica Kincaid's *Lucy*." *Modern Fiction Studies* 44, no.1 (1998): 164–183.

Medalie, D. "'Such Wanton Innocence': Representing South African Boyhoods." *Current Writing* 12, no. 1 (2000): 41-61.

Minh-ha, T. T. "Not You/Like You: Post-Colonial Women and the Interlocking of Identity and Difference." *Inscriptions* 3, no. 4 (1988): 71–77.

Ross, D. "Celie in the Looking Glass: The Desire for Selfhood in *The Color Purple*." *Modern Fiction Studies* 34, no. 1 (1988): 69–84.

Stevenson, G. "On Constructing Useful Realities: The Uses of Popular Culture in the Uncertain World of the Adolescent." In *Young Adult Literature: Background and Criticism*, edited by M. Lenz and R. M. Mahood, 107-117. Chicago: American Library Association, 1980.

Timothy, H. P. "Adolescent Rebellion and Gender Relations in *At the Bottom of the River* and *Annie John*." In *Caribbean Women Writers*, edited by S. Cudjoe, 233–242. Wellesley, Massachusetts: Calaloux Publications, 1990.

Whitlock, G. "From Prince to Lorde: The Politics of Location in Caribbean Autobiography." Unpublished paper. Griffiths University, Brisbane, Australia, 1995.

Willis, P. 1990. *Common Culture: symbolic work at play in the everyday cultures of the young*. Milton Keynes: Open University Press, 1990.

PART II

Knowing Girls

CHAPTER EIGHT

Reclaiming Girlhood: Understanding the Lives of Balkishori in Mumbai

Balkishori Team of VACHA Women's Resource Center
with Jackie Kirk

Introduction

She is standing on threshold
Of adulthood.
She has been pushed, harassed
Forced to stand still.
Punished for violation of norms by
Crossing the threshold on her will and accord,
She has no right to have a wish and a will
She is Balkishori. (Vacha 2002)

In a culture that is saturated with film imagery, film stars, and film story lines, the images the industry is promoting of girls and women cannot be ignored by anyone interested in girls and girlhood studies. Even the poorest of families in Mumbai regularly watch Bollywood-style films and videos and the clothes worn by the stars, reproduced in magazines, in TV commercials and on advertisement hoardings quickly get turned into cheap copies to be bought on market stalls and in the many clothing stores throughout the country. The film industry, however, rarely gives girls of the pre-adolescent age group (9–13) any particular attention. When it does, they are presented as premature adults who talk in the tone of, and with the understanding of, adults or of how adults perceive them. We have seen this in one of the Bollywood hit films, *Kuch Kuch hota hai* (Some Thing Happens) where an eight-year-old girl behaves like a mature woman, helping her father marry his old girlfriend. She successfully manipulates the situation with the help of her grandmother. In another film, *Kairee* (Raw Mango), the pre-adolescent female protagonist gets carried away with her problems between her mother and her foster mother, through her perspective and child-like manner. Her life revolves around the adult women and the child identifies with them although in a way which maintains her innocence and which allows her to remain natural. Her identification with an adult woman brings her a sense of independent thinking and helps her appear to be a rational person.

Situating the Balkishoris—Pre-adolescent Indian girls

The invisibility of pre-adolescent girls in film and popular culture mirrors their invisibility in policy. The Mumbai-based NGO, Vacha, has responded in very concrete ways to the critical issues of poverty, gender discrimination, and marginalization that combine to limit the opportunities for young girls [1] The empowerment of women begins with girlhood, and there is a particular need to work with girls who are at the threshold of adolescence.

The Indian constitution and government policies are protective of and promote the principles of child rights. However, in everyday life, these provisions mean very little because they lack gender perspectives and ignore the realities of children's—and especially girls'—lives. A child is defined in the Indian constitution as a person below 18 years, but most programs focus on children below 5 years. These early years are a critical time in a child's development, and this is a serious issue in India, where malnutrition and lack of hygiene account for 90% of children's diseases, for 60% of infants' deaths and 40% of mental and physical problems (Chowdhary 2002). The needs of older children, and especially pre-adolescent girls, also require specific attention, but the reality is that they fall into a gap.

Indian health policies for women focus on the issue of family planning, and mainly contraceptive distribution, and therefore target older, married women. The policies are in keeping with international trends. However, in the Indian context, most girls marry and reproduce between the ages of 13–19. Such early marriage and motherhood would suggest that girls in the age group of 9–13 should be a focus for reproductive health information, advice, and interventions. The average age at which a woman is sterilized in India is as low as twenty-six and in Maharashtra, Mumbai, it is twenty-five. Anemia is prevalent in 60%–75% of women in the reproductive age group (International Institute of Population Sciences 1995). The National Nutritional Policy focuses on children below six years, and only in a very small way caters to girls in the adolescent age group. Pre-adolescent girls (i.e., those between 9–13) are again invisible.

With increased international attention to girls' education and to reducing the gender gaps in school enrolment, retention, and achievement, a number of significant policy and programming initiatives have taken place in India.[2] Specific learning programs have been developed, targeting out-of-school girls in Rajasthan (Rajagopal 2000), and India has been included in UNICEF's special '25 by 2005' campaign to improve girls' education in twenty-five countries in which the gender gap is significant. Emphasis is placed on enhancing learning achievements, promoting a quality teaching-learning environment, and mobilizing community involvement in schools (UNICEF). The Government of India, in collaboration with different partners, is working to implement a national plan of action for Education for All (Government of India 2003) which includes specific attention to disadvantaged girls.

However, despite these initiatives, the challenges are huge and the reality remains that the educational opportunities for many Indian girls are extremely limited. A Marathi writer has expressed the situation of girls in schools as follows: if one hundred girls enroll in the first grade of a school, eighty-two drop out by the seventh grade, and only one girl reaches the twelfth grade (Panse 2001). Education policy and programming for girls tend to be narrowly focused on the school—for example, improving sanitary facilities for girls and replacing stereotypical images found in textbooks and materials with images of boys and girls, men and women doing a variety of tasks. Training teachers to be gender sensitive in their pedagogy is another important strategy being used. Yet, the stories that girls tell of their lives indicate the interconnectedness of family, school, and community and of the ways in which discrimination and marginalization in one context impact on their life experiences in another.

The Study

Vacha undertook a large-scale survey to find out more about the lives of poor urban girls aged 9–13. Even to start to talk about these girls, a new term—*Balkishori*—had to be coined in order to articulate the experience of being a girl of this age. These girls are at a stage when they are close to being *balika*—a girl child but at the same time are on their way to being women. The term *Balkishori* makes visible a group of vulnerable girls, girls who are often omitted from policy and programming in different social sectors such omitted from policy and programming in different social sectors such as education and health and child development. There is generally no special recognition of this age group or of their particular needs. From a feminist perspective which recognizes the interconnectedness of the issues that affect girls' and women's lives, the survey aimed find out more about their lives as a whole. This included school, but the experience of school and education can only be understood if looked at in relation to the girls' family and community lives and issues. The imperative was to reach out to girls who were not from any special group, like orphans or children of women in the sex trade (who sometimes do receive special attention) but 'normal' girls. Because of their invisibility in policy and programming initiatives, research documents, popular culture and media, it was difficult to comprehend the experiences of young Indian girls from the city of Mumbai—especially those from an economically underprivileged background.

The girls from poor family backgrounds who were involved in the survey experience quite different lives from those portrayed in the Bollywood films. Their mothers and the women around them are also leading very different lives. The stories the girls tell—of their likes, dislikes, and plans for the future—reflect at the same time the realities of the material conditions of their everyday lives as well as the images and notions of gender, beauty, and power that are portrayed in the films they love to watch. The survey findings, and Vacha's subsequent programming and activities for Balkishori, have some important implications for further research and action with preadolescent girls in India. In the first phase of the study, 2,600 girls were interviewed from 33 municipal schools (local government), studying in seven language mediums spread over Mumbai. The questionnaire contained questions on the girls' personal data, their likes and dislikes, their perceptions of their health status, their future aspirations, and their families' socio-economic status. This was done in order to understand the socio-economic and health status of these girls as perceived by them. It was also a chance for researchers to interact individually with the girls, to hear their stories, and to start to understand their lives. The study then provided a basis for a series of follow-up interventions.

In the second phase of the study, more information was sought about the girls' families and their backgrounds. These interactions provided more insights about their homes, neighborhoods, and social environment as well as their own needs as children growing to be adolescents. Social, cultural issues were incorporated as part of the study. There is no one cultural pattern for being female in Indian culture; as a child, if you are the first-born girl you may experience a different socialization than if you are the third daughter. In some castes and cultures, it is not a taboo to give birth to girl. But in most of them, it is. Therefore, the sex ratio in India is dwindling at the age of 0–6 years of age. In this age group, there are currently an average of 927 girls per thousand boys, with lows of 793 and 865 girls in the states of Punjab and Rajasthan (Mishra 2001).

The Girls

The Girls' Stories

Sushila wanted to become a lawyer so that she could fight for the rights of the people of her community. Unfortunately after the 7th grade, she had to discontinue her studies and work as a domestic help. Most municipal schools are only up to grade seven. She came from a large family of nine brothers and sisters who were almost all employed as sweepers either in private houses or in the Municipal Corporation. There is tuberculosis in the family. She herself has polio in her left leg, but in spite of that, she came along with Vina and taught the Vacha class a folk dance—which made them heroines of sorts!

In the Marathi medium, Seema—a bright and serious student—was way ahead of her class; she would often lose interest because of this. She represented the school in various competitions. She joined a private school after the 7th grade but didn't keep in touch as she had a lot to study. We are told she is doing well. Her father works in a factory and her mother is a domestic worker. Seema has four sisters and two brothers. Her older sister is working in a private firm. Seema is fond of cycling and wants to become a doctor when she grows up.

Nazia, from the Urdu medium, had endeared herself to us all by her sheer energy and charm. Her father is employed in the railways. Her older brother works in a garag, an older sister is married, and a younger and an older sister are in the village in U.P. along with their mother. Nazia lives in the Railway colony in Mumbai with her father and younger brother. Nazia would do the household chores and come to school neatly dressed and smiling. She was full of fun and enjoyed every aspect of school life. She went on to a private school after the 7th grade and visited us when she came to pick up her brother. While she was in the 8th grade, she had an affair with the bar-

ber. *This cost her dearly: the school asked her to leave, and her father— unable to cope—packed her off to the village. We hear she is studying, but there is no Urdu medium school in their village.*

Zainab was a little older for her class. A talkative girl—she was more interested in the affairs of others than her studies. Zainab was always well dressed and seemed well off. Her father sells eggs. She wants to study to get a college degree. Her elder sister, who had dropped out of the school system after grade five, would come to Vacha to learn English. Because her father desired it, Zainab joined a private Urdu school. She failed in grade eigh, but continued to study in the same school.

Tanu, a delicate and charming girl, took an interest in all activities. She had lost her father. Her mother was working in Dubai. She stayed with her maternal uncle along with her two sisters and brother. Her mother wants her to become a religious teacher, whereas she would rather join the police force like her late father.

Ayesha, a very serious and well-behaved student, was determined to learn English so that no one would laugh at her when she spoke. She has good support from her family to study. She is the youngest of a family of four sisters and a brother. Her elder sister is in college and her brother is studying to become a religious teacher. Her father had studied until grade twelve. He is employed in a five-star hotel. He is a devout Muslim. She said her parents did not like it if she danced. They had no television at home. We observed that she was fond of dancing and took part in all activities. Ayesha was the teachers' pet and generally topped the class. After grade seven, she joined the Municipal school near by. She continued to do well but like the others found it difficult to do Mathematics, Science and English. We were very happy to learn that she had topped the 10th board exams in her school— followed by Niloufer, another bright and motivated student.

Gender, Beauty, and Power

Images of beautiful film stars, beauty products and beauty tips, fancy fabrics, sarees and suits are a constant presence in the popular culture of urban Mumbai. But how do Balkishori perceive beauty? To what extent are their notions of beauty shaped by the images around them, and how do they understand the linkages between power and beauty? These were important questions to pose. When girls were asked what or whom they imagined as a "Beautiful Woman," the question evoked two main types of responses. One set of responses typically named actresses who are generally considered good-looking. A second type of response related the concept of beauty with qualities and included women the girls see and interact with on a daily basis. Some of these responses included:

They are those who obey the parents and do not give trouble to them.

A beautiful woman is that woman who is simple and not proud.

A beautiful woman is one who cares for and respects elders. She also speaks with others respectfully and in a sweet way.

A beautiful woman does not do any dirty business and she is friendly with everyone.

She does is not interfere while crossing the road.

She is clean and does not fight with others.

She is not very fashionable and is simple, as being simple is the most beautiful thing in the world.

I like a beautiful woman who has beautiful hair, has a beautiful walk, and speaks beautifully.

My neighbor is the most beautiful woman, and whenever I listen to her orders then she is very happy

She should make people envious. She should have beautiful face. She should have a killing style of walk. She should have beautiful clothes and she should dance well.

She should not talk with unknown men and should behave well with men.

These questions were asked to understand the way ideas are constructed in girls' minds. These responses are indicative of a normative construction of female identity characterized as passive, obedient, and submissive to the wisdom of age and experience.

The Girls' Lives and Experiences

Girls in urban areas of India may have an advantage over girls in rural areas, as access to education is much higher in the towns and cities. The Balkishori study findings compare to another path-breaking study on Primary Research on Basic Education (De and Dreze 1999) conducted in five underdeveloped states, which found that almost 90% of parents want their sons and daughters to get primary education. This is the case in the Balkishori study where, in keeping with Municipal schools across the country, more than 90% of the girls surveyed are economically underprivileged, with the more affluent parents sending their children to the better-resourced private schools. The atmosphere in the girls' homes and bastis (the small huts in which poor families live) is generally constrictive—both physically and mentally. In contrast, school offers them at least some free physical and mental space. They have a definite liking for school and a desire to be in school. For the Balkishoris, whatever little is available at school is important and valuable. In today's textbook-oriented education, these girls who have no extra resources at home have a definite need to receive some special inputs that go beyond exams and textbooks. It became clear to Vacha that the girls need better exposure that would help them deal with questions arising in their minds. They are curious to know about the adult world which lies beyond their school world. They are eager and receptive but do not get much chance to explore knowledge that lies beyond the routine classroom culture.

The study showed that the girls are keen to study and also to read and write but that their concerns are not catered to by the present education system. Many of them were unable to write anything beyond their name, and yet, 90% of them stated they like their studies. Another significant finding was that by the 7th grade, almost 90% of the girls in the survey could not give their complete addresses. Though they are born and brought up in city of Mumbai, many were unaware of their date of birth. Knowing one's address means having one's own identifiable place in the world, and there are various reasons other than ignorance that make it impossible for the girls to have this sense of place. Regular displacement, not having one's own permanent house, the unnumbered small lanes, and complex mesh of the unmarked roads in the shanty town all contribute.

The nutritional status of girls in the survey is alarming. Severe malnourishment—based on Body Mass Index (BMI), that is, weight in kilograms divided by square of the height in meters—was found in 1,352 girls, i.e., 72% out of the 1,853 for whom height and weight were recorded. Only two girls were found to be overweight, and 183 girls were found to be mildly malnourished. So there is a total of over 83% of girls who are malnourished. The girls' responses showed that most often they attend school having had just a cup of black tea. One of the girls interviewed said she would be happy when she gets enough to eat.

Discrimination is built into these girls' lives and has been accepted by them. For example, a question was asked about whether they got enough to eat and whether they ate with the family. The girls generally answered that they did get enough and that they ate with the family. It is only later that it was realized that they did not consider eating less or late as anything different. It was 'normal' and so not worth reporting. Even the discrimination in doing housework was similarly invisible. Boys were reported by the girls to be sharing housework when all they did was merely pick up things that they had let fall in spite of the fact that it was the girls who worked the whole day at 60% to 70% of the housework. The work that girls do in most of these households is manifold. It engages a large part of their lives and leaves very little—if any— time for play. Similarly, it is an accepted norm that girls and women should eat less—even on special occasions. Girls are made to fast before, as well as after, marriage: before, in the hope that fasting will get them a good husband and after, to ensure his well-being.

This trend of the revival of discriminatory traditions is being increasingly and aggressively preached through Indian films and television and is an issue of concern. The violence it does to women is incalculable. The *Kadwa Chowth*—a fast for the well-being of the husband—has become part of almost every Hindi and regional-language family-centered soap opera. This trend of fasting is growing rapidly and seems to be happening in every community. What is clear is that there is an increasing, sustained pressure to adhere to rituals and practices.

One of the most important issues relates to how girls are socialized to internalize a female identity that accepts as normal oppression and subordination; the material conditions in which they grow up and, for example, the workload this demands of girls and their mothers only reinforce this process. Shelter and permanency for these girls are sought in marriage, the earlier the better. They have little opportunity to learn or to earn. Their lives revolve around their families and community, and caste pressures also exploit them in subtle ways. If a girl is dark and simple, she is doomed to a dreary existence and has to suffer many indignities, as finding a husband becomes even more difficult. There are also cases where girls have to undergo being seared or other such tortures in the name of exorcising evil spirits residing in their bodies. What is curious is that one rarely hears of the same thing happening to boys. These girls are the ones who perform 60% of the work in the household. Yet they are the ones who do not have say in the house because they are girls. The men in the house, even younger brothers, can dictate to them because they are responsible for the chastity of their sisters and are allowed to regulate their actions.

In effect, the girls' lives are shaped by their experience of the power of others and their own powerlessness. Vacha is working towards a better understanding of these processes and towards ways of constructing more positive and proactive ways of being a woman. These are girls who have lost their childhood at the age of nine and see a bleak future—in spite of the dreams that they nurture in their hearts to become doctors, teachers, and even police officers. There is so much that is hidden about them but so much we can come to know if only we talk with them and allow them to express themselves. When engaged with them, it is heartening to see that though they may have lost much of their childhood, they have not lost their smiles, their mischievousness, or their spirit.

Given their socio-economic circumstances and the lack of opportunities and resources for these girls to extend their formal learning outside of the school, it is vital to equip Balkishoris with information, skills, and attitudes to deal with the realities of life. This has to be done as soon as possible because they are shortly to be considered as adult women and therefore to become wives and mothers. Five of the girls in the survey talked about getting married soon. One was engaged and was to get married within six months. One was betrothed in childhood. Many others did not reveal in so many words but hinted that families had started planning for their marriages. With or without marriage, more than 60% would drop out from school after the 7th grade.

Implications for Girlhood Activism and Scholarship
In an Indian Context

There is clearly a long way to go to better understand and the help to fulfill the potential of the pre-adolescent girl child. The research was a concrete step in making the girls visible and in intervening in some aspects of their lives, but now subsequent interventions need to be developed and awareness raised about the experiences and needs of these girls. By making sure that the Balkishori see that people are interested in them and their lives and are concerned to address their needs, we can promote the development of a stronger sense of self and self-respect. Interaction with the Municipal authorities showed that—like most other policy-makers—they were unaware of the special educational needs of Balkishoris but also that they were open to knowing more about the issues. The research findings have been shared with them and with health and welfare authorities in the cities. Doing so facilitates policy and programming dialogue relating to pre-adolescent girls.

This kind of work takes place in the context of the increased international attention given to girls and girlhood, particularly girls' education. In the context of Education for All (EFA), girls have become a focus for policy attention, [3] and yet there are many thousands of girls who are attending Municipal schools but whose opportunities within the school, and whose lives beyond the school, are constrained by issues such as poverty, gender discrimination, and marginalization. The girls surveyed attend school on a regular basis, but their learning there is extremely limited. This is not surprising when they rely on minimal learning materials and do not receive adequate nutrition. Another issue of particular concern is the lack of awareness the girls have about their own bodies and about menstruation in particular. Such findings create an imperative for focused yet holistic programming and activities such as the training module subsequently developed and implemented.[4]

Working as girlhood activists in the Indian context, it is very relevant to draw on the scholarship relating to girls and popular culture and to identify where and how work with pre-adolescent girls in quite different cultural contexts, such as the UK and North America, is relevant to local understandings of girls and popular culture in India. Inspired by the work of scholars such as Ewald (2001) and Mitchell and Reid-Walsh (2002), for example, there is much potential for more participatory and creative ways of working with girls in order to engage them in the research process. At the same time, there are culturally specific methodological challenges of attempting more participatory approaches with girls whose learning experiences—and relationships with adults—have so far been characterized by passivity, obedience, and submission to the wisdom of age and experience.

The pervasive film culture, with its glamorous women, its stars, and its fantastical story lines is a context in which the lives of poor urban girls have to be understood. Working with girls requires a critical engagement with such images and ideals. However, there is an urgent need to concretely address the material issues that affect the lives of poor and marginalized girls, and limit their life opportunities. This implies providing girls with the sorts of information, awareness, and skills with which they will be able to assume more control of their lives, to make effective choices, and to assert their own individual identities, dreams, and desires. The Balkishori are invisible in a gap between nutritional policies for young children and reproductive health policies for older women and so busy with housework and other chores that they are rarely seen playing out on the street like their brothers. For children who rarely have time or opportunity to just enjoy growing up as girls, ways also have to be found to engage playfully and creatively with them, to sing, dance, and have fun with them:

"I want to get back my childhood, that is my dream."

Notes

[1]   Vacha is a women's resource center in Mumbai, established in 1987. Vacha's main areas of activity are research and documentation and publications, training, and programs for girls and women. Its center includes a women's library and resource collection. Girls have always been of concern to Vacha, but the move in 1995 to the present premises in a Municipal school in a poor suburb of the city and the interaction with the girls in that school made it clear that more needed to be done.

[2]   The targets set in the Dakar Framework for Action for Education for All (EFA) and the Millennium Development Goals (MDG) articulate an internationally agreed upon imperative of closing the existing gender gaps in education. EFA target 5: "Eliminating gender disparities in primary and secondary education by 2005, and achieving gender equality in education by 2015…"   MDG 3: "Promote gender equality and empower women: Eliminate gender disparity in primary and secondary education, preferably by 2005, and to all levels of education no later than 2015."

[3]   See note 2.

[4]   Subsequent to the Balkishori survey, Vacha has developed a Training Program, with a number of different modules that provide the girls with information and skills useful for the real world. These modules include: *Health Awareness & Communicating with One-self* (including an introduction to menstruation and importance of menstrual hygiene); *Knowing One's Own Address; Map Drawing & Reading; Communication; Everyday Math; and Career Possibilities*. Diaries were also prepared for each girl to have a book of her own, complete with a photograph and with space to include personal information. Vacha has also held a series of very successful *melas*—or fairs for girls—at which a number of different fun yet also instructive activities are set up for girls to enjoy (hat-making, body measuring, etc.).

References

Brown, L. M. "Cultivating Hardiness Zones for Adolescent Girls." Keynote Address. Girls' Health Summit, 1 June 2001.

Chowdhary, R. *Children, the Family and Health: What It Takes to Give Children Long Life. The Silent Crisis: The Singapore Workshop.* All India Women Conference, PPSEAWA India, November 2002. http://www.ppseawa.org/Reports/CFH/silent.html.

De, A., and J. Dreze. *Public Report on Basic Education in India (PROBE Report).* Oxford and New Delhi: Oxford University Press, 1999.

Ewald, W. *I Wanna Take Me a Picture: Teaching Photography and Writing to Children.* Durham and Boston: Lyndhurst Books in association with Beacon Press, 2001.

Gilligan, C., N. P. Lyons, and T. J. Hanmer. *Making Connections: The Relational Worlds of Adolescent Girls at Emma Willard School.* Cambridge, Mass.: Harvard University Press, 1990.

Government of India. *Education for All: National Plan of Action, India.* New Delhi: Government of India, 2003.

International Institute of Population Sciences. National Family Health Survey (MCH&FP), India 1992–93. Mumbai: IIPS, 1995.

Mishra, B. "Sex Ratio Reveals Anti-Female Trend." The Times of India News Service. Delhi, 2001.

Mitchell, C., and J. Reid-Walsh. (2002). *Researching Children's Popular Culture: The Cultural Spaces of Childhood.* London and New York: Routledge, 2002.

Orenstein, P. *Schoolgirls: Young Women, Self-Esteem, and the Confidence Gap.* New York: Doubleday, 1994.

Panse, Ramesh. *Shikshan Anand Kishan. (Education Moment of Joy).* Bombay: Granthali Publications, .2001.

Ramesh, P. *Shikshan: Anand Kshan (Education: Moment of Joy).* Bombay: Granthali Publication, 2001.

Rajagopal, S. "Closing the Gender Gap in Education. The Shikshakarmi Programme." In *Institutions, Relations and Outcomes: Framework and Case studies for Gender-Aware Planning,* edited by N. Kabeer and R. Subrahmanian, 266–288. London and New York: Zed Books, 2000.

UNICEF. "At a Glance: India." New York: UNICEF, 2004. http://www.unicef.org/infobycountry/india.html.

Vacha. *Balkishori: The Preadolescent Girl. Health and Education Status of Girls in the Age Group 9–13 in Municipal Schools in Mumbai.* Mumbai: Vacha, 2002.

CHAPTER NINE

"I *do* know who I am": Writing, Consciousness, and Reflection

Relebohile Moletsane

Introduction

In an article recently published in *Agenda*, Jeanne Prinsloo (2003) appropriately concludes that the social identities of individuals and groups do not suddenly materialize in adulthood but are cumulatively constructed from birth. Thus, the ways in which childhood is constructed in our society, and in which children themselves experience it, are important factors in molding the social identities they have and perform as adults. With this in mind, contemporary notions of childhood and the ways in which the diverse children living in a complex post-apartheid South Africa experience it need to be understood and transformed.

Conceptions of childhood in the West seem to be built around age. Consequently, it is through concepts of age that the life experiences of children are shaped and controlled (James and Prout 1997). Yet, most studies in this area tend to focus on early childhood (birth to seven years) and adolescence. The research agenda of those working with and on behalf of young children locally and internationally tends to neglect the notion of childhood as experienced and understood by tweens (children between the ages of 7 and 12).

To address this gap, using Vygotsky's notion of the relationship between writing, consciousness, and reflection, (cited in Faragher 1995) this chapter aims to analyze the ways in which a group of tween girls from a primary school in the greater Durban area describe and reflect on their childhood, particularly on their encounters with violence and crime, through writing. The chapter analyses the discourses that the girls construct about their experiences of their childhood and in particular about how as young children and girls they experience incidents of crime and violence in their communities and school. The chapter investigates the possible impacts these children's everyday experiences and the meanings they make of them might have on the ways in which they construct and perform their social identities. Such an understanding might inform school-based interventions aimed at averting and reversing the negative impacts of such experiences.

Conceptions of Childhood

In the above-mentioned article, Prinsloo also concludes that childhood is socially constructed and is performed through practices and social relations in families, communities, and social institutions. Citing Jean Jacques Rousseau's definition of childhood in *Emile* (1762), Prinsloo reflects on conceptions of childhood as:

> [drawing] on notions of the child as in a state of nature, of innocence and purity...as uncorrupted and thus special in certain ways...the child should be protected from premature exposure to the corruptions of society to have a chance of developing naturally. (2003: 27)

This is in contrast to the realities of living in contemporary South Africa, where young children, particularly girls from marginalized communities, have to construct and live their childhood and social identities amid violent crime and gender-based violence. This is evidenced by media reports, which are inundated with stories of, among others, domestic violence, xenophobia, robberies, drug abuse, sexual and other forms of violence, particularly against women and children from poor and marginalized communities. In the first instance, as a social group, children experience this violence in three ways. First, they either are victims themselves or are witness to significant others' attacks. Second, they are consumers of violent programming in the media (e.g., in the form of local and international television and other electronic media programs). Third, as media reports and studies in schools (e.g. Griggs; Mahlobo, cited in Moletsane 2000) have concluded, children are often perpetrators of violence themselves.

In the second instance, as researchers have concluded (e.g., Bhana, 2003; Prinsloo 2003), as a social construction, childhood is also gendered. It defines and delineates different identities and ways of being for boys and girls, often governed by unequal power relations between the sexes. Thus, as a social group, young girls would experience childhood in general and incidents of violence and crime, in particular, in significantly different ways, often in silence and powerlessness. It is for this reason that tween girls were selected as a unit of analysis in this study.

The above suggests that, at the least, children will employ some form of agency depending on the social environment in which they exist. As James and Prout suggest:

> children [might] locate themselves flexibly and strategically within particular social contexts...through focusing on children as competent, individual social actors, we might learn more about the ways in which 'society' and 'social structure' shape social experiences and are themselves refashioned through the social action of members. (1995: 78)

Therefore, this chapter contends that a proper understanding of the meanings tween girls make of their everyday experiences, particularly as they relate to crime and violence, forms an authentic base on which schools and others working with children can intervene successfully.

Data Selection

Data for the analysis in the chapter were drawn from the Crime Reduction in Schools Project (CRISP), a multi-disciplinary research and development project co-coordinated by the University of Natal, Durban (now called the University of KwaZulu-Natal). The intervention aimed at finding reasons for, and dealing with, the unprecedented levels of violent crimes against and by learners in schools. To illustrate, research referred to above has shown that most learners in South African schools are either victims or perpetrators of violence, particularly gang-related crime, rape, assaults, theft, and hijackings (e.g., Griggs; Mahlobo, cited in Moletsane 2000). The Human Rights Watch (2001) concurs: While schools should be safe havens for all children, the reality for many, particularly girls and other socially marginalized individuals and groups (gays and lesbians, HIV-positive individuals, etc.), is different. Classmates and teachers are implicated in gender-based violence against them. The emerging picture is that gender-based violence in schools is tolerated and that "[girls] are disproportionately the victims of physical and sexual [and emotional] abuse at school..." (cited in Coombe 2002: 10).

Two primary and two secondary schools in the greater Durban area were involved in the CRISP partnership (see Moletsane 2000). The data were selected from children's writings for a competition sponsored by the project under the topic: *The crimes I have seen*. The competition was an attempt by the project partners to generate data aimed at gaining a greater understanding of the extent to which learners are exposed to crime in the course of their lives (Leggett 1999: 1).

For this chapter, 15 pieces of writing, in the form of letters to friends, parents, relatives, and fictitious characters as well as essays by girls aged from 11 to 13 years from one of the primary schools were randomly selected for analysis. The school, Roadside Primary (a pseudonym) is a formerly white institution located in one of Durban's formerly segregated suburbs. At the time of the research (2000), while the student population was almost totally African (98 percent), the teaching and administrative staff were 95 percent white, with the remaining five percent made up of people of Indian and Colored (mixed-race) descent. Thus, while servicing mostly African children from the surrounding townships and informal settlements, Roadside Primary could be considered 'white English' in its ethos and teaching and learning culture. Most of these children come from traditional African backgrounds, where children are mostly still 'seen but not heard.' Instead of empowering them, it is my contention that attending school in a different cultural and educational environment may function to further silence them.

In the intervention project (CRISP), writing was used not only as a data collection method but also as a means through which the children might be enabled to freely express themselves regarding issues that affect their lives in the school, their families, and communities. Using Brink's (1998 cited in Stein 1999: 6) notion of "excavating the silence," which, through writing, provides some distance and protection between the powerless individual and those in power, the children's experiences regarding crime and violence were acknowledged and analyzed.

In an earlier publication, writings by high school girls from the same project, in which they described, interpreted, and responded to their experiences of violence and crime, were analyzed (Moletsane 2000). The article acknowledged that it is possible that in constructing their stories, most of the girls had to confront real experiences of crime and violence against themselves and others. However, it is also conceivable that not all of the learners' constructions reflected first-hand personal experiences. Nonetheless, their constructions of their own stories might be useful in exploring the meanings they make of their lives and their school and community environments. The same applies to the letters and essays in this chapter.

Data Analysis

This chapter explores the meanings young girls in a Durban primary school make of their everyday experiences, particularly as they relate to crime and violence in their school and communities. The chapter investigates the possible impacts these children's everyday experiences and the meanings they make might have on the ways in which they construct and perform their social identities. Such an understanding might inform school-based interventions aimed at averting and reversing the negative impacts of such experiences.

To capture these representations, 15 pieces of writing by girls from Roadside Primary were selected and qualitatively analyzed. Content analysis, which involved a systematic and interpretive analysis of the girls' texts to understand their underlying meanings (Esterberg 2002), was used. The following themes emerged from the analysis.

The Social Context

In order to understand the diverse and often complex conditions in which the children whose essays were analyzed in this study live and in which they construct their identities, a brief overview of their social contexts is necessary. The first aspect of this social context is the family structure and the important role played by families. To illustrate, of the 15 girls in the sample, six lived with both parents, seven with one parent, with only one living with a father, and two with extended family members (an aunt and grandparents). One girl highlighted the significance of the family structure and support in her essay:

> *I live with my mother, father and brother. I enjoy having both my parents because I can get a lot of love and attention.*

This is not to say that single parents are not capable of giving love and attention to their children. However, the effects of the multiple and complex demands usually made on single parents, particularly mothers, in terms of work, family, and social commitments, cannot be underestimated. For example, writing about the socio-economic difficulties of getting to and from school every day, one girl reflects on her single mother's efforts:

To get to school I travel by bus and it is difficult because I have to buy a ticket. I also need to think about my mother [as] she works hard and she is the only person who works [is the breadwinner] and she works very hard.

The second aspect of the context is the geographic location of the girls' residences in relation to the school. Reflecting the general trends in the school, 10 of the girls in the sample (67 percent) lived in townships (an average of 50 kilometers from the school) around Durban and commuted to school every morning. Only five lived in the neighborhood around the school. In line with the apartheid history and the (still) segregated social (settlement) geography of South Africa, experiences of crime and violence tend to be higher in poorer communities, particularly in African townships and informal settlements around the country. Consequently, children living in these areas are likely to experience crime and violence more frequently and intensely than their counterparts who reside in formerly white towns and suburbs. Predictably, most of the girls in this study wrote about a lack of security in their neighborhoods. To illustrate, one girl wrote:

I do not like where I live because it is not good for me to grow up in this crime. I do not think it is good for me to grow up in a [place where there is] swearing and fighting.

Another reflected on similar circumstances and how they affect her:

I do not like the place I live in because I've seen people dying and sometimes there would be a burglary at somebody's house. The place I live in is not good for me because sometimes there are people shooting each other or a street bash (party) and then I can't concentrate on my schoolwork.

South Africa is plagued by high incidence of road accidents, which often result in injuries and deaths. For the many township and rural residents who commute to the city for work and business, travel on the country's roads exposes them to these daily hazards. In terms of the daily commute to and from school in the suburbs, schoolchildren who travel by bus or other means of transport are not spared. The media has often reported on minibus loads of children killed on their way to or from school. Reflecting on this reality, the girls in the sample often referred to their own experiences and hazards of commuting. One girl whose mother drives her to school from one of the townships wrote:

When we are driving to school every morning we always have to be very careful because of taxi drivers who drive fast. I remember one morning when we were coming to school and we were forced off the road by another vehicle. We went down an [embankment] and nearly overturned.

Others wrote of speeding taxis, pedestrians, including children, who are hit by cars on the roads.

To escape these conditions, most black families who can afford to move to the more expensive suburbs often cite crime and violence as their main reason for leaving. The perception is that the suburbs are safer and that there is more visible and efficient policing as well as other social services than in the townships. To illustrate, one of the girls cited the same reason for her family's decision to move to the suburbs and wrote that, "We now live in [a suburb] where we think it is safer."

This chapter is not arguing that crime and violence do not exist in the suburbs. Like all the children in the rest of the country, suburban residents do experience unacceptably high levels of crime and violence. One of the girls whose family had also moved to the suburbs from the township corroborated this:

...But it is not safe here. Old grannies get raped and stores are robbed. We will never be free. We can't go to the shops at night because it is not safe.

However, it is my contention that because of the legacy of apartheid and the resultant poor quality of service delivery, poorer communities tend to experience crime and violence more frequently and intensely than their counterparts in the better-served, formerly white areas.

Related to the geographic location of residences, a third aspect of the social context of these children's lives is public service provision in their neighborhoods, particularly police and educational services. The legacy of apartheid and its racial segregation policies meant unequal provision of public services according to race. This means that children living in the townships still experience non-existent or inefficient service delivery. To illustrate, reflecting on the poor educational service provision in her township as the reason why she was moved from the family home in the township to live with an aunt in the suburbs, one girl lamented:

At the moment I live in [the suburb] with my aunt and her family. I do not live with my parents. They live far away and they wanted me to live in the suburb with my aunt so that I can [go to schools] which have good facilities and most important, a good education.

Unfortunately, this is not an isolated case. Many families in the townships and rural areas often send their offspring off to the city to live with relatives during the school year so that they can go to what are perceived as good schools in the suburbs. The negative impact this might have on the children's lives is a cause for concern. The girl quoted above contemplated the negative impact of her living away from her parents, particularly her mother:

The problem that I have is that I am not happy where I live because if bad things happen to me, I tell my aunt and her eldest daughter but they laugh at me and ignore me. I cannot live with people whom I can hardly even talk to. I feel that a young girl growing up needs to be close to her mother so she can talk 'woman' things.

Policing is another area of poor service delivery in poorer areas. As expected, in this study, suburban and township girls' experiences of police services differed, with the former reporting quick responses from the police and the latter reporting very slow or no response at all. To illustrate, one girl from the township recalled a shooting incident in which her neighbor's grandmother was killed by burglars after the police failed to respond in time to a call for help:

*My granny quickly called the police...then we heard a gunshot...The police came but they were too late, the thieves were gone with all the property. My granny explained to the police what happened, and they said they will contact us **if** they have any evidence [emphasis added].*

In contrast, a girl from a suburb recalled the quick response from the police after a neighbor's young child was abducted while being looked after by the nanny:

She [the nanny] ran inside as fast as she could to dial the police. In about five minutes time, the police arrived. They took fingerprints...

Another expressed feelings of gratitude and relief at the quick police response after a robbery that saw everything of value taken from a neighbor's house:

...Luckily we called the police and we found everything except the mother's watch.

It is within this context that children in South Africa in general, and the girls in this writing in particular, have to grow up and construct and perform their social identities. The impact of this context on the growing-up process is the focus of reflection in this chapter.

The next section examines the particular experiences of crime and violence the girls in this study described and reflected upon.

Everyday Experiences of Crime and Violence

This section does not aim only to list the numerous and varied experiences the girls wrote about. Rather, the purpose of the section is two-fold: First, the seemingly hopeless and apprehensive descriptions of violence and crime by most South Africans and the girls in this study will be presented and the apparent acceptance of these as inevitable examined. Second, the girls' responses to their experiences of violence and crime in their communities will be discussed. Third, the girls' agency and intended approaches to 'taking back the streets' and fighting crime will be explored.

Representations of Crime and Violence

Reflecting the violent context in which South African children live, of the 15 essays analyzed in this writing, only one reflected on what might be considered a 'normal' childhood experience, that of falling off a bicycle and hurting herself badly:

> *I remember when I fell off a bicycle. It was really bad because I was poked by a piece of metal. There was a big hole…My neighbour and my mother took me to McCord Hospital…*

As expected, the rest of the essays reported and reflected on varied and numerous incidents of crime and violence in communities. The essays painted a hopeless picture through vivid descriptions of armed robberies, murder, domestic violence, child abuse, assaults, car hijackings, rapes of young children and the elderly, child abductions, theft and muggings, and victims and a society unable to respond effectively. As one girl aptly put it:

> *Nowhere to go. Everything you do you are watched. I hate it! I wish it would change.*

Three categories of violence and crime can be identified from the girls' essays. These include house breakings and burglaries, gender-based violence, as well as personal attacks (assaults and robberies) within homes and in communities. First, on the one hand, most of the essays referred to theft, robberies, and burglaries, which may suggest that these acts are a function of unemployment and poverty in the country (see Chisholm 1996). These included descriptions of boys as "bag snatchers," thieves leaving with "a radio, iron, food for Christmas, and the TV," an uncle getting stabbed and "killed with a knife for his money," and the more daring and notorious car hijackings. To illustrate, one girl sadly recalled how hijackers killed her uncle in a shopping mall parking lot:

> *My aunt [had] run in to buy a cold drink. Ten minutes later she came out looking for my uncle. Then she saw three males approaching the car and telling my uncle to get out. He refused and he still had his seat belt on. They shot him and ran away. I can't believe they could shoot an innocent man for his car and not even take it. All they took was my uncle's life.*

Another vividly recalled an attack on her uncle and his family who were holidaying on the coast:

> *The next night my uncle heard a noise outside his caravan so he went to go see what it was. There were five men; my uncle got shot...the bullet got stuck five inches away from his spine. I must say that I had never felt more afraid.*

A second category of the girls' descriptions involved gender-based violence—which came in the form of domestic violence, child abuse, and rape of women. A girl described an incident in which an uncle stabbed a cousin who was trying to stop him from fighting with his mother:

> *When he got there he saw his cousin fighting with his mother for a beer. My uncle doesn't like fighting...he went to his cousin very anxious to know why he [was] doing a thing like that to a person who cared for him since the day he came into this world. His cousin [responded] angrily and with hatred and ...quickly stabbed him on the arm...*

Another lamented but preferred her parents' divorce to their frequent fights during their marriage:

> *I do not live with my parents because they are divorced. Some children whose parents are divorced cry because they want their parents to get back together again but*

not me. In my own mind I don't think they were meant to be. The reason…is because when I was a small child my mother and father always used to fight. There could not be a day when they never used to shout at each other.

Outside the family, gender-based violence was also discussed in a few essays. Descriptions of child abuse and rape were often vivid and filled with disgust, fear, and anger. One girl referred to the notorious child rapes we often read about in the media:

I think crime is nasty…Children are being abused by their own parents. Some are 3 years old, 10 months, 8 years and even adults.

Another reflected on a specific case she had recently read about:

I remember a couple of weeks ago I read about a 14-year-old girl who had been raped by several men and I also remember how scared I felt because I am almost the same age as her. What if that had been me? Before I read the story I used to walk to the shop without worry, but now I am terrified to walk alone.

Personal attacks in the form of assaults and muggings within homes and in communities formed a third category of the crimes described in the girls' essays. One girl wrote:

There was a man who was killed for his money by two men. He tried to fight them but he did not succeed. They stabbed him on his stomach and shoulder. They took his money and left him lying on the ground.

Another wrote:

I remember when my mother was coming home and a man came out of the bush and tried to take her bag but only [managed to] cut the strap and ran off.

How did the girls respond to these experiences?

Writing, Consciousness, and Reflection

Vygotsky's notion of the relationship between writing, consciousness, and reflection sees consciousness as a mental activity that aims to transform an individual's representation of the reality he/she lives in (cited in Faragher 1995.) This is achieved through intellect, affect, and change. Using this approach, this chapter has examined how, through the medium of writing, the girls in this study represented their consciousness of their realities and their emotional responses to these.

So how did the 15 girls in this study represent and respond to their realities of living and studying in communities riddled with violence and crime? In the publication referred to earlier (Moletsane 2000), I suggested that there seems to be an acceptance and normalization of violence and criminal activity, especially by youth in various communities across South Africa. Quoting a 1997 newspaper article that reported a Durban township teacher as declaring: "The horror is no longer the violence. It is the acceptance of violence as normal that is so tragic" (*The Sunday Times*, 16 November 1997, quoted in Moletsane 2000: 65), I concluded that the high school girls in that study indicated disgust and shame when community members failed to intervene in incidents of crime and violence.

The same holds true for these younger girls. While the most dominant response to experiences of violence and crime was fear and a sense of resignation and defeat, a more positive was a call by the girls to 'fight back.' In terms of the former, one essay captures the sentiments expressed by most of the girls in the sample:

All these things make us scared and threaten our lives and others' too. Now we are scared to go into our own garden. I have also seen things that happened to other people and hope it never happens to me.

Another expressed the same fear and the negative impact it was having on her life:

Sometimes I just cry because I get so scared that something might happen to me and my family. I am not even allowed to go to the beach with my friends.

A response that aptly reflects the hopelessness expressed by some sectors of our society and the girls in this study came from a girl who recounted an incident of an uncle who was shot by robbers:

After that my parents decided that they want to move to Australia because of the high crime rate in South Africa. I also want to move because I would like to be able to live.

Another agreed, and stated:

Crime affects me…I would not like to grow up in a place where people fight and swear.

However, not all the essays expressed hopelessness. The most heartening representation of the girls' realities and their responses came from a girl who began her essay by declaring, "I *do* know who I am!" This was in spite of the difficult circumstances of living in a violent neighborhood in which she had often been witness to deaths, burglaries, and shootings. In addition, a few of the girls expressed some agency in the fight against crime and violence and described a number of ways in which they and others might intervene. The essays suggested that there had to be individual as well as collective responsibility in resolving crime in the country. To illustrate, one suggested that:

South Africans should work as one community to stop crime. If we don't, we will live in fear for the rest of our lives. We should stop looking at the colour of each other's skin and work together to save our beautiful country!

On the one hand, some might argue that this is too much responsibility for children this age and that, as suggested long ago by Jean Jacques Rousseau in *Emile*, children must be left to 'develop naturally.' On the other, this signifies hope and the existence of a 'fighting' spirit that may sustain these children in the midst of complex and seemingly hopeless conditions.

Conclusion

This chapter has examined the ways in which young girls at a Durban Primary school represented the realities in which they lived, particularly in the context of crime and violence in their communities. Through writing, this study aimed to engage the girls in a mental activity, first, to 'excavate' their silences around their lived realities and responses to them. A final question that remains to be addressed is: What are the implications of the girls' representations for school-based interventions aimed reversing the effects of negative experiences on their lives?

Informed by the frameworks used to analyze the writings, like several before it, first, this study points to the gendered nature of violence, with men and boys as perpetrators and victims of violent crime, and women and girls as mostly victims. Second, it upholds findings from previous studies and media reports which suggest that most children in South Africa often experience and are traumatized by incidents of crime and violence against themselves and significant others in their lives. Third, the ways in which children receive and respond to these experiences tend to vary from fear and hopelessness to hope and a sense of agency to intervene as individuals and as groups.

As a social institution in which children spend a significant amount of time (an average of eight hours a day in South Africa) and which, in some cases functions as the only space where children could feel safe and protected, the schools have a huge role to play in positively intervening in the lives of children affected by violence. Thus, this chapter contends that schools locally and internationally might benefit from a thorough understanding of the complex experiences children have of their everyday lives as well as of the ways in which they respond to such encounters. From such understanding, using media of communicating other than oral communication in the classroom and in research projects might play a significant role in the development of effective interventions for transforming such responses. It is therefore encouraging that at least one of the girls in the study recognized and acknowledged the value of engaging in the writing exercise. After describing the negative effects of crime on her life, she declared:

> *I am so honored that you are giving me this opportunity to show my inner feelings about crime.*

Specifically, at the forefront of the research and teaching agenda of those interested in developing and implementing school-based interventions aimed at addressing the negative effects of crime and violence must be the development of effective ways of communicating in schools. These must include more effective ways of enabling children, particularly girls—who are often silenced by the unequal power relations that favor boys in the school, the community, and the home—to construct their own representations of their realities and their responses to them. It is from such authentic representations that relevant interventions might be developed and implemented effectively.

References

Bhana, D. "Children are Children: Gender Doesn't Matter." *Agenda* 56 (2003): 37–45.

Chisholm, L. "Out-of-School Youth Report: Policy Provision for Out-of-School and Out-of-Work Youth." Johannesburg: University of the Witwatersrand Educational Policy Unit, 1996.

Coombe, C. "HIV/AIDS and Trauma among Learners: Sexual Violence and Deprivation in South Africa." In *Lifeskills within the Caring Professions: A Career Counselling Perspective for the Bio-technical Age*, edited by J. G. Maree and L. Ebersohn. Cape Town: Heinemann Educational Publishers, 2002. Available from http: //www.zimaids.co.za.

Esterberg, K. G. *Qualitative Methods in Social Research*. Boston, Montreal, and London: McGraw-Hill, 2002.

Faragher, L. "Reading for Riches: A Vygotskian Analysis of Learners' Writing." In *Reading Change: Education Policy Research: Kenton 1994*, edited by G. Kruss and H. Jacklin, 117–125. Kenwyn: Juta & Co, Ltd, 1995.

James, A. and A. Prout, "Hierarchy, Boundary and Agency: Toward a Theoretical Perspective on Childhood." *Sociological Studies of Childhood* 7 (1995): 77–101.

James, A., and A. Prout. "Re-presenting Childhood: Time and Transition in the Study of Childhood." In *Constructing and* Reconstructing *Childhood: Contemporary Issues in the Sociological Study of Childhood* (2nd edition), edited by A. James and A. Prout, 230–250. London: Routledge/Falmer Press, 1999.

Leggett, T. "Preliminary Report on the "Crime I Have Seen" Contest." University of Natal, Durban: The Crime Reduction in Schools Project, 1999.

Moletsane, R. "Talking Back to the Masters: Girls' Writing about Experiences of Violence." *Agenda* 46 (2000): 59–69.

Prinsloo, J. "Childish Images: The Gendered Depiction of Childhood in Popular South African Magazines." *Agenda* 56 (2003): 27–36.

Stein, P. "Drawing the Unsayable: Cannibals, Sexuality and Multimodality in a Johannesburg Classroom." *Perspectives in Education* 18, no. 2 (1999): 61–82.

CHAPTER TEN

"Show Me the Panties": Girls Play Games in the School Ground

Deevia Bhana

My boyfriend gave me peaches
My boyfriend gave me pears,
My boyfriend gave me 50c
And threw me down the stairs.
I gave him back his peaches
I gave him back his pears
I gave him back his 50c
I made him wash the dishes
I made him scrub the floors
I made him kiss a pretty girl behind the kitchen door.

By the time young girls begin attending primary school they have already embarked on the lifelong process of constructing their gender and (hetero)sexual identities. Sexual and gendered cultures are pervasive in primary schools—even among seven- and eight-year-old-girls. A public example of young girls' sexual cultures is the games they play. Girls' play in the early years of the primary school often involves singing and clapping to the sounds of rhythmic tunes about girls, boys, kissing, love, and a cozy life. Girls' play is an exciting activity and yields a great deal of pleasure for the players. What is the power of a girl in the games she plays? Drawing from an ethnographic study of the manifestations of gender and sexuality in primary schooling (Bhana 2002), this chapter seeks to examine the question by focusing particularly on young girls' play in two primary schools in South Africa. The particular focus here is on young girls, the games they play, and the complex performance of gender identities.

Traditional primary school games are often considered innocent or frivolous 'girlie' activities without sexual and gendered knowledge. A key way in which sexuality and gender is made absent in young people's lives is through the notion of childhood innocence. Children are believed to be immune to knowledge about sexuality and unable to discuss it (Renold 2000). The presumption of childhood innocence sustains the perceived immunity to sexual knowledge: young children are innocent and play is innocent.

In contrast, this chapter will argue that girls' play culture is invested in heterosexuality and offers a strategic space through which young girls resist, contribute, and contest their sexual and gendered identities. The construction of play as trivial and innocent masks the power structures, the pleasure principles, and the contestation that young girls experience against the backdrop of danger. Through play, girls learn to take up their places in the complex web of power. They conform, fight, and resist. This will be demonstrated through ethnographic evidence from two schools: KwaDabeka Primary School (a poor black township school) and Westridge Primary School (a predominantly white middle-class school). For a period of a year, I visited these schools, sat in on lessons, observed, and talked to young boys and girls in the playground.

The contention that children know a great deal about sexuality does not imply that they all know the same things. Their particular context and local cultures strongly influence what they know and believe. Girls are knowledgeable about sexuality and interested in sexuality, but, in specific contexts, they are also aware of violent gender relations. They derive a great deal of pleasure in singing and clapping to the rhythmic beat of traditional games and in shooing away troublesome boys. This is a strategic practice of seven- and eight-year-old girls in primary schools. Within the tensions of pleasure and the knowledge of danger in the broader space of primary schooling, girls' agency is highlighted.

Playing (Hetero) sexual Games

Children's play is complexly gendered (Thorne 1993; Grugeon 1993). Thorne (1993) suggests that children learn to become gendered (and heterosexual) through play. As girls play at kissing, love, marriage, and babies, they show themselves and others what they think about boys (and men) and what girls (and women) can and should do.

An example of one of the traditional rhymes that girls recite is:

Emma and Dave [names are always changed]
Sitting on a tree

K I S S I N G [alphabets are recited]
First comes love then comes marriage.
Then comes the baby in the golden carriage.
That's not all. That's not all.
  Then comes the baby drinking alcohol [can be changed to playing basket-
  ball].

Confronted with these discourses of gender and their related implications for femininity, the girls can be seen to be reproducing the 'love 'n marriage' discourse without consciously thinking of it as such. Here the girls can be seen as preparing for the heterosexual courtship and its associated activities, which include marriage. They are also preparing for the kitchen sinks, babies, and buckets to come (Rhedding-Jones 1996). Yet, the cacophony of sounds and rhythmic clapping associated with the rhymes are not audible as heterosexual discourses in schools but as natural and as 'just what girls do.' Heterosexuality is normalized. Epstein (1999: 31), however, suggests that the rhymes "certainly produce part of a culture of heterosexuality in which girls grow up to be women who marry men, go on honeymoon, have babies and otherwise perform their gendered, heterosexual female parts." In other words, through the rhymes, they are not simply clapping and singing—they are also exploring their positionings in gendered society. They do this by the narrative constructions of femininity. The rhymes that they sing can be seen as their own but also of other girls past and present. They sing the rhymes with the support of the other girls. That they sing with the support of friends means that one girl gives another the point of access to a gendered discourse. Thus, the rhymes are heterosexually desirable through the validation of other girls. They enjoy it; they do it for their own enjoyment and for other girls. The girls take delight and pleasure in the fantasies that are projected through these rhymes. In this way, the insertion into the rhyming culture becomes a part of girls' early childhood experience through which particular forms of femininity are fashioned. Yet, they are also able to position themselves with power over boys who stand watching and mocking. The very public space of the school fields provides the space through which moments of power can be experienced, thus disrupting adult–child relations, disrupting innocence, and subverting unequal gender power relations.

Kissing and Farting

The games girls play are important in sustaining particular feminine positions: little girls become tomorrow's women. At the same time, however, the rhymes can also validate and make tangible a range of alternative feminine positions. At KwaDabeka Primary School the following rhyme is a favorite amongst girls:

> *Ofuna ukungigaxa*
> *Makeze kithi*
> *Hayi umfana*
> *Sifuna intombazana*
> *Ngoba umfana*
> *Ushipa izidwedwe*

Translation:

> The one who wants to hug me must come to us.
> Not a boy.
> We want a girl,
> Because the boys are farting, filthy rags.

This rhyme can be seen as breaking free from the rigid stereotypes of love and marriage and thus testing out other ways of femininity. The girls make things happen to their advantage by associating boys with things that adults consider uncouth: farting, dirty rags. In this way, the girls mock and resist traditional forms of femininity. They laugh and shout as they perform this rhyme. Such rhymes provide powerful moments through which femininity is redefined and re-evaluated against the patriarchal investment in heterosexuality. Here normative meanings are defied, and schoolgirls can triumph within the rude spaces that they make available for themselves. Newkirk (quoted in Tobin 1997) writes that children's predisposition for poop jokes and farts can open up newer transgressive spaces in schools. The girls who chant this 'farting rhyme' are no different. They open up spaces through which heterosexual patriarchy is challenged and play with the normative boundaries through which children are constructed as innocent and rule abiding.

Sexuality pervades games girls play, and girls actively draw on it as a resource for constructing their gender identities. Within the normative boundaries of gender (and heterosexuality), they are not simply reproducing the schoolgirl culture that makes available a discourse preparing them for marriage, babies, and husbands, but they have the potential to recast themselves as powerful.

Show Me the Panties

I have suggested that playground rhymes are contradictory discourses that serve to reproduce schoolgirls' heterosexual culture but also, within constraints, allow girls to position themselves with power—which goes against the patriarchal discourses of the school. This makes it impossible for schooling to ignore sexuality. Through rhymes, girls are able to transgress the normative boundaries under the convenient cover of childhood innocence. Through rude suggestions, the girls are able to position their femininities in different ways.

In this section, I show how 'show me the panties' works at KwaDabeka Primary School to provide girls with a space to contest boys' domination. The girls engage in rhythmic performances in pairs or groups. Other girls and, sometimes, boys watch. The girls develop a sense of being together through which their collectivity is asserted. This is especially the case as they try to create a space for themselves away from the (mocking and sometimes violent) boys. Fuelled by their desire to amuse themselves and others, and create a space for themselves, the girls raise their dresses to the boys. In response, the boys either move away or make misogynistic comments. I illustrate this through different cameos:

(1)

Khanyasile: *The girls don't swear at the boys because they are scared of them. We say, "he's mad in the head" and we show them our panties. [Giggling]*

Me: *And what do the boys do?*

Khanyasile: *They laugh and tease us.*

(2)

Me: *Do the girls show you their panties?*

Siyabonga: *Yes. They think that the boys love girls. They say, "Hey, do you love me?" and they mock us.*

Mncedo: *The girls say, "He's mad in the head". They say voetsek [get lost]. The girls say, "Come here" and they raise their dresses. [He shows me what he means.]*

(3)

Me:	*Do you play with the girls, Sibonelo?*
Sibonelo:	*No.*
Me:	*Who do you play with?*
Sibonelo:	*Mbatha.*
Me:	*Why don't you play with the girls?*
Sibonelo:	*They show me their panties.*

The above cameos suggest constant struggles between boys and girls to make things happen to their own advantage. 'Show me the panties' is a position that girls inhabit to make things happen for themselves. It is clearly a powerful moment of female conspiracy against (swearing) boys. Khanyasile suggests unequal power relations between the girls and boys. But, even though the girls are scared at school, they are not powerless. Girls adopt a strategy of resistance to mocking and violent boys by acting out an aggressive sexuality and investing in rudeness, lifting their dresses in concert to 'show their panties.' Their moment of power rests in 'show me the panties,' which tries to create a safer place through which their desires can be lived out. This moment of power is enabled through constraint. Within constraint there exists a freer position that pushes the boundaries and transgresses the norms of patriarchy and childhood innocence of everyday school life. As they show the boys their panties, the girls laugh hilariously as if in a surge of camaraderie, a spirit of oneness joined by laughter. The boys react by saying, "voetsek" [get lost] and some move away while others just continually say, "voetsek, voetsek." 'Show me the panties' provides the girls with an opportunity to display their own power. The fact that this takes place within a discourse through which girls are scared of boys is a paradox. "Hey, do you love me?" is a power moment made to mock and humiliate boys, while paradoxically it happens within the power relations of heterosexuality. The girls are able to use the heterosexual discourse to their advantage while at the same time being positioned in it. 'Show me the panties' questions the relative passivity and innocence of schoolgirl discourses (Walkerdine 1996).

'Show me the panties' is an ambivalent moment that is shocking both in terms of its explicit sexual reference and the power it asserts over the troublesome boys. The girls—who are cast as powerless, scared of boys in general, scared of boys who swear in particular—are able to recast themselves as powerful in the public space of the school as they privately recast boys as powerless objects whom they humiliate through their performance. There are definite limits to this transgression. In South Africa, sexual violence against schoolgirls is a daily experience. Girls are raped, sexually abused, sexually harassed and assaulted at school by male classmates and teachers (Human Rights Watch 2001). The convenient cover of childhood innocence makes the recognition of this sexual violence difficult. But children are neither ignorant nor innocent of sexual knowledge. Childhood innocence is an excuse for keeping children ignorant, denying them access to power, and justifying their powerlessness (Epstein, O'Flynn and Telford 2003). The supposed innocence of young girls in particular is problematic, as it constitutes what Kitzinger (1990) calls an eroticisation of children.

In foregrounding heterosexual games, I have argued that young girls draw upon sexuality in the construction of their gender and sexual identities. Children are active makers of sex/gender identities through which unequal gender power relations are contested, challenged, and maintained as groups of girls stick together.

But, not all games are based on sticking together. There are different types of chasing and catching games that carry explicit sexual meaning. One such game is based on entry into the classroom. Both boys and girls stand at the door. The girl who is selected has to kiss a boy if she wants to enter the classroom. If the girl refuses, then the boys run after her. Another game is called 'I propose.' In this game, a girl starts the play by touching another girl's pinky [small finger]. Girl 1 says, "I propose that you hug and kiss Bongani [name of a boy]." If the Girl 2 says "no," then Girl 1 hits Girl 2. Torture is not simply a boy's domain, as girls too resort to painful activities that construct their femininities with hardness. If Girl 2 says "maybe," then she has to hug the boy. If she says "yes," then she hugs and kisses the boy who has been proposed. Another game involves a boy taking a girl's shoe and running. The girl runs after the boy, and she has to kiss him in order to get her shoe back. This game in particular also involves running and catching, which become transmuted into arenas of sexualized chasing. I consider 'kiss-kiss chase' as the complex experience of sexualized chasing,

Kiss-Kiss Chase

'Kiss-kiss chase' was not something I saw during playground activity, but it was talked about in the classroom at Westridge Primary School:

(1)
Me: *Which pre-school did you go to?*

Mariella:	*Westridge Pre-primary.*
Me:	*And you, Keith?*
Keith:	*Westridge Pre-primary*
Me:	*So you two should be friends?*
Mariella:	*No.*
Keith:	*Yuck.*
Me:	*Why?*
Mariella:	*Yes, but just in class I talk to him, but I don't have any boy who is my friend. No. My friends are girls.*
Angelique:	*No, Miss Bhana, Mariella does play with boys. We play kiss-kiss catches. Mariella runs after them.*
Me:	*Do you, Mariella?*
Mariella:	*Er....Ja, sometimes.*
Me:	*What's this kiss-kiss catches?*
Angelique:	*It's a kiss-kiss catching game. Mariella kissed Alex. [laughing]*
Mariella:	*Angelique, you're rotten.*
Me:	*So what is this game?*
Mariella:	*It's when girls are on, and boys are on.*
Me:	*Do you enjoy it?*
Mariella:	*Yes I do…*

(2)

Me:	*Do any of you play kissing catches?*
Nguleko:	*Yes we do.*
Sarah:	*But, Mrs. B doesn't know 'cos she said that it's not allowed.*
Nguleko:	*All the boys say, "Can I play? Can I play?" and I say, " yes" because it's a fun game.*
Me:	*So what's this game?*
Angelique:	*The girls run and catch the boys and they catch the boy for me if I'm the queen and then we swap. The boys catch us.*
Nicholas:	*Oh, and then we kiss them on the lips.*
Angelique:	*But Leo is the roughest. He is like a rugby player...*

In both vignettes, games of 'kiss-kiss chase' are described as pleasurable moments in children's lives. A major contradiction surrounding the production of gender identities is the ambivalence regarding sexual knowledge and childhood innocence. But 'kiss-kiss chase' and other games are part of the stuff of everyday culture in primary schooling. Girls actively challenge the rules; they seek out pleasure and playing heterosexual games is a pleasurable performance. As in the other (hetero)-sexual games, gender difference in 'kiss-kiss chase' was marked as a heterosexual binary. 'Kiss-kiss chase' produced heterosexual desirability and was part of the complex network of heterosexual activities: Mariella kisses Alex, and Nicholas claims that boys kiss the girls on the lips, though sometimes the girls told me that the boys kissed their hands. For both boys and girls, kissing and kissing on the lips is an ordinary experience, but it happens within a discourse which tries to bring it under siege "...cos she [Mrs. B] said it was not allowed..."—perhaps another strategy to not deal with childhood sexuality.

For the girls, 'kiss-kiss chase' provides the opportunity to perform heterosexuality. Within this matrix, one girl is queen while the other girls are worker bees who do the hard work and catch the prey (boy) that the queen has chosen. Engaging in kiss-kiss catches does empower girls, but it does so within the boundaries through which girls' heterosexuality is regulated. For example, kissing a boy means facing the danger of being identified as less than innocent. This is clearly evident as Angelique lets the secret out and mocks Mariella for kissing Alex. Thus, the girls operate in contradictory discourses: constructing heterosexual femininities while guarding against overt heterosexuality. 'Kiss-kiss chase' is invested with power relations. Angelique is wary of Zo, whom she constructs as a rugby player: wild and rough. I illustrate this with another cameo:

Megan: *Yes, except for the big boys. They [boys] are bullies. My big brother bullies me all the time. Girls aren't bullies.*
Bryce: *Yes, except that they have long hair.*
Me: *Do you play with girls, Bryce?*
Bryce: *We play kissing catches.*
Me: *What's that?*
Bryce: *[embarrassed] No, just catches.*
Megan: *Don't lie, Bryce. He always wants to play kissing catches. He always runs and doesn't give us a chance to eat our lunches...*

Sexualized running occurs with knowledge of the "more general relation of gendered power" (Epstein 1999: 33). While learning that kiss-kiss catches is an enjoyable and pleasurable moment entwined with power positions, the girls are also learning that its enjoyment happens within unequal relations of power.

Conclusion

Sexuality pervades primary schooling, and girls draw on it as a resource for constructing themselves as young heterosexual girls. Games are strategic in promoting normative heterosexuality and breaking the myths about childhood innocence. Games are sites of energy and a creative force for young girls. But there are also dangers and restrictions as unequal gender power structures manifest. Girls' play highlights their agency, and their play speaks of the things that really matter to them. In certain schooling contexts, forms of abuse against young girls are more severe. Differences in gender identities are structured through power and resistance in complicated patterns of inequality (Epstein, O'Flynn, Telford 2003). At both KwaDabeka and Westridge Primary School, girls deploy heterosexuality and use it as a resource in the construction of their gendered identities. However, patterns of violence and abuse at KwaDabeka Primary School make life much more difficult for young girls. Play is pleasure and danger too.

References

Bhana, D. "Making Gender in Early Schooling. A Multi-Sited Ethnography of Power and Discourse: From Grade One to Two in Durban." Ph.D. diss., University of Natal:Durban, 2002.

Epstein, D. "Sex Play: Romantic Significations, Sexism and Silences in the Schoolyard." In *A Dangerous Knowing. Sexuality, Pedagogy and Popular Culture*, edited by D. Epstein and J. T. Sears, 25–42. London, New York: Cassell, 1999.

Epstein, D., S. O'Flynn, and D. Telford. *Silenced Sexualities in Schools and Universities.* Oakhill: Trentham, 2003.

Grugeon, E. "Gender Implications of Children's Playground Culture." In *Gender and Ethnicity In Schools 'Ethnographic Accounts,'* edited by P. Woods, and M. Hammersley, 11–33. London and New York: Open University Press, 1993.

Human Rights Watch. *Scared at School: Sexual Violence Against Girls in South African Schools.* USA: Human Rights Watch, 2001.

Kitzinger, J. "'Who Are You Kidding?'" Children, Power and Sexual Assault." In *Constructing and Reconstructing Childhood,* edited by A. James and A. Prout, 157–183. London: Falmer Press, 1990.

Renold, E. "'Coming Out': Gender, (Hetero)sexuality and the Primary School." *Gender and Education.* 12, no. 3 (2000): 309–326.

Rhedding-Jones, J. "Researching Early Schooling: Poststructural Practices and Academic Writing in an Ethnography." *Gender and Education.* 17, no. 1 (1996): 21–38.

Thorne, B. *Gender Play, Girls and Boys in School.* Buckingham: Open University Press, 1993.

Tobin, J., ed.. *Making a Place for Pleasure in Early Childhood Education.* New Haven and London: Yale University Press, 1997.

Walkerdine, V. "Popular Culture and the Eroticization of Little Girls." In *Cultural Studies and Communications*, edited by J. Curran, D. Morley and V. Walkerdine, 254–264. London: Edward Arnold, 1996.

CHAPTER ELEVEN

Tween Worlds: Race, Gender, Age, Identity, and Violence

Yasmin Jiwani

Introduction

As scholars, activists, and advocates, we often take for granted the ability to be able to speak in our own voices—the freedom to be able to articulate our perspectives, experiences, feelings, and visions. However, such is not the case for all of us. In fact, doing research with girls and young women under the legal age is often difficult, given the existing university-based research ethics requirements which ensure that such research is only permissible with the signed consent of parents and care-givers.[1] This is in spite of Canada's official signed assent to abide by the UN Convention on the Rights of the Child. Article 13 of the Convention explicitly states that:

> The child shall have the right to freedom of expression; this right shall include free-dom to seek, receive and impart information and ideas of all kinds, regardless of frontiers, either orally, in writing or in print, in the form of art, or through any other media of the child's source.

In doing research on issues of violence, belonging, and identity, obtain-ing the permission of caregivers can constrain a young girl's willingness to participate in the research process. Oftentimes the caregivers themselves are the perpetrators of violence—whether it is psychological, physical, sexual, or financial forms of abuse. In such cases, they are not likely to give permission for those in their care to participate in a research process that can potentially result in disclosures of violence or incrimination. When the research involves girls and young women from racialized immigrant communities, the situation is worsened by the reality that in many cases, these communities themselves are marginalized, criminalized, and stigmatized (Lucashenko 1996; Razack

1998). A code of silence prevails in these communities as a way towards defusing any potential public scrutiny on deviant behaviors. The communities themselves often feel embattled and hence turn inward to protect themselves from negative societal sanctions. In such cases, institutional requirements such as those of obtaining permission for doing sensitive research become significant barriers—both from the institutional contexts of universities and from within communities that want to shy away from any potential disclosure of deviant or negative behavior.

Nevertheless, given the types of institutional constraints and normative pressures that young women experience in general and that girls and young women who are differently located (as a result of race, class, age, sexuality, and ability) face in particular, it is imperative to research girls' lives with respect to their experiences of violence, belonging, and identity. However, because of the barriers outlined above, it is extremely difficult to conduct research with tweens (girls aged between six/seven and eleven) on such issues as violence, belonging, and racism. Thus, the content of this chapter focuses on the experiences of girls and young women between the ages of thirteen and eighteen from racialized immigrant communities. Not only are these young women more accessible in the sense of being able to speak in their own voice without parental consent, but they are often more interested in participating in the research process itself and becoming agents of social change. Further, unlike their younger counterparts, girls who are older than tweens have often acquired the language by which to name their particular experiences of oppression. In contrast, while some tweens may feel the pain and trauma of racism, they are often unable to articulate racism or contextualize it as a systemic phenomenon. Rather, the tendency to want to belong to a peer group often masks experiences of racism in the language of various kinds of differences, which are either perceived as unvalued or unwanted or simply denied and suppressed. Nonetheless, recalling experiences of their lives as tweens growing up in Canada often works, methodologically, in terms of capturing the latter and situating it within their own cognitive and social psychological development as young women of color located within a predominantly white society.[2]

Nonetheless, we cannot forget that the social category of 'tweens' is itself a market-driven construction based upon the meanings that adolescence has in the West and the disposable income possessed by this particular group. As the concepts of childhood and adolescence become more universalized because of globalization, migration, and westernization, the rituals marking the change from girlhood to womanhood are becoming increasingly complicated and sometimes imbued with contradictory meanings. So for instance, while adolescence may mark the transition from girlhood to motherhood in some societies, in the west, there is a tendency now to see adolescence as an extension of girlhood—not quite girl but not quite woman either—a young woman in an 'in between stage.'

In the context of this transition from girlhood to young womanhood, migration has a particularly harsh impact. The dislocation resulting from migration—and it depends whether the migration is voluntary or enforced—can be highly traumatic. There is a sense of grief as one leaves what is familiar, euphoria as one experiences relief and novelty from being a new situation, disillusionment as the reality of uprooting sets in, and finally a sense of settlement that comes with integration or adaptation to the new space. This cycle of grief, euphoria, disillusionment, and settlement is not peculiar to young women—it is a cycle that most immigrants and refugees experience as a result of dislocation. However, that sense of dislocation is highly pronounced when the individuals involved are marked by physical and cultural differences, in other words, when they are racialized. It influences the cycle resulting in adjustment and continues to impact individuals in terms of their social and economic mobility not to mention their acceptance and integration into the milieu in which they have relocated. As the Working Group on Girls noted in its report (Friedman with Cook 1995), immigrant and refugee girls also experience higher rates of violence because of dislocation, racism, and sexism from both within their own communities and the external society. Caught between two cultures, where their own is devalued and constructed as inferior and where the cultural scripts in both worlds encode patriarchal values, these girls face a tremendous struggle in trying to 'fit in' and often suffer intense rejection and backlash as a result of their failures to do so.

This chapter begins by outlining some of the key issues regarding gender and race-based violence. It then examines the various kinds of violence that are experienced by young racialized women from immigrant and refugee backgrounds today. Contributing factors that increase their vulnerability to both intimate and systemic forms of violence are explored. Data from an extensive study involving racialized girls and young women conducted under the auspices of the BC/Yukon FREDA Centre for Research on Violence

Against Women and Children are used to highlight the main themes concerning violence, identity, belonging, and racism that influence and shape the lives of racialized girls in Canada.[3]

Statistics reveal that young women are particularly vulnerable to gender-based violence. For example, adolescent wives between the ages of 15 and 19 are three times more likely to be murdered than older wives (Rodgers 1994). A survey of secondary school students in British Columbia revealed that an average of 32% of girls and 15% of boys have experienced a history of physical and/or sexual abuse. It has been found that girls are likely to be sexually abused in their teen years between the ages of 11 and 14 and boys between the ages of 4 and 6. Research also suggests that 94% to 100% of the abusers are men in cases of child sexual abuse involving girls, with men also accounting for 85% of the perpetrators in cases involving child sexual abuse involving boys (Duffy and Momirov 1997).

The vulnerability associated with gender in the context of family violence is also reflected in the following statistics, which demonstrate that girls and young women are more at risk for physical violence from family members as compared to boys, and equally at risk for sexual violence.

Table 11.1: Assaults

	Females	Males
Sexual assaults committed by family members	31%	29%
Physical assaults committed by family members	30%	16%

Source: Daisy Locke. "Violence Against Children and Youth by Family Members." *Family Violence in Canada: A Statistical Profile, 2000*, 31–37. Statistics based on police reports.

Many factors contribute to the vulnerability of children and youth to violence and principal among these is their dependency on caregivers. The literature suggests that older boys are better able to protect themselves against sexual abuse by expanding their sphere of influence and spending more time outside the home. With girls however, the dependency in the home continues and is reinforced by gendered notions of what it means to be a girl. Girls are also more vulnerable to sexual violence because of their gender—as girls and young women. The vulnerabilities of girls to violence can be partly attributed to their subordinate position as girls as well as to associations of innocence signified by their young age and the knowledge among abusers that young women and girls are not likely to be believed and can be coerced to remain silent.

Race

While gender and age are associated with commonly accepted vulnerabilities, race and racism have not been examined in the same way. In reality, there are no defined biological races. However, in social reality, people are defined by the color of their skin. The sociological value of race as a construct is that it draws our attention to the phenomenon of racism at the institutional and individual level. It alerts us as to how people are treated differently because of their ascribed or physical differences. A considerable body of research details the racialization of specific groups and attests to the racism prevalent in Canadian society (Fleras and Elliot 1996; Henry et al. 1995). Aboriginal peoples, people of color, and many new immigrant groups are racially marked and subjected to institutional and everyday racism (Essed 1990).

Racism can be defined as a form of systemic violence that is often expressed in daily reality through acts of exclusion, stigmatization, and devaluation and institutionally through exclusion, ghettoization, and genocide. The intersection of racism and sexism compound the vulnerabilities of Aboriginal women, immigrant and refugee women, and women of color. Age complicates the situation given that many girls and young women from these communities are doubly vulnerable—dependent on their care-givers (legally and institutionally) and dependent on their communities for a sense of belonging and protection from what can often be a hostile and racist world (Jiwani 1998). Racialization can be defined as "any process or situation wherein the idea of 'race' is introduced to define and give meaning to some particular population, its characteristics and actions" (Miles 1989: 246). The idea of 'race' is now commonly understood as signifying a difference in skin color. However, historically, it has also been used to refer to peoples of a different religious orientation and geographic location. Through racialization, physical differences become signified with particular valuations and connotations. Those who are racialized are often the targets of racism—an institutional and everyday practice of othering based on perceived physical and cultural differences.

In November 1997, a fourteen-year-old South Asian girl, Reena Virk, was brutally murdered in Victoria, BC. Since that time, there have been other such murders, including those of Dawn Marie Wesley in BC in 2000, Aylin Otano-Garcia in St. Andre-est, Quebec, in 2001, and more recently, the murder of seventeen-year-old Amandeep Atwal in Kitimat, BC. What is common in these four cases of murder is that three of the victims were young women of color from immigrant communities and one was part aboriginal. All of them had spent the majority of their lives in Canada or were born in Canada and were well versed in the dominant languages of English and French. Yet, this did not protect them from the violence enacted by their peers in two cases or by the family in Amandeep's case. These murders highlight the complex ways in which race, gender, and age interlock to create vulnerabilities to violence. They further illuminate the sites in which systemic forms of violence, such as racism, sexism, ageism, ableism, and sexuality intersect with intimate forms of violence within the family and from intimate partners.

Dominant frameworks for understanding the lives and realities of girls of color tend to focus on cultural differences (Jiwani 1992). As Narayan (1997) argues, within these paradigms, culture becomes the terrain upon which colonial binaries are constructed. With regard to immigrant and refugee girls, and more particularly girls of color, the tendency has been to understand their lives through the prism of 'cultural conflict.' Here conflict is used to explain the dissonance and dissatisfaction that girls experience in dealing with the supposedly contradictory and opposing normative structures of the dominant 'host' society on the one hand and their own cultural communities on the other (Hutnik 1986; Miller 1995; Onder 1996; Rosenthal et al. 1996). Deeper questions regarding why this conflict exists in the first place or its underpinnings are rarely examined in terms of the structural relations of power that inhere in the dominant, host society—i.e., the subordination of minority groups vis-à-vis the hegemonic power of the dominant society. More recent studies have followed this line of inquiry and have demonstrated how racialized girls are inferiorized and how they internalize dominant values which embody a rejection of the self and their cultural communities (Bourne, McCoy and Smith 1998; Handa 1997; Matthews 1997). This rejection varies and is compounded by strategies of negotiation wherein girls try to 'fit in' to the normative standards imposed on them by the wider society whilst simultaneously adhering to the culturally prescribed standards of their own communities.

In her study of South Asian girls in Canada, Amita Handa (1997) demonstrates how the girls' lives are shaped by competing discourses. On the one hand, they have to deal with the pressures of assimilation in the context of school, employment, and acceptance in the wider society. On the other hand, as signifiers of culture by their families and communities, there is an emphasis on protecting them from the westernizing influence of the dominant society and ensuring their conformity and maintenance of cultural traditions. Western traditions are perceived as weakening the moral fabric of community life. Yet, in order to belong and gain a sense of acceptance, the girls have to engage with the dominant western norms and mores in the public domain of their lives. This is the site of the 'cultural' conflict. However, Handa problematizes the notion of culture that is couched within the conflict paradigm. In the latter, culture is perceived to be static and 'frozen' rather than dynamic and relational. The discourse of cultural racism and cultural violence marks the lives of immigrant girls and young women. But cultural racism and cultural violence are predicated on the gendered and racialized context of immigrant and refugee girls and young women. Racism becomes culturalized by virtue of its use of culture as the signifier of inferiorized difference (Gilroy 1991; Hall 1990). Cultural norms and traditions that are perceived to be 'different' and negatively valued become the vehicles through which the hierarchy of preference and privilege is communicated and sustained. Violence is similarly culturalized because it is understood as stemming from a cultural conflict rather than a structural inequality (Razack 1998). In other words, violence is perceived to be an inherent feature of the racialized culture and its failure to adapt/assimilate to the dominant, western context.

Methodologies

In conducting the larger and more extensive examination of the lived realities of racialized girls and young women, multiple methodologies were employed. First, research into the applicability of various international instruments as well as national and provincial policies was undertaken with respect to their adherence/compliance regarding services and protection for girls from immigrant and refugee communities. This analysis revealed marked disparities between the obligations set out in various international accords to which Canada is a signatory and the lived realities of girls from communities of color—whether they were recent immigrants or born in Canada.

Specific areas of disjuncture between policies and realities dealt with issues pertaining to the lack of gender-specific data on immigrant and refugee girls, vulnerability to trafficking and sexual exploitation, and experiences of violence as a result of isolation, othering as well as systemic and interpersonal racism.

The second phase of the research — and this is what this chapter focuses on—involved conducting focus groups and individual interviews with girls of color and women of color service providers who work with girls from immigrant and refugee communities. Five focus groups were conducted in total. These included a focus group and individual interviews with girls from the Iranian community in Vancouver, two focus groups with Afro-Caribbean girls, one with Latina girls, and a focus group with a mix of racialized girls. In addition, individual interviews were conducted with 14 girls in rural and urban areas. A total of 52 girls/young women participated in the project. The majority of the girls were between 15 and 16 years of age.

The focus group and individual interview questions were drawn up in collaboration with an advisory group of girls convened through various community organizations. Many of these girls had participated in an earlier experientially based two-day workshop using various tools of popular education. The following analysis includes quotes from the transcripts of this two-day workshop and focuses on the young women who were between the ages of 13 and 18.

Findings

In talking to the girls in both the focus groups and individual interviews, it was apparent that they negotiate multiple realities. To highlight the element of negotiation, I use the term "Walking the Hyphen" from Indy Bath's illuminating thesis on South Asian girls (Batth 1998). In her thesis, Batth makes the point that Indo-Canadian girls negotiate multiple realities. My point of departure in mapping the links between social cohesion and violence in the lives of racialized girls from communities of color rests on this notion of negotiation, which implies multiple-subject positions and the fluidity of identity as mediated by structural location and systemic factors. In the sections below, some of the main findings of the project are detailed. Many of these support the existing literature, but other themes emerging from the interviews and focus groups demand a more complex analysis.

First, none of these girls identified 'cultural conflict' as the major issue confronting them. Rather, the majority of the girls and young women identified racism as the dominant and most pervasive form of violence they encounter in their daily lives. They defined racism in interpersonal and systemic terms—from discriminatory treatment by teachers in schools, to the dismissal of their participation, the silencing of their voices, and the erasure of their histories and cultural realities in the school curriculum. On the other hand, they also identified racism as acts of verbal and physical abuse that cause pain and that result in their othering, inferiorization, and exclusion.

Some of the other themes that emerged from the data dealt with their notions of belonging, fit within the dominant culture, the hierarchy of racism, and the various ways in which they are othered. A significant theme was the impact of the media in negating and stereotyping their communities. This latter theme resembles what Kobena Mercer (see Cottle 2000: 106) has called "the burden of representation," whereby they are made to feel ashamed when others of the same race are criminalized and negatively stereotyped.

Notions of Belonging

In negotiating a sense of self and their own positionality vis-à-vis their communities and the dominant society, many of the girls and young women reveal a relational identity—in other words, they are Iranian in one context and Canadian in another. Overwhelmingly, they did not see themselves as 'Canadian' in Canada but only when they were visiting their cultural homeland or within the context of their own group. For some, their perception of authentic 'Canadians' was based on the latter as being white and of European origin. As this Iranian girl noted, "I think they see me as Iranian. Like the brown people, Moroccan, Iranian are like all one...they don't see me as white like they call Canadian." (Interview 2)
One of the South Asian girls reported:

> Like if someone was to ask me where I was from, I'm still from Pakistan. I'm always going to be from Pakistan and ultimately, somewhere deep down inside, that's my baseline foundation. But I have a Canadian flag on my backpack and if I were to backpack for a year...I'd be Canadian.

A dominant distinction emerged in the focus group with Afro-Caribbean girls dealing with the issue of 'birthright'—whether they were born here or not. Those that were born here felt that they were Canadians; those who had immigrated did not feel the same level of comfort in calling themselves Canadian though they were often referred to as such when they went to visit their relatives in their country of origin. The notion of a birthright is one of the ways in which the differentiation between the newly arrived and established communities is maintained, often in the interests of the dominant society, and one that resonates with state policies regarding definitions of 'immigrants' versus 'Canadians.'

Racism

Everyday experiences of racism reinforced the notion of otherness that many of the girls and young women reported in the individual interviews and focus groups. Many of the girls and young women immediately defined racism as a form of violence they are most likely to experience, inclusive of physical and emotional abuse. As this young woman from the Afro-Caribbean focus group defined racism:

...it doesn't have to be physical. It can be...like if someone calls someone a Black bitch or something, that's still violent because obviously that pissed you off because you went and busted the girl in the head. So obviously anything that breaks someone down, that doesn't make them feel good.

For many of the focus group participants and individual interviewees, it was difficult to confront overt incidents of racism because of the pressures they felt at home—with parents having immigrated in order to provide them with a better future. Nevertheless, as this young woman recounted, there was an explicit rejection of Canadian identity when it involved associations with overt racism:

My parents...they're constantly [saying] like I'm giving my kid a better [life]. But what is better? That's not to say it doesn't happen in our countries. We hear it con-stantly, ethnic warfare and political strife but they think that it's so much better here and then you hear things like that [incidents with the Ku Klux Klan] and it totally breaks down your faith in human-kind and Canadian nationalism and pride. I don't want to have pride in that. If that's Canadian, I don't want to be Canadian. (Jump-start Workshop with Girls of Color)

This kind of critical interrogation of their identities and location was apparent in a number of interviews. But, the majority saw their identity as Canadians in graduating and evolving terms—not one that was inherently theirs but rather as one that could possibly be acquired over time via an increased fa-cility with English, broader networks with European Canadians, and 'know-ing the system.' In addition, acquiring identity as Canadians was also predicated on being differentiated from those 'others'—notably those more recent immigrants who were newly arrived and who had not yet assimilated. As this young woman from the Iranian focus group commented:

> But I have Canadian friends too. But then they, Canadians, make fun of my friends. Like, "Are you hanging out with those FOBs again. Come hang out with us. Why are you hanging out with those FOBs?" I'm like, "They're not FOBs just because they can't talk English, or...you know?" But that's just making fun. That's not really...I don't think that's really racist.

Here, the experience of differentiating between the FOB's versus the more established immigrants is not understood in terms of racism but rather is imputed to the ignorance of members of the dominant society. Again, as this young woman's quote reveals, the distinction is hierarchical. At the top of the hierarchy of acceptance and authenticity, are the 'true' Canadians, defined by their skin color and access to informal and formal social knowledges. At the bottom end of the ladder are the 'FOBs'—defined by their newness, lack of such knowledge and their cultural/racial difference, or as one young woman described them: "FOB is like "fresh off the boat." It means that you're really...geeky and you don't know how to speak and stuff. You dress stupidly or whatever, right?" (Iranian focus group participant). In between, are the assimilated, relatively accepted but culturally/racially different categories of girls and young women. However, this hierarchy was not simply confined to the register of 'Canadian' identity and access to knowledge but rather extended to include other racialized groups.

The Hierarchy of Race

The hierarchy of race was most clearly expressed in terms of the inter-ethnic/racial conflict that was endemic in most schools. Most participants and interviewees reported witnessing considerable inter-group violence in their schools. Girls reported that that they often hung around in groups consisting of members from their own communities as a form of protection and because they could communicate more freely with those that shared their own cultural affiliation. The hierarchy of race was also implied in terms of perceptions and differential treatment accorded to particular groups vis-à-vis other groups:

> I know because I remember Chinese people had the day off because they had Chinese New Year. But when we asked if we could have our day off, Persian New Year,

they said no, we can't. Or we wanted to have a party or something, we wanted to use a little room in our school. And we wanted to use that to just party during lunchtime for our New Year, but we couldn't do that either. (Individual Interview #2, Iranian girl)

The girls and young women reported that in many instances, white students were given more attention, allowed more privileges, and treated better than students of color:

And then also, I don't know what it is but my teacher, when we come in late, she starts yelling at us, she starts saying, "Why are you late again? La, la, la, la." But some white girl comes in, she goes, "Oh, where have you been." She goes, "I was out with my friends, I'm so sorry," and she starts laughing. I would be like, "What the hell was going on?" Why is she yelling at us and not her and she's not saying anything. Or assignments. You hand them in one day late, "Oh that's a zero for you." But then Canadian people, I don't know what they do, suck up to them or whatever, and then they can get the marks. (Iranian girl, Individual Interview #2)

Despite being aware of the ranking and differential privileges accorded to different groups, the girls and young women who participated in the study did not perceive this as a systemic issue. On the contrary, many attributed the interracial violence and hostility to the innate characteristics of different groups and to a competitive and violent school environment.

Fitting In

The aspects of fitting in that the girls described were also factors grounded in systemic and everyday racism. As this young woman from one of the focus groups commented: "Yeah, like sometimes I feel like I have to lose my true identity to fit in."

Clothes—as in wearing trendy clothes—constituted a major signifier of acceptance. This is something shared by other girls who are not immigrants or racialized in the same way. However, for immigrant and refugee girls of color, the issue of poverty makes it very difficult for them to acquire clothing that would facilitate their fitting in. As well, informal knowledge about the normative values ascribed to clothes is something that they can only acquire over time. 'Fitting in' requires fluency in the dominant language and the ability to remain silent in the face of dismissal and erasure—in other words, knowing how to 'stay in one's place.' Many of the young women we talked to were cognizant of this implicit demand. Others, however, saw it as a normalized response to a situation of having little knowledge of the rules or access to social resources.

Othering through Inferiorization and Exoticization

Aspects by which girls and young women of color were othered included strategies of highlighting their differences, which were devalued, exoticized, or distanced as 'different.' One Afro-Caribbean girl commented that, "If you have hair like [name of another girl], they always ask you, "Did you wash it? How do you wash it?""

Stereotyping and criminality were often the two main strategies by which difference was underscored and devalued. Stereotyping was most often attributed to the media and to the ignorance of peers. Criminalization was more pronounced in that girls were often followed if they were in stores or perceived to be prostitutes if they were hanging around a street corner or waiting for a bus:

> *I was in Super Store with a couple of Black people and we were talking. And this one lady that worked in the store, she walked by us like 10 times. She kept on walking by and looking at us as if we're going to hijack her store or something. Who would try to hijack Super Store?* (Afro-Caribbean girls Focus Group Participant)

Inferiorization was also communicated through the institutional streaming of girls and young women of color into ESL classes. As this participant noted:

> *When I first came here, it was my second year at school. And they're like taking me to this room. I speak English because they were going to put me in ESL. I'm like, "I speak English. In my country, I speak English. That's the only language I know. English."* (Afro-Caribbean Focus Group Participant)

The Burden of Representation

For many, the stereotypes they encounter are mainly through mainstream media representations. Many of the girls and young women, by virtue of being minorities, carry with them the burden of representation. This refers to their feelings of shame resulting from the association of oneself with a devalued and stigmatized group or individual. One of the Afro-Caribbean focus group participants provided a poignant example of this when she said:

For example, I'm reading this book in school, To Kill a Mockingbird. *And it was about the Black guy, they thought he raped the girl or something. The whole time I had my head down because maybe it's nothing big. It's just my personal feelings because it just makes me feel like all Black people, they're the ones who are the rapists and the killers. And I'm the only Black girl in my class, so and then they have all these white people.*

Another Iranian girl mentioned in her interview that she was highly embarrassed and shamed by the teacher's screening of the film, *Not without My Daughter*, which portrayed Muslim cultures as backward and brutally patriarchal. One of the South Asian girls pointed to the discrepancies between exoticized and depressed representations of India, contrasting it with her experiences of visiting her cultural homeland. As she put it:

[The media] shows it [India] being very exotic, with Madonna and her mendhi [henna] and saris being turned into drapes and the masala and everything being exotic. When I went to India it was not like that, it seems very exotic. On the other hand, it's shown as a welfare culture. It's the kids on the UNICEF ad. So on one hand, it's like this big rich silk industry which does henna on the side and on the other hand, it's the nude baby with the over-swelled tummy on the UNICEF ad.
(Jumpstart Workshop with Girls of Color)

Conclusion

These interviews and focus groups reveal the complexity of negotiation that girls and young women are engaged in, both in terms of identity formation and in securing a place for themselves in society as a whole. They also reveal a number of interesting parallels when viewed in the larger context of issues concerning violence against women. First, many of these girls articulated definitions of violence that equated it with racism. They perceived racism as a major form of violence that they encounter in their everyday reality. Second, like women who experience intimate violence, the tendency among many of these girls was to overlook or negate any systemic factors except those that dealt with curriculum and the school structure. For instance, they were not able to perceive the hierarchy of races that was in place and that served the interests of the dominant group. Further, they often attributed racism to ignorance on the part of their peers—this reinforces elite notions of racism which are relayed by the media—that racism is due to the ignorance of a few or the lack of education of the 'loonies out there' (van Dijk 1993).

The antidote to this is then increased education rather than a systemic change in the institutional and structural matrix of society.

Third, as with women who experience violence, there are few services or safe places available to girls or young women from racialized communities of color. Rather, they are often faced with little choice except to turn to their own communities—via friends and family to deal with these issues. In most cases, the girls turned to their immediate friends as they thought their families would blame them for causing various incidents.

The theme of 'caution' was one that came across strongly in the various interviews and focus groups. Parents did not want their girls to be identified as 'problems' and, hence, not only monitored but reprimanded girls if they were caught in problem situations. Like other forms of violence, racism was also often individualized by the parents—resulting in a strategy of retreat and silence: ignore the problem and it will go away. In part, the parents' reluctance to engage in this at the systemic level was itself a function of their fear of being branded as problems and of having to watch themselves to find acceptance within the institutional framework of the school and society.

None of the girls we interviewed or those who participated in focus groups disclosed experiences of intimate violence. They were aware of sexism within their own families and communities and had bought into notions that Canadian society was indeed more egalitarian with regard to the status of women and that women enjoyed far more opportunities here than in their countries of origin. A few were skeptical of this view, but it remained a dominant theme and underpinned their belief in the Canadian dream—that with enough education, they could surmount the barriers that might confront them. However, even this view was tempered somewhat with the knowledge that white girls and young women were more likely to be chosen for positions in the end. As this one interviewee put it:

> *Like maybe if I finish my education, I have my degree and I'm a lawyer or whatever, if they have to hire me or some Canadian person, I don't know, I'm afraid they're going to choose the Canadian person over me. I don't know why but maybe because I think…"* (Interview #2, Iranian girl)

Finally, none of the girls reported incidents of 'cultural conflict.' While many mentioned the differential values regarding gender relations that prevailed within their homes as compared to the wider society, none reported this as being a 'problem' as such, and many felt that any similar problems could negotiated with over time. However, in examining the transcripts, it appears that intra-familial conflict may have more to do with the pressures that girls and young women from communities of color experience in terms of gaining acceptance and finding a 'fit' within a normative order that imposes hegemonic values and that demands compliance with these values—even if they are antithetical to those of the cultural communities. The tendency to focus on culture tends to detract attention from the deeply embedded sexism prevalent in the larger society, a sexism that is so encoded in the hegemonic structures and values that it tends to be normalized and hence rendered unproblematic. In such a context, sexism from within a cultural community is more noticeable and hence more liable to be cast within an orientalist, binary framework. In the latter case, dominant Canadian society is cast as more egalitarian, liberatory, and progressive while racialized communities are perceived as being excessively traditional, repressive, and rigid (Berman and Jiwani 2001).

Nevertheless, as advocates, researchers and service providers, we need to be cognizant of these normalized binary distinctions and transcend them in the interests of better serving and working with young women of color. More than that, we need to recognize the structural conditions that make these binaries possible in the first place, and guard against catch-all terms such as cultural conflict. We must also simultaneously recognize the specific vulnerabilities that accrue from dependency, isolation, and inferiorization that define the experiences of being raced and gendered in a hierarchical society where whiteness is dominant and privileged as a sign of normativity.

Notes

This research was made possible by a grant from the Social Sciences and Humanities Research Council (829-1999-1002).

[1] The legal age varies across provinces in Canada. Hence in British Columbia, where this research was conducted, the legal age of consent was deemed to be nineteen. In other provinces, it is sixteen. The legal age also varies with regard to access to services and the government's mandate with regard to the care of children and teens.

[2] See also Mitchell and Reid-Walsh (2002) for a further discussion of the utility of revisiting previous experiences of growing up.

[3] The Centre is one of five research centres on violence. A more detailed report concerning this project is available on the FREDA website: www.harbour.sfu.ca/freda/.

References

Batth, I. "Centering the Voices from the Margins: Indo-Canadian Girls' Sports and Physical Activity Experiences in Private and Public Schools." Master's thesis, University of British Columbia, 1998.

Berman, H., and Y. Jiwani., ed. *In the Best Interests of the Girl Child, Phase II Report*. London, Canada: Centre for Research on Violence Against Women and Children, University of Western Ontario, 2001. http://www.harbour.sfu.ca/freda/reports/gc203.htm.

Bourne, P., L. McCoy, and D. Smith. "Girls and Schooling: Their Own Critique." *Resources for Feminist Research* 26, no. 1, 2 (Spring 1998): 55–68.

Convention on the Rights of the Child, 20 November 1989, 1989 UNTS 1992/3. http://www.unhchr.ch/html/menu3/b/k2crc.htm.

Cottle, S. "A Rock and Hard Place: Making Ethnic Minority Television," in *Ethnic Minorities and the Media*, edited by S. Cottle. 100–117. Buckingham, England and Philadelphia: Open University Press, 2000.

Drury, B. "Sikh Girls and the Maintenance of an Ethnic Culture," *New Community* 17, no. 3 (1991): 387–399.

Duffy, A., and J. Momirov. *Family Violence: A Canadian Introduction*. Toronto, ON: James Lorimer and Company, 1997.

Essed, P. *Everyday Racism, Reports from Women of Two Cultures*. Translated by C. Jaffe. Claremont, CA: Hunter House, 1990.

Fleras, A., and J. L. Elliot. *Unequal Relations: An Introduction to Race, Ethnic and Aboriginal Dynamics in Canada*. Second Edition. Scarborough, ON: Prentice Hall, 1996.

Friedman, S. A. with Cook, C. *Girls, A Presence at Beijing*. New York: NGO Working Group on Girls, 1995.

Gilroy, P. *There Ain't No Black in the Union Jack, The Cultural Politics of Race and Nation*, 2nd edition. Chicago: University of Chicago Press, 1991.

Hall, S. "The Whites of Their Eyes, Racist Ideologies and the Media." In *The Media Reader*, edited by M. Alvarado and J. O. Thompson, 9–23. Britain: BFI Publishing, 1990.

Handa, A. "Caught Between Omissions: Exploring 'Culture Conflict' Among Second Generation South Asian Women in Canada." PhD diss., University of Toronto, 1997.

Henry, F., C. Tator, W. Mattis, and T. Rees. *The Colour of Democracy: Racism in Canadian Society*. Toronto, Canada: Harcourt Brace Canada, 1995.

Hutnik, N. "Patterns of Ethnic Minority Identification and Modes of Adaptation." *Ethnic and Racial Studies* 9, no. 2 (1986): 150–167.

Jabbra, N. "Assimilation and Acculturation of Lebanese Extended Families in Nova Scotia." *Canadian Ethnic Studies* 15, no. 1 (1983): 54–72.

Jiwani, Y., with N. Janovicek, and A. Cameron. *Erased Realities: The Violence of Racism in the Lives of Immigrant and Refugee Girls of Color*. Vancouver, CA: FREDA, 2001.

Jiwani, Y. "To Be or Not to Be: South Asians as Victims and Oppressors in the Vancouver Sun." *Sanvad* 5, no. 45 (1992): 13–15.

_____. *Violence Against Marginalized Girls: A Review of the Literature*. Vancouver, Canada: FREDA, 1998.

Locke, D. "Family Homicide." In *Family Violence in Canada; A Statistical Profile*, produced by Canadian Justice Statistics, 39–44. Ottawa: Statistics Canada, 2000.

_____ "Violence Against Children and Youth by Family Members." In *Family Violence in Canada: A Statistical Profile*, produced by Canadian Justice Statistics, 31–37. Ottawa: Statistics Canada, 2000.

Lucashenko, M. "Violence against Indigenous Women: Public and Private Dimensions." *Violence against Women* 2, no. 4 (1996): 378–390.

Matthews, J. M. "A Vietnamese Flag and a Bowl of Australian Flowers: Recomposing Racism and Sexism." *Gender, Place and Culture* 4, no. 1 (1997): 5–18.

Mitchell, C., and J. Reid-Walsh. *Researching Children's Popular Culture*. London: Routledge, 2002.

Miles, R. *Racism*. London and New York: Routledge, Key Idea Series, 1989.

Miller, B. D. "Precepts and Practices: Researching Identity Formation among Indian Hindu Adolescents in the United States." *New Directions for Child Development* 67 (1995): 71–85.

Narayan, U. *Dislocating Cultures/Identities, Traditions and Third World Feminism*. London and New York: Routledge, 1997.

Onder, Z. "Muslim-Turkish Children in Germany: Socio-cultural Problems." *Migration World Magazine* 24, no. 5 (1996): 18–24.

Razack, S. H. *Looking White People in the Eye, Gender, Race, and Culture in Courtrooms and Classrooms*. Toronto.: University of Toronto Press, 1998.

Rodgers, K. B. "Wife Assault: The Findings of a National Survey." *Juristat* 14, no. 9 (1994). http://www.hc-sc.gc.ca/hppb/familyviolence/html/femnational_e.html.

Rosenthal, D., N. Ranieri, and S. Klimidis. "Vietnamese Adolescents in Australia: Relationships between Perceptions of Self and Parental Values, Intergenerational Conflict, and Gender Dissatisfaction." *International Journal of Psychology* 31, no. 2 (1996): 81–91.

Van Dijk, T. *Elite Discourse and Racism*. California: Sage, 1993.

Vertinsky, P., I. Batth, and M. Naidu. "Racism in Motion: Sport, Physical Activity and the Indo-Canadian Female." *Avante* 2, no. 3 (1996): 1–23.

CHAPTER TWELVE

"Losers, Lolitas, and Lesbos": Visualizing Girlhood

Shannon Walsh

> Who would ever think that so much can go on in the soul of a young girl?
>
> —Sally Mann, *At Twelve*

By the time I hit twelve, I was certain I had the world all sorted out. Growing up in a middle-sized city in Ontario, Canada, I had lots of opportunity to dream about the many mysteries that lay beyond the city limits. The world yawned open before me. I felt as though I was already a part of it, yet at the same time, I was still far 'too young' to engage with the real world. I raged inside when labeled a mere 'child.' I felt I could not shake the adult world's condescension, and no amount of shouting and protesting seemed to make any difference. In reaction, I dived into books to fill in the other side of the conversations that adults or older teens did not want to have with me. In the cultural representations around me I saw only the children of television sit-coms or the teenagers full with brimming sexuality, conflicts, confidence, and violence—like those found in Judy Blume novels, Betty and Veronica comics, or John Hughes teen movies like *Sixteen Candles* and *The Breakfast Club*. Neither of these representations reflected the moment I was in—the tween space. I knew I was not just 'between' something—I was in the middle of it.

Remembering who I was during that turbulent period gives me pause to reflect on how the tween girl is represented today. Who is this in-between girl? In the Western visual representation the tween rests somewhere between a cocky explorer and a sensual princess. Lewis Carroll's Alice gazes at us, bold and inquisitive, from beyond the Looking Glass. The tween is 'the only girl on the boy's summer softball team' in Sally Mann's photographic portraits of girls in her hometown in Virginia. Frankness, innocence, and androgyny are set out against long stares and outthrust hips.

At eleven, the tween girl is Dawn Wiener, "sometimes hated, often reviled, [and] seldom understood" (Solondz 1992: introduction). The awkward central character in the feature film *Welcome to the Dollhouse*, she bumbles her way through failed first loves and hallway bullies with a witty defiance and gall even when the cheerleaders call her 'lesbo.' We find her in Hellen van Meene's portraits of girls in Holland: a tween sullen and listless, yet defiant and independent.

As Chris Townsend muses, "Perhaps we do not construct our children in our own image, we construct our children in our images of them" (1998: 14). And our images of them construct innocence in flux, a space of contradiction and change. Sexual and social scripts are being written, and in our mind's eye, we see the woman lurking within the girl strain and contort with internal growing pains. While she is sometimes represented as the ideal strong and independent woman, the tween girl is also represented as locked in a state of unabashedness about her own prowess and womanhood, sometimes not quite understanding the social script she is meant to play or choosing to ignore it.

Ann Higonnet (1998) points out that images have been used to create cultural and social understandings of children and adolescents from paintings to photography and film. It is through visual culture that I wish to situate my investigation into the pre-adolescent girl both in the way she has been represented and the meaning we can glean from that representation. In the works I explore in this chapter, the pre-adolescent girl occupies a particular space—within and beyond that of the girl-child or the adolescent girl. I am calling her an 'outsider' tween—the tween who contests our notions of childhood and innocence and defines a space that is very much her own.

In her book, *Picturing Innocence*, Ann Higonnet argues that childhood has been represented in visual modes throughout the modern period as pure and innocent. She maintains that the collective fantasy of idyllic innocence is undergoing a crisis of representation since the 1990s as visual culture increasingly dominates Western lives. Children are no longer represented as blank slates of innocence: from jean ads to high art, children are being pictured as violent, sexual, hurt, sensual, knowing. Higonnet reminds us that, "the change…seems dangerously unfamiliar because it is so visual" (1998: 8). Thus, it is necessary to look to the visual in order to uncover what this change means for tween girls. In this chapter, I draw extensively on Higonnet's understanding of the shifting representation of childhood and, in turn, girlhood.

Of course, visual culture exists on multiple levels of understanding and creation. I draw on Annette Kuhn's understanding of "texts as producers of meanings, as producing meaning in the moment of reading," in which the "reader is inserted into the meanings produced by the text and is thus in a sense produced by them" (Kuhn 1982/1994: 12). This dynamic conception of reading a text (in this case film as text and photograph as text) will allow us to investigate the way that meaning is inscribed and proscribed through an active relationship to culture, reading, and readership.[1] This 'reading' is also complicated through the performative nature of tween representations (Mavor 1995). The girls themselves lend an additional component to their images through performative relationships towards the image-maker. These performative aspects of representation are discussed in the work of Carol Mavor, Roland Barthes, Craig Owens, and Peggy Phelan amongst others. Self-representation can be further unearthed when we consider that mothers, friends, or family members are often the ones creating images of girls (such as in the work of Hellen van Meene, Sally Mann, and Collier Schorr, and, of course, the thousands of images of girls made for family albums and snapshots). In that context, we can imagine the space and comfort to 'create' the self must be tangibly present. Keeping these various intersections of reading and performance in mind, I turn to the texts.

Welcome to the Dollhouse: Pre-Adolescence in Crisis

Todd Solondz's dark film about junior high school life follows Dawn Wiener, an eleven-year-old bumbling through the horrors and agonies of being a girl loser. *Welcome to the Dollhouse* is an intelligent film, one that leaves us both sympathizing with and disliking the main character, Dawn. Dawn is not a pretty, put-together young Miss. She is hung up on her life, often mean, , unpopular and uncomfortable in her own skin. She is also cocky, cynical, presumptuous, and outspoken. Dawn is most definitely an outsider tween— she is a loner, an independent agent with little or no access to 'normal' girlhood.

With *Welcome to the Dollhouse*, Solondz hit on a version of girlhood that many parents were uncomfortable with. As he writes in the introduction to the screenplay for *Dollhouse*:

Although there is no sex, nudity, or violence in the movie, many parents were re-
luctant, if not unwilling, to allow their children to participate in it.... [We] described
the material as 'unsettling,' prompting some of the parents to retort, 'sick' or 'depressing,' which I took as a compliment, as that reflected the world I was trying to
portray. (1992: introduction)

Girlhood, especially tween girlhood, was not meant to be sick or depressing.
It was suppose to be full of pink flowers, dollhouses, and laughter. In fact,
Dawn's younger sister, Missy, is exactly the image of the perfect, innocent
girl that adults wanted so much to believe in. Dawn embodies Higonnet's
idea of a shift in representation insofar as she is always undesirable, never
innocent, often shunned (even by her own parents). This shift sits against a
modern visual precedent in which "children could only become desirable if
they were genuinely believed to be innocent" (Higonnet 1998: 132). The tension between Missy and Dawn captures the crisis of visualizing the girl.
Missy fits into our understood notions of childhood, while Dawn departs
from them. She exists outside the existing representation.

The ease with which Missy glides through life brings Dawn close to
murderous impulses towards her 'perfect' sister. Her ill wishes fatefully
manifest when Missy is kidnapped partially due to Dawn's negligence. The
kidnapping itself seems to allow Solondz to poke more fun at our idealized
version of girlhood, as the faultless Missy is whisked away by a 'regular
family man who would often dress up as Santa at Christmas' who tapes her
doing pirouettes in his basement. Solondz draws on both our fears of the
violation of a perfect innocence as well as the melodrama of American culture hyperconcerned with the child-snatcher lurking in the shadows:

DAWN   Did he rape her?
MARK   Nah. I think he videotaped her doing some pirouettes, but that's it.
DAWN   Is she in the hospital?
MARK   No, she's here. And she's the same. Y'know, actually, I think she may
       have liked being there, 'cause she had her own TV and total control over
       the pusher. And she also got to have as much candy and McDonald's as
       she wanted. (1992: 82)

In fact, it was Dawn who had narrowly escaped a rape and was now alone on
the streets of New York. Yet her troubles are seen as minimal compared with
the potential for horror experienced by Missy, the idyllic girl.

We can analyze Dawn's various romantic misadventures through Mary
Beth Haralovich's discussion of the way in which dominant cinema finds

narrative closure through "a resolution of enigmas centering on heterosexual courtship" (cited in Kuhn 1982/1994: 34). Haralovich explains, "[If] a woman is in a non-normative role…she will cede that control to a man by the end of the film. Romantic love seems to be the normative role which most strongly influences her decision" (ibid.). As Kuhn points out, "not only, then, is the woman recuperated into the male/female bond by the closures of these films (Dalton), but the courtship process itself constitutes a structuring element of their entire narratives" (1982/1994: 34). In this understanding, Dawn is being read as a woman despite the fact that she is far from being a woman yet. Her conflict in courtship exists as a counterpoint to her young age.

Through looking at these dominant storyline constructions, we see how the outsider tween represented in the character of Dawn is thrust into a narrative ideal that she can never fully realize. Dawn must wrestle with the fact that it is through romantic, heterosexual love that she will be normalized (both in the film and in her own narrative reality), yet this is forever beyond her reach. The outsider tween is powerful only in her adoption of adult female norms, and so her inability to access those norms leaves her isolated and alone. In contrast with the way pre-adolescents and children have typically been represented, again we see Dawn as a sexual being, although still somewhat innocent given her limited experience.

While this narrative moment may be seen as a transition period in Dawn's life to some readers, I would argue that this moment is a defining aspect of the outsider tween's dilemma, one that puts her beyond the realm of a completed normative narrative. *Welcome to the Dollhouse* both reaffirms her confined position as outsider, while at the same time, causes us to question the very premise that this narrative is structured upon. One of *Welcome to the Dollhouse*'s strengths comes from the way it takes advantage of dominant forms of narrative cinema, but still manages to twist and play with them. The film gives us both the modern version of girlhood (in the character of Missy) and the post-modern tween girl (in Dawn). The tensions between the two girls are also the tensions within a society that is still coming to terms with the gritty details of girls' experiences and sexuality. The implicit irony in the film and its dark, post-modern humor cast Dawn as an anti-hero in a hopeless quest bound for failure.

What pushes Dawn Wiener's narrative misery forward centers around her (un)desirability to various male characters throughout the film. Her sexuality is constantly at the crux of her agony. Again, it is important to draw attention to the fact that Solodnz chose to represent an eleven-year-old girl as a sexual being—it is part of her narrative and part of her persona, even though she is unsuccessful at fulfilling her sexual quests. These 'less-than-Kodak' moments (Higonnet 1998) are part of what resonates within the film and within pre-adolescent representation—the dirty details better left out of sight and out of mind.

The film begins with Dawn being teased as a 'lesbo.' She proves her heterosexuality through a series of 'frustrated love affairs' with boys, yet her queered self remains part of her ugly identity throughout the film—unfeminine, awkward, and unwanted—an unsuccessful girl.

Throughout *Welcome to the Dollhouse,* we trace Dawn's overwhelming hopelessness at not being an innocent tween girl—the role of the 'right-kind-of-girl' that her sister masters so effortlessly. Dawn is silent about what goes on inside her. She has learned that her complaints get her nowhere. Her 'ugliness,' distasteful nature, and lack of childish innocence make those around her, including her parents and siblings, assume an attitude that tells her she deserves no better.

Hellen van Meene: An Ordinary Girl

Hellen van Meene[2] presents us with an emergent sexuality in her photographic portraits of girls who maintain traces of childhood. Her subjects are awkward, small-town girls who seem wrapped in a struggle for feminine identity. Rather than seeming caught between childhood and adulthood, these pictures illustrate for us an identity that has vestiges of both but is neither. Much like Dawn Wiener, the tween has been abandoned by innocence. She is Higonnet's 'knowing' child, one who is "far from being psychically or sexually innocent"(1998: 12). Van Meene's pictures draw to mind the growing body of visual work that represents pre-adolescence and adolescence as a space of conflicted meaning, gender bending, and fraught realities, juxtaposed with fictions and created narratives (see the work of Collier Schorr, Sarah Jones, and others).

The girls van Meene photographs are almost always depicted alone. Something in their postures speaks to a very stark individualism: a solo journey within the self. This representation seems to be a key aspect of the tween—the struggle for individuality but also a reference to an individuality fully defined. A self that is anxious, lonely, awkward, and emotional. These pictures, too, are of outsider tweens.

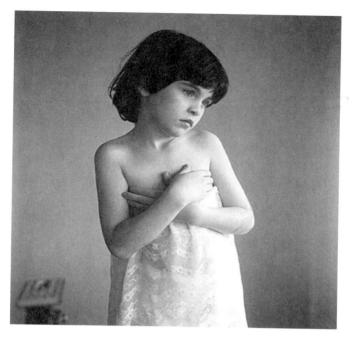

Figure 12.1 Untitled, Hellen van Meene

Figure 12.2 Untitled, Hellen van Meene

In van Meene's *Botticelli in the Lowlands* series a chubby girl rests her head on a windowsill, her eyes cast down at the dull white paint on the window frame.[3] In another portrait a girl looks sadly into the camera, her knee flung over a lone metal bar, her cheek on her leg and hair falling across her shoulders. Another striking portrait (figure 12.1) presents us with a girl of nine or ten, hair cut in a childish bowl, who crosses her arms around her (as yet) undefined breasts, holding up a thin nightie. Her head is slightly bent in the style of a turn-of-the-century oil portrait and her eyes cast off frame. She seems quite old with her look of absent complacence, her sullen gaze.

There is a sense in these portraits of a girlhood quite fraught, sensual, awkward, and graceful. The pictures draw forth a very contradictory and complex styling of the tween years, one that rings uncomfortably true. Perhaps this emerges from van Meene's closeness to her subjects. She was still an adolescent when she began photographing girls she knew from her hometown of Alkmaar in the North of Holland. As she has said of her working process, "the 'best' kind of adult is one who is able to keep some bond with childhood, and this bridge is adolescence" (MOCP 2004: n.p.). The sense of a performative aspect of girls' self-representation seems especially poignant in these pictures and draws to mind other photographers who work in the same vein, such as Wendy Ewald's work with children, and Collier Shorr's photographic work with her niece, Karin, and Karin's community of friends.

Again it is useful to think of Higonnet's discussion of the multiple meanings that intersect in representations of girls, retaining perhaps traces of innocence but mixing as well with meanings of sexuality, loss, longing, violence and politics. (Higonnet 1998: 148) The girls in van Meene's portraits occupy a space of identity that is very particular to a certain moment in their lives. They are not Spice Girls. They are not cheerleaders. While certainly part of the reason that their time/space seems fraught comes from their struggles with the onrush of adulthood, it is not only adulthood that preoccupies their quiet spaces and sulky glances. The portraits attest to something outside the version of childhood and womanhood that we find comfortable and familiar.

As in all transformation, there is an element of sadness. Something very familiar, very comforting is being left behind for the unknown, which beckons her, siren-like and irresistible. She is, as Rilke observed, seated before her own heart's curtain. It allows the tiniest peek (Mann 1988: 22)

One of van Meene's portraits (figure 12.2) seems like a character study for Dawn Wiener. The image depicts an unnamed girl who wears an ill-fitting red tracksuit. Her back leans against a long thin tree. Her bright red track top is zipped around the tree behind her, effectively locking her to it. The tree holds her back straight like a puppet, though her head dangles forward with a look of dejection. The picture seems like a macabre play in which the girl is the school dunce, trapped in a corner. It brings to mind the ritual humiliations of junior high. Did some ill-meaning boys rope her to this tree? Is the tree her support in the midst of the rejection of being a not-so-pretty girl? The image is puzzling and disturbing: a perverse look into the outsider girl who is not often pictured at all. The girls in these portraits seem less on their way somewhere else than utterly confined to their present state.

Bruises, bad complexions, awkwardly applied make-up, and bleached hair are all exposed to view. These details, and others more troubling, are corporeal reminders that van Meene's models are real girls who, like the rest of us, are imperfect as human specimens (MCOP 2004: n.p.).

What is interesting in these portraits is that the girls are only partially trying to fit into the glossy magazine image of glamour, style, and intellectual power that is associated with teen girls and women. The girls are on their own trip, watching where it will take them, as yet unafraid of their androgyny, their isolation. They reside in a space outside childhood but still are unable or unwilling to enter the space of adulthood. They retain their traces of innocence and mingle them with their reflexivity, sure postures, and inquiring glances. They seem at once strong-minded and at the same time vulnerable. They stare out at us with a banality and thoughtfulness — they return our gaze.

Sally Mann: *At Twelve*

What knowing watchfulness in the eyes of a twelve-year-old...at once guarded, yet guileless. She is the very picture of contradiction: on the one hand diffident and ambivalent, on the other forthright and impatient; half pertness and half pout. (Mann 1988: 14)

A young girl stands staring at the camera. A tall man in a black suit (her father?) wraps a protective arm around her from behind. They stand on the mini-porch of a dollhouse, surrounded by ridiculously tiny chairs and tables set with china. His head is hidden in the shadows. She stretches one arm to rest on the doorframe behind her, opposite foot balanced casually on her knee. She gazes listlessly, longingly, at the camera. The image is part of Sally Mann's series *At Twelve: Portraits of Young Women*. It is an untitled work perhaps best referred to by the Lewis Carroll quote Mann has placed on the page opposite the portrait: "Fringe of the Shadow of Sorrow" (1988: 152).

Mann writes, "Repeatedly, I found girls like her who, despite the protective postures that their parents and society assume, already have begun to shoulder the weight of adult reality"(1988: 52). Her portraits of tween girls are at once gorgeous and disquieting. They speak to girls' toughness and defiance but also their fears, their burdens, their conflicts.

Sally Mann's photographic work of her own young children and of girls from her environment has drawn both reverence and controversy for more than a decade. Tracing her own children's growth towards adolescence in sensual large- format black and white images, Mann has often had to justify whether this staged and sensualized approach to children is appropriate—both in the realm of art and in the realm of parenting. As Higonnet asks:

> Had [Mann], consciously or unconsciously, exploited their family intimacy to create sensational images that would further her own career? Had she sold her children's bodies to cater to an abusive public, just as surely as any advertiser or sports agent, or even as any pornographer? (1998: 196)

Mann's photographs evoke society's fear of representing girlhood as sexual, of the appropriate positioning of photographer to subject, especially in cases when the photographer is actually the intimate friend, relative, or mother of the child depicted. From family album snapshots to Hollywood films, representations of children and girls are guarded by adults' desire to represent childhood in a particular, often glossed over, ideal. Essentially, it is a childhood free of pain, violence, trauma, sex, and politics. As we saw in van Meene's and Solondz's work, images like Mann's disrupt a static version of childhood in which children and pre-adolescents fill an idyllic, modern understanding of innocence, both psychologically and sexually.

In 1988, Mann produced a collection of portraits of girls around the age of twelve who lived in her community. *At Twelve* is an intimate glimpse into the contradictions of tween girlhood. Photographed in Mann's hometown of Virginia, the images sit ambiguously between being staged and being captured moments of lives lived. The tween girl is represented (by Mann and by the girls' own performative self-representation) both with love and with objective observation through a number of juxtapositions—from boyish to feminine, sensual to innocent, from object to subject. The images again test the boundaries of how we conceptualize the tween girl.

In Mann's portrayals of her own children, the contradictions and tensions of girlhood are constantly at the surface of her images. For example, in *The New Mothers*, two girls between the ages of four and eight pose for the camera. They stand in "provocative and defiant positions" and look "much more like young women" than children (Mitchell, Walsh and Larkin 2004). The elder holds a cigarette in her left hand, hip outthrust towards the camera, right hand casually and elegantly poised on her baby stroller's handle. The younger stands defiant, hand on her hip and head cocked at a don't-mess-with-me angle. Higonnet observes:

> Mann's work is not easy to look at. Whether in confrontational or visionary modes, her images upset cherished conventions of idyllic childhood. A photograph like her *New Mothers* (1989) drives cuteness into bankruptcy. Some right elements are there: the ruffled print dresses, the jolly dolls, the two sisters out together playing mommy. Some wrong elements are there too: the cigarette, the Lolita heart-glasses, and above all the tough stances, turned to us in harsh sunlight (1998: 204–205).

At play here is the tension between the way that "the community often wishes to see young people—innocent as in non-sexual and in need of protection (from sex itself)—as opposed to the way young people actually are" (Mitchell and Reid-Walsh: 2002). These images disrupt our stereotypes while also presenting us with young women who are, at this moment in their lives, strong and fearless. It is also their lack of complacence, their unwavering selfhood, and quest for self-definition that disturbs our ideas of young women in need of guidance—in need of adults.

This tension is not easily resolved at a time when young women are the fastest-growing group world wide vulnerable to HIV infection, both due to their biological vulnerability, gender inequality, and sexual violence (UNICEF, UNAIDS and WHO 2002: 17). Girls are in serious need of information about safe sexual practices, yet this can only be effectively achieved through an acknowledgment of their existing sexuality. Attempting to protect girls from sex and, in turn trying to protect ourselves from seeing young women as sexual beings can quite easily have grave, even deadly, consequences. In fact, it may only be through an acknowledgment of girls' sexuality, both in visual modes as well as educational contexts, that we can actually 'protect' girls. Protecting the images of sexualized girls from the public gaze emerges from a fear of sexual predators but also of girls' latent sexual desires, one which many parents and adults hope will remain idle.

Real children seem to be endangered when photographs imply, however ambiguously, that children are not completely sexually innocent or when photographs allow predatory adult sexual projections onto children. For the last two centuries, the social protection of children has been based on the assumption of their innocence, an innocence whose sexual component turns out to be crucial and whose credibility turns out to depend rather more on images than we had realized. (Higonnet 1998: 133)

Images are not reality, but they create a certain understanding of reality in their representations. How can we understand protectionism in an age where sex is potentially deadly? Girls are having sex at increasingly younger ages, and a continued denial of this reality may potentially endanger their very survival. Our representations also must meet with a reality where some girls are sexually active. (UNICEF, UNAIDS and WHO 2002: 11)

Mann's luscious photographs of her children's beautiful bodies, bloody noses, and sullen gazes challenge us with their truthfulness. They confront our expectations and stereotypes and force us to recognize in them children who *are* sexual beings, tweens who *are* comfortable in their bodies, and girls who have not yet learned to turn the gaze away. It seems an easy criticism to level at Mann that she is being negligent to portray her children as sexual beings for the world to see (and implicit in this criticism: 'for men to locate, stalk, or potentially abduct'). This moral panic must be tempered with a look at the images themselves, at the way in which these girls are not being created as passive objects but as active agents in their own depictions. No amount of coaxing could thrust out that hip just so, lend that gaze its penetration, and set that mouth in defiance. These girls are real tweens, and tweens are rugged, strong, defiant, sexual, beautiful, awkward, uncertain, and confident. They are a bundle of contradictions- and changes. To disregard the actual and perfomative aspects of girls' self-representation blinds us to a deeper understanding of the tween.

Mann's work has an oscillating relationship with the 'real.' Her large-format camera affords no spontaneity, necessitating complicity and performance from her subjects. As Craig Townsend writes about Mann's work, "the 'natural' flow of childhood is interrupted to fix a particular performance, perhaps instigated by the adult, perhaps one in which the child is complicit"

(1998: 16). The element of performance adds to an already dense meaning etched onto the girls' bodies.

In the *At Twelve* series, Mann plays with the contradictions of girlhood through a group of portraits that defy standard representations of childhood. *The Only Girl on the Boys' Summer Softball Team* (1988) leans sensually against a brick wall. She dangles her bat behind her, eyes closed, hip out-thrust in dirtied baseball pants, hair stuck in sweaty curls around her face. She is a young girl, but her androgyny, her sensuality, and her independence—her contradictions—arrest the viewer: "She disarms me with her sure sense of her own attractiveness and, with it, her direct, even provocative approach to the camera. Impossibly, she is both artless and sophisticated; and child and yet a woman" (Mann 1988: 14).

The Mann girls' raw sensuousness set them, too, outside our conceived notions of girlhood. While perhaps they could be seen as standard visions of beautiful girls, the ownership they display in relation to their own sexualities and identities has caused controversy and discomfort in viewers. Again, we see that the 'normative' version of girlhood, which rests on a supine and modest femininity, is rocked and shaken by images of girls who transgress. I would argue along with Cindy Patton that part of the trouble for adults and parents with this kind of frank sexualization (and the acknowledgment of the sexuality) of young people is the latent threat that their innocent children might somehow "so easily go queer" (1996: 37). In this case I wish to play with Patton's meaning of queer to suggest that queer is not only the bullying 'lesbo' comments, but also implies the queering of identity, an identity that is transgressive, and breaks the boundaries of what is socially comfortable. [4]

Visualizing Girlhood

As Higonnet argues, representation has become "more emotionally resonant than it had been, not losing its meanings of innocence but also acquiring others, exchanging and mingling commercial, sexual, and political forms of power in an increasingly tight knot of private and public forces" (1998: 148). Understanding this, it is vital to develop a more extensive analysis and deconstruction of visual culture in order to understand pre-adolescent girlhood. The works looked at here continually evoke the shift in representation that pictures children (and pre-adolescents) as somehow outside innocence. It is not always a comfortable transition and can bring to the fore the real-life spaces of child pornography and violence against young people. Under these conditions, analyzing the changing state of depiction becomes a question of vital relevance. In these cases, visual representations are seen as powerful transformers and instigators in a society that may so easily step out of bounds.

An image is not reality, but it is part of a construction of reality that influences the society in which it is created. Images of tweens abound in contradictions and tensions. Tweens are not just 'in between' but they *are* somewhere. And that somewhere is an interesting, difficult, personal, and conflicted space. A more rigorous integration of the way that tweens have been visually constructed is necessary if we are to understand the position that they occupy in Western culture. The visual is important not only in defining for adults where these girls exist but also for the girls themselves in juxtaposing their self image with the images 'out there'. It is critical that we take the time to examine the visual culture of tween girls and the particular position that they occupy in girlhood studies more generally.

Notes

[1] Angela McRobbie has also leant a great deal of insight into the idea of girls as 'readers' in her text, *Feminism and Youth Culture* (2000). While this chapter will not explore how girls are actually reading these texts, I think it is important to keep in mind that my analysis is limited without girls' own input. Further insight into how girls themselves view these images and films would allow us to unpack how resonant they are to 'real' tweenhood.

[2] For more examples of van Meene's work, go to http://www.hellenvanmeene.com/photos/.

[3] See http://www.postmedia.net/01/vanmeeneB.htm.

[4] Think, for example, of girl video artist Thirza Cuthand. In her work, she challenges and takes up notions of 'queer.' Cuthand's self-identification as a lesbian is a major subject of her work and has allowed her to explore the 'lesbo' comments in a very direct way. The Saskatchewan- born Cree girl started making films about herself and her own struggles with identity while she was still a girl of sixteen. Her work is interesting in how it shows us that girls *are* sexual beings, that they are active agents in their own self-representation, and that they are challenging female stereotypes. For more information about Cutland's work, see http://www.videopool.org/frameset/index.htm.

References

Higonnet, A. *Picturing Innocence: The History and Crisis of Ideal Childhood.* London: Thames and Hudson, 1998.

Kuhn, A. *Women's Pictures: Feminism and Cinema*, 2nd edition. London and New York: Verso, 1982/1994.

Mann, S. *At Twelve: Portraits of Young Women.* Turin, Italy: Aperture, 1988.

Mavor, C. *Pleasures Taken: Performances of Sexuality and Loss in Victorian Photographs.* Durham: Duke University Press, 1995.

McRobbie, A. *Feminism and Youth Culture.* New York: Routledge, 2000.

Mitchell, C., and J. Reid-Walsh. *Researching Children's Popular Culture.* London & New York: Routledge Taylor Francis, 2002.

Mitchell, C., S. Walsh, and J. Larkin. "Visualizing the Politics of Innocence in the Age of AIDS." *Sex Education* 4, no. 1 (2004): 35–47.

Museum of Contemporary Photography [MOCP] (2004) "Hellen van Meene." in *The Museum of Contemporary Photography's Exhibitions Catalogue.*Chicago:MOCP, 2002.http://www.mocp.org/mocp062500/viewhellen.htm.

Patton, C. *Fatal Advice: How Safe-sex Education Went Wrong.* Durham, London: Duke University Press, 1996.

Solondz, T. *Welcome to the Dollhouse: The Screenplay.* Boston and London: Faber and Faber, 1996.

Townsend, C. *Vile Bodies: Photography and the Crisis of Looking.* Munich and New York: Prestel-Verlag, 1998.

UNICEF, UNAIDS, and WHO. *Young People and HIV: Opportunity in Crisis.* New York: United Nations Children's Fund, Joint United Nations Program on HIV/AIDS, World Health Organization, 2002.

PART III

Marketing Girlhood/ Consuming Girlhood

CHAPTER THIRTEEN

In a Girlie World: Tweenies in Australia

Anita Harris

Introduction

Tween culture includes many elements that bring together youth, femaleness, and consumption in a distinctive combination. This culture can be discerned in pop music, TV shows, magazines and websites, fashion, make up and accessory lines, and youth products such as games and toys. It engages pre-teen girls as entitled to a culture of their own that distinguishes them both from boys their own age and older females as well as situating them as sophisticated and often sexualized consumers. Here I argue that it is in the intertwining of these last two features that tweenie becomes problematic for feminist theorists, although these are often negotiated deftly by girls themselves. I suggest that the main criticisms of tweenie: that it sexualizes girls and that it commodifies girls' identities and cultures, reveal as much about the changing construction of girlhood in late modernity as they do about issues facing girls in negotiating young, female identities in a consumer-oriented and hetero-sexualizing environment. My objective is to open up a conversation about the uses, problems, and pleasures of 'tween cultures' for girls and for those who study them. Rather than develop a single position on either the value or problem of tweenie, I attempt to unpack why it engages both young consumers and older researchers at this moment.

The key question that forms the basis of this inquiry into tweenie in the Australian context is what developmental and classist assumptions lie behind panics about this phenomenon? I conduct my exploration mainly by looking at the September 2003 issues of three Australian tween magazines: *Barbie, Total Girl,* and *Australian Girlz Klub*. I also include reflections offered by a nine-year-old Australian girl, Elena, who reads these magazines and is knowledgeable about tweenie culture more broadly, to enhance and complicate my analysis. Elena's thoughts are not, of course, intended to be illustrative of all girls' views and are not presented here to be read as research data. Rather, she offered her opinions, in a role perhaps best described as a one-person reference group, when I was mulling over these issues, and our conversations deeply influenced my analysis of tweenie.

Tween Culture in Australia

Just as in other Western countries, Australia has seen changes in the representation and experiences of pre-teenagers that have contributed to a distinctive identity for this cohort. Tween culture has formed, and been formed by, these changes. These include earlier onset of puberty, greater responsibilities in the family and at school, and an increase in personal income. For example, a recent survey of Australian children found that the average twelve-year-old has about $17 per week at their disposal (Robinson 2002).[1] Girls aged 5–12 years old average between $5 and $20 per week in pocket money (Nikas 1998). Along with this, they are both influential on family purchases such as groceries or holiday choices and have considerable 'pester power' in terms of convincing parents of their need for particular products and clothes that they cannot afford to buy from their own money. In some markets, such as the US, tweens have been found to have more discretionary purchasing power than both younger children *and* older adolescents, and one third do the family's weekly grocery shopping (see Simpson, Douglas and Schimmel 1998; they define tweens as 12–14-year-olds). Tweens have emerged as a demographic in their own right as previously adult experiences and interests such as sexuality, popular culture, money, and the occupation of public space are pushed back further and further into youth. Tween popular culture draws on and contributes to these changes by offering specific products and services for girls in the pre-teen age bracket who are now apparently interested in personal appearance and sexual attractiveness, like to shop for themselves, and experience a public identity in shopping malls, the Internet, and through images of girls like them in the media. Tween is, however, fundamentally a marketing device to create a consumer cohort out of these girls. Because of this, tween culture in Australia does not have a distinctive local identity—in fact, to do so would be to undermine a fundamental element of its function. As Catherine Driscoll (2002: 282) argues,

> The globalization of certain modes of production/consumption demands stable cross-cultural categories that could be used to explain how people could be brought

to consume products not differentiated along specific cultural lines. By constructing certain consumer groups as innately, naturally, interested in specific products it is possible to sell an idea of belonging to groups, such as girls, which can cross cultural boundaries although they do not always do so.

Tween culture itself has specific cultural reference points and origins but presents the tween world as a total system in which these specificities become universalized. The products, images, and heroes of tweenies do not differ significantly across national boundaries because they are selling a fantasy of global girlness and a mythical belonging to a community of like-minded girlfriends, which is supposed to be equally accessible to all girls around the world. As tweenie is a subset of a globalized youth market, it is sold through the same media and the same sales techniques of any youth culture that is constructed and/or utilized by multinational advertisers. For example, Australian tween magazines such as *Disney Girl, Barbie,* or *Total Girl* either are simply local versions of American or British publications or are indistinguishable in terms of content and presentation from other titles available elsewhere. These magazines promote US pop and film stars (current favorites are Reese Witherspoon and Beyonce Knowles), Disney films, and generic 'girlie' products like hair accessories, lip-gloss, and nail polish. Toys are also advertised (Shimmer Puff Fairies, Rainbow Kidz, Bratz dolls) and fashion spreads are common ("A friend asks you for fashion advice. You say: Hello! A miniskirt of course!" [*Total Girl,* September 2003]). In the construction of this generic tween world, local differences are eliminated as girls are encouraged to engage in a fantasy community with its own lingo ruled by "pink power!" and where there are "no boys allowed!" (*Total Girl*). This community is populated by friends and celebrities who sing and dance together, go on picnics, do each other's make up and outfits, ride horses, make "yummy treats" and win "brekkie dates!" (*Barbie*).

Ostensibly, only age and gender determine membership, but, in fact, class and cultural privilege saturate tweeniness. As Rachel Russell and Melissa Tyler (2002: 632) write in the context of the UK girl retail store Girl Heaven:

> Girls are invited to participate in a shared, clean, safe, bright and glittery atmosphere divorced from the messiness and apprehensions of the world outside…[this] presupposes a shared cultural experience of "girlhood." Divisions disappear, girls are girls, they are the same.

This analysis stands not only for the specific places where tween culture is performed, such as Girl Heaven but also for the tween ethic itself. Where 'difference,' especially cultural diversity, is acknowledged, it is represented merely as a yet another style that can be purchased. For example, *Total Girl* includes a quiz to ascertain "which dance diva are you?" whereby answers to questions about preference in hairstyles and fashion will determine if girls are most like pop stars Jennifer Lopez (Latina), Beyonce Knowles (African American) or Delta Goodrem (blonde, white Anglo Australian). In spite of the culturally diverse Australian population and especially the significant number of third-generation migrants of South East Asian origin, Australian tween culture reproduces an ideal of white, Anglo girlness whereby other cultural identities are either ignored or constructed as a fun, optional style.

In a Girlie World

There are two significant elements in the creation of this homogenized tween world: first, it is a girl space, and second, it is a space of consumption. Russell and Tyler (2002: 621) argue that being a young girl in contemporary consumer society means "to be a child, to be a consumer and to be feminine." Tweenie is the site within which feminine child-ness, that is, girlness, is entwined with consumption. Girlness is represented in tween sites (magazines, shops, music video clips) through the color pink; fluffy, glittery, sparkly and shimmery objects and fashions, and the use of words like 'princess,' 'fairy,' and of course, 'girl.' Girlness is also something that is inherent but can (and to some extent, ought to) be acquired through the purchase of the right products. For example, the New Zealand fashion website *fashionz* advertises clothing ranges for the over-8s with the message:

> Girls can do anything—RIGHT!—girls just want to have fun- RIGHT! So get a life- get clothes that are bright, fun and easy to wear. There are clothes out there just right for YOU. You don't need to look like a kid, you don't need to look like your mum or even your big sister.

Marking out a young female consumer identity that is not like one's mother or older sister (or younger brother) is the work of tweenie. Advertising campaigns for every imaginable product—hats, bags, clothes, toys, cosmetics, and snack foods—tap into this notion of distinctiveness about being an 8- to 12-year-old girl.

The existence of a special community marked by age and gender, which is fun loving and global, is a compelling notion. It takes the least controversial aspects of 'girlpower' and offers a discourse of pleasure and confidence and a pre-made community of girlfriends to pre-teens. I would suggest that tween culture is so successful because it creates a way for girls to stake a claim for themselves as young and female. In this way, tween does the same work for young girls that female teen culture did for teenagers a decade or so ago: acknowledges them as having different interests and ideas from older females as well as boys their age. In this sense, nothing new is going on in the relation between popular culture and girls beyond a simple mechanism of downshifting in response to and as part of broader processes of juvenescence. Arguably, tweenie is merely evidence that ever-younger people are being taken seriously and given opportunities to express their desires, styles, and opinions in the public world or, at least, its markets. However, this take on tweenie, that it reflects an increasing regard for children's cultures, rights, and voice, is less common than a discourse of anxiety, represented by rising concerns about exploitation of minors and the phenomenon of 'growing up too fast.' Part of the concern about tweenies is not dissimilar to an earlier anxiety about the constitution of female teenagers as consumers, as needing to construct limited feminine identities for success, and as (hetero)sexualized at too young an age. Today, however, the 'adult-eration' of girls takes place with an ever-younger cohort. It also occurs within the context of a far more sophisticated global economy that relies heavily on a youth market for sales in the burgeoning industries of non-essential, 'lifestyle' and 'identity' goods and services.

Thus, what have caused considerable disquiet amongst feminists, social commentators, teachers, and parents are the secularization of children's identities and the commodification of their cultures. In other words, tweenie is criticized for inappropriately sexualizing girls and drawing them into a world of feminine display, artifice, and the imperative to attract male attention at far too young an age. Whereas once, young women did not have to grapple with the requirements and constraints of hetero-normative femininity until they were well into their teens, today they must confront these patriarchal realities while they are still children. Second, tweenie has been seen to trivialize, commodify, and universalize girls' cultures, reducing play, leisure, learning, fun, and friendship to the experience of purchasing a normative image of girlness and suggesting that a successful identity is achieved through consumption of the right items. However, rather than seeking to decide whether or not these criticisms are valid, here I am interested in establishing how they have been produced and where they leave a feminist analysis of girls' agency and desire for hegemonic expressions of femininity.

Too Much Too Young: Innocence Lost

One of the key concerns about tweenie is that it inappropriately positions girls as 'grown up': that is, they are inculcated into a world of money, sex, image, and lifestyle when they are in fact children who should be enjoying the innocent and more simple pleasures of a child's life experience. Chris Griffin (2001) suggests that, on the one hand, tweenies interfere with straightforward feminist analyses of the nexus of consumption and the presentation of a desirable self for the male gaze simply because they are pre-teen. That is, the purpose of their consumption cannot be to attract male attention because they are too young for (hetero)sexual encounters. However, this is complicated by the overt sexualization of children in the tweenie market, as Griffin points out in her analysis of the British pre-teen girl magazine *Mad About Boys*. As the British *Daily Telegraph* puts it, "Sex, Boys and Make-Up: Is This What Tweenie Girls Want?" (Barwick 2001). This issue has also received attention in the Australian context, partly due to the success of 8-year-old model Morgan Featherstone, who poses for fashion spreads "smoldering under a Heidi Klum-style fringe with nightclub eyes and full woman war paint" (Halfpenny 2003: 30). A recent edition of *Who* magazine declares her "too young to be 'sexy'," but also uses an image of her at "eight years old and posing like a woman" on their cover. Tweenie is thus commonly criticized for its sexualization of girls for an adult male audience.

As I have suggested, this argument has been well rehearsed in the context of earlier feminist critiques of teen girl culture and has considerable validity. However, rather than re-visiting this analysis here, I would like to add another way of looking at the issue of inappropriate grown-upness through the work of Nancy Lesko (2001). Lesko draws on Homi Bhabha's insights about modernity and temporality to illustrate how ideas about progress and the social order are produced through concepts of linear time, and in the case of her own work, through assumptions of natural, age-related stages of linear development in youth. She argues that youth is produced as a life stage in a series of progressive steps towards an adult future. Young people are therefore constructed as 'becoming' (see also Wyn and White 1997; Harris 2004).

She uses the example of teenage mothers to open up the workings of a discourse about appropriate stages towards grown-upness, arguing that the issue of teen motherhood acts as a "disjunctive moment, a moment when conceptions of adolescents and youth are revealed as 'staged' or produced" (Lesko 2001: 137). Teen mothers disrupt the orderliness of youth as a linear developmental process by acting 'out of time,' and in particular, through acts of precocious sexuality. The furor about teen mothers is in part the expression of a profound anxiety about contained, linear progress and a social order grounded in a clear demarcation between childhood and adulthood.

Lesko offers a method for examining instances of outrage over girls who act in adult ways in order that we can begin to see how normative ideas about what it is to be young and to grow up are produced. The tweenie phenomenon also acts as a disjunctive moment that reveals our assumptions about childhood and youth and shows them to be ideas that must be worked on and produced rather than natural. Part of the anxiety over tweenie is also an anxiety over the disruption of linear and controllable notions of correct ways to grow up, which are under considerable strain in current times where 'transitions' to adulthood seem much less clear and assured than they once were. The desire to keep children and teenagers 'forever young,' in Lesko's words, is a desire for adult control of young people's lives, but more than this, 'out of time' acts by girls must be worried over and punished because they stand in for broader fears about flux, insecurity, social disorder, and the breakdown of the teleological project.

The other piece of work that is useful to add to this way of perceiving the panic over tweenie is that of Valerie Walkerdine (1997). Her work suggests that the tweenie phenomenon may be an extension of the sexualization of working-class girls—itself a project with a long history—to all preteens. In other words, the positioning of young girls as sexual, as consumers of popular culture and as knowledgeable actors in an adult world of sex and money has perhaps only become problematic now because it has reached out in a process of upscaling to the white and middle class. This phenomenon itself has been going on for a long time but is only now starting to target privileged girls.

Walkerdine suggests that the coquettish little working-class girl as represented in popular culture through talent quests, movies such as *Annie,* and advertisements that invite an eroticizing gaze is an image associated with two important meanings. First, the sexual working-class girl is utilized to reveal the fiction of childhood innocence and then personally blamed for causing this corruption of cultural fantasies of childhood as a time of idyllic pre-sexuality. It is her class that brings vulgarity and overt eroticism to innocent girlhood—a state that is thereby reserved and protected as middle class. However, and perhaps controversially, Walkerdine also argues that the child-woman is an important figure of fantasy and hope in working-class female childhoods. The wish for a personal transformation through celebrity is an important means by which successful futures can be imagined. She says (1997: 154):

> These girls struggle in a world full of apparently glamorous options to 'be' some-body and that is an adult, sexual woman. Middle-class girls, as our research shows so clearly, do not need to fantasize being somebody; they are told clearly at every turn that they already are…

I would suggest that contemporary readings of tweenie are also very much class dependent. However, current times emphasize self-invention and the importance of the project of working on the self for success for all girls. Middle-class status is no longer assured through marriage or inheritance but must be secured anew by anxious families and their daughters, who are ne-gotiating a very different economic and social order from a generation ago. The importance of creating a successful 'choice biography,' in Beck's (1992) words, is brought home to all girls living in a late modern world that no longer offers fixed structures or pathways to assure an economically secure adult life. The absence of predictability and linear transitions to adulthood ushered in by late modern socio-economic conditions thus comes to bear on girls in particular ways (see Harris 2004). In this context, the fantasy of suc-cessful self-invention is no longer a purely working-class experience. More precisely, the fantasy of success through celebrity has been shifted up to the middle class in the absence of more traditional means such as inherited wealth or good marriages. It is in a world of pop stars, supermodels, actors, and entertainers that all young women are encouraged to become somebody by introjecting aspects of a glamour celebrity lifestyle into their everyday lives. Reality TV, 'search' style programs, and makeover shows all demon-strate how celebrity can become ordinary. Susan Hopkins (2002: 4) argues:

> The new hero is a girl in pursuit of media visibility, public recognition and notoriety. She wants to be somebody and 'live large.' In the postmodern world, fame has re-

placed marriage as the imagined means to realizing feminine dreams…fame is the ultimate girl fantasy.

In this context, celebrity becomes an important means of self-invention and feminine success for the middle classes, and because it is middle-class girls who are involved, tweenie (as emblematic of girlie glamour culture) has become perceived as both a new phenomenon and a dangerous one at that.

Thus the panic about tweenie may have more to do with anxieties about social change and the loss of predictability as represented in conventions about linear adolescent development and the loss of the innocent girlhood reserved for the middle classes rather than anything inherently problematic in girls' fantasies of glamour, feminine celebrity, and performance. Quite the contrary: tweenie may well be in some respects empowering for girls. As Walkerdine (1997: 183) writes:

> The popular culture place, which admits the possibility that little girls can be sexual little women, provides a place where adult projections meet the possibility for little girls of being Other than the rational child or the nurturant quasi-mother, where they can be bad. It can then be a space of immense power for little girls...

In introducing these ideas and the important work of Lesko and Walkerdine, I am not arguing that concerns about the inappropriateness of tweenie culture should be dismissed. Rather, I am suggesting that the emergence of these concerns also gives us important information about how we conceptualize and invest in female childhood and youth as meaningful to a late modern social order and how class (and ethnicity) cut across popular anxieties about 'innocence lost.'

Commodifying Girl Culture

The other major criticism of tweenie is that it commodifies girl culture and connects the achievement of a successful identity as a girl with looking the 'right' way and buying the 'right' things. Broader debates about the construction of youth as consumer citizens also touch on this idea that success and power for young people are increasingly linked to good consumption practices rather than other forms of civic engagement (Miles 2000; Côté and Allahar 1996). However, Chris Griffin suggests that the figure of the tweenie problematizes the meaning of girls' consumption as either empowering or oppressive. She says (2001):

Patriarchal cultures are relatively comfortable with the notion that female consumers
are shopping for their families, but are likely to be more unsettled by the image of
the consuming female subject, expressing and acting on her own wishes and desires.

I asked Elena what she would do if she received $100 as a gift. She said she
would put $30 in the bank and spend the rest on CDs, clothes, dolls, and
sweets. Tweenies are thus indeed managing their own money and shopping
for themselves; buying clothes, accessories, cosmetics, toys, games, music
and magazines for their own leisure. Significantly, these products are marketed directly at them as young girls, so there is no ambiguity about the intention of their shopping practices as self-focused. On the one hand, there is
something very positive about the possibility of girls proudly embracing their
young femaleness and identifying with other girls around the idea of a global
girl community. However, the reduction of this possibility to consumption is
disquieting, and as has been seen in the debate about girlpower, the political
and agentic elements of girl communities are often the first to disappear in
the process of the commodification of a 'girls rule' ethic.

What is perhaps productive in this context is to move beyond the debate
about whether tweenie, like girlpower, is 'good' or 'bad' for girls, and to
consider instead the extent to which girls are able to negotiate and positively
draw upon the pervasive and compelling consumer culture within which they
live. Bettina Fritzsche (2001) uses this approach in her analysis of the Spice
Girls, for example, concluding that the image of this girl group functions as a
'toolbox' for girls to use in their identity work, including their resistant identity work. Similarly, Russell and Tyler argue that "the intended meanings of
the producers of texts such as *Girl Heaven* seem to have only a partial impact
on girls' actual engagement with practices of consumption, childhood and
femininity" (2002: 633). Elena agrees. She says that girls her age are generally into tweenie culture. For example, she buys *Total Girl* magazine every
month and visits its website regularly; she likes to shop and to buy music and
clothes; she owns Bratz dolls and is a fan of Beyonce Knowles, Christina
Aguilera and Avril Lavigne. However, she adds that this is not *all* that she is
into. She also spends her time playing many sports, riding her bike, reading
books, playing with friends and hanging out with her family and suggests
that most of the girls her age are similarly occupied. Her interest in tweenie
does not undermine the multifaceted nature of her identity, in particular, her
ability to position herself as 'not girly' and yet still a successful girl.

Elena emphatically dismisses the idea that tweenie puts pressure on girls to look a certain way or to worry about having trendy clothes or fitting in. She also does not feel that the commodities associated with tweenie are the most important aspects of this culture. For example, even though magazines offer lip gloss, jewelry, and other trinkets as 'freebies,' she does not make her reading choice based on these giveaways. Nor does she buy things from the associated websites or pay particular attention to the places she can purchase the clothes featured in the fashion spreads. After all, her current pocket money is only $2 per week (although her parents do buy her extras like magazines—for example, *Total Girl* costs $4.40). Although she likes looking at the fashion pages and enjoys shopping for clothes, I would suggest that what is compelling to her is the girl culture that is offered rather than its associated products.

Elena seems to be suggesting that it is fun to be a girl, to be valued as a girl, and to be part of a special culture that is both female and young. Importantly, as Walkerdine suggests above, tweenie offers a space of play that gives girls possibilities outside of their positioning as 'the rational child or the nurturant quasi-mother,' and as Griffin adds, it also offers an identity of powerful, self-interested (if consumer-based) autonomy. This is not to say that Elena or other girls therefore eschew the glamour and self-making, that is, the other kinds of hegemonic femininity that are on offer in tweenie. Rather, I would suggest that they enjoy it and play with it much as older women do, and in fact, perhaps because of their age, they may be better able to incorporate this as play and take it less seriously than older women. Although children's play through dress-ups and performance is well established as gendered and gendering (see, for example, Davies 1989), it also contains possibilities for resistance, humor, excess, performance, and insight. Play is less invested in as identity work than 'serious' pursuits, which means that it may simply be more a more covert site for gender positioning but also a freer space. Pam Gilbert and Sandra Taylor (1991: 122) suggest that it is especially girls' play—as it is enacted on the sites and with the discourses of hegemonic gender positionings—that can be particularly effective as resistance. They write:

> 'Play' becomes more powerful, however, and more useful to young women, if the conventions that are being played with are linked to their discursive power bases, and to broader semiotic systems constructing gendered identities.

Tweenie offers an excessive, performative representation of young femininity that enables girls to play with its conventions.

Alternatives to Tweenie?

This being said, and although I can see the playfulness at work in dressing up, performing glamour, flicking through magazines, and so on, I remain concerned about the commodification of girl culture insofar as tweenie seems to tie identification as a girl with excessive consumption in a pop culture market of hegemonic and hetero-normative femininity. What have been some feminist solutions to this issue? One common answer to the limited subject positions offered to girls by tweenie is the creation of other cultural products for them to engage in. Feminist experiments in manufacturing alternative media and culture for girls have had mixed results.

For example, in competition with the transnational tween magazines is the local *Australian Girlz Klub* magazine. This magazine offers many of the same features as the others: quizzes, recipes, letters, and stories from readers, movie reviews and so on. Its slogan is "making friends and sharing dreams." Unlike the others, however, it has almost no content related to celebrities, fashion, or popular girl culture. Instead, it includes stories about animal welfare, interviews with female scientists, crafts and activities for girls to do, and information about girls' lives in other cultures. Its September 2003 cover features three 'regular' looking young girls of apparently Anglo and non-Anglo ethnicities in a shot that is casual and relaxed rather than posed and artificial—more like a holiday snap than a cover girl shoot. By contrast, in the same month, the cover of *Total Girl* depicts Reese Witherspoon as her *Legally Blonde* film character, and *Barbie* features the winner of its national cover girl competition, a blonde pre-teen in lipstick and eye shadow who also appears in that issue's fashion spread. Although *Australian Girlz Klub* is not explicitly feminist, it does offer a very different version of tweenie to girls than that of the consumption-oriented and image-conscious *Total Girl*.

Elena says that even though she had never seen *Australian Girlz Klub* before, it looks good and she would like to read it. She especially likes the Australian focus. If she had to choose between that and *Total Girl*, however, she would choose *Total Girl* because she is familiar with it. She added that *Total Girl* does a better job of promotion, as its cover is bright and grabs your attention. She also thinks that *Total Girl* stands out because it includes stories about celebrities. In terms of her current reading practices, she buys

Total Girl every month and checks its related website about once per week. She used to read *Barbie* but does not any more because she has outgrown it. The main attractions of *Total Girl* are that it is pitched directly at girls, and it includes the things that she is interested in, namely, fashion, movies, books, and music.

From one perspective, this preference demonstrates a feminist failure on the part of *Australian Girlz Klub* and a win on the part of the hegemony. However, as Marnina Gonick suggests, a strict dichotomization of feminist versus feminine discourses about girls and popular culture has proved unhelpful for understanding and challenging the power and pleasure of engaging in hegemonic girlness. The long history of feminist attempts to get girls to 'see the light' and understand how popular culture socializes them into subordinated femininity has been painful and to some extent misguided. Gonick says (2001: 171):

> ...as feminists, we need to rethink our sense of certainty about having 'gotten it right' once and for all. We need to find forms for our work with girls that produce a multiplicity of discourses, including some that allow for the investments girls might have in conventional expressions of femininity.

This is particularly important in the context of popular cultural forms that deliberately draw on and play with feminism itself as tweenie often does. If we cannot do as Gonick suggests, we find ourselves back in old and essentially irresolvable debates about resistance and false consciousness that deny the agency of girls, the fun of participating in conventional femininity, and the complexity of this experience as both constraining and enabling.

This chapter has been intended as an exploration rather than a strongly defended argument about the pros, or as is more typically articulated, the cons of tweenie. My feeling is that tweenie is in some respects a cause for concern but is perhaps more interesting for what it reveals about the changing construction of girlhood in late modernity and anxieties generated by these changes. Although I cannot therefore conclude with a resolution, I do offer an idea about moving feminist analysis of tweenie forward. I asked Elena what part of *Total Girl* she tended to look at first. She said she always turned to the "Jessie's diary" section, an ongoing serial-type story written in diary form about everyday events in a girl's life. This is an interactive feature whereby readers can go to a website and write what they would like to see happen next, and the story's development is shaped by their suggestions. As

Gilbert and Taylor (1991: 126) argue, this kind of activity is commendable as a feminist pedagogical tool, because it enables girls to engage actively and directly with the discursive conventions of feminine story lines. They write, "once the stability and apparent permanence of a story are disrupted, then the conventions that have held it together can be unpacked, re-read and then re-written." Without wanting to overwork the metaphor, I believe that at the very least, older feminists need to listen carefully to the multiple story lines girls write for themselves, including those that incorporate tweenie props and plots (see Gonick 2003). This involves recognizing an important shift in young feminine identities that is offered by tweenie, one that allows girls to move from a purely passive position to one of active protagonist, from consumer and 'reader' of popular culture to agent and 'writer.' To recognize this is not to concede defeat in the face of patriarchal pop culture but to take seriously the ways tweenie offers girls an agentic, albeit limited, subject position that they are able to negotiate and play with.

Notes

Many thanks to Elena for our conversations about tweenie and to Jacqui Reid-Walsh for her editorial suggestions.

[1] As of November 29, 2004 one Australian dollar is worth approximately 78.5 US cents and 41.4 UK pence. http://www.xe.com/ucc/convert.cgi

References

Barwick, S. "Sex, Boys and Make-Up: Is This What Tweenie Girls Want?" *Daily Telegraph*, February 8, 2001.

Beck, U. *Risk Society: Towards a New Modernity.* London: Sage, 1992.

Côté, J. E., and A. L. Allahar. *Generation on Hold.* New York: NYU Press, 1996.

Davies, B. *Frogs and Snails and Feminist Tales.* Sydney: Allen and Unwin, 1989.

Driscoll, C. *Girls: Feminine Adolescence in Popular Culture and Cultural Theory.* New York: Columbia University Press, 2002.

FashioNZ. "Girl Power". In Fashion New Zealand. ChristChurch, NZ: FashioNZ. http://www.fashionz.co.nz/designers/article/2053.html

Fritzsche, B. "Spicy Strategies: Pop Feminist and Other Empowerments in Girl Culture." In *All About the Girl: Power, Culture and Identity*, edited by A. Harris. Routledge: New York, 2004.

Gilbert, P., and S. Taylor. *Fashioning the Feminine: Girls, Popular Culture and Schooling.* Sydney: Allen and Unwin, 1991.

Gonick, M. "What Is the 'Problem' with These Girls?: Youth and Feminist Pedagogy." *Feminism and Psychology* 11, no. 2 (2001): 167–171.

Gonick, M. *Between Femininities*. Albany: SUNY Press, 2003.

Griffin, C. "Good Girls, Bad Girls: Anglo-centrism and Diversity in the Constitution of Contemporary Girlhood." In *All About the Girl: Power, Culture and Identity*, edited by A. Harris, Routledge: New York, 2004.

Halfpenny, K. "Way Too Little Women." *Who*, August 25 2003, 30–33.

Harris, A. *Future Girl: Young Women in the Twenty-First Century*. New York: Routledge, 2004.

Hopkins, S. *Girl Heroes: The New Force in Popular Culture*. Annandale, Australia: Pluto Press, 2002.

Lesko, N. *Act Your Age!* New York: RoutledgeFalmer, 2001.

Miles, S. *Youth Lifestyles in a Changing World*. Buckingham, UK: Open University Press, 2000.

Nikas, C. "The Power of Girls." *Ragtrader*, April 13–16, 1998, 20–21.

Robinson, F. "Pre-Teen Believers." *The Age*, June 9, 2002, 24–27.

Russell, R., and M. Tyler. "Thank Heaven for Little Girls: 'Girl Heaven' and the Commercial Context of Feminine Childhood." *Sociology* 36, no. 3 (August 2002): 619–637.

Simpson, L., S. Douglas, and J. Schimmel. "Tween Consumers: Catalog Clothing Purchase Behavior." *Adolescence* 33, no. 131 (fall 1998): 637–644.

Walkerdine, V. *Daddy's Girl: Young Girls and Popular Culture*. New York: Harvard University Press, 1997.

Wyn, J., and R. White. *Rethinking Youth*. Sage: London, 1997.

CHAPTER FOURTEEN

Girl-Doll: Barbie as Puberty Manual

Catherine Driscoll

Tween

This chapter aims to consider the 'pre-adolescent girl' at an intersection of two different dominant discourses on 'the girl' as an embodied identity—Barbie® dolls and puberty manuals.[1] I want to consider the Barbie doll and the puberty manual as influential manifestations of the 'tween' space in public and popular representations of girlhood—one of them much discussed and the other too rarely considered. The category of 'tween' girl is not easily defined in terms of age or development, and this slipperiness is an element of tween girlhood that both Barbie and puberty manuals foreground and negotiate. In general terms, however, the tween girl is a school-age girl prior to adolescence, and puberty thus marks one of the most influential endpoints of the tween stage. In fact, it often seems that the tween girl can only be mapped by analyzing what she is not, by locating her as the gap between the formation of social identity, and thus gender identity, in early childhood and the crescendo of bodily and social change in adolescence.

The tween girl has not been subject to the same kind of attention as other stages in a girl's or a woman's life. When the tween girl is discussed—by psychologists or popular guidance writers, for example—she is often considered in terms of what comes before or comes after her. From many different analytic perspectives, the tween girl seems to fall 'in between' crucial developmental crises. While it is possible to dispute this positioning of the tween girl as a minor part of this developmental trajectory, this essay proposes that the tween girl might be considered in other than straightforwardly developmental terms. 'Tween' might be a space rather than a stage—a cultural position that not only girls of a certain age occupy or transit. In considering a map of the tween girl space, I am still drawing on cultural forms that are associated with either end of that developmental model that has defined tween girlhood. But both Barbie and discourses on puberty extend into the tween girl space and might help consider its content and significance as well as its limits. This intersection of Barbie and puberty manuals will not provide us with an accurate portrait of tween girlhood as if one were possible, but it might provide some interesting questions about what characterizes tween girlhood.

The range of available discourses on girlhood produce distinguishable fields of girlhood, even if we can debate how much they arise from a developmental norm. Each of these girl territories is filled with objects and activities, with practices of being a girl. Even the baby girl, prior to any recognized place as a speaking subject, has practices of play and behavioral norms thought specific to her 'stage,' although the gendering of those practices seems to be largely imposed on her. Even if the exact relation between the establishment of gendered identity and self-identity remains open to debate, it is indisputable that gender has already arrived for the tween girl, who knows that a great deal is at stake in being a girl rather than a boy. On the other side of tween girlhood is the territory of feminine adolescence, in which gender—the gendered body as much as gender roles—is continuously and consciously being reiterated and renegotiated.[2] There are thus good reasons why psychology, including academic theory, therapeutic practice, applied psychology in fields such as education, and the pop psychology of family guidance manuals, talks extensively about the tween girl in terms of where she fits between these other girl territories. Before looking at the tween girl space, then, it seems important to make some reference to the figuration of the tween girl as a space that is, in fact, a gap.

The tween girl is subject to a range of specialized discourses about being on the edge and in between, being a gap or pause between childhood and adolescence. The most famous of these is Sigmund Freud's theory of latency, in which the girl is prepared for her mature roles by early childhood and enters into an extended period of waiting for sexual maturation, at which point the crucial questions of sex and gender identity will be raised again. The close of Freud's famous essay on "Femininity," which claims that present knowledge is insufficient to discuss pubescent girls, in fact avoids discussing girls during latency either but with the implied caveat that there was nothing to say about them in any case.[3] The latency theory has not only been taken up by psychoanalysts and other psychologists but also converted into other kinds of academic and public analysis of the tween girl. For feminist theory,

hormonal differences hold this girl at an infantile stage, with puberty intervening to help constitute the subject of feminist analysis as a transformation
of sexuality and consciousness simultaneously. For Simone de Beauvoir, for
example, the adolescent girl "becomes an object, and she sees herself as object; she discovers this new aspect of her being with surprise: it seems to her
that she has been doubled; instead of coinciding exactly with herself, she
now begins to exist outside" (1988: 361).

In popular guidance manuals directed at adults, the girl is often figured
as a stable positive space stretching between childhood and adolescence.
While books like Emily Hancock's *The Girl Within* or Mary Pipher's *Reviving Ophelia* represent the girl as a field of potential endangered by the demands of adolescence, they nevertheless conform to the latency model in
which no dramatic changes affect girlhood between childhood and adolescence. Such guidance manuals represent popular culture as a hostile force
directed primarily at adolescents but a step back from developmental models
based—however loosely—on the latency theory reveals a wide range of
popular cultural forms directed to the tween girl, the most visible of which is
Barbie. Barbie is a wonderful example of the contentions around girlhood,
gender norms and identities, and the cultural economies that circulate ideas
about girlhood. This chapter considers how Barbie positions the tween girl in
relation to this dominant developmental model. The comparison of Barbie to
puberty manuals will help stress this focus, positioning the tween girl at a
nexus of social networks of discipline and powerful ideologies of gender,
body, and self.

Barbie

Barbie is a girl—not only resolutely gendered but also a game about gender.
But the kind of girl Barbie is can be very difficult to pin down.[4] If she is a
girl, why does she have her own jobs, houses, cars, and holidays? If she is a
woman, why is she constantly trying on new roles and then giving them up
for new games? I have argued elsewhere that Barbie is fundamentally adolescent because of the difficulty of pinning her down to a representation of
any age or type of girl rather than a *trajectory* of girl-doll desire, and that is a
suggestion I want to expand on here. Barbie is successfully marketed in two
directions: to tween girls, and to consumer groups for whom the ideal of the
tween girl who loves Barbie is highly desirable. In this chapter, I am principally interested in Barbie as a part of the tween space, where in many ways

she represents feminine adolescence and female puberty for the tween girl. Sometimes this relation between Barbie and puberty is explicit in Barbie's production and packaging. Growing Up Skipper™ (1975) is a spectacular example, given that winding her arm causes her body to lengthen and breasts to protrude from her rubber chest, thus enacting the puberty foreshadowed for tween girls, but Skipper represents this puberty as a game of reversible development as an experiment with performing puberty.

Many critics have used Barbie to discuss socialization, body-image, desire, pleasure, and corporate motives, but Barbie is rarely discussed as a mode of becoming a girl. Even when consumed nostalgically, as an erotic object, as an historical text, or as an object for feminist and other cultural critique playing with gender, Barbie represents girls playing with gender. The interesting paradoxes built into Barbie depend on the fact that Barbie play slips away from any specific age categories or clear positions in terms of sexual development. Barbie becomes a figure of gender ideals and gender experimentation at once only as an object of tween doll play. An older collector, a child psychologist criticizing Barbie, or a culture jammer undermining Barbie's self-evidential femininity are all exchanging images of Barbie as a girl-doll relation that presumes the girl-doll relationship.

Not all Barbie play is girl-doll play or even doll play; this chapter focuses on that situation without imagining that all girl-doll play is the kind prescribed by Mattell and modeled in Barbie merchandising or spin-off products like *Barbie Magazine*. Even within the field of girl-doll play, Barbie gets contradictory press and at the beginning of the twenty-first century has become a standard for debating relations between popular culture, dominant ideologies, and developmental models. Not only feminist but also dominant public discourses on Barbie express anxiety about why and how girls play with Barbie. Not only Prom Queen and Astronaut Barbie ™ (1985), but also forcibly 'liberated' Barbies are all Barbie. This is true of anti-consumerism activism like the Barbie Liberation Organization, or of small circulation zines like *We Girls Can Do Anything, Right Barbie?*, as much as feminist cultural studies.[5] All too often, however, such critiques of Barbie begin with an all-too, recognizable devaluation of girl culture and position girls as definitively malleable consumers.

In this chapter, which is not a study of Barbie consumption or Barbie play but a critical contemplation of what these say about tween girlhood, I am more interested in how Barbie is understood to be an influence than in what kind of influence she might be. Nevertheless, blanket dismissals of Barbie as oppressive femininity simplify the practices of Barbie play. The specific gender games played with Barbie are not as predictable as they might seem, but girls do produce gendered identities and practices in relation to Barbie, who is less a thing girls use than an intensely social gender machine.

There is never in any one moment of Barbie play a singular gender but rather as full as possible a range of potential Barbie performances of gender, including disruptive versions of Barbie's gender games. A range of disciplinary discourses shapes this multiplicity, but Barbie is nevertheless an assemblage of girl-doll relations that denaturalizes gender as well as framing it normatively. Barbie's multiplicity is not a matter of the number of Barbie bodies, faces, styles or releases but emerges in moments of play and other interactions with Barbie as idea or object. Even critiques of Barbie are also a deployment of Barbie that must comprehend and acknowledge what Barbie claims to stand for in order to undermine her authoritative model of a girl lifestyle. The assumption that Barbie's multiplicity is a marketing practice and precedes her purchase is too simplistic. On the other hand, the idealization of Barbie play that represents her multiplicity as created by users after purchase misses the way that Barbie is sold as a multiplicity. Barbie successfully articulates gender norms across periods and cultures by being unfixed, and by emphasizing their mobility.[6] Barbie does not teach or impress upon girls any particular set of norms about gender as the sheer multiplicity of Barbie play attests, but girls cannot play Barbie with absolute creative freedom as to her meaning. Girls play Barbie with both respect and passionate disregard for her hegemonic positions. In thinking about how this works, the work of Michel De Certeau (1984) on consumers is still useful. De Certeau rejects the passivity implied by the label "consumers" and focuses on instead on how "users" subvert dominant meanings, "not by rejecting or altering them, but by using them with respect to ends and references foreign to the system they [have] no choice but to accept" (xii). Following De Certeau's lead, we do not need to ignore either the formal structures imposed by economies or existing normative gender roles, or even Mattel's strategies designed to shape Barbie play, in order to recognize the tactics of Barbie play in practice.

Although Barbie always involves an allusion to girl-doll play, there is not only one mode of such play. Barbie is not a baby doll but a fashion doll even if some of her detachable fashions represent mothering. According to the vice president of design and development of girl's toys at Mattel: "Barbie has no fixed identity, no 'self.' Barbie *is* change...There was Barbie the model (1959), Barbie the career girl (1963), Barbie the surgeon (1973), and Barbie the aerobics instructor (1984)" (quoted in Carter 1993: 54). There are strategies by which Mattel supports certain versions of Barbie, highlighting elements of Barbie most amenable to the disciplinary identification that has made her such a success. For example, Prom Queen Barbie™ appears not just as a doll (various releases up to 2001) but also as a Mattel board game—Barbie Queen of the Prom™ (1961, 2000), as a Halloween costume for girls, and in diverse merchandising, including such ephemera as key chains (1999). And yet the success of Prom Queen Barbie is not determined by Mattel, nor is the meaning of Barbie for her consumers or in any instant of Barbie play. Ann Ducille's analysis of 'ethnic' Barbie friends foregrounds an important example of this complexity. The absorption of the specific identities implied by Colored Francie™ (1967) into the umbrella Barbie of Hawaiian Barbie™ (1975) or African American Barbie®, which Ducille discusses, is not necessarily a greater homogenization of Barbie, let alone Barbie play. It certainly re-centers the ethnic primacy of the white Barbie, although that was never in doubt, but it also positions 'Barbie' as the girl-doll relation rather than as a definitive whiteness. Ducille correctly points to this marketing ploy as "an easy and immensely profitable way off the hook of Eurocentrism" (1994: 52), but it also leaves Barbie's specific identity open to an even wider range of Barbie play. Nevertheless, more realistic or egalitarian production of Barbie models will not determine which dolls girls want to play with or how identification with Barbie works, because the influences on Barbie play are not limited to Barbie herself.[7] Barbies appear to be punched out at different points on a developmental line—Kelly, Skipper, Prom Queen Barbie, Teacher Barbie™ or Mommy Barbie—but there is no sequence involved. Barbie is stamped out in a pose, and you can move her forward or backward by new purchases or new Barbie games. The specifics of Barbie's production do shape Barbie play, and Barbie roles are fashions that come and go but not arbitrarily. Mommy Barbie, significant as a representation of the typical developmental mode of doll play, is an occasional side role for Barbie compared to roles that are more relevant to the tween space. Like Growing Up Skipper, the maternity of Mommy Midge (1993) is entirely reversible, and her magnetic detachable pregnant stomach makes Barbie's role as gender manipulation explicit while also more strictly regimenting modes of Barbie play. The fashion doll idea is derived from centuries-old games with dolls dressed in adult fashions or regional costumes, which came in both two- and three-dimensional versions and were not necessarily about childhood play. While Barbie does not invent a new kind of doll play in this sense, Barbie packaged dollhouse play with fashion doll play and the new hyper-visibility of the teenager as a commoditized object of desire in the 1950s. Entire life-styles can be constructed in Barbie's games with gender, and Barbie's suc-cess lies partly in this conjunction of recognizable young girl's games and the teenage ideal that is so important to tween culture. A genealogy of Barbie might also produce a genealogy of the tween girl, intersecting discourses on puberty, girlhood, feminism, consumption, and the teenager and marking movements in the public images and ideals of girlhood.[8] While such a history of Barbie is not possible here, overlaps between Barbie and puberty manuals might add to the available work on historicizing Barbie some of the defining practices of the tween girl space: negotiation of what the body means, the emergence of new forms of discipline, and the performance of both gender norms and marginalized gender roles.

Leaving aside the preferred and implied roles for Barbie and Barbie play, Barbie may not in the first instance seem to represent girls' bodies or identi-ties. Assessing her bodily form in realistic terms, Barbie has preternaturally large breasts, a narrowing waist that implies a womanly figure, and facial features that are closer to adolescent or adult. However, these references to a more 'developed' or 'womanly' body are contradicted by other elements of the Barbie body mould. She has underdeveloped hips, disproportionately long legs, and genitals and overt references to other sexual characteristics are excluded from the Barbie body. Barbie's very confusing body resembles the confusing body-image experienced and imagined in puberty. Barbie repre-sents, as if from the outside, the pubescent confusion of bodily form and bodily change. Barbie might thus seem to fit psychoanalytic models of a fantastic bodily coherence represented through ideal femininity, but an alter-native frame for understanding the reality of Barbie's body might be found in the work of Gilles Deleuze and Felix Guattari. Using their critique of psy-choanalytic models of subjectivity, we could argue that Barbie is a surface on which identities can be produced rather than a representation of any embod-ied self. Deleuze and Guattari reject the psychoanalytic idea that subjectivity is founded in "lack"—on separation from the other and loss of the fantastic coherence of infancy (1977: 26). For Deleuze, lack does not found subjectivity, body image, or desire, and the subject's development is not about negotiating between lack and fantasy. Barbie is never either complete or lacking but accessorizes everything, including semiotic and pragmatic functions: occupations, families, names, ethnicities, and identities. Even Barbie's most famous companion, Ken™ (1961), is an accessory and could thus be discontinued in 2004, although this is not necessarily a closure because anything that looks like lack on Barbie is really the potential for further attachment. Girls can thus attach to Barbie in powerful ways without seeing Barbie as having or being something they lack, and Barbie functions as a recording surface for diverse desires and identities.[9] The possibility that Barbie is a goal is what concerns many critics about girls desiring Barbie, but Barbie play doesn't necessarily position Barbie as either a separate object for the girl or as a role to be imitated or position to occupy. Instead, Barbie is produced "on the periphery, with no fixed identity, forever decentred, defined by the states through which it passes" (Deleuze and Guattari 1977a: 20).

Thinking about Barbie this way rather differently frames Barbie's notorious impact on 'body image.' Barbie is not responsible for the 'tyranny of slenderness' in which she participates although Barbie certainly reinforces the normative power of particular bodily norms despite there being nothing normal about her body. Such normative force is just as clearly about the racial marking of Barbie's body as it is about representation of slenderness or sexuality, but in none of these cases is Barbie an image to be imitated. Despite the repeated appearance in mainstream media of adult women who claim to want to look like Barbie and the recurrence of girls dressed in Barbie costumes, Barbie play is not about imitating Barbie but rather identification with elements of her. Viewed through psychoanalytic models of identification, Barbie play belongs to a developmental model wherein girls are almost quintessentially impressionable and all doll play is about imitation.[10] But identification with Barbie can be detached from this model if understood as a mode of gender discipline. Both doll play and the invocation of a Barbie/girl lifestyle in Barbie packaging and in associated merchandise exemplify this disciplinary identification.

Like girls' magazines directed to an older audience, *Barbie* magazine encourages girls to identify with 'their' magazine and *the* Barbie-girl lifestyle through prizes and competitions, reader contributions, and advice columns.[11] *Barbie* cultivates self-examination and self-improvement that transcend as well as conform to the aesthetic and social norms laid out in the magazine's pages. This is not a site for limitless self-expression but represents what Foucault (1988: 18) terms "technologies of the self," discourses that permit "individuals to effect by their own means or with the help of others a certain number of operations on their own bodies and souls, thoughts, conduct, and way of being, so as to transform themselves in order to attain a certain state of happiness, purity, wisdom, perfection, or immortality." Such technologies are underpinned by disciplinary regimes, and this theoretical model allows us to recognize both girls' individual desires and the systematic exercise of disciplinary power. Foucault notes that the "chief function of the disciplinary power is to train" but not by creating a "single, uniform mass." Instead, disciplinary power "trains the moving, confused, useless multitudes of bodies and forces into a multiplicity of individual elements" (1980: 188). In just such ways, Barbie does not represent girls but is a place for representing girls, demonstrating the limits and possibilities of gender as produced by tween girls. If Barbie still operates with reference to wider discourses on gender and thus may be a relatively minor element of the way in which girls negotiate with normative roles offered to them, another example will hopefully help elaborate the significance of the tween space as a site for the production of multiplicitous gender roles.

Puberty Manuals

Paradoxically, puberty defines the tween girl rather than erasing her, and, as Barbie exemplified, the process of adolescence is always part of the tween space. Puberty manuals are generally presumed to be proper to adolescence rather than the tween girl, but in fact, the purposes of puberty manuals are only served by their being directed at those who are anticipating rather than experiencing puberty. 'Puberty manuals' explain puberty to those who do not yet understand it but who must become familiar with the disciplines attached to puberty in contemporary Western culture. They are a product of the same scientification of human development that produced modern discourses on adolescence. In *Birth of the Clinic: An Archaeology of Medical Perception*, Foucault discusses the emergence of a new perception of the body as anatomical through a collaboration between language and the gaze he calls "the clinical optic." In elaborately defining the body through an expanding anatomical vocabulary, this optic produced new modes of the body's visibility. Foucault argues that this collaboration of language and gaze restructures the threshold of visibility so that what is seen appears to be self-evident and thus grounds for particular kinds of social analysis. The starkest example is perhaps the anatomical diagram, which claims to be a set of essential facts about the body rather than an interpretation of the body. This collaboration of seeing and knowing, an "ideal of an exhaustive description" (Foucault 1973: 112–113), underlies the way puberty is distributed in public, popular, and theoretical fields as a field of explanations that explain their own necessity as they explain the difficulty of puberty.

Puberty manuals are directed not only to those awaiting puberty but also to people charged with authority over them, including books and other media explaining puberty to parents, teachers, and counselors of different kinds. The genre generally emerged in the late nineteenth century, inheriting elements of both earlier medical discourses on physiological development and philosophies of citizenship. So, for example, a text like Rousseau's *Emile* or the nineteenth-century books designed to explain puberty to the newly expanding field of teachers always positioned puberty not just in relation to the development of social agency and skills in citizenship but as part of that development. Puberty in the puberty manual is not entirely about bodily change but also about the changed social position of the adolescent. Contemporary discourses on puberty endorse this interaction of physiological change and psychological development ordered according to sexual dualism, a pattern evident in the 'emotional' symptoms attributed to puberty's hormonal flows and bodily reshaping. It is also crucial that the majority of puberty guidance explains feminine adolescence, either finding more to say about it or focusing exclusively on it. For example, Llewellyn-Jones and Abraham's popular puberty manual, *Everygirl,* presents puberty as a surreptitious emergence of the body that is more "exactly defined" in girls than in boys but for which "[the] changes begin quietly" (1987: 30).

The premise of puberty guidance is that girls lack knowledge about their own bodies or the means to attain it, and while Barbie is clearly not a realistic representation of any body, neither are puberty manuals. As bodily change in puberty is often represented as sexual development, sexual organs remain definitive indices of puberty. And yet, the diagrammatic explanation of even this most clinically described element of puberty condenses puberty into clean and proper lines, concealing rather than representing bodily form as much as Barbie's own version of the feminine body. Like the discourse on puberty, Barbie maps the constitution of the body as a space marked and crossed by lines of inclusion and exclusion. Barbie may in fact be the ultimate clean and proper body, the perfect management of puberty without bodily residue, but puberty guidance regularly resorts to the diagrammatic to emphasize the objective knowability and everyday invisibility of the adolescent female body. Scientificity is often inferred by linearity and highly selective detail, and in this genre diagrams are thus opposed to the identificatory possibilities of photographs, which might raise other than objective didactic relations to the illustration. While Barbie's body makes far fewer claims to empirical realism, she might be understood as a site for greater 'emotional realism,' for playing out situations and possibilities within an ideal girl world.[12] Barbie also attests that puberty and both adolescent and adult gender roles are visible and experienced long before puberty.

The clinical optic that Foucault discusses was not merely a new way of organizing knowledge about the body for medical discourses on the body. In fact, Foucault links it to the emergence of what he calls "biopower," the politicized power over life. Governance over life extends in many directions via this knowability of the body, and health and education policies, for example, often rely on clinical knowledge of puberty. These powerful discourses ground not only the content of puberty manuals but also what kind of puberty manual is permissible, and in this sense too Barbie works as a puberty manual. Barbie articulates parameters for and tendencies within what is appropriate to young girls and their bodies, and Mattel's policing of how Barbie should be understood and represented not only protects intellectual property rights but also keeps Barbie's paradoxical sexiness within the realm of what is allowed to girls (Rand 1995: 41–64). As with puberty manuals in general, this outline of what is normal and permissible is specifically focused on sex, as distinct from other practices that might mark maturity/immaturity like careers or family roles. Barbie can be President Barbie™ (2000) "with an action agenda and a Girls' Bill of Rights in every box" (Haley 2000), but she must not cross the important sexual boundaries around puberty. Barbie's plethora of gender roles does include sexualized roles, in dating games for example, but explicit sexual activity is either unsanctioned or confined to forms deemed appropriate to tween girl play.[13]

The discourse on puberty is shaped by the power and knowledge systems of a given context, a mapping of the sexed body which just as concretely maps a gendered body, entangled in what gender theorists sometimes call the sex/gender system, which is always culturally specific. The first obligation of the contemporary puberty manual is to describe or map this body in a didactic way, representing puberty as the arrival of sexuality out of the latency period and thus part of the post-Freudian understanding of Western adolescence. But this kind of historical context is never made explicit in the puberty manual, and, understood as mutely biological, it seems impossible to think of puberty as subject to and a process of power although it is lived as such. The reconstitution of a girl's body in puberty is both beyond her control and obsessively controlled by herself and others. Rather than a natural emergence of the mature body, puberty is a set of narratives about social positions, about lived bodies, identities, and power.

Dominant discourses on puberty, including the puberty manual, present puberty as a physiological development that is less straightforward for girls and has more pervasive social implications for girls. This greater complexity and obscurity thus requires more extensive guidance and discipline. A puberty manual does not have to claim to educate about puberty as do books like *Everygirl*. The relationships between embodiment and selfhood that define female puberty are evident in a wide range of tween girl culture. For example, the trans-national genre of teen girls' magazines also includes many conventions of the puberty manual. Girls' magazines prioritize the monitoring of puberty in their interrogation of girls' maturity, but they are generally directed towards a much younger audience than the girls represented in the magazine. Girls' magazines describe for themselves an audience of adolescents, but the plethora of information explaining menarche, puberty, and 'early' sexual experiences (like kissing) indicates both the educational rubric of the girls' magazine and that the actual audience of the genre is presumed to be prepubescent. The girl of girls' magazines is in the field of puberty and yet not in control of it—she is in need of instruction, guidance, and helpful illustrative models.

Puberty is a period of training that explicitly constructs knowledges about the body, but the educational premise of the puberty manual is only one of its disciplinary modes. The genre instructs girls in how to know their body's limits and responsibilities and how to monitor it for the correct procession through puberty, but the rhetoric of self-production embraced in the puberty manual—giving girls the tools to manage their puberty—is a mode of disciplined self-observation. Collapsing the public and private obligations of self-control into this representation of the gendered body, these manuals present girls with a fantasy of control over that body. The 'facts' of puberty are cast in disciplinary terms, with those anomalies and variations that are named as acceptable marking limits beyond which difference is by default unacceptable or abnormal. The technologization of puberty is thus complimented by a care and practice ethic that constitutes a dominant theme of girl culture, and which Barbie's array of carefully equipped selves reinforces. Barbie's emphasis on disciplined care of self and body is not confined to grooming and fitness regimes but encompasses Barbie's happy girl life, managed across diverse roles and life styles. Considered through Barbie's representation of puberty, the puberty manual represents the tween girl as not yet sexual or fully gendered even while it understands her as already a girl. The puberty manual affirms that body, desire, and gender are the most significant areas of tween girl life, but at the same time insists that the tween body is transient; her desires are incomplete, and her gendered identity is as yet unfixed. This representation also overlaps in interesting ways with the forms that Barbie takes in Barbie play.

As Judith Butler famously argues, the gendered body is "the repeated stylization of the body, a set of repeated acts within a highly regulatory frame that congeal over time to produce the appearance of a substance, of a natural sort of being" (1990: 33). The gendered body is a norm to be cited, a repetition which is recognized as taking on a definitive form with puberty but can clearly also be seen in the processes of Barbie play. Puberty is an educational space where an already but incompletely gendered subject learns which gender norms are available for what kinds of citation and which body-styles are acceptable or possible, and Barbie play also works in this way. The conditions that make modern puberty possible not only forcibly categorize girls but, even through those categories, enable girls in producing themselves, and Barbie play is an exemplary instance of that production in the lives of tween girls.

The Intermezzo

When Deleuze described "the little girl" as always moving between surfaces of meaning, this was a very serious proposition about the way in which the little girl, excluded from "making sense," models a way of operating in relation to the major regimes of power in her world. This works strictly by refusing any attempt to incorporate the little girl into developmental schema, seeing her as discontinuous with the development of Woman: "It is not the girl who becomes a woman; it is the becoming-woman that produces the universal girl" (Deleuze and Guattari 1977b: 277). Setting aside for a moment the feminist contentions around this sidelining of Woman, what Deleuze wants to recognize is not merely a serious respect for play in the little girl, but the way she slips in between the identities taken as important subjectivities in her world. For Deleuze, that so-called "latency" is an assemblage of possible trajectories, and when considering Barbie play, that seems a useful contention despite its utopic overtones. Deleuze takes Lewis Carroll's Alice as a model and example, and the limitation of this work for considering the little girl is Deleuze's assumption that she has no gender. Alice, like Barbie and like all tween girls, is already gendered but in a contradictory, multiplicitous sense. This is part of the fascination of the little girl packaged into Alice and Barbie; the fascination with gender games that dominates both the potential and limitations of the tween space.

In conclusion, I want to suggest that the 'in-between girl' might provide a useful position from which to rethink current popular and academic discourses on socialization and embodiment. Barbie and puberty manuals demonstrate that the tween girl is clearly both a product of and template for processes of embodiment, and it is not adequate to think of her as suspended between more cathartic periods of self and body constitution. More specifically, I want to suggest that the materialization of a gendered embodied self, usually associated with dramas in early childhood and adolescence, is not developed in anything like those linear terms. The idea, supported by not only Hancock and Pipher but by psychoanalytic and feminist theory in general, that the young girl comprehends a range of possibilities that are narrowed down with the arrival of puberty is compatible with the latency paradigm. But, I have suggested, Barbie indicates an explosion of gender possibilities around the tween girl that cannot be fully determined by either dominant gender norms or Mattel's marketing strategies, and which are clearly not finalized by puberty but in fact continuous with puberty. The difficulty of disentangling the possibilities and limitations of Barbie as a socializing force might be most easily resolved by removing Barbie, and the tween girl, from a developmental understanding of the way in which she is 'in between.' Barbie's typical development is not linear but is instead what Deleuze would see as a series of incorporeal events which is not merely reversible but discontinuous.[14]

The developmental frame for understanding the tween girl as between one stage and the next relegates the malleability of time and development within tween girl culture and the difficulty of marking the borders between girl-child and tween or tween and adolescent to the realm of ideology. The non-linear organization of the tween space is important for understanding how Barbie play works and thus how the multiplicity of Barbie's gender is performed by girls. It therefore may be helpful to think of 'tween' less as a developmental stage which girls enter and leave behind after the physical dislocation of puberty than as a space in relation to which girls are positioned by their particular knowledges about gender and practices of being gendered. There is no necessary chronological or developmental slot into which Barbie and Barbie play fit or even to which 'tween' as a cultural position is incontrovertibly tied.

The tween girl defined as prior to puberty and as delimited by puberty is crucial to the overt address of the standard puberty manual. However, the extent to which Barbie herself functions as a puberty manual, instructing girls as to the form, purpose, and limitations of their imagined and lived body, and training them in the complicated disciplines of femininity, indicates that these were discourses in which the tween girl was already participating. Moreover, they are not discourses through which she passes, never to revisit or be named by on the other side of puberty. I am not proposing that Barbie is an explication of tween girls or a model for girls' subjectivity. Rather, Barbie is an index of the tween space, mapping some of its changes and always subject to reinterpretation and redeployment from different perspectives on tween girlhood, and she allows us to think about the constitution of gender as a field of ongoing processes in which embodiment is always a set of disciplined games.

Notes

[1] The idea of 'tween,' even more than the hotly debated category of adolescence, is culturally and historically specific. For the purposes of this chapter, I will merely note that this is a Western, and even generally American, construction proper to late modernity and perhaps to the late twentieth and early twenty-first centuries. What kinds of girls are eligible to become tween girls is relevant here, but I will discuss them within the frame of contemporary Western culture.

[2] I have discussed the adolescent girl at length in *Girls: Feminine Adolescence in Popular Culture and Cultural Theory* (2002), which discusses both Barbie and puberty manuals in that context. I am grateful to the editors of this volume for the opportunity to look at these discourses from another perspective.

[3] See "Three Essays on Sexuality," for discussion of latency. Freud saw the games and peer friendships of the latency period as an outlet for libidinal energy but saw throughout

latency a continuation of a "masculine sexuality" formed in the "phallic stage" which must be abandoned at puberty. There is thus, even for Freud, an active, power-centered, and egotistical content to the latency period belied by the term.

4   See Rand's discussion of Barbie's age and independence (1995: 21–27). Rand discusses Mattel's move in the 1970s to divest Barbie of all narrative fixity, including her name, parents, and a clear context for her age or "developmental" position (58–64). Despite celebration of Barbie's birthdays, making her now past forty, Barbie is twenty, or twelve, or fifteen, or somewhere in between, and she always will be.

5   *We Girls Can Do Anything, Right Barbie?* is a small-circulation art and text zine produced by ten U.S. high school girls in 1997. For information on the Barbie Liberation Organization, whose Barbie/G.I.Joe voice box switch has become an exemplar of culture jamming, see "Barbie/G.I.Joe Home Surgery Instructions."

6   Considering the possibility that 'tween' is in fact specific to white Western (American) girlhood, it is also possible to see the consumption of Barbie even by young girls excluded from white Western (American) femininity as a kind of fetishization of Barbie's special resonance for the tween girl. Relevant discussions of Barbie's cross-cultural consumption include Ducille (1994) on African American girls consuming Barbie and Hegde (2001) on Barbie in India.

7   Barbie is an interesting point for considering whether tween girl culture is always 'Americanized.' The category of 'tween' is certainly much more recognizable in the U.S., and Barbie's emergence as a girl culture ideal is attached to the globalizing wave of U.S. youth culture in the 1950s. Her American-ness is not, however, just about ethnic codes or standard gender roles but also about factories. The raised plastic mark on Barbie's body traces a history of exploitation and 'development' that has a very different relation to girls' lives—from made in America to made in Japan, Hong Kong, Korea, Taiwan, China.

8   Among many publications containing elements of a Barbie historiography, see Rogers' *Barbie Culture* (1999), Rand's *Barbie's Queer Accessories* (1995), and Mitchell and Reid-Walsh, "Historical Spaces: Barbie Looks Back," in *Researching Children's Popular Culture* (2002).

9   Deleuze's philosophy provides different approaches to Barbie. She might resemble the "Body without Organs," the body that is not organized in hierarchical terms, or the "desiring machines" which move across such a body, always producing and never final or coherent. Desire operates in relation to the Body without Organs through the connective/disjunctive processes of "desiring machines," which are not goal or object-directed and suggest a desire that does not emanate from an individual but is produced on the body amongst fluxes of "associative flows and partial objects" (Deleuze and Guattari 1977b: 287). Barbie could alternatively be understood as an assemblage of girl-doll relations, a way of approaching the group-individual relations of Barbie differently than peer and object-based development studies. But from a Deleuzean perspective, it is not a matter of cohering these into a unified representation of what Barbie means—instead, each of these approaches suggests some new approach to Barbie that is useful in specific contexts.

10   Freud's tripartite model of identification associates the third form of identification—"the possibility of putting oneself in the same situation" (Freud 1922: 64–5)—with schoolgirls and understands it as a regressive or immature placement of the self, which is insufficiently coherent or individuated.

11   *Barbie* magazine is explicitly directed at tween girls—"Australia's premium lifestyle mag for girls aged five-to-12" (http://www.emap.com.au/). First issued in 1996, licensed to Mattel and with substantial Barbie® content, the magazine has moved into more general girls' magazine content, with a target audience as hard to pin down demographically as Barbie's own age. *Barbie* still includes some Mattel content in advertising and still relies on the almost denotative link between Barbie and a tween market to identify its audience.

12   I take this distinction and these terms from Ien Ang's discussion of soap opera: "what is recognized as real is not knowledge of the world, but a subjective experience of the world: a "'structure of feeling'" (1989: 45).

13   This does make Mommy Midge a little problematic, but she is sanctioned under a now rarely used "Friends" name and carefully framed as married. *Barbie Magazine*, drawing on this trademarked image, stresses that it is "parent approved" and part of a reading program "promoted in schools around the nation" (http://www.emap.com.au/).

14   I take this idea from Deleuze's discussion of "the little girl" in *The Logic of Sense*. This "state of affairs," according to Deleuze, is "incorporeal" in the sense of being detached from a corporeal cause and "insofar as it is a way of being" (1990: 147). See my essay "The Little Girl" (1997) for further discussion of this figure.

References

Ang, I. *Watching Dallas: Soap Opera and the Melodramatic Imagination*. Translated by D. Couling. London: Routledge, 1989.

Barbie Liberation Organization. "Barbie / G.I. Joe Home Surgery Instructions." http://users.lmi.net/~eve/download/barbiedir.pdf.

Barbie Magazine. http://www.emap.com.au/.

Butler, J. *Gender Trouble: Feminism and the Subversion of Identity*. New York: Routledge, 1990.

Carter, S. "Real Simulacra Redux: Barbie and Jane Versus the Wooden Nutmegs of Connecticut." *Journal of Popular Culture* 27, no. 3 (1993): 41–59.

de Beauvoir, S. *The Second Sex*. Translated by M. Parshley. London: Picador, 1988.

de Certeau, M.. *The Practice of Everyday Life*. Translated by S. Rendall. Berkeley: University of California Press, 1984.

Deleuze, G. *The Logic of Sense*. Translated by M. Lester. Edited by C. V. Boundas. 1969. New York: Columbia University Press, 1990.

Deleuze, G., and Guattari, F. *Anti-Oedipus*. Translated by R. Hurley, M. Seem, and H. R. Lane. Vol. 1, *Capitalism and Schizophrenia*. Minneapolis: University of Minnesota Press, 1977a.

Deleuze, G., and Guattari, F. *A Thousand Plateaus*. Translated by B. Massumi. Vol. 2, *Capitalism and Schizophrenia*. Minneapolis: University of Minnesota Press, 1977b.

Driscoll, C. "The Little Girl." *Antithesis* 8, no. 2 (1997). Time and Memory: 79–100.

Driscoll, C. *Girls: Feminine Adolescence in Popular Culture and Cultural Theory.* New York: Columbia University Press, 2002.

Ducille, A. "Dyes and Dolls: Multicultural Barbie and the Merchandising of Difference." *differences* 6, no. 1 (1994): 46–68.

Foucault, M. *The Birth of the Clinic: An Archaeology of Medical Perception.* London: Tavistock, 1973.

Foucault, M. *Power/Knowledge: Selected Interviews and Other Writings 1972–1977.* Translated by C. Gordon et al. New York: Pantheon Books, 1980.

Foucault, M. *Technologies of the Self: A Seminar with Michel Foucault.* Edited by L. H. Martin, H. Gutman, and P. H. Hutton. Amherst: University of Massachusetts Press, 1988.

Freud, S. "Three Essays on the Theory of Sexuality." Translated by J. Strachey. 1905. *The Standard Edition of the Complete Psychological Works of Sigmund Freud.* Vol. VII. London: The Hogarth Press, 1953: 123–243.

Freud, S. "Femininity." Translated by J. Strachey. 1905. *The Standard Edition of the Complete Psychological Works of Sigmund Freud.* Vol. XXII. London: The Hogarth Press, 1953: 112–135.

Freud, S. *Group Psychology and the Analysis of the Ego.* Translated by. J. Strachey. 1921. Vol. VIII. London: The Hogarth Press, 1922.

Hancock, E. *The Girl Within.* New York: E. P. Dutton, 1989.

Haley, K. "Barbie Gets a Political Makeover." *AlterNet.* 1 April, 2000. http://www.alternet.org/story.html?StoryID=9064.

Hegde, R. S. "Global Makeovers and Maneuvers: Barbie's Presence in India." *Feminist Media Studies* 1, no. 1(2001): 129–133.

Llewellyn-Jones, D., and Abraham, S. *Everygirl.* Oxford: Oxford University Press, 1987.

Mitchell, C. and Reid-Walsh, J. *Researching Children's Popular Culture: Childhood as a Cultural Space.* London and New York: Routledge Taylor Francis, 2002.

Pipher, M. *Reviving Ophelia: Saving the Selves of Adolescent Girls.* New York: G. P. Putnam's Sons, 1994.

Rand, E. *Barbie's Queer Accessories.* Durham, NC: Duke University Press, 1995.

Rogers, M. F. *Barbie Culture.* London: Sage Publications, 1999.

We Girls Can Do Anything, Right Barbie? Walker Art Center, 1997.

CHAPTER FIFTEEN

Consuming *Hello Kitty*: Tween Icon, Sexy Cute, and the Changing Meaning of 'Girlhood'

Amy T.Y. Lai

"Kitty has a mouth," Yamaguchi states flatly. Spread open on the table is an issue of the glossy magazine/catalog, *Kitty Goods Collection*. I look again: The damn cat has no mouth.

"It's hidden in the fur," Yamaguchi insists.

"But—"

"She has one."

> —This dialogue is taken from Mary Roach's interview with Yuuko Yamaguchi, the designer in charge of Hello Kitty for 19 of the character's 25 years of life, at Sanrio, Japan.

Once Upon a Time

I spent my early childhood in the late seventies yearning for Sanrio characters and products, but particularly Hello Kitty. At that time, the lovely cartoon cat had not yet gone through endless metamorphoses and reincarnations like those that it has today. Hence, she always appeared in four or five primary colors: white body, black eyes, yellow nose, red ribbon, blue or red attire. My earliest memory consists of her image on my schoolbag: she sits sideways, her head turned to the audience, occasionally holding up her thumb to her face where her mouth should be. For some mysterious reason, like many of my fellow classmates, I was instantly drawn to her at first sight.

My craze for her nonetheless died as I matured t hroughout the years, despite the fact that her popularity has soared in Asian countries since the eighties to the extent that she has become the crown jewel of Sanrio characters. Probably owing to feelings of nostalgia, I continued to keep a close eye on this childhood 'friend' of mine and to pay attention to whatever was written about her. I discovered that we were born in the same year—1974—the year of the Tiger. In fact, this should not be surprising—cats, after all, belong to the tiger family. And no, she was not born in Japan, but London, England, and lives with her parents and her twin sister, Mimmy. Her hobbies include traveling, reading, eating yummy cookies, and making new friends.

However, it was after I had long become an 'adult' and developed what is known as my 'career,' that I started to research her history and discovered her origin, including the name of her inventor, Yuko Sakiyama. I have also started to complicate the kitty's motto "You can never have too many friends," the meaning and significance of which is one of the things that I will try to explore in this chapter. All the while, I am fully aware that the skepticism essential to every cultural scholar and critic might also indicate my betrayal of her, hence marking the end of our 'friendship.'

Kitty's Life, a 'Kitty Life'

For such commercial goals as profit maximisation, and as if for the sake of promoting the Kitty's Life—which is essentially defined by a cheerful and positive attitude—Sanrio has actively extended the Kitty product-line. Since the nineties, the company has covered many everyday commodities and, in many cases, by joint venturing with other big companies. In the past, we took pride in the Hello Kitty pencil-cases and pencil-sharpeners that Mom bought for us; now not only are there Hello Kitty cosmetics, toasters, microwaves, mobile phones, computers and small furniture, but even automobiles with the Hello Kitty logo on them. And, yes, there are Hello Kitty anti-SARS facemasks, which appeared within a week after the outbreak of the epidemic. As some remark, "You name it, and they have it." Along with the proliferation of Kitty products, the Kitty image has undergone many metamorphoses: now we seldom find her in simple red and blue, but dressed up like a snow angel, riding on Pegasus, and even transformed into a mermaid.

As far as things go, it seems that as long as you are willing to pay, it is not difficult, after all, to live a 'Kitty Life.' One event, which testifies to the charisma of Kitty, is particularly worthy of attention and discussion. In the late nineties, McDonald's launched a promotional campaign, the "Hello Kitty Meal Package," in Asian countries and cities such as Singapore, Taiwan, and

Hong Kong. Within a short time, the Kitties went out of stock. In Taiwan, those who had been waiting to purchase this celebrated stuffed animal since early morning complained and even got into a nasty fight, which made its way onto the evening news of several television channels and eventually accelerated into the so-called 'Hello Kitty Mania.'

Sanrio has also expanded its Kitty merchandise to the West. Forty Sanrio stores have opened in the US, and there are subsidiaries selling merchandise in Brazil, Germany, France, Italy, and Britain. In 2001, on my last visits to PaperChase, a chain stationary store in the UK, I found Hello Kitty postcards and birthday cards on the shelf, and I felt terribly homesick— and nostalgic. On these cards, Kitty appears in her primary, original form, hence very similar to the one I first saw as a five-year-old kid.

"Hello, Kitty!" How Americans Hail the Cat

For many people, the round, hence childlike features of Hello Kitty make her a symbol of cuteness. In fact, save her ribbon that indicates that she is a 'female,' there is not a single sign that betrays her real 'biological sex'—and this also makes her 'asexual.' Overall, her immaculate whiteness connotes an aura of incorruptible innocence. It is not very surprising indeed, for many people to hold a rather scornful attitude towards the 'Hello Kitty fandom/ mania,' seeing the collection, seeing even simple liking, of the Kitty as a sign of childishness, even naiveté. It is their derision, however, which subsequently drew me to study the fandom. For quite some time, I have discovered something even more interesting, which is the different receptions and consumptions of Kitty products in Western and Asian countries. The scope of this chapter allows me to explore mainly the case of the United States versus those of Japan and Hong Kong.

For Americans, Hello Kitty is no more than a 'cartoon cat,' generally liked and consumed by pre-teenage girls ('tweens') but having much less impact among adolescents, let alone adult women. People beyond pre-teenage who collect Hello Kitty items risk being derided for suffering from what is known as a 'Hello Kitty Problem,' some sort of 'obsession,' or 'fixation.' Anna Hanks' article (1999) begins by offering a parody of a 'Hello Kitty maniac' by using a first person voice:

> Hello, my name is Anna, and I have a problem. And I am not alone. There are a lot
> of us who share the same addiction. There are few men in our world. And for the
> most part, we are in the closet. Few people know the depths of our obsession until

they come into our homes. You can find us at online auctions and novelty stores, plunking down big cash to score elusive items to feed our need. Hello, my name is Anna, and I have a Hello Kitty problem. And I am not alone....

When I invite my Hello Kitty support group over, they drink out of Hello Kitty mugs, eat with Hello Kitty forks, and have ice cream in Hello Kitty bowls. They eat unlicensed Hello Kitty cookies from Dobie Mall. When things get too intense, they dry their eyes with Hello Kitty tissues. If they get overexcited at my decorating scheme, I turn on my tiny Hello Kitty fan to cool them down. <1>

The article then moves on to describe what the Kitty means in the US:

In short, Kitty is *a paradigm of the preadolescent female self*, before young women are forced to internalize the images of what society promotes as necessary to become beautiful or appealing: uncomfortable shoes, control-top pantyhose, a cow-like Nancy Reagan gaze, and those twin demons—silicone and Stairmasters. Kitty is *eternally uncorruptible*. [emphasis added] <2>

Mary Roach (1999) further attributes the popularity of Kitty items among pre-teens to American culture, where 'cute' is generally thought of as 'kid stuff.' "The further you get from elementary school, the heavier the American resistance will be to cute in its purest incarnation." Roach explains. She also quotes Mari Yakushiji, Sanrio's Tokyo-based head of design for US products, who observes that "American kids demand to be entertained; cute is a secondary selling point" (5).

Sanrio has been trying to hit the adult market in the US all the same. While Hello Kitty used only to be found in specialty stores, Sanrio opened its first US adult-merchandise store, Vivitix, in October 1999 in Berkeley, California, and mass retailer Target now carries their own Hello Kitty line. "We used to just sell the character to children 13 and under," says Randall Patterson, a vice president at Sanrio, "but in the last four or five years our customers have included college age kids" (Gallegos 1995 <1>). Fans can tell that Mariah Carey is a devotee, and so are Courtney Love and US punk queen Exene Cervenka (Spreckley 1999).

Nonetheless, a lot of those adolescent and even adult customers, as it seems to me, have collected Kitties more out of their love for cats in general than because they find Hello Kitty 'cute' (for instance, see Gallegos: 1995). Nostalgia is another major factor: those who loved Kitties when they were children have continued to show their loyalty. For Hello Kitty to really make a big splash in the US adult world and for a real merging of tween and adult popular cultures, it would definitely take some years for 'tweens' to grow up.

For the time being, Hello Kitty generally remains a tween icon, and the consumption of Kitty products is largely a practice among pre-teens, and to a lesser extent, early teens. This is very different from the case of Japan, which I will address in the following section.

'Cute' Is 'Sexy': Hello Kitty and Japanese Women

Kitty products are popular among different age groups in Japan. According to Roach, their popularity in Japan is not only due to nostalgia (Kitty has appeared in Japan for almost thirty years) but also to the 'cute' (*kawaii*) factor, which exerts "a powerful and omnipresent force" in Japanese culture:

> The Japanese are born into cute and raised with cute. They grow up to save money with cute (Miffy the bunny on Asahi Bank ATM cards), to pray with cute (Hello Kitty charm bags at Shinto shrines), to have sex with cute (prophylactics decorated with Monkichi the monkey, a condom stretched over his body, entreating, "Would you protect me?"). Cute is everywhere. They're soaking in it... (1)

Roach even attempts to research the 'cute culture' in Japan, tracing its history and origin:

> According to Sharon Kinsella, a Cambridge University researcher who has written on the subject, the cute craze began around 1970, when a fad for writing notes and letters in *rounded, childish characters* began to catch on among teenage Japanese girls. Scholars who studied the phenomenon dubbed it *Anomalous Female Teenage Handwriting*. Kids called it burikko-ji, translated as *"kitten-writing" or "fake-child writing."* At one point in the mid-80s, some 55 percent of 12- to 18-year-old girls was using it [emphases added]. (1)

She further accounts for the appeal of 'cute' to the Japanese, which is, in large part, the appeal of childhood in itself. She quotes Merry White, author of *The Material Child: Coming of Age in Japan and America*: "Childhood, in Japan, is a time when you were given indulgences of all kinds - mostly by your mother, but by society too"(2). Hence, Japanese want to go back to childhood, mother, and home, and this is different from the case of the US, which White calls an 'adolescence society.' In fact, many anthropologists have also observed that Japanese adulthood is, perhaps more so than in most cultures, a time of onerous responsibilities, expectations, and pressure to conform. This further accounts for the Japanese yearning for childhood and its innocence.

This nostalgia for childhood also goes along with Anne Allison's experience in and observation of Japan (2000), which is the proliferation of sexual imagery in the country's visual culture. In fact, tween culture and sex are not separate and tied to the cute culture—the well-known Lolita complex, or 'Lolicom.' Even to the eye of the random tourist, the phenomenon of the little girl as sexual object apparently abounds in Tokyo. There are vending machines selling schoolgirls' used panties, which the girls sell to middlemen; 'image bars' specialising in escorts dressed in school uniforms; telephone clubs featuring bored adolescent girls earning spending money by talking dirty. And then, of course, one should never forget that the country is virtually the first empire of VCD's full of (pre) teen sex. The 'cuteness' of Kitty is not merely for cuteness' sake but has turned into a weapon to increase the sex appeal of its owner. The cuteness of a giggling girl clad in a Hello Kitty jumper may not be all that innocent; in fact, this is sexually alluring to those with Lolicom.

The consumption of Hello Kitty, therefore, is testimony to the merging of adult and children's cultures—a phenomenon visible all around the world but much more apparent in Japan than elsewhere. Hello Kitty is not a tween icon in Japan as it seems to be in the US: the Kitty products being popular among tweens, adolescents and adults, its crazy consumption by pre-teens already marks their entry and absorption into the adult world of materialist culture. Anna Hanks claims that Kitty "doesn't resort to sex appeal," because "flat shoes and a big red bow do not a come-hither look make," and you do not find the cat "purring on anyone's lap" (2). However, the culture of Japan provides an interesting illustration of how the Kitty is in fact fully incorporated into the highly sexualized adult world. In addition, given the popularity of Kitty products in Japan and considering that many Japanese teenagers have acquired more liberal sexual attitudes than earlier generations, it would not be too much to deduce that many Kitty fans or owners of Kitty products nowadays are also those who are into all types of casual sexual behaviors. It should not surprise anyone that Sanrio has in fact extended its Kitty product line to cover items such as the electronic vibrator.

Beyond Sexy and Cute: What's in a Cat?

As one can see from the above discussion, Kitty is not merely 'gendered' but also sexualized. It has naturally become the target in feminist politics. Attention has been drawn to its mouthlessness, which Sanrio sees as accounting for its popularity. Sanrio's Nakajima Seiji says, "Without the mouth it is easier to imagine Kitty-chan shares whatever feeling you have at that moment. If Kitty-chan was smiling all the time, and you'd just broken up with your boyfriend or something and were very sad, the last thing you'd want to look at was a grinning Hello Kitty. Without a mouth you can imagine she is sad with you" (Spreckley 1999). Nonetheless, feminists are quick to read the mouthlessness (of not only Kitty, but also many other Sanrio characters, such as Pochacco, Cathy the bunny, Chococat) as an element of passivity, submissiveness, and little-girl helplessness, which is, after all, in tune with, and already accentuated by their generally rounded features. Cambridge researcher Sharon Kinsella, in her study of Japanese culture, contends that the connotative meanings of "kawaii" include "helplessness and vulnerability" (cited in Roach 1999, 1) In Kinsella's argument, what can be more tempting than a cute and submissive tween girl, whose aura of vulnerability is reinforced by her hugging a Hello Kitty plush toy? As far as 'cuteness' goes, even an adult female hugging a Hello Kitty becomes more appealing.

At this stage, however, I would like to probe the question of whether Kitty is always necessarily 'girlish' and 'childish,' or whether it can, like many objects, contain many meanings. I would like to turn to Ko Yu-fen's conference paper (2000) on Hello Kitty and identity politics in Taiwan. Ko addresses in length the commonly held suspicion, even accusation that Hello Kitty fans are destroying feminists' decades of advocacy on gender politics. Not only does the 'Kitty style' call for an animated girlish look but it also has no expression or mouth:

> Mouthlessness is her crucial mark (or the mark that is not there, the un-mark). The lack of a facial organ arouses an *uncanny feeling of repressed incompleteness*. Mouth, the ultimate symbol that defines personal character, is an organ that governs in/out relationship of the interior corporeal self and the exterior other. Without a mouth one cannot devour nor vomit, not swallow nor speak. A mouthless face bears an even more significant sign for something that is uncommonly at lack. This explicit speechless and actionless character of Kitty worries some intellectuals. They think that the empty face represents the *infantisation of the Kitty fans*, that a mouthless cat represents the *dull and docile femininity that always remains silent, and that soft pink and blue colors stereotype female as fragile and weak* [emphases added]. (9)

Nonetheless, Ko argues against the grain, first by claiming that in the social practice of consumption, there is no natural equation between consumption and cultural identity. He makes use of Barthes' concept of the "sign" and "signification" and quotes Baudrillard to describe "consumption" as "an active mode of relations (not only to objects, but to the collective and to the world)" and "a systematic act of the manipulation of signs" (see Ko 5–6, and Baudrillard 1988: 21–22). Hence that which can be consumed is never the object but the meaning that it bears, which is obtained through its signification process. Second, taking Baudrillard's (de)constructionist stance, Ko fleshes out the idea that both the value and meaning of a commodity are determined by the consumers, not pre-determined by the system:

> The meaning of an object is not assembled on the production line or completed in the advertising package: nor is it finished after the monetary exchange. For an object to mean something, it has to enter our lives, enter our relationships, being used, interpreted, articulated, through touch, sight, and spoken words (20).

Third, Ko goes on to argue that since all consumers are actively participating in a production process of a sign—in this case the cat that is no longer a cat but is made into an 'elusive sign' by the fans themselves. Rejecting the idea that the consumption of Hello Kitty necessarily equates the 'Japanisation' of a culture, Ko even goes so far as to suggest that the cat in fact does not attach itself to any national or cultural origin in any way, at all:

> Hello Kitty rarely appears in anything Japanese except the love of Kyoto pair in McDonald's Meal Package: most of the profits don't necessarily contribute to its Japanese franchise, the Sanrio Company, because the ubiquitous counterfeits are made by local factories: the equivocal meanings and ambiguous positions of Hello Kitty upset us: the poverty of meaning and the impossibility to fix it onto a stable relation upset us. (13)

Hello Kitty, therefore, has no essential meaning. Its meaning(s) ultimately depends on whatever its consumers are willing to bestow on it in the process of consumption, to the effect that its 'mouthlessness' should not be disturbing after all:

> Hello Kitty is not Japan, nor is it (a) mouthless teenage girl. That Hello Kitty has no mouth doesn't mean that consumers don't have anything to say about it: Hello Kitty doesn't and is unable to advocate a silent submission.

It should not sound contradictory, therefore, that Kitty was 'born in London,' but not Tokyo. I would also like to bring in some personal anecdotes. I recall that Kitty was once quite expensive in Hong Kong (as it was in Taiwan, according to Ko's conference article). In the early 80s, it could only be found in a few boutiques, such as Gift Gate and Gift Gallery, where I visited with a whole month's savings in my pocket; in the early 90s, it had become more 'affordable,' hence more 'popular.' At the same time, many counterfeits could be spotted in night markets and vendor stands. I tried to avoid them, but it was sometimes hard to distinguish between the real and the fake. Very often, the fake ones had mouths and the colors were 'not quite right.' Ironically enough, in a television production that stars the 'real' Kitty along with her family members, she was also given a 'mouth' so that she could speak! Needless to say, Sanrio has also hybridized the Kitty's appearance to make it 'less original,' and in one of the company's re-inventions of its image, the cat was actually dressed in black, hence no longer associated with the girlish blue and pink.

I also recall one of my favorite primary school teachers, probably in her fifties when she taught my class, who actually helped to promote the Hello Kitty ballpoint pen: "Especially those of you whose handwriting is awful—it truly works! I bought one for a past student as a present, and her writing improved drastically afterwards—another reason being that she probably worked on it out of gratitude to me!" So, Kitty products are not 'fancy' gifts—they do have practical purposes, and as a loyal fan of the Kitty ballpoint pen, I concur with her that it might actually function better than other brands. When I was attending college, an Engineering sophomore and a schoolmate of mine was famous for his craze for Keroppi, a fellow character at Sanrio and also 'mouthless' most of the time. And no, he was neither gay, nor 'girlish/ feminine'—character-wise or appearance-wise. I did not ask him about Keroppi's appeal, but now I cannot help but dwell on the possibilities. Did he find it (or 'him') cute? Did the character remind him of his childhood? Or, was there a story behind his affection for it? Did he feel attracted to girls who craved Hello Kitty?

Paradise Lost, or No Paradise? A Hong Kong Nightmare

I believe that despite the popularity of Hello Kitty in Hong Kong and among various age groups, the love of the cartoon cat is generally taken as a sign of immaturity—privately, if not publicly. My general impression has found its backup in various postings—anonymous, hence relatively 'honest'—on an English-language chatboard, IceRed, which has been set up especially for college-educated working professionals. In fact, the majority of them are overseas educated—those whom the society believe to have cultivated 'fine tastes' in life. One good example is "Why Gals Like Hello Kitty," an excerpt of which I have included below:

> Don't know Posted: 27 August 2001 3:47 pm
>
> --
>
> Why so many not-so-young gals like Hello Kitty?

> Eskimo Bob Posted: 27 August 2001 3:53 pm
>
> --
>
> Because like everything in HK/China
> People have no taste or style
> Be it in music, films, architecture
> Its shite around here

> [omitted]

> Anonymous Posted: 28 August 2001 9:03 am
>
> --
>
> I'm not obsessed with Hello Kitty, but I think it is cute and sometimes I can escape from the stress by just looking at some of my cute collection. Which reminds of my childhood. I'm 22 yrs old and Hello Kitty has always been around ever since I was young. It's no big deal.
>
> It's not like I have Hello Kitty socks or a Hello Kitty shoes that I'd wear to public. But things like shower curtains, carpets, pajamas are cute.

> [omitted]

> Psycho-analyst Posted: 28 August 2001 10:36 am
>
> --
>
> Idols are a way of saying to the world one's preferences.
>
> In the case of hello kitty, gals who like them are saying, "gee, i'd like to look cute and be loved by many, whether it's just hay or air in the head is irrelevant. i live in a feckin dream world. joining?"
>
> That's why avoid hello kitty lovers if you are not into stupid, characterless, bimbos.

It is quite ironic that those who deride Hong Kong women simultaneously participate in the re-appropriation of the cat's image, and in Ko's argument, they share in the generation of the sign's meanings or the "signification" process. In "To All the Hello Kitty Girls," their attempt to sexualize it is not original but is already an on-going process prompted and undertaken by inventors and consumers of Kitty products:

> Smakelijk Posted: 23 June 2001 3:44 am
>
> --
>
> Do you think that Hello Kitty will bang Keroppi? Have some wild inter species sex. What kind of new Sanrio character they will produce? Something better than Hello Kitty, so all the stupid Hellow Kitty [sic] fans can dump bunch of their daddies $ to buy toys, pens, books etc. Why ? Because she's the love child of Keroppi and Hello Kitty.
>
> Another fantasy i have is Hello Kitty to have orgy w/ Pochacco, Pippo, and Pekkle. Or better yet have mad lesbian sex w/ Spottie Dottie? After all she's a dog!
>
> If Hello Kitty is not up for it I 'd love to see Little Twin Stars do oral on each other, while My Melody watches, play w/ herself and joins in later. Nothing hotter than 2 twin sisters showing love and passion for each other. God i Love bestiality!!
>
> [omitted]
>
> Slim Posted: 24 June 2001 10:33 am
>
> --
>
> Erm, what i meant was i'm sure he'd offer to bang hello kitty... mmm, on second thoughts maybe not.,
>
> Moi Posted: 24 June 2001 10:37 am
>
> --
>
> One of my friends has a hello kitty vibrator. What do u think of TAT? =p
>
> Anonymous Posted: 25 June 2001 11:47 pm
>
> --
>
> The one act i really want to see is Spottie Dottie and Hello Kitty do the doggy style. Did i may the Hello Kitty girls cry yet?

I have come across countless reports that urge me to realize that Hello Kitty is being continuously dislocated from the tween culture and its familiar contexts of innocence and cuteness. For instance, I can still visualize magazine photographs that show pimps and 'mammasans' keeping Kitty products at homes. The reasons are unknown, though: it might be for the sake of luring under aged girls into prostitution, but it might well be out of their genuine affection for these plush toys—and no one has any reason to dispute such a possibility after all.

A particularly shocking and extreme example of this featured in an online magazine called *Bizarre*. The report featured in the magazine, notwithstanding the possibility of sensationalism, described a violent case in Hong Kong involving Hello Kitty. Its graphic details might evoke abhorrence and disgust—do not complain that you have not been forewarned.

In 1998, three triad gangsters brutally tortured and beat a young woman for a whole month until she died. Then they dismembered and cooked the body and threw most of it out along with the garbage, fed the legs and arms to stray dogs, but hid the skull inside the head of a giant-sized Hello Kitty mermaid doll. The horrible crime was disclosed only when a 14-year-old girl turned up at the police station in 1999. She confessed that she was being haunted by the ghost of a woman whom she had helped torture, kill, and butcher a year earlier and then took them up to a third-floor apartment in Hong Kong's shoppers' paradise, Granville Road.

What demand special attention are the teenager and the victim. Since the teenage girl had run away from home and been introduced to Chan (the triad head), she had embraced a horrid world of sex, drugs, and violence. Chan's place, a seven-room apartment above Granville Road, was his headquarters for loan-sharking, pimping, porn, and drugs. It not only contained cable TV, video games, Hollywood and Hong Kong movies, sex movies and lots of drugs—sufficient to block out reality—but also Hello Kitty curtains, bedsheets, kitchenware, and dolls. After the victim was kidnapped for failing to return the stolen money and the 'high interest,' the 13-year-old joined the guys in torturing her. "Well," she told the court, her face blank, her voice devoid of emotion, "I did it for fun. Just to see what it was like to hurt someone." The victim's tormentors even made her laugh aloud and pretend to be happy while she was being beaten. "It was a game they played," she said. "If she didn't pretend to be happy they would beat her harder. They told her to laugh while they burnt her. It was a fun atmosphere."

The life of the 23-year-old victim was no better. Abandoned as a child, she was raised at Ma Tau Wai girls' home. By her teens, she had settled into a life of petty crime, prostitution, and drug addiction. The triad head was in fact one of her triad clients, who never forgave her for stealing his wallet. In the reportage of the crime in Hong Kong's press, all newspapers ran the story on the front page, all of them showing similar images. First, there was the court-issued photo of the victim holding a child: her eyes are tired; her face is drawn, and she is not sexy. Next to this, the papers had other pictures generated on a computer. Here, she was transformed into the kind of thin-armed, pert-breasted, chisell-cheeked cyber-babe found in any Japanese video game. The newspaper story says it is a representation of a real event, but the pictures look as if they had been taken from graphic Japanese pornography or X-rated Manga. It was as if the news writers were living in a simulated world (as the murderers did), and imposing such a world on its readers.

Bizarre's article calls Hello Kitty the "perfect icon" for "an amoral age" such as the one that we are living in, pointing out that the whole crime was overlooked by the huge Kitty mermaid plush toy all along, which did not hate the murderers, let alone frown on their behavior. Its cat head and fish body also make it a perfect symbol of a crazy world turned-upside-down. Indeed, the cartoon cat has never been so far removed from its original context and culture; as a sign, it has never been re-appropriated so violently for the setting up of a simulated world where the murder took place before finally turning into a monstrous symbol of brutality and death.

I believe that the 'premature' entries of both the 13-year-old torturer and the victim into a world of sex and violence, as indicated by their backgrounds, also flesh out a further significant dimension to the symbolic meaning of the Hello Kitty plush toy in this tragedy. Enveloping the entire flat where the murder took place, it indicates the changing meaning of 'girlhood' and 'tween' experiences, which I will further address in the next section.

"Girl" or "Woman": Does Silence Bespeak Many Words?

The definitions of 'tween' and 'girlhood,' like those of other age periods, can be problematic in themselves. Allison James writes, "The age at which childhood ends and adolescence begins, when adolescence turns to adulthood, is both fluid and context specific, despite attempts to bind it legally" (1986: 157). As Kathleen Woodward (1999: x) also observes, "Old age and middle age are part of the larger continuum of a discourse on age itself, a system of age that includes infancy, childhood, adolescence and young adulthood."

Nonetheless, speaking as a Hong Kong-born and bred Chinese and from personal experience, I believe that delineating periods in age studies might have an added difficulty in Chinese culture. I hereby provide my reader with a handy example of the fluidity of 'age.' This is the 'naming' of females in

Hong Kong Chinese culture, which is more problematic than in Western cultures in general. While rather clear definitions of 'girl' and 'woman' can be found in any Western dictionary, they are relatively vague for Chinese. For Hong Kong Chinese, the term 'girls' (*nui jai*) spans different age groups, from kids to anyone in middle age who happens to be still single. 'Women' (*nui yahn*) refers to those already married. Therefore, if you chance upon a young-looking female whose marital status is yet unclear to you, you had better call her a 'girl' instead of 'woman.' I recall a friend of mine in her late twenties was extremely offended when a Western acquaintance called her a 'woman,' and she even told him that a single female in Hong Kong would not want to be addressed in that way.[1]

Given the fluidity of 'age,' hence 'tween,' and the contested nature of Hello Kitty, which is consumed by people of different age groups, the cartoon cat as a cultural icon can in fact serve as a mirror of the changing meaning of the former. Hello Kitty is, for the time being, a much more contested cultural text in Japan and Hong Kong than it is in the West—it is being readily appropriated and re-appropriated for different purposes and in different contexts. As such, it turns into a fine symbol of the constructed—and particularly shifting and unstable—categories of 'tween' and 'girlhood' in Asian cultures.

Notes

[1] I would like to return to the quotation that marks the beginning of this chapter. It does not matter whether Kitty has a mouth or not. It does if you think it does. It speaks if you give it a voice. "You can never have too many friends": call it a friend, and it is 'yours.' An attentive reader should have discovered by now that I have replaced the pronoun 'she/her' with 'it' in my discussion of my long-time 'friend.' As a sign, it/she can be gender-neutral, gendered, and de-gendered. Likewise, as a Hong Kong Chinese who shares similar backgrounds with the aforementioned female friend of mine, I certainly do not care whether I am called a 'girl' or a 'woman.' I can be both, one at a time, or neither, can't I?

References

Allison, A. *Permitted and Prohibited Desire: Mothers, Comics, and Censorship in Japan.* Berkeley: University of California Press, 2000.

Barthes, R. *Mythologies.* New York: The Noonday Press, 1992.

Baudrillard, J. *Selected Writings*, edited by M. Poster. Stanford, California: Stanford University Press, 1988.

Bizarre. "Hello Kitty...Goodbye World." *Bizarre: A Magazine about Life in the Extreme.* http://www.bizarremag.com/truecrime/kitty.php.

Gallegos, L. "Kash Kitty." *Prism,* (November 1995), Pacific Rim issue. http://www.journalism.sfsu.edu/www/pubs/prism/nov95/16.html.

Hanks, A. "Say Hello to Kitty." *The Austin Chronicle*, (November 5 1999). http://www.austinchronicle.com/issues/dispatch/1999-11-05/xtra_feature.html.

James, A. "Learning to Belong: the Boundaries of Adolescence." In *Symbolising Boundaries*, edited by A. P. Cohen, 155–170. Manchester: Manchester University Press, 1986.

Ko, Y. "Hello Kitty and the Identity Politics in Taiwan." Seminar paper presented at the Re-mapping Taiwan Conference, UCLA, October 13–15 2000. http://www.international.ucla.edu/cira/paper/TW_Ko.pdf .

Mitchell, C., and J. Reid-Walsh. *Researching Children's Popular Culture: The Cultural Spaces of Childhood.* London: Routledge, 2002.

Roach, M. "Cute Inc." *Wired Magazine* 7, no. 12 (1999). http://www.wired.com/wired/archive / 7.12/cute_pr.html.

Spreckley, C. "Tokyo Feature Stories: Here Kitty Kitty! The Comeback Cat Turns 25." *Metropolis*, (1999). http://metropolis.japantoday.com/tokyofeaturestoriesarchive299/272/tokyofeaturestoriesinc.htm .

Woodward, K. "Introduction." In *Figuring Age: Women, Bodies, Generations*, edited by K. Woodward, ix-xxix. Bloomington: Indiana University Press, 1999.

CHAPTER SIXTEEN

Mediated Consumption and Fashionable Selves: Tween Girls, Fashion Magazines, and Shopping

Farah Malik

Over the last thirty years, there have been various explorations into the relationship between mediated messages and the development of femininity and identity (David Buckingham 1993; Dawn Currie 1997; Susan Douglas 1994; Catherine Driscoll 2002; Sharon R. Mazzarella and Norma Pecora 1999). Theorists have elucidated that fashion and consumption images are pervasive in girls' magazines (McRobbie 1991, 1997) and that female magazine reading, as well as fashion and beauty practices, is a site for the production of feminine selves (Joanne Hollows 2000; Angela McRobbie 1999; Myers 1987; Valerie Steele 1996). However, the aspects that require further exploration are the formation of girls' consumption habits and girls' active construction of style informed by their interpretation of the images and information that they obtain from magazines. A dialogic understanding of younger girls' perspective—in particular their experience with the conscious negotiation of subjectivity—is also necessary.

In the existing body of feminist research there still seems to be a lack of sufficient evidence to discern whether girls "challenge, negotiate, or ultimately accept what fashion magazines have to offer" (Diana Crane 1999, 544). Accordingly, this study attempts to determine just how much of a role the mediated messages of consumption, the selling of style and the marketing of fashion in magazines play in girls' consumption habits, in the construction of their individual style and fashion, as well as how they might enact a transitional route to adulthood.[1]

Although there is an array of theoretical research that explores magazine reading's contribution to identity and sexuality, questions about appearance, construction of style, the production of selves and fantasies about self-invention are not adequately observed. Most studies on girls' consumption of fashion have located girls in sub-cultures and offered analyses on style as a resistance to traditional femininities (Dick Hebdige 1979; Lauraine Leblanc 1999; Joanne Hollows 2000; Angela McRobbie and Jenny Garber 1976; David Muggleton 2000). Consumerism too, is merely summed up as "the seduction of buying" (McRobbie 1991: 176) without taking into account the impact of magazines on the gendered practices of shopping and buying.

Consequently, this exploration attempts to complement the existing scholarly work by addressing girls' consumption practices as they are bound up with issues of agency as well as how consumption might enact a rite of passage, concentrating on how the act of consumer choice (whether real or falsified) can serve as a transition into adulthood. To further explore this transition, there will be an elaboration of the subtle ways in which magazines exert their symbolic power to naturalize the dichotomy between the ordinary world of young girls and the extraordinary world of commodities and teen-hood. The manner in which magazines erect a boundary that girls feel compelled to cross, and the manner by which they make girls believe that they are exercising their own choice and agency, will also be deliberated on. The subsequent section will address how the representations within magazines that girls confront unconsciously impact their self-constructs or "projects of the self" (John Thompson 1995, 233) and how, if at all, the representations may provide a means for self-individuation. Finally, the discussion will extend into the idea that consumption and all its possibilities for active and conscious self-construction can provide girls a route to the "perfect self" (Sharon Zukin 2004: 10). The analysis will begin by addressing how the practice of consumption for tween girls is implicated in adult anxieties about their vulnerability as consumers by briefly presenting a synopsis of previous examinations of girls' identity and magazines, girls and popular culture, girls and media as well as girls and consumer culture.

Locating Tween Girls and Mediated Consumption
within the Terrain of Girlhood Studies

Angela McRobbie suggests that "teenage magazines are always read by an age range below the target readership the editors officially aim at, for the simple reason that they perform the role of guides to girls as to what is in store for them at the next stage of growing up" (1997, 197). Girls' magazines are implicated in forming early shopping, fashion, and style habits and mediating consumption, for it is through magazines that "girls [are] being introduced to and educated into the sphere of feminine consumption" (2000, 109). Indeed, magazines are sites where messages of consumption intersect with images of fashion and the proliferation of advertisements to present utopian possibilities for the construction of self-style, but as McRobbie insists, it is the "energy and vitality" within magazines that should also be attended to (1997, 190). The simple view that "all women's fashion and beauty magazines are mere manuals for particular kinds of training in femininity" (Ingeborg Majer O' Sickey 1994, 23), needs to be problematized.

What has been recurrently hypothesized, starting with McRobbie (1977) and in much work since hers (Diana Crane 1999; Marjorie Ferguson 1983; Elizabeth Frazer 1987; Joke Hermes 1995; Leslie Rabine 1994) is that magazines, through ideological messages, socialize girls into gendered roles and a world of fear and neurosis. Such hypothesizing has meant that the context-specific reception and decoding of these inscribed messages have been neglected. Studies of text and content analysis are ultimately problematic in that they overlook (except McRobbie 1997, 198) how magazine editorial boards can also present a tongue-in-cheek, subversive and ironic style to girls, working with the awareness that girls are not easily manipulated and that to win their interest, it is often necessary to employ humorous or indirect tactics. Textual readings seem to now be less and less conclusive because alongside seductive messages of consumption in magazines, there exists a self-reflexive and deadpan cynicism that girls identify with.

Accordingly then, here I want to offer a reconciliation between what is prevalent on the one hand — a sense of apprehension in scholarship regarding young girls as victims of media and marketing manipulations with a constant emphasis on girls' "complicity and vulnerability" (Driscoll 2002: 280) — and what exists on the other — the voices of young girls that exhibit how they are not unknowing and naïve, indicating that there is room for celebration and empowerment through fashion and shopping.[2] Perhaps through shifting our perspective, we too can come to view the consumption of style for some of its liberating self-inventive qualities.

Methodology

In order to complement the theoretical hypothesis at the base of this examination, a total of thirteen tween girls who "really love to shop" were allowed to speak at length—and openly—about their views on the role that magazines play in their lives.[3] To reveal an array of meaning making, two groups of five girls were interviewed in focus group settings and three girls were interviewed in individual, conversational interviews. The individual interviews followed a set of shopping trips on which I accompanied the girls, letting them act as tour guides through shopping malls and large stores. I allowed the girls to act as my informants on everything from trendy accessories and clothing color schemes to celebrity hairstyles. The more I presented myself as unknowing and unaware, the more the girls offered to inform me.

Rationale for Type of Interview and Its Content

The content of the interview, arranged according to five main themes, was devised on the basis of the gaps found in the above literature. Primarily, I was interested in observing whether tween girls in their route to a creation of style and image through shopping are influenced by and incorporate the mediated messages of consumption offered by girls' (teen) magazines. Stemming from that question, my main inquiries were posed within the interview in a semi-structured manner.

The first topic area, *Relationship and Interaction with Shopping*, was designed to invite the participant to talk about her habits and views on shopping. The second area, *Shopping and Autonomy*, ascertained the extent to which what girls gather from magazines contributes to their shopping habits, their notions of fashion commodities and of teenhood. The third area, *Influence and Inspiration*, explored whether girls accept, interpret, contest, or reject the images of consumption that are dispersed through magazines. The questions posed here were designed to reveal details of the self-reflection, personal empowerment, or experimentation with modes of expression that the participants take part in, focusing on any possible links between these processes and their self-constructs. Emulation and role models were also discussed. The fourth area under discussion, *Shopping and Fashion as Fantasy and Escapism*, aimed to capture details about the weight of expectations that magazines create in girls. Do magazine portrayals of glamour create the sense that an ideal self can be attained through shopping? How much of what girls see in magazines is perceived as fantasy and how much as realistic was also assessed. The last area *Contradictions*, dealt with the main mixed messages or contradictions within magazines. How do girls deal with these contradictions? Do they feel that any negative structure of the magazines that preys on insecurities is juxtaposed with a positive structure that offers empowerment and encouragement?

The following report will briefly outline some of the responses, providing insights into the main research questions posed above.[4] What this research also endeavors to reveal is that questions about girls and the mediation and consumption of fashion and femininity have to be rewritten and readdressed, drawing the focus away from arguments about victimization and more towards a conceptualization of changing modern identities and new theories of consumer culture.[5]

Shopping to Be Adult: All Grown Up and No More to Grow

> I like going to malls, I like shopping even on the computer. When I go I bring friends along. I love stores like Claires and Forever 21. I don't like adult stores. When I grow older I want to move to some place where there is a mall—there definitely has to be a mall. When I see ads all I say is: I want that, I want that. I have a wish list all year long. I listed every single page from the catalogue... (Chloe, 7 years old)

Shopping, in the United States, is the second largest leisure activity after television viewing. As such, its impact on the formative years of girlhood cannot forego theorization. Among the few theories pointing to the increasing pervasiveness of shopping is Sharon Zukin's, attributing its growth to an increase in our desire for aesthetic pleasure and cultural goods (2004: 38). Zukin's thesis capitulates that shopping has become more compelling. The culture for it has globally broadened to the level that it now induces in us the view that the entire world is a shopping experience (257). "Consumer culture translates even our most idealistic desire for beauty, equality, and social acceptance into a need for commodities" (263). Most importantly then, Zukin's postulation that "we learn to be adults by learning to shop" (30) is a significant premise underlying the argument at hand: that the consumption habits of tweens are bound up in a search not only for self but also for an older self and as an eventual route, via teenhood, to adulthood. Let us now shift our focus to a conceptualization of shopping as a symbolic act. What, then, is the nature of the dialectical relationship that is formed between girls and the activity of reading, their internalization of the presented messages, and the act of shopping?

Can it be simply concluded that the power of the media (fashion magazines in this case), the absence of parental supervision, and the influence of peer groups all augment the downward trajectory of fashion consumption? Indeed the in-between nature of the transitional space between childhood and adulthood aggrandizes scholars' tensions about girls and their ensuing loss of innocence. Susan B. Kaiser suggests that the marketing of smaller versions of fashionable adult clothes to tweens has further truncated the "years of childhood" and that the "'age of protection' has given way to the 'age of preparation'" (Marie Winn, cited in Kaiser, 156). Paradoxically, not only our own anxieties about girls in the transition phase but also marketers' segmentation of clothing and makeup brands into age-specific stores as "classifying categories" "demonstrate how variable, context-specific and gendered these definitions of where childhood ends and adulthood begins are" (Valentine et al, cited in Driscoll 2002: 215; 204).[6]

The prevalence of hysteria in theoretical discourse and news media about 'tweensploitation' and the loss of childhood innocence appears authenticated when we acknowledge the impact of magazine representations and magazine- mediated consumption on girls. Undeniably, anxieties may also seem granted when we learn how much girls view the simple act of shopping to be capable of enacting a route to adulthood and when we comprehend that through magazines, girls may be taught that the acquisition of material goods of style and beauty can provide them an entry into a more extraordinary world.

Shopping for Our New 'Selves'

I'm not a girl, not yet a woman. (Britney Spears)

You're too old for the "Angel Is Sleeping" pillow and too young for the T-shirt blazoned with the word "Hottie." (Ann Gerhart, *The Washington Post,* 1 September 2001, p. C.01).

I can't wait till I'm 13, cause then I could just walk outta the house whenever I want and not tell anyone. Oh and I could get a cell phone. (Saira, 7 years old)

I want to be like my older sister because I want to copy her style—she's crazy and wild. (Nina, 8 years old)

For tween girls the anticipation of teenhood is indeed bigger than its arrival. This preparation for adolescence through consumption and fashion can perhaps illuminate how it is that "feminine adolescence [is] channeled into and constituted in consumption" (Driscoll, 218). The girls' statements in the study here expounded how the inauguration of shopping for clothes and style symbolized a transgression from childhood. The moment in which each girl was able to shop for herself was seen as the ultimate moment that an independence associated with older girls had arrived:

> I always had to stay by my mom's side when we went shopping and now she just lets me go off with my sister or with friends. I never even had fun or even liked shopping when I was going to boring stores with my mom but now it's my favorite thing to do (Ginny, 8 years old).

All the girls' sentiments reflect how shopping is a predominant recreational and social activity for them, providing a sharing and enriching experience away from the home or schoolyard. The accounts also amplify the salient view in girls that the surfacing and inception of shopping for image and beauty products for the 'self' is regarded as a turning point towards adulthood and autonomy.

If it is through commodities that the very idea of "participation in girlhood" and the route to a feminine adolescence is marketed (Driscoll: 268), I would like to propose that the whole field of preteen consumption of images, fashion, and beauty products can be expressed in terms of a rite of passage over a boundary.[7] This can be articulated in two senses: First, it is a means by which tween girls, in their interaction with magazines, easily cross the boundary into an extraordinary world of glamour and fantasy that the magazines open up to them. This enacts a daily transgression from their 'ordinary world' to a more 'sacred' one of the magazines, and as a result, they are transformed by the experience. Second, this interaction can be understood as a life-stage progression from preteen to teen and eventually into adulthood— a commoditized rite of passage between girlhood and eventual womanhood. Indeed then, the act of shopping to 'be adult' is actualized specifically in how "the steps toward autonomy are measured by exercising a consumer's choice" (Zukin, 54).[8]

Ingeborg Majer O'Sickey states that change happens through buying, that magazines only act to "teach girls that women, like cars, must be restyled each year" (1994, 24). Elaborating on *Barbie Magazine*, she suggests that the magazine, through each issue, acts to convince its readers that they are in perpetual need of renovation. How is it, then, that magazines construct the dichotomous boundary between young and old or "sacred" and "profane" (Emile Durkheim 1912, reprinted 1995) and naturalize the route to growing up? Perhaps it is precisely through exercising their "symbolic power," defined by Pierre Bourdieu as "the power of constructing reality" (1990, 166), and employed by Nick Couldry to explain the organization of media that use symbolic forms like writing and images to exercise domination (whether ideologically manipulative or not) (2003, 54). The term further evinces how there is a power involved in these symbolic forms because the privilege and ability to produce them is not available to everyone. It is media institutions' symbolic power that allows them to uphold categories that readers understand themselves through and also enables them to construct a boundary separating the two worlds, reinforcing all that is sacred and extraordinary (teen and older; magazine world of glamour) by placing the profane (girl readers; non-magazine world) in relation to it. Therefore, by marking the boundary between the inaccessible and the ordinary world and by utilizing their own power to construct reality in terms of a "media world" versus "ordinary world" dichotomy, magazines offer the sense that it is important to cross this very boundary that has been fabricated and enforced by them in the first place (Couldry 2000).

Essentially, magazines strengthen and reinforce the two types of boundaries explained above and then market the crossing over as a product. Subsequent to that then, magazines bolster the view in their readers that their worlds are merely simple and childish and that only by way of consumption can they access the route to adulthood and sophistication. Hence, the triangulated acts of magazine reading, internalization of the messages of consumption and the shopping experience, can be seen to offer girls a rite of passage through which they enter an unfamiliar and exciting world, leaving behind a familiar and mundane one, emerging transformed by their experience.

> Sam: I know it sounds really bad, but sometimes I feel that those [teen] celebrities and models in those magazines and on TV look so happy with all the clothes they have and I think that if I had as many clothes as they have then I'll be just as happy. Sometimes I get something and then I see someone get something that is just a little better and I get frustrated.

Perhaps this quote from an eleven-year-old can highlight the extent to which magazines' symbolic power to construct an hierarchical boundary between average girl readers and the world of extraordinary and 'special' teens (special because they appear 'in' the media) having fun, dressed in fashionable clothes and accessories, becomes naturalized. Through presenting childhood as boring and passé, by drawing attention to the sacred world of commodities and what they represent to the reader as her more profane world lacking such commodities, and by deeming and declaring that which is in style and that which is "OUT" or last season, magazines make childhood appear as if it should be thrown into the pile with the clothes of yesteryear. By looking down on all that is young, magazines only further affirm the superiority of womanhood and of older girls (Bourdieu 1984).

Couldry suggests that it is simply because of the space between the spheres of media consumption and media production that the symbolic division and magazines' ability to exercise symbolic power are strengthened (2000, 53). In addition to enforcing the dichotomous division, magazines also mislead girls to believe that they exercise their own free will—choosing for themselves out of all the choice that is given to them. This fact is further intensified as girls' readings become transferred onto the act of shopping. The tactics used by marketers and magazines convince readers that they have power, control, and choice. But in actuality, one could consider, as Mazzarella indicates, magazines are merely presenting a form of power (and a sense of agency which is false) that is acquired through commodities, painting the picture that identity is all about what one purchases and how one dresses the self in these commodities (106).

According to this viewpoint, girls' will to buy is falsified, when in reality the magazines and marketers have already done the work of deciding what the 'must haves' and the 'can't live withouts' are. Furthermore, commodities— presented as playful fantasies and options among many for a better and more grown-up self—as well as the presence of positive and empowering messages in magazines could also be perceived as "commodity feminism" a phenomenon that translates "feminist goals of individuality, independence, and control over one's life" into "the freedom to choose commodities to define one's independence" (Roberet Goldman, cited in Mazzarella 109).

Even Driscoll, who grants girls an agency, highlights that conformity and complacency are disguised and sold as agency: "any marketing strategy works by trying to manipulate conformity, including conformity to the image of nonconformity" (269). A thorough analysis of tween consumption cannot be complete without acknowledging that "the girl market describes a demographic wrapped up in negotiating their own power and powerlessness through consumption" (269).

Subsequent to that then, magazines—by mediating consumption, by portraying that teenhood is better than childhood, and by convincing tweens of their autonomy in consumption choices—can be perceived to actualize the relationship among commodities, consumer agency, and the route to adulthood. But representations in magazines also serve as unconscious mechanisms through which identities are formed in conjunction with the conscious consumption of fashion and style commodities, promising the deliverance of sophisticated, new, and improved selves.

Shopping and Dressing to Be What *They* Show Me I Should Be: Identities Formed in Magazine Representations of Consumption and Fashion

Mediated consumption and magazine representations

> At my school everybody looks like each other and like what they see in magazines, and then it makes you feel like you should look like that too. It's crazy because that's probably how I'm supposed to look like if I want to be like the people in the magazines with their perfect lives. (Zia, 9 years old)

Even as this quote reflects an acknowledgment of conformity, it does amplify how girls become increasingly aware of their selves in relation to the media and in relation to others around them. Magazines, thus, are recognized by most theorists as a barometer of how women and girlhood are represented in the popular media (McRobbie 2000, 191), the media being "both a principal focus of imagination, creativity and identification *and* a principal source of information and representation," helping to "define both the facts of our social reality *and* our individual desires" (Couldry 2000, 40). John Thompson indicates that the development of the media has heightened and accentuated the reflexive organization of the self by opening it up to outside knowledge and rendering audiences dependent on material symbolic systems that are not within their control (1995). Concurrently, Susan J. Douglas (1994) writes that "by pitching so many things to us all the time that were only and specifically for us the mass media insisted that *we* mattered" (25), that "we were desperate to know which type we were, to know ourselves, and we looked to the mass media for answers" (99). While Douglas is referring to a bygone era, the impact of the mass media on girls' lives and identities has only become stronger and more persistent (there are now more monthly magazines for girls than at any other period in time).

We are informed that through magazines girls are inevitably taught how to measure and perceive themselves, their personal style, and their own bodies. Valerie Walkerdine, in her work on comics as texts that girls' desire is formed on, reflects on this trend: "girls do indeed form ambitions and desires around aspects of femininity which are presented to them" (1997, 50). Driscoll, too, asserts that the "girl market" uses pop culture to mediate identification and "generic conventions for becoming a woman" (284).

If magazines have the capacity to act as a means by which girls are sold an image and an ideal of what they should or ought to be, how then, do tween girls interact with what is offered up for their visual and imaginative purposes? As this study asserts, strictly deterministic views of tween girls and media influence are often inconclusive. One prominent finding here provides evidence that perhaps social relations—in addition to magazines—are also significant for the development of image and identity. In other words, how girls feel they are perceived by others reinforces how they view themselves. The *self as it is defined in relation with others* is particularly evident in participants' statements indicating that self-approval often comes as a result of the approval of others.

Constructs of the self too are formed based in part on the views or support of others (mostly peers and sometimes magazines). The following assertion reflects the common theme in all the participants' comments: even though magazines affect girls' views, ultimately the people around them and their acceptance are much more significant. The statements also indicate to what degree magazines play a role in shaping girls' self-fashionings:

> Most people I know either dress like their sister or their other friends. Sometimes I do get confused because I don't know whether to wear this kind of style or the other and it's mostly because of what my friends would like or what they would say is better. (Tabitha, 10 years old)

By contrast, for twelve-year-old Tania (as was the case for a few of the other participants) a construction of identity and appearance also came in relation to her mother, who wasn't concerned about her appearance and provoked, in Tania, a desire to be the opposite:

> Tania: I know that all my friends think I am obsessed with clothes and hair. I feel that I should always be looking my best because my mother isn't that way. I guess I learned all of my hair and makeup tips from those magazines. I never thought about that, but I guess it is like my role model for beauty.

Another prominent theme in all the participants' responses describes how they construct their appearance in relation to trends or as contrary to trends and 'other people':

> Amy: And you see maybe a celebrity or maybe a model wearing something and looking great and then I'd see maybe people on the street wearing it and I'd think ok so there's ordinary people also looking really nice and that's when I say, "Oh I really want it." In a way I'm like, "Oh that's fashionable, everyone's going to be wearing it maybe I should buy those shoes or whatever." And then I'll be like very happy when I've got them. If I dress up to go shopping I've got to feel like I'm wearing what I like and that it is kind of fashionable so that the people in the stores also see me as fashion-y. (10 years old)

Aiming for individualism—to not be a 'clone'—was also a key factor in the determination of 'style' for all the participants:

> Zia: I don't want to turn myself into some kind of a clone or I'll totally look like every other girl at school who bought the same at all the stores. (9 years old)

Similarly, Chloe noted:

> We don't have a uniform at my school so hardly nobody wears the same clothes twice. My friend ended up wearing the same outfit as somebody else on picture day—the same shoes, same pants—it was like a whole outfit that came together. It was funny that they had the same ones….My school had the choice to vote for having uniforms but we voted against it because it's better to have everyone look individual. (7 years old)

To that, eleven-year-old Minah added:

> My school has a uniform and so we have free days when we can wear whatever we want to. But there are rules about what we can't wear like jeans and hoodies. They don't let us wear those things because they don't want us to express our personalities now do they [sarcasm].

Consequently, as a few of the prevalent themes in the interview data for this study have indicated, how girls construct their style is not solely determined by magazine representations; the social relations in their lives contribute quite strongly to their 'projects of the self.' Another essential factor in shaping the participant girls' appearance and style is the way in which they negotiate their *desire to be glamorous* (stemming from magazine representations and messages) as well as the positive encouragement and insecurities that arise out of this desire. The effect of this fascination with glamour has a positive influence: images of glamour can encourage the participant to 'be all that she can be'; they can create aspiration and emulation; they can broaden the girls' world-views and sense of place by presenting possibilities for the attainment of success, and they can provide opportunities for elevation, escapism, or fantasy. Eight-year-old Ginny phrased this well: "Magazines can tell me what is happening outside of my little world." Contrarily, the desire to be glamorous can certainly encompass negative attributes. All the participants substantiated that the portrayal of glamour could have an authoritative effect and that ultimately magazines aim to sell consumption through the guise of glamour. Ginny said: "Magazines always make me feel like I am not ever stylish enough."

While mediated consumption socializes girls into a commodity-identified womanhood, the consumption of fashion can also be regarded as an activity that affirms and strengthens collective status or performs a self-affirming and individual quality-related act (Zukin, 195).[9] Hence, although there certainly are detrimental attributes to the early formation of consumption habits among girls, as has been outlined above, there are indeed openings through which girls resist the kinds of control that theories of media effects concentrate on. What follow are instances of the empowering and liberating possibilities of self-invention through style and fashion, highlighted through the voices of young girls.

Eleven-year-old Kate's remarks reflect how significant the ideal of 'glamour' is for her self-image and appearance, how being glamorous seems to make opportunity accessible, and how simple attempts at being glamorous can offer escape, elevation, and an alternative to the banality of everyday life:

> What I don't have…it's to be really trendy and to be really kind of glamorous….I guess it is some sort of fantasy world of the very glamorous girls going to costume parties, proms or even the movies. There's a part of me that likes to escape into that world and the clothes are kind of a part of that. Like, if I'm going to school and I'm wearing beautiful shoes that have like a little bit of a heel, it makes me feel better— not like better than everyone else but it makes me feel cooler and better about my

day and takes away the boringness of just wearing the same old boring things to school.

Tabitha (10 years old) offered:

> The magazines may look like they are telling you: you should wear this makeup, and these kind of clothes, you should follow this kind of style, you should be doing this with your boyfriend, that you should want to travel to these places. But really that's why me and my friends buy them. That stuff is very inspiring and even the make-over stories are so encouraging.

While we may conclude that girls do not entirely have the tools with which to deconstruct negative cultural stereotypes, ultimately the manner in which mediated messages and representations of consumption are recontextualized by girls cannot be overlooked. Just as representations can be decoded in alternate ways, commodities too can be readapted once bought. Hollows states: "consumption is not simply identified with shopping but also the ways in which 'commodities are taken "home" and adapted and reinterpreted in establishing relationships and social positions'" (J. Clarke, cited in Hollows 116). It is important, then, to draw our attention to how consumption does play a role in defining girls, not only as groups and in terms of demographics but also as individuals. For instance, even the conscious picking and choosing that occurs in girls' construction of self through fashion and style commodities is ripe with definitive possibilities for experimentation and self-invention. Since demographics ultimately only exist as marketing categories, it is more productive to understand girl culture and consumption in terms of self-production and "identification" (Driscoll, 269).

Thus far, it has been illustrated that girls' styles and self-constructs are shaped as a consequence of mediated socialized consumption, marking the consumption-influenced rite of passage from childhood to adulthood. It has been proposed also that girls' selves are formed from identification, in contact with representations and with others around them. Let us focus now on the ways in which girls' consumption of fashion (whether *in* magazines or prompted by magazines) can be understood, in effect, as a conscious and active production of selves.

Fashion Consumption as a Route to the Perfect Self

There are theoreticians who draw attention to the fact that magazines (like much of the rest of the media) create a split in their audience. Even with the recognition that magazines are not one coherent monolithic entity and that indeed there are many contradictions within them (contradictions that girl readers have to reconcile), the views of the participants in this inquiry indicate, how as receivers, they take charge of the ultimate meanings that they want to derive from magazines. For example, it was revealed that girls might find empowerment from the very same representations that are theorized to be embedded with ideologies and messages that prey on their insecurities (Hermes 1995). Magazine messages that compel girls to be glamorous, sophisticated, and uninhibited may be considered to impose on them unachievable standards of perfection and ideals of womanhood and femininity. However, they could also be regarded as encouragement for girls to realize their full potential and to cultivate a fun-filled girlhood—to be 'all that they want to be.'

For the girls that participated in this analysis, the ways in which *the rituals of fashion and beauty* hold an importance in their lives, and are promoted by magazines, are a crucial aspect in the construction of a fun and style-aware self. These rituals offer opportunities for self-expression, nurturing, pampering, and celebrating girlhood. The following statement demonstrates participants' recurrent allusions to experimentation with modes of expression:

> Francesca: I like magazines telling us things, like about a nice papaya bubble bath, or showing ways to do hairstyles. I like the make-up and fashions. It can be so much fun and a great way to express yourself. (8 years old)

Furthermore, while postmodernist readings of consumer culture would conclude that the magnitude of choice in consumer goods hinders the creation of a fixed identity, such a view also salutes the use of fashion and style as a guise wherein an artifactually constructed self is just as significant as one that may be formed through social experience. Ultimately, then, according to such a reading, one is free to self-produce, constructing identities from "looks, images, and consumption" (Douglas Kellner 1992, 153–154). Kellner's thesis on the self, formed in interaction with the media, negates the notion that identities are handed to us; it proposes instead that each person changes roles and takes on various images in accordance with what she interprets from media messages (153). Similarly, John Thompson explains the manner by which receivers appropriate messages and incorporate them into their own self-formations: "individuals increasingly draw on mediated experience to inform and refashion the project of the self" (1995, 231–233), in the process selectively filtering or ignoring those materials that are not of interest to them (209). Thompson offers that the media's intrusion has neither dissolved nor destabilized the self as a coherent entity but rather that the self is multiple and that it is merely the nature of the self that is changing as it is opened up and made vulnerable to media messages (232).

If, as Hollows, too, speculates, "our sense of who we are increasingly comes from what and how we consume," then "our identities are not fixed but something we can play with, construct and reconstruct through our use of commodities" (132). Following from that, fashion and clothing can be understood as cultural markers that not only allow a purchase of an individual or group identity but also a real or imagined one (Jennifer Scanlon 2000, 7). Contrarily to the aforementioned dichotomous perspective, in which the fashion world's sacred and the reader world's profane are polar opposites, Leslie W. Rabine states, "imitated from magazines, movies or videos, and worn in daily life, fashion erases the boundary between the 'real' and the 'fantastic'" (1994, 63). Although magazines may be assumed to destabilize girls' selves only to present them with new products through which to restabilize themselves (Kellner, 166), there are also "endless possibilities of reinvention" (Zukin, 9) available through the ideas presented within them—ideas for restructuring of the self and for emulation, via advertisements which depict lifestyles, utopian images, and assurances for more glamorous selves (Kellner, 159–163). Can tween girls consciously use these ideas and images as empowering tools for the construction of a self-fashioned individual style? And what potential can we see in tween fantasies about goods as a way to the perfect self (Zukin, 263)? The following quotes from the informants might offer some insight:

> Sam: I mean a lot of people would say it's not good to be worried about makeup or whatever. But I think it is because it does make you feel good about yourself if you are wearing something nice or looking good. Why shouldn't you spend time or money on yourself? I don't think magazines are like: you should dress like this to try and get a boy. (11 years old)

> Francesca: Magazines can help you with your appearance, and make you feel good about yourself and tell you what is the fashion. And I can know that I can buy something and wear it and feel trendy in it because I've seen it in magazines and I can feel quite good about how I look. (8 years old)

Amy: Do you know they're always doing stories about "I had this and I'm so much happier now?" Just in the same way as "Oh I had my haircut in some sort of new style and now I feel awesome." And those can really get you excited about following the trends and dressing up. (10 years old)

While it is all too easy to wax poetic about the victimization intrinsic in magazine-induced consumption, there are also sensual aspects inherent in the activity of shopping—it can offer a liberating quality. Within studies of consumer culture, theorists are now beginning to regard consumption as less passive and more active and even an "heroic activity" granting access to "new frontiers" and allowing people to "construct meanings and create a sense of identity" (Hollows, 129). Ultimately, in their interaction with magazines ("and the branded stores, boutiques, discount chains, and websites where [they] shop") girls can indeed shape their "dreams about a perfect society...and about a perfect self"—real or ideal (Zukin, 10).[10]

Towards a new conceptualization of consumption

Taking from this embracing of the liberating aspects in shopping (Zukin; Scanlon; Hollows) and Scanlon's proposal that consumption is a collaborative process wherein the consumer is not just a dupe (9), this exploration, by revisiting a familiar site of examination, has attempted to investigate how tween girls resist, negotiate, and/or accept imposed messages of fashion and beauty consumption. The goal was to ascertain how much has changed for girl readers of magazines as well as to decipher the complex value that tween girls, in particular, can derive for their own construction of identity (especially in terms of fashion, image, and appearance). By exemplifying some of the diverse reasons that make mediated messages of consumption and fashion both a meaningful aid and a hindrance in the construction of girls' own style and image, it has been illustrated here that girls can and do devise their subjectivity from the mixed package of magazines and fashion marketing. Surely, girls read magazines for many differing reasons. Magazines and the related act of shopping provide more than just "momentary enjoyment" (McCracken 1993, 164) to tween girls. Even with the contradictions explicit in magazines and their inherent manipulations, the ways in which they can offer a challenging ground for the contestation and negotiation of ideas about a rite of passage from girlhood to adulthood, can encourage the actualizing of each girl's potential, can offer openings and possibilities for girls to relate to fun-filled and ironic portrayals of fashion and can offer a celebration of

selves require appreciation.[11] Hence the inclusion of girls' perspective in sociological, cultural, and feminist thought has to be, not a temporary measure,
but a normalized one.

Notes

[1] Consumption as considered by Pierre Bourdieu can be understood here as a process of communication that presupposes practical and explicit mastery of a cipher or code. By giving this code away, magazines inscribe the social order (1984).

[2] McRobbie wisely insists that feminism, by focusing only on girls' victimization, overlooks the chance for debate on girlhood popular culture, desires, and identities (1997, 208).

[3] The sample, which is ethnically and socio-economically diverse, is intentionally limited to tween girls who enjoy shopping and partake in it without always being accompanied by an adult. Due to the limitations of this small project, no generalizations are made about race and class.

[4] The interview data were analyzed based on the predominance of themes and concerns in the respondents' statements. The most cohesive way to understand the views of tween girls in a true social and cultural analytical context was through thematic analysis, which entailed deriving a coding framework from the interview data.

[5] Mediation can have varied meanings: "ranging from neutrally informing, through negotiation, to attempts at manipulation and control" (Dennis McQuail 2000, 66). Here it will be used to describe "the fundamentally, but unevenly, dialectical process in which institutionalized media of communication (…) are involved in the general circulation of symbols in social life" (Silverstone 2002, 3).

[6] As Sonia Livingstone et al. elaborate, children as young as toddlers start being targeted and trained to consume, either through the use of cross-promotional practices wherein marketers use television programs to tie in and promote toys and products or through the toy gifts that come with their hamburger happy meals (2001, 10). Furthermore, marketers understand that it is primarily girls who 'go shopping.' They have learned that a tween girl will go through copious wardrobe, style, and bedroom décor changes, rarely showing loyalty to any one brand, because in tween culture brand status and trends are fickle.

[7] See Bourdieu (1990).

[8] Sharon R. Mazzarella presents a case of magazine-driven consumption where the high school prom is used to lure readers into buying products to assuage 'prom panic' and fulfill their dream of a 'perfect' prom. Similarly, preparations, by tweens, for teenhood or 'pre-teen panic' happen on a daily basis, where girls—prompted by magazines—take to purchasing goods to achieve the perfect look.

[9] What is an "economic" or "practical" function is transformed into a "cultural" practice of consumption (Zukin, 260).

[10] Zukin (40) even suggests that one can derive cultural capital from the democratic activities of shopping and browsing in opposition to Bourdieu, who defines cultural capital as the product of a privileged upbringing and education (1984).

[11] Further development is still required, however, to fully make comprehensible the extent to which consumer agency and magazines—in a global as well as local context—can play a role in imparting girls tools for self-expression and self-empowerment beyond questions of image and appearance.

References

Bourdieu, P. *Distinction: A Social Critique of the Judgment of Taste.* London: Routledge, 1984.

——. *Language and Symbolic Power.* Cambridge: Polity Press, 1990.

Buckingham, D. *Reading Audiences: Young People and the Media.* Manchester: Manchester UP, 1993.

Couldry, N. *The Place of Media Power: Pilgrims and Witnesses of the Media Age.* London: Routledge, 2000.

——. *Media Rituals: A Critical Approach.* London: Routledge, 2003.

Crane, D. "Gender and Hegemony in Fashion Magazines: Women's Interpretations of Fashion Photographs." *The Sociological Quarterly* 40, no. 4 (1999): 541–563.

Currie, D. "Decoding Femininity: Advertisements and Their Teenage Readers." *Gender and Society* 11, no. 4 (1997): 453–477.

Douglas, S. J. *Where the Girls Are: Growing up Female with the Mass Media.* New York: Penguin Books, 1994.

Driscoll, C. *Girls: Feminine Adolescence in Popular Culture and Cultural Theory.* New York: Columbia University Press, 2002.

Durkheim, E. *The Elementary Forms of Religious Life,* 1st edition 1912. Translated by K. Fields. Glencoe: Free Press, 1995.

Ferguson, M. *Forever Feminine: Women's Magazines and the Cult of Femininity.* London: Heinemann, 1983.

Frazer, E. "Teenage Girls Reading Jackie." *Media, Culture and Society* 9 (1987): 407–425.

Goldman, R. *Reading Ads Socially.* London: Routledge, 1992.

Hebdige, D. *Subculture: The Meaning of Style.* London: Methuen, 1979.

Hermes, J. *Reading Women's Magazines.* Cambridge: Blackwell, 1995.

Hollows, J. *Feminism, Femininity and Popular Culture.* Manchester: Manchester University Press, 2000.

Kaiser, S. B. "Fashion, Media, and Cultural Anxiety: Visual Representations of Childhood." In *Mediating the Human Body: Technology, Communication, and Fashion,* edited by L. Fortunati, J. E. Katz, and R. Riccini. 155-162. Mahwah, New Jersey: Lawrence Erlbaum Associates, 2003.

Kellner, D. "Popular Culture and the Construction of Postmodern Identities." In *Modernity and Identity,* edited by S. Lash and J. Friedman, 141–177. London: Blackwell, 1992.

Leblanc, L. *Pretty in Punk: Girls' Gender Resistance in a Boys' Subculture.* New Brunswick, New Jersey: Rutgers University Press, 1999.

Livingstone, S., L. d'Haenens, and U. Hasebrink. "Childhood in Europe: Contexts for Comparison." In *Children and Their Changing Media Environment: A European Comparative Study,* edited by S. Livingstone and M. Bovill, 20–27. London: Lawrence Erlbaum Associates, 2001.

Mazzarella, S. R. "The 'Superbowl of All Dates': Teenage Girl Magazines and the Commodification of the Perfect Prom." In *Growing Up Girls: Popular Culture and the Construction of Identity,* edited by S. Mazzarella and N. Pecora, 97–112. New York: Peter Lang, 1999.

Mazzarella, S. R., and N. Pecora., eds. *Growing Up Girls: Popular Culture and the Construction of Identity.* New York: Peter Lang, 1999.

McCracken, E. *Decoding Women's Magazines: From Mademoiselle to Ms.* London: Macmillan, 1993.

McQuail, D. *Mass Communication Theory: An Introduction,* 4th edition. London: Sage, 2000.

McRobbie, A. *Feminism and Youth Culture: From Jackie to Just Seventeen.* Basingstoke: Macmillan, 1991.

———. "More! New Sexualities in Girls' and Women's Magazines." In *Back to Reality? Social Experience and Cultural Studies,* edited by A. McRobbie, 190–209. New York: Manchester University Press, 1997.

———. *In the Culture Society: Art, Fashion and Popular Music.* London: Routledge, 1999.

———. *Feminism and Youth Culture,* 2nd edition. London: Macmillan Press, 2000.

McRobbie, A., and J. Garber. "Girls and Subcultures." In *Resistance Through Rituals: Youth Subcultures in Post-war Britain,* edited by S. Hall and T. Jefferson, 112–120. Essex, England: Hutchison University Library, 1976.

Muggleton, D. *Inside Subculture: The Postmodern Meaning of Style.* New York: New York University Press, 2000.

Myers, K. "Fashion 'N Passion." In *Looking On: Images of Femininity in the Visual Arts and Media,* edited by R. Betterton 58–65. London: Pandora, 1987.

O'Sickey, I. M. "*Barbie Magazine* and the Aesthetic Commodification of Girls' Bodies." In *On Fashion,* edited by S. Benstock and S. Ferriss, 21–40. New Brunswick, New Jersey: Rutgers University Press, 1994.

Rabine, L. W. "A Woman's Two Bodies: Fashion Magazines, Consumerism and Feminism." In *On Fashion,* edited by S. Benstock and S. Ferriss, 59–75. New Brunswick, New Jersey: Rutgers University Press, 1994.

Scanlon, J., ed. *The Gender and Consumer Culture Reader.* New York: New York University Press, 2000.

Silverstone, R. "Complicity and Collusion in the Mediation of Everyday Life." *New Literary History* 33 (2002): 745–764.

Steele, V. *Fetish: Fashion, Sex, and Power.* Oxford: Oxford University Press, 1996.

Thompson, J. *The Media and Modernity.* Cambridge: Polity Press, 1995.

Valentine, G., T. Skelton, and D. Chambers. "Cool Places: An Introduction to Youth and Youth Cultures." In *Cool places: Geographies of Youth Cultures,* edited by T. Skelton and G. Valentine, 1–32. New York: Routledge, 1998.

Walkerdine, V. *Daddy's Girl: Young Girls and Popular Culture.* Cambridge, Massachusetts: Harvard University Press, 1997.

Zukin, S. *Point of Purchase: How Shopping Changed American Culture.* New York: Routledge, 2004.

CHAPTER SEVENTEEN

Constructing the Digital Tween: Market Discourse and Girls' Interests

Rebekah Willett

Market analysts tell us that tweens in Britain have more disposable income than ever before, coupled with greater influence over parental purchases (Bradberry 2003; Casselle 2001). Commercial companies have seen this buying power as an opportunity for creating a profitable new niche in the market. As a result, specialist tween products have emerged, which include everything from clothes to cosmetics, magazines to websites. We know that material objects are used by young people as markers of identity, defining their specific social groups and distinguishing class, race, and gender as well as age (Lury 1996). However, it is not clear whether tweens in Britain are buying into the market discourse and using objects to mark their age or, indeed, whether they wish to classify themselves as a distinct audience. Asking a group of girls aged 11–12 in Britain if they know of the term 'tween' or 'tweenager,' they say 'Oh, you mean teenager' or they ask with a hint of distaste, 'Like in Tweenies?' (a BBC TV show for under-fives), or finally hypothesize that they may have heard the word in Scotland. The construction of the tween, therefore, may be nothing more than market discourse.

Although tween marketing is capturing the pocket money of the girls I will be discussing in this chapter, the concept of a 'tween' as a separate group of young people has yet to hit the consciousness of the tweens or the general public in Britain. This chapter looks at British girls' perceptions of the tween market as constructed by new media, using data collected from focus groups of 11–12-year-old girls in which the girls researched, discussed, and designed websites targeted for tweens. The chapter will start with a textual analysis of websites targeted specifically for tweens and contrast that with an analysis of the websites tweens actually use. These textual analyses will provide a basis for the third section of this chapter, which looks at tweens' productions of personal websites. In all three sections, the focus is on the different ways the distinct social identities are constructed for and by tweens and how tweens interact with those constructions.

Researching Digital Tweens

The data for this chapter were collected in two different research sites over the course of 18 months, from September 2001–April 2003. Both sites were located in urban areas within mixed socio-economic and ethnic communities. One site was a cyber café at an arts center in London, which offered arts classes on the weekends to children from low-income families. The other was a state secondary school located on a large housing estate just outside London. In the arts center, I observed children ages 3–13 interacting in the cyber café every Saturday over the course of the academic year (September 2001–June 2002). In the school, I ran an intensive two-day workshop for thirteen girls aged 11–12 in which we researched the term tween, analyzed websites constructed for tweens, and then designed and constructed personal websites. The girls for this workshop were chosen first through a process of elimination based on who had returned their parent/carer permission slips, and then by the teachers, who put together a group with a mix of abilities and ethnicities. In both research sites, I used ethnographic-based research methods, attempting to downplay my position as an authority figure and setting up mini-disk players with microphones as a regular feature of the computer rooms. Data collection included recordings of conversations between children of various ages, observations of tweens on the Internet, semi-structured small-group interviews, formal written research done by tweens, and website designs (on paper and live on the Internet).

Tween-only Websites—Cyberspace Constructions of Tweens

Websites targeted only at tween girls (i.e., websites that have specific statements about tweens or preteens on their home pages) are certainly present in cyberspace. However, with the enormous assortment of cyber activities available to tweens, targeting this one audience on the Internet is difficult, and, given the limited amount of online spending a tween can do without a credit card, tween-only sites do not yield huge profits. In my research, I did not see a tween choose to go on a website targeted solely for tweens, and when I provided lists of tween-only sites for them to look at, the girls quickly moved on to their own favorites. It is worth looking at the tween websites and comparing them with favorite websites of tweens to see how the tween is constructed on the sites and perhaps to locate how tweens are identifying themselves within the cultures available on the Internet. This section will give a brief textual analysis of three tween-only websites (a Public Broadcasting Service site, It's My Life, and two commercial sites, Go Goddess Girl! and Kylie Klub), focusing on how the tween audience is constructed on each site.

The first site by PBS, It's My Life (http://pbskids.org/itsmylife/), obviously has a different background and objective than commercial sites. With public funding, the site was designed under an initiative that aims "'to create safe, engaging, and educational online media for kids aged 9 to 12'" (http://pbskids.org/itsmylife/about_us.html).[1] The site offers games, advice, articles, polls, quizzes, and movie clips, which all canter around issues or problems faced by tweens. Although there are visual elements, the site is heavily text based, and the site does not attempt to use specialized tween vocabulary. Even the games require reading and are centered on topics such as how tobacco affects your body, caring for a younger sibling, and bullying. This site, therefore, constructs the tween within an educational framework. Tweens here are in need of advice and guidance for the many changes that they are experiencing in their lives, particularly in relation to social and emotional situations. They need to read, talk about, and practice tricky situations they are likely to encounter, for example, experiencing peer pressure to smoke. Above all, the site constructs the tween as facing innumerable risks in every area of life: for example, under the heading 'body,' where one might expect information about sexualities, masturbation, or menstruation, the topics include drug abuse, eating disorders, and smoking. This construction of the tween is supported by popular discourse concerning the developmental stage called adolescence. According to Frost (2001), "Adolescence has now for more than a century been pathologized by adults as a time of difficulties and disturbances, needing a variety of kinds of interventions and reforms" (81). *It's My Life* draws on this discourse and positions the tween as vulnerable and suggests that risks are to be avoided through access to information and social and emotional support (via an adult). However, one could also argue that the tween is addressed as a serious and intelligent Internet user—nothing on this site is 'dumbed down,' and there are no condescending attempts to appeal to tween popular culture.

Although the other two sites I will analyze are both commercial ones, they construct their tween audience in ways that are entirely different from each other as well as from the PBS site. Go Goddess Girl! (http://www.gogoddessgirl.com) centers on a game and book for tween girls. The game and site are designed by three women and three tweens (ages 7–10), the daughters of one of the women. The game is based on an adult game connected to a "communications company" which promotes "empowerment, enrichment and entertainment" for women (http://www.gogoddess.com/about/). The splash page on the site is strikingly different from on the PBS site—the introduction includes music, psychedelic colors, and tween words such as "wazzup" flashing around the screen. The message here could be interpreted as one of acceptance of tween culture, or it could be interpreted as an overly simplified and stereotyped attempt to appeal to tweens. The home page addresses tweens with the message that they are powerful—"the game where you know ALL the answers," "tell the world what you can do!!!" (http://www.gogoddessgirl.com/splash.html). The concept of the company is based around discovering which 'goddess' you are. For the tweens, the 'goddesses' are depicted as fairies with trendy clothing—another attempt to appeal to tween culture.

This combination of tween culture and New Age spirituality is reflected in a speech bubble from one of the tweens on the site: "I'm brave and bold like Aphrodite and I've got great hair too!" The text on the website describes tweens as facing changes and issues, and the solution is getting tweens to turn inward through discussion with peers:

> Go Goddess Girl! Tween Talk gets girls sharing their feelings, learning from each other and understanding that they are going through all these changes together. With gab and giggles, tweens turn their focus to what's inside their heads and hearts and finish knowing that they can be whatever they want to be.... (http://www.gogoddessgirl .com/aboutus.html)

There is a striking contrast between the ways tweens are constructed on this site and the PBS site. The girls' culture is celebrated through the tween-based images and text, unlike the PBS site, which contains very few references to popular tween culture. At first glance, the Goddess girls are depicted as powerful, and they can get their support through their peers and themselves; they are not vulnerable or in need of adult guidance as on the PBS site. However, one could also interpret the Go Goddess site as depicting an underlying anxiety about tween girls. Girls are in need of empowering, because they feel powerless. The girls on the site are depicted very carefully by their mothers—which, in fact, renders them powerless. The parents see themselves as starting the girls on their path to self-confidence, but instead of telling the girls how to lead their lives, the 'goddess' gimmick is used by the parents as a way of guiding the girls through adult-approved means disguised as peer culture. Looking at popular discourse that constructs adolescence as a difficult stage of life, parents are often implicated in this discourse as the key to guiding their children, particularly as an assurance against the dangers of peer pressure (Frost 2001). In contrast to the PBS site, therefore, one could argue that the audience on the Go Goddess site is seen as powerless, easy to manipulate, and vulnerable.

The last site I will discuss, kylieklub.com, is connected to a British department store (Mackays) and promotes their range of tween clothing and accessories. (The use of the name Kylie immediately brings to mind the pop star Kylie Minogue, but there is no connection between the site and the pop star). The extensive website contains sections on fashion, beauty, music, TV and movies, magazines and a members' zone with games, e-cards, and special offers. Similar to Go Goddess Girl!, the home page of the Kylie Klub site is immediately recognizable as a tween site, with bright purples and pinks, Manga-style cartoons sporting the latest fashion and key words in tween talk (e.g., 'fab features'). However, the homepage indicates that the site goes further into tween culture with pages on pop groups, fashion and beauty tips, and celebrity gossip as well as interactive elements such as games, polls, e-cards, and downloads. The site contains few overt messages about tweens as a separate group apart from the banner on the homepage, which says "the klub for girls 9–13+, the klub for girls who want to know more, the klub for funky cyberbabes." The site offers little advice (apart from fashion and beauty tips), and there are very few references to any risks tweens are likely to experience in their lives. On the contrary, the site offers features that encourage risk taking, such as tips on flirting, ideas of how to earn money and interviews with boys about how they see girls. On this site, tweens are constructed in a celebratory manner: tweens are actively appropriating popular culture; they are curious about a variety of topics, and they are expressing and enjoying their sexual identities.

To summarize this section, tween-only sites construct their audiences in different ways: as vulnerable, sexual, potentially powerful, curious, in need of guidance, and having their own valid popular culture. These constructions reflect the underlying concerns of the producers of the sites: the PBS site is concerned with educating tweens; the Go Goddess Girl! site reflects parental concerns and anxieties, and Kylie Klub is foremost a commercial site concerned with selling products to tweens. These various constructions of the tween reflect the definitions of the 'child' and the 'adult' in Western society, which, as Thorne (1993) describes, are marked by "a series of dualisms: irresponsible/responsible; dependent/autonomous; play/work; asexual/sexual" (154). As I will describe in the following sections, tweens are often caught within these dualisms, trying to position themselves as adults, yet being pulled by various practices to remain as children.

Tweens on the Net—Defining a Social Space

As I have alluded to, the tweens I observed did not find any of the tween-only sites captivating. They said Kylie Klub was too girlie and babyish; the colors and cartoon characters reminded them of Barbie or Polly Pocket, and there were not enough interactive elements on the site. Although their favorite sites were not specific to tweens, the girls argued that their preferred sites and their ways of interacting with sites are distinctly different from those of younger children or of teens. Very simply, the tweens saw younger kids' digital activities as connected to their play and popular culture—Barbie, Noddy, *Bob the Builder,* and other television shows. The girls argued that tweens are particularly interested in games or interactive elements. Therefore, according to the tweens, their use of the site based on *Eastenders*, a widely watched evening soap opera, is distinct from younger children's use in that tweens make use of video clips, downloads, e-mail and newsletters, whereas younger users 'just play around' on the site. Teenagers, on the other hand, are viewers of *Eastenders*, but they are 'too cool' to be seen on the site, according to the tweens. Teenagers have a different cultural capital, which includes music and celebrities. Finally, although tweens and teens use chat rooms, the tweens made a distinction between the kinds of chat rooms they use and the kinds of conversations they have compared with teens. Tweens use what they describe as "safe chat rooms" which "treat us like real people" and listed MSN (instant messaging) and Habbohotel as tween chat rooms. (Unlike text-based chat rooms, Habbohotel is a moderated avatar-based chat room with cartoon animations.) According to the tweens, teen girls in chat rooms talk about boys and 'having it off,' and several tweens mentioned swearing as far more prevalent in teen chat rooms.

In these discussions, tweens are arguing for a distinct identity in terms of the way they use the Internet. A next step, therefore, is to analyze the sites tweens use and the interactions surrounding their use of particular sites. Several extremely popular websites have emerged through my work across the two different research sites including the *Eastenders* website, dress-up sites, flowgo.com, and Habbohotel. In this section, I will discuss three popular websites and attempt to locate the elements that make these websites more appealing than tween-only websites.[2]

Dressupgames.com is an index of links to dress-up games or doll-maker sites, a particular genre of web interaction that is popular with many of the children I observed, boys and girls, but particularly girls. Dress-up sites are a cyber version of paper dolls—the user is offered a page with various 'dolls' to choose from and then is able to 'drag and drop' clothing and accessories onto the chosen doll. The girls I observed in London would save the doll, put it in a paint program, make a background and print the final creation. Many of the dolls are cartoon-like and feature highly exaggerated body shapes, which can be accentuated with the trendy clothing choices. Looking just at how the audience is constructed, the overwhelmingly curvaceous bodies on offer and choice of clothing including thongs and high heels are clearly not sending a protective/conservative message to the user. The message is encouraging the user to experiment with sexy images. The doll-maker sites respond to an interest in girls playing with the appearance of idealized figures, much in the way that Barbie or paper dolls do. In comparison with other websites, doll-maker sites offer simple interactive choices (drag and drop), which draw on popular culture (trendy clothing, hairstyles, and accessories) and give users a way of playing with a powerful medium—the sexy female body. One could speculate that users are playing with power and fantasizing about their future bodies. These fantasy materials are similar to the girl pin-ups in teenage girl magazines. McRobbie (1991) argues that fantasy materials offer spaces for girls to move away from their position as children and towards the exciting and new position of adolescents (184). Similarly, Walkerdine (1997) looks at girls' fantasies as spaces in which girls play with and insert themselves into various discursive practices, and therefore fantasies "'become discursive and material in the social world'" (188). Doll-maker sites also provide a visual cultural reference point for tweens and their peers.

The girls I observed were all working in social situations (peers within a room of computers)—so the work they did on the screen was part of their social environment. Girls would often share a computer and decide on an activity together, or they would work side by side on separate computers, maintaining constant dialogue with their friends. When using doll-maker, the girls often discussed their choices with peers, showed peers their finished products, or tried out racy choices for a joke with their peers; and the printed versions remained as tokens of their social experience. Doll-maker here is a means of social interaction, a way of discussing and playing with sexually provocative clothing, in some cases a way of discussing other issues such as skin color, and a way of displaying interest in something that has high cultural capital for tweens—an interest in all things trendy.

The next site I will discuss, flowgo.com, was described by the tweens as "the funniest site ever" and contains links to short videos and simple games, many of which draw on potty humor, slightly rude or racy jokes and innuendoes. The importance of 'having a laugh' with friends is a characteristic of adolescent girl peer groups (Blackman 1995; Griffin 1985), and therefore we can see the girls' choice of Flowgo as a favorite website as typifying their alignment with teenage girls' interests and ways of relating. The site offers a large selection of material, some of which is interactive (e.g., games, writing messages on an image and e-cards). Many of the materials have sound (which alerts other users in the computer room to one's activities). This site is not geared specifically toward tweens or girls: there are no messages for the user on the home page (apart from advertising), the top half of the page consists of orange stripes (not particularly a tween colour), and the site contains a wide range of categories including inspirational, cartoons, patriotic, angels, parodies, and fun. The bulk of the home page is devoted to spotlights on favorite animations which include "time to bomb saddam," "blubber boobed bertha," and "pooey louie." These spotlights are the types of animations that were most popular with the tweens I observed. As the site is not geared toward tweens or girls, the tweens' interest in this site indicates that they are identifying with a larger group of peers in cyberspace. I would guess that the site has a wide audience, as it offers a variety of materials for different tastes and uses. However, the home page clearly is aimed at users with a particular sense of humor. The material which is highlighted (and used by tweens) is a careful balance of naughty but not too naughty. The "nude doodle," for example, features a cartoon of a nude muscle-bound man with no genitals. The user can draw on the cartoon, and the girls experimented with rudimentary phallic additions. The bulk of the home page is devoted to rude potty humor, but the lack of more sexually explicit material perhaps indicates that the user is seen as young and in need of protection. The adverts on the pages, however, are aimed at a mixed-age audience. Through their viewing of these slightly rude cartoons, the tweens used this site to play with the boundaries of the semi-formal setting of the workshop I was running. But it is important to see the girls as pushing the boundaries as peers, not just as individuals. The naughtiness came partly as a shared experience. When the girls found something risqué, they immediately shared it with friends. This shared experience became part of the tween girl culture, something that bonded them as friends and gave them a certain amount of clout.

The last site I will discuss is based on an extremely popular evening soap opera called *Eastenders*. The tweens I worked with all watched *Eastenders* and insisted that everyone in their families and in the school did as well. The website (http://www.bbc.co.uk/eastenders) was popular with the tweens at the school and with all ages (3–13) at the arts center cyber café, and both boys and girls used the site. The website contains an extensive range of fan material including interviews, competitions, e-cards, a newsletter, a message board, a webcam, acting advice, educational information, and games. The most popular page for all the children I observed in both sites was a dress-up page. Similar to doll-maker, the page features cartoons of characters from the show with various outfits to drag and drop. Another popular page was movie maker, which allows the user to construct a cartoon comic strip of the show. I saw very few users on other pages of the site. Similar to the use of flowgo.com, the tweens saw themselves as part of a much larger audience than with tween-only sites. The *Eastenders* television show offers tweens easy access to a form of cultural capital (knowledge and interest in a very popular item), giving them a certain amount of kudos with their peers. Similarly, the website offers the cultural capital and at the same time, interactive elements (also present in the tweens' website designs). In both research sites, children were hesitant to express their fandom for less mainstream items but found the *Eastenders* site an easy, familiar, and socially acceptable way to express their interest in popular culture. If we look at how the TV show, *Eastenders,* constructs its audience, in spite of the fact that the audience covers a very large age range, the show has featured various mature topics such as rape, abortion, teenage pregnancy, HIV/AIDS, prostitution, and drug addiction. The show, therefore, constructs the tween as a serious viewer who can handle mature topics. As described at the beginning of this section, the website offers users of varying ages different ways of interacting with the site, and the tweens see themselves as using the site in an age-specific way.

To summarize the tween cyberspace arena as I have described up to this point, websites aimed specifically for tween girls can be identified by overt statements regarding their target audience age range as well as by the presence of particular topics, colors, stylized language, images, and sound. These websites construct the tweens in various ways, including the tween in need of guidance, the tween at risk, the tween as a consumer, and the tween as a powerful and sexual person. Although the implied readers of the websites are tweens, these sites were not used by the tweens I observed. In contrast, the sites tweens used were aimed at a wide audience. On these sites, the tween was constructed as a serious user of popular culture, and the sites provided a kind of cultural capital that tweens used amongst their peers for discussion, shared jokes, experimenting with sexuality, and playing with boundaries. Therefore, the marketing technique used by tween-only websites appears to miss its target by constructing a narrow version of the tween and not providing the cultural capital desired by the girls.

The Ideal Tween Website: Designs on Paper

One of the first activities I did at the school was to have the girls look at tween-only websites and do further research on the term tween or tweenager. The girls analyzed the websites, searched for the terms on the Internet, and then compiled, analyzed, and shared what they had found. The girls listed specific details that characterize tweens within various categories including language, colors, clothes, topics of conversation, accessories, and shops. Kylieklub.com appears to meet many of the criteria the girls outline as markers of tweens, so it is interesting that the girls were not interested in the site. To get a better sense of what elements appealed to the girls, I had them design their own ideal website. The designs were first done on paper, partly so that the girls were not restricted by any technology, given that we only had one day for the design aspect of the project. I wanted to see what their ideal website would look like. After the paper designs, the girls used a simple web-authoring site, matmice.com, to make live personal webpages. The live pages resembled some of the paper designs, to an extent, but because I chose a design site that would give us a product and would be easy to use (involving no programming), the final live designs were much simpler than the paper designs. As the girls were missing classes to do research on tweens, and over the two days, I referred to them as a group as 'tween girls,' the emphasis on tween and tween culture is most likely exaggerated in their designs.

I do not have room here to analyze the paper designs, so I will give a summary to indicate some of the similarities and differences amongst the site designs (see table 17.1). Although I emphasized to the girls that they could design any type of site they wanted, many of the titles and elements indicated that their target audience was tween or teenage girls.

Comparing the site designs with the sites that the girls actually visit, there are striking differences. The girls' designs contain a wider variety of interactive elements than on a site such as flowgo.com, which features QuickTime movies. Furthermore, the subject matter, although specific to tweens, shows more variety than on the sites they use (which focus on one subject such as jokes or one particular television show). Also, interestingly, the site designs incorporate elements that the tweens said were of more interest to teens (particularly music and celebrities). In a way, the girls' designs represent a hybridity of their experiences on the Internet combined with other 'real life' experiences and ideas. The girls are incorporating the best of all possible worlds, combining chat with fashion, for example. These hybrid designs can be seen as a reflection of the girls' experiences, particularly with new media forms such as interactive digital television, and they also tell us about how they wish to represent themselves, their interests, and their desires. The website designs, therefore, can be seen as part of the social interactions that surround the girls' use of digital media.

Tween Girls' Live Websites: Online 'Vanity' Pages

After drawing designs on paper, the girls constructed live web pages. These online designs, which center on girls' culture, reflect an image of the girls which is perhaps more ideal than real. The content of the designs are similar to the 'vanity' pages discussed by O'Hear and Sefton-Green (2003) in which the website authors are focusing more on their image than the art of web design. The tweens' paper designs were incorporated into their live designs, but the girls were limited in terms of graphics and interactive elements. The web-authoring tool we used (matmice.com) allows the designer to write text, display pictures, add links to other websites, and have a guest book. There is a choice of colors for text and background, and pictures can be imported or the

Table 17.1. Summary of Website Designs

Names of sites		Go Girlz, Tween Girls.com, Tweens Aloud[3], Gossip Girls, Chillin.com, Tween Style, Tweens Rock 4ever, Tween girls Rule!, just hangin out.com
Most common subjects		Music, fashion, shopping, film/TV/celebs, games, makeup, chat, advice
Sharing		Problem page, embarrassing moments, my secrets, submit stories/letters
Interactive elements		
	Communication	E-mail, chat, agony aunt/advice, give feedback, message board
	Games	If U dare, hang-man, crossword, spot the accessories, puzzles, coloring in
	Dating games	Perfect match, spin the bottle, lad of the week
	Information gathering	Competitions, quizzes, surveys, voting
	Other	Listen to music and sing along, make your own videos, make your own games, beauty salon and fashion passion (doll-maker type activities, including putting on makeup), baby sit me (simulation), shopping, photo editing
Other elements (in each case, these appeared on only one site)		Search engine, log on and password, join the club, Bratz (a line of fashion dolls), sleep-over tips, top 10 websites, top 10 authors and books, 'about the Internet,' funny pictures/videos, hobbies, editorial on Michael Jackson, screen savers

designer can choose from a library on the site, which includes animated pictures. Because of the limits of the authoring tool, the girls' sites all look very similar. I showed the girls how to download an image off the Internet and put it on their sites, but they preferred to use images in the library, making the sites appear even more similar. The pictures the girls chose were most frequently 'cute' animals (kitten, horse, pig, dolphin, animated dog and cat). These images, though different than the ones the girls drew on their paper designs, are popular amongst girls and therefore signify a particular form of femininity. Similar to the magazines girls choose to read as discussed by

McRobbie (1991), the girls' designs, though drawing from a limited range of available subject positions, reflect their alignment with a mainstream feminine position. However, the girls do not go into hyper-feminine mode and deck their websites in pink. On the contrary, only one site has a pink background, the others being blue and purple.

Links to other sites was a popular section of the pages (see table 17.2). Most girls had links to a chat room, a music-related site, a games site, and a television-based site. These links are a reflection of the image the girls would like to present of themselves, which perhaps is slightly different than their real interests. Although chat rooms were filtered at the school, I noticed a tendency for the girls to pretend that they knew more about chat rooms than they actually did (for example, they told about elements of Habbohotel which do not exist). When I gave the girls free time on the Internet, they inevitably used the fun/games sites listed here and also spent time on Barbie.com. In interviews with the girls, they said they were keen to identify themselves as a distinct age group and for stores to recognize their identity, because "we're not exactly going to be seen wearing Barbie outfits." However, they also described themselves as able to draw on cultural goods from a wide age range, as these girls describe:

Girl 1   I went through a phase of Winnie the Pooh
Girl 2   I like the Barbie website—there are really nice jigsaws on it and every-
          thing and they're hard
Girl 3   And you put Barbie's make-up on ready for a photo shoot it's really cool

Table 17.2. Links on Tween Websites

Chat rooms	habbohotel.com, buzz-chat.com
Music- related sites	kiss100.com, capitalfm.com (radio stations), ggates.co.uk (Gareth Gates, a teenage pop idol), bbc.co.uk/totp (Top of the Pops)
Fun/games	flowgo.com, bigfatbaby.com, dressupgames.com, whatsher-face.com, fullofjokes.com
Television based sites	bbc.co.uk/cbbc (children's BBC), bbc.co.uk/eastenders (soap opera)
Other	Ring tones (ringtones.com, mrtones.com), friends' sites

The girls' websites, therefore, are reflections of a slightly idealized self, one that perhaps fits more with discourses around teenagers.

The text on the pages came partly from the text they had written on their paper designs. Most of the text, however, was written at the computer as they were setting up their sites. Several of the girls wrote introductions aimed specifically at tween girls that expressed a particular feeling of empowerment. For example:

> I think that kids grow up too fast so you should be proud to be a tween as we're not yet teenagers but we're not little kids.

> I want tweens to find out how much better they are than teens and kids and that you don't have to wish that you were older to get more things from your mum and dad.

This feeling of empowerment is also reflected in the interviews I conducted with the girls. The girls remarked on the importance of having a term that describes them as a group that is distinct from younger children and from teenagers. This prevents people calling them 'kids,' and according to one tween, "you're like out from the crowd" by identifying with the tween age group. Furthermore, although one group hypothesized that stores invented the term tween, the tween identity allows tweens to purchase clothes which are not too babyish "like with Barbie on them" and not too 'mature.' This pull between appearing babyish and appearing "too old too soon" is reflected on their live websites, as mentioned earlier, particularly when compared with their digital practices. The above quotes from the websites also reflect an awareness of discourses around childhood, particularly references to 'the loss of childhood,' which is often used in arguments about children's media cultures (Buckingham 2000). One of the girls in particular, reiterated this discourse in the interviews, saying, "A lot of [tweenagers] are losing their childhood because they've been caught up in show biz or they've been, you know, mixing with older people....They'll have no childhood to look back on when they're older." From statements like these one can see that the category of the tween represents an uneasy and unstable compromise: while apparently empowering tweens by distinguishing them from mere 'children,' it simultaneously defines them as innocent and in need of protection.

Conclusion

The analysis presented here provides a variety of answers to the basic question, what is a tween? The websites aimed at tweens have particular sets of concerns, which therefore construct the tween in different ways. For example, the PBS site is concerned with educating tweens about risks they may encounter. The tween, therefore, is constructed as curious but also vulnerable and in need of guidance. In contrast, the girls' own websites, which are also aimed at tweens, are concerned with creating an idealized image of the author (and the audience). Here the tween is part of a cohesive group whose interests and knowledge lie in things that give them status within their peer group (e.g., fashion, music, soap operas, and celebrity gossip). Therefore, the various discourses that are defining the tween offer 'symbolic resources' for identity formation that are quite ambivalent in their consequences. In some contexts, and for some purposes, tweens may be keen to appropriate the definitions of identity that are made available through marketing discourse, but in other contexts and for different purposes, they may be inclined to dismiss them as too narrow and constraining. The process of identity formation (at least specifically for children in this age group) is ongoing and perhaps inevitably contradictory. As such, it involves a continuing negotiation between structure and agency, between the market discourse and the girls' interests.

Notes

I would like to thank to David Buckingham for his valuable input on this project.

1. All website quotations were taken from 21 — 24 April 2003.

2. There is not room for a discussion of chat rooms here. For a discussion of the data on tweens in chat rooms, including *Habbohotel*, see Willett and Sefton-Green 2004.

3. When asked if she meant 'aloud' or 'allowed,' the author confirmed she meant aloud, as in "giving tweens a voice."

References

Blackman, S. J. *Youth: Positions and Oppositions: Style, Sexuality and Schooling.* Aldershot, UK: Avebury, 1995.

Bradberry, G. "Tweenagers in Love." *The Observer*, July 13, 2003. http://observer.guardian.co.uk/review/story/0,6903,996955,00.html.

Buckingham, D. *After the Death of Childhood: Growing Up in the Age of Electronic Media.* Cambridge: Polity Press, 2000.

Casselle, T. "Don't Count out UK Teens." *International Market News*, April/May 2001. http://www.tdctrade.com/imn/imn189/feature6.htm.

Frost, L. *Young Women and the Body: A Feminist Sociology.* Basingstoke: Palgrave, 2001.

Griffin, C. *Typical Girls? Young Women from School to the Job Market.* London: Routledge and Kegan Paul, 1985.

Lury, C. *Consumer Culture.* Cambridge: Polity Press, 1996.

McRobbie, A. *Feminism and Youth Culture: From 'Jackie' to 'Just Seventeen.'* Basingstoke: Macmillan, 1991.

O'Hear, S., and J. Sefton-Green. "Style, Genre and Technology: The Strange Case of Youth Culture Online." in *Doing Literacy Online: Teaching, Learning and Playing in an Electronic World*, edited by C. Beavis and I. Snyder, 121–143. Mount Waverly, Victoria: Hampton Press, in press.

Thorne, B. *Gender Play: Girls and Boys in School.* Buckingham: Open University Press, 1993.

Walkerdine, V. *Daddy's Girl: Young Girls and Popular Culture.* Basingstoke: Macmillan, 1997.

Willett, R., and J. Sefton-Green. "Living and Learning in Chatrooms." *Éducation et Sociétiés*10 (2004): in press. [For the English version see www.wac.co.uk/sharedspaces/research.php.]

CHAPTER EIGHTEEN

Imported Girl Fighters: Ripeness and Leakage in *Sailor Moon*

Hoi F. Cheu.[1]

As strange as it may sound, tween television programming in North America is facilitating an intense cultural exchange with Japan. Indeed, tweentoon is the only area in North American television that is dominated by foreign productions. This strange phenomenon resulted because of an underdeveloped tween market in North America. America's film and media industries are accustomed to having two age divisions: children and adults. In this system, 'betwixt-ness' refers to adolescents from thirteen to seventeen, those caught between PG–13 and NC–17. 'G' (general admission) or 'F' (family) includes both children and the tweens. The self-regulated rating system does not only reflect social-moral values but also denotes industrial perceptions of the market. In the early 90s, when the industry began to recognize the tween age group as a powerful consumer and cultural force that behaves differently from younger children, there was virtually a vacuum in the business world to deal with the newly distinguished and easily manipulated market. North American television programming, instead of creating more cultural products for this age group, decided to import from Japan.[1]

A successful early import is the *Sailor Moon* series. The series fills two gaps: first, the lack of production for the tween market (in the Japanese system, it is considered to be suitable for ages 7 and up), and second, in response to public demand since second-wave feminism, the desire for girl fighters. *Sailor Moon* is a work of 'tween schoolgirl fiction.'[2] The central characters are about thirteen years old, at the end of tweendom and the beginning of adolescence, and its intended audience is early tweens in search of a role model. As an action hero, Sailor Moon fulfils the feminist agenda in American popular culture's demand for strong female figures. As one may expect, however, the incorporation of this foreign media product is not just a matter of filling a gap in the market; willingly or not, underlying Japanese ideology embedded in *Sailor Moon* culturally affects its audience.

Of course, one television show is not going to change the general ideology of a society. My study is more concerned with the psychological effects that come along with the ideological impact. Assuming that social and cultural values are not simply reinforced through a single-ended circuit running from the media hegemony to its submissive audience, I presume a dynamic interaction between an inconsistent (or sometimes politically conflicting) media domain and a heterogeneous audience. This approach is rooted in the theory of cultural negotiations. In her famous essay, "Video Replay," Valerie Walkerdine (1986) tells her story of watching a working-class girl participating in her father's ritualistic replay of the last round of boxing in *Rocky II*. In her analysis, she describes the six-year-old Joanne as a quiet child. Although she is a 'tomboy,' and her father encourages her to fight for herself, she remains a silent victim of her family's fantasy structure. Her father only teaches her to be a fighter *in his own image*, and, being a girl, she has every feminine quality he rejects in himself. Interestingly, in her notes published along with the essay, Walkerdine has no record of Joanne taking pleasure in her father's male fighter fantasy. Perhaps that explains why Joanne is quiet: she has no voice in her family; she does not have a fiction of her own. In her silence, she has little power to negotiate her own identity with her family and culture. I am interested in how a girl like Joanne can break her silence. Can she find the necessary stories for the formation of her own identity? *Sailor Moon* is interesting because it is constructed for tween girls. It is not countercinema: it neither presents "the 'cold' aesthetics of high culture" (Walkerdine 1986: 197), nor does it deliberately reject the general social-economic values of the globalizing consumer society. Yet it is different from *Rocky II*. On a textual level, I would like to examine *Sailor Moon*'s metaphoric and ideological content. I propose the multicultural exchange can enrich narrative resources for personal and cultural transformation.

The frame of my investigation is a modification of the theory of cultural negotiations in light of complex systems narrative therapy. This approach is not incompatible with the postmodern discourse and poststructural psychoanalysis behind Walkerdine's works. It is, nevertheless, a shift of focus. In *Conversation, Language, and Possibilities*, for example, Harlene Anderson (1997) summarizes her "postmodern collaborative approach" to systems therapy (3):

1. Human systems are language—and meaning—generating systems.
2. Their construction of reality is forms of social action rather than independent individual mental processes.
3. An individual mind is a social composition, and self, therefore, becomes a social, relational composition.
4. The reality and meaning that we attribute to ourselves and others and to the experiences and events of our lives are interactional phenomena created and experienced by individuals in conversation and action (through language) with one another and with themselves.
5. Language is generative, gives order and meaning to our lives and our world, and functions as a form of social participation.
6. Knowledge is relational and is embodied and generated in language and our everyday practices.

These assumptions support my inquiry of how the multicultural exchange can enrich narrative resources for personal and cultural transformation. If these assumptions are 'postmodern,' one may ask, why do we not simply adopt existing critical paradigms instead of bringing in systems therapy? It is because Anderson's systems spin emphasizes the constructive side of language. Her assumptions may seem similar to contemporary theories used to proclaim the death of the author (Roland Barthes), to deconstruct hermeneutics (Jacques Derrida), to expose truth and knowledge as a construct of power (Michel Foucault), to revolutionize gendered symbolic languages (Julia Kristeva), to analyze the fetish of the male gaze (Laura Mulvey), to problematize individualism (Donna Haraway), to destabilize the codified cultural fiction in the postcolonial world (Gayatri Chakravorty Spivak), to reveal the ideological infrastructure of the arts in late capitalism (Frederick Jameson), etc. When developed into critical applications, contemporary theories, however helpful in exposing the hegemony of mass media, often fall into the problem of what Walkerdine describes in "Video Replay" as "pathologizing popular culture" (198). Walkerdine's argument is an attempt to find an exit within the negativity of critical theory. Anderson's approach shows a way out by underscoring story-making as a continuous and shifting process of identity formation. Complex systems theory implies that cultural materials do not have to be symptomatic of the society; instead, language acquisition can function as an explosive ingredient of ideological transformation.[3]

Psychological Ripeness and Girlhood Fantasy

Sailor Moon's character is realistically inconsistent. In everyday life, Sailor Moon's name is Serena. Serena is a clumsy, noisy, boy-crazy crybaby. She overeats. Her hairstyle makes her the brunt of teasing and malicious comments. Her immaturity makes my six-year-old daughter laugh. Most young viewers will not have all of Serena's flaws or commit her errors in judgment; however, they can always identify with some of Serena's problems—her social awkwardness, her struggle to adapt, to grow, and to find potential in herself for personal transformation. Because Serena is the sum of ordinariness, tween girls identify with her. In an interview, Takeuchi Naoko (the woman who created the original *Sailor Moon* comics) revealed that she chose the sailor suit because it is a common school uniform in Japan's junior and senior high schools: "[it] is a widely recognized symbol of young girls. I wanted to turn it into a super hero that everyone could relate to."[4] This motive is certainly recognized by Naoko's audience. Fans around the world give three consistent reasons for loving the show: first, it is a rare show of female superheroes; second, it has complex plots and character developments; third, most important, the characters are ordinary.[5] Sailor Moon is not a fantasy about an unreachable superpower; instead, she is a metaphor, a work of schoolgirl fiction that provides escape and relief from the struggle of growing up.

By growing up, I refer to the process of coming to both physical and psychological ripeness. Usually, the intense process of maturation is identified with adolescence. Although this stage of human development is very important, it is grossly understudied in psychoanalysis and its subsequent critical theories. In *Adolescence: The Farewell to Childhood*, psychologist Louise Kaplan asserts that adolescence is indeed more important than infantile development to the formation of adult characters. Unfortunately, adolescence has always been a 'stepchild' of psychoanalysis because of its neglect in traditional Freudian disciplines. Kaplan argues:

> When Freud announced his discoveries of infantile sexuality and the infantile Oedipus complex to a reluctant and disbelieving scientific community, it was partly to demonstrate that the sexual life of human beings did not commence at puberty or sexual maturity. It was far from Freud's intention to diminish the impact on adult mental life of the unique sexual and moral changes that occur at puberty. Nevertheless Freud's revolutionary emphasis on the influences of the infantile past had the long-term effect of obscuring the monumental changes that occur during the adoles-

cent years, changes that may, in fact, have a more decisive and immediate impact on the evolution of the human mind than the events of infancy. (81–82)

According to Kaplan, adolescence should not be overlooked because it is a stage of life when a person is most actively exploring possibilities, struggling with social conformities, and seeking changes:

> When adolescence is over, the young adult's character is etched with the inner struggles she has undergone. The changing woman has not been a passive recapituator of infancy; she has been an active reviser. Her strategies, her losses, her defeats, her triumphs, her new solutions leave their imprint on the adult form....In adolescence the forces of growth are a spur to innovation and moral renewal. Adolescence is the conjugator of a human life. When it is over, who we are and what we might become are not as open to change. We are never as flexible again. (347)

Not only is the adolescent 'imprint' necessary for healthy individual development, but it is also vital to human survival. It preserves in humanity a space for nonconformity, rebellion, and imagination that can transform self-awareness into social consciousness. Active revision is a strategy of adaptation; it inspires societal transformation:

> [In] order to make life on this harsh and confusing planet more bearable, she must find a way to preserve the resting places, beyond society, pleasure, or reality. Organized human societies could last a while without cultural aspirations, but no society has survived for long without them. (346)

In Kaplan's book, tweendom is not a topic (tweendom had not yet been identified as a special developmental stage in psychology back in 1984). Based on the book as a whole, however, I argue that what Kaplan means by 'adolescence' really refers to puberty; her book's subtitle, "a farewell to childhood," is certainly applicable to tweendom. Concretely, the study of tween girlfiction can relate to Kaplan's insight into adolescent development in two ways. First, tweendom can be regarded as a transitional period from childhood to adolescence. To prepare the way for the bewitching magic of adolescent rebellion, tweendom is a stage where infantile fantasy is called into question and dissolved into oblivion. Second, perhaps more accurately, what we mean by tweendom now is actually what Kaplan meant by adolescence then. According to a study in the medical journal *Pediatrics*, 48.3% of Afro-American girls and 14.7% of Caucasian girls have begun the development of breasts and pubic hair by age 8.[6] This discovery challenges the generally accepted definition of puberty that is based on studies from the 1960s,when signs of physical maturation only showed as early as age 12. Alongside early maturity, common social and emotional characteristics attributed to adolescence—including 'deviant' and 'risky' behaviors of teenagers (as described in a Global National's documentary, *Tweens: Too Fast, Too Soon*)—are now applicable to tweens.[7]

Not accidentally, since puberty is now a growing element of tween development, the first successful tweentoon imported to North America is about a transforming girl. In order to fight, Serena, the ordinary girl, has to change into Sailor Moon. Transformer tales are successful not simply because transfiguration enhances the escape from mundane reality to unreachable fantasy, but also because the fantasy eases the anxiety over the scarily changing body. Unlike the male line-up of transformers in which transformation is technological and power oriented, Sailor Moon's transformation is mystical. Rather than enveloping herself in armor and munitions, Sailor Moon relies on the energy from a crystal from a legendary past. From season to season, as Sailor Moon meets greater challenges, the power of her crystal grows. The Japanese version uses the word 'make-up' instead of 'transform' to describe the change. Sailor Moon does not have super powers without her 'make-up.' If we use poststructural feminist film theory to psychoanalyze the latent content of *Sailor Moon*, we may criticize that the girl fighter fantasy is subjected to the male gaze—the girl power is in the cosmetics—Serena must put on her 'make-up'—her masquerade—to *be* a fighter—while symbolic of her masquerade is a wand, a phallic possession which she waves to cast her spell—she is a fairy with a phallus—her crystal, which is fixed in a secret compartment in the bow of her middy blouse between her developing breasts, is a symbol of the feminine subjugation to the male gaze.

But not everything fits the poststructural reading. For the male gaze, a sexualized female image does not grow up. The girl cannot be a wife or a mother. She has to be fixed in purity, idealized in virginity, or presented as a fairy. Freudian analysis is a useful key with which to unlock the patriarchal projection of femininity: infantilism is a male fantasy. As Kaplan criticizes Freud, however, his model of psychology is limited by the recapitulationist myth, which states that the adult mental life is driven by the desire to return to infantile fantasy. During puberty, as Kaplan insists, the return to the past is indeed a revision, not a recapitulation: "The adolescent revision helps to assure that adult existence will not be consumed by repeating the past" (98).

Similarly, in the tween girlfiction, the fantasy presents a non-linear intermix of the past and the future. Sailor Moon lives in fairytale-like imagination, but she also craves adulthood. She has a grown-up boyfriend (Darien, who transforms into Tuxedo Mask). In the second season, Sailor Moon's daughter, Rini, comes from the future and stays with her, which makes her a teen mother.[8] In *Sailor Moon*, fantasy does not exist apart from living experience, for she continues to struggle with the same sorts of challenges that any schoolgirl would encounter—infatuation, confusion, insecurity, fear, defeat, ridicule, etc. It is true that the power of Sailor Moon's scepter is like magic in fairytales; it is a wand (very much similar to the one in *Cinderella*) that turns the ordinary girl into a princess. But the magic opens a world where the search for strength, friendship, and maturity is the ultimate aspiration.

In *Sailor Moon*, traditional fairy archetypes of childhood fantasy suddenly decompose as the imagination of ripeness strikes puberty. The iconography and the symbolism of fairytales work only to the extent that they are connectors; they ensure the viewers' identification with their infantile fantasy. This identification is important because the cultural context surrounding children's psychic reality remains traditionally gendered and patriarchal. Children around the world grow up with the Disney versions of *Snow White*, *Cinderella*, and *Little Mermaid*. Female infantile fantasies are filled with the desire to be princesses, to be protected, adored, and treasured. These fantasies are life-long investments; even buried in adulthood, they remain influential, twinkling in the twilight of the unconscious as guiding stars of female perversions—to be a 'woman' in the patriarchal cultural context, one has to subvert one's genuine identity so as to conform to a gender stereotype of 'womanliness.'[9] *Sailor Moon* connects to the viewers' childhood fantasies with its fairytale-like elements; however, it also moves beyond the naiveté to capture life in transition. Childhood fantasy does not diminish, but it is not idealized either. Submissive romantic fantasy is treated half seriously and half mockingly most of the time. Serena perceives Darien as a prince; her understanding of heterosexual relationships evokes a juvenile perception of ideal love. But this childhood ideal is complicated when alternative female possibilities join Sailor Moon in her fights. Sailor Moon has a group of loyal friends who can transform into Sailor Scouts. They fight as a group, not as individuals. Each of the Sailor Scouts emphasizes a certain virtue: Sailor Mars, spirituality; Sailor Jupiter, bravery; Sailor Mercury, intelligence; Sailor Venus, love. If Sailor Moon were the sole scout, she would be like Superman, projected as the one ideal of truth and power. However, when the girl fighters are presented as a group, multiplicity becomes possible. The presence of the Sailor Scouts opens up a variety of femininities: my older daughter models on Mercury, my younger on Jupiter.

Indeed, resistance to role modeling is an inherent moral in the show. In the beginning of the episode "Dreams of Her Own," for instance, Serena and Rini are window-shopping. Struck by a wedding dress on display, Serena exclaims, "Every girl dreams about the day she can wear her wedding dress!" "Serena," Rini asks, "You dream of being a bride?" "Of course," Serena adds, "I also want to be a biologist, a teacher, an actress, a food taster, a super fashion model, and wah!!!" She remembers that a fashion magazine is supposed to be newly available and runs to find it.

In the same episode, the Sailor Scouts fight a monkey monster that gets its fighting power by stealing energy from the "dream vortex" of a little girl who abandons her own dream because of low self-esteem. The little girl looks up to Raye as a role model, mimicking Raye's appearance and taking on her identity to fill her psychological void. With the little girl's dream energy, the monster fights like a mirror, reflecting every move of the Sailor Scouts, which makes it impossible to defeat. The hardest enemy to fight is one's own self-image. Through the monster, the psychological darkness of the girl is revealed. The Sailor Scouts begin to realize the pain and the desperation behind the little girl's self-deception and her struggle for acceptance. After the attack, the little girl lies on the ground writhing as if she is having a nightmare. As her painful story is revealed, tears come out of her eyes while she begs the Sailor Scouts to stop the monster. Compassion inspires Raye to summon raging fire that surpasses the monster's imitative capacity. The Sailor Scouts break the spell and dissolve the monster as they realize the sadness and pain that the girl goes through in order to live another person's dream.

In her efforts to diversify female possibilities, Takeuchi Naoko includes the possibility of a lesbian relationship in the third season (*Sailor Moon S*) through the creation of two relatively more grown-up fighters, Sailor Neptune (Michiru, or Michelle) and Sailor Uranus (Haruka, or Amara). In the Italian magazine, *Kappa* (September 1996), she reveals:

> The relationship between Haruka and Michiru is quite special....The friendship between them is so strong that it becomes love. There is not only heterosexual love, but there also can be a homosexual love, in this case between two girls.

In Japan, strong girls are very popular. The tradition of my country has the Tarazuka, the Japanese theater in which only women take part, the maximum level of
feminine emancipation. These actresses cover all roles of the plays, even male ones.
I was inspired by them to create Haruka.

The creation of Sailor Uranus was not by consumer demand. Naoko knows
very well that "it wasn't easy to make children understand how there could
be true love between two women." Nevertheless, she makes her attempt by
creating a tomboy who is so attractive that the Sailor Scouts are attracted to
her.

   Though toned down from the comic books to a certain degree, the TV
series preserves the characterizations of the comic books and presents the
same challenges to childhood gender perceptions. In an episode of the *Sailor
Moon S* series, "Driving Dangerously," when Amara's female identity is still
ambiguous, Serena and Mina (Sailor Venus) spy on 'him' because of their
sexual attraction. In an awkward encounter, as Amara tries to brush off the
two young admirers, the issue of fairytale ideology is raised:

> Amara: You know, you guys seem really sweet and I'm sure you'll find your
> princes someday.
> Mina: Like today?
> Michelle (just entering the scene): There you go again Amara, giving love advice.
> Amara: Hi Michelle.
> Michelle: Amara's got this thing about people living happily ever after.
> Amara: And there is nothing wrong with it either.
> Michelle: Except that it only happens in fairytales. If you ask me, anyone waiting
> for Prince Charming is not living in reality.

While the scene seems to sympathize with the two younger Sailor Scouts, the
subsequent scene further questions their heterosexual idealism by way of
mockery. Waiting for the two Sailor Scouts, the other scouts wonder why
they are late for their gathering. "If you know them," Raye (Sailor Mars)
speculates, "they probably got sidetracked by some cute boy they met at the
game arcade or something." "No way," Amy (Sailor Mercury) defends her
friends, "they are not total geeks." There is a long silence. Then, they agree,
in unison, "Oh, yes, they are."

   By the time Sailor Uranus and Sailor Neptune are introduced, Darien and
Serena's transfiguration as Prince and Princess of the Moon Kingdom has
already been established. All of a sudden, as Serena is finishing junior high,
she chases a tomboy. Where is her belief in happily ever after, true love?

Evidently, there is a plot-character discrepancy. But such a discrepancy is realistic if we take into account that the fantasy is parallel with the degeneration of childhood fantasy. Successful tween fiction has to find its way to embody the fading efficacy of fairytales and the heightening intensity of psychological metamorphosis. Infantile fantasy does not disappear with the dissolution of childhood fairytales; instead, with the intervention of social realities, it becomes richer and therefore more embroiled than ever. Imagination forms a hybrid of demystifying myth: role-playing games turn into career planning, animal songs into love lyrics, etc. The social-psychological contradiction and physical changes at puberty are key challenges for the tween audience. As a piece of schoolgirl fiction, *Sailor Moon* reflects the psychological complexity in the process of growing up: identity is in flux and in doubt, gender is ambiguous, imagination is wild, and physical transformations materialize the anxiety over the fast-changing body. *Sailor Moon* is not 'sugar, spice and everything nice.' It articulates the search for individuality, self-expression, and self-approval through confronting the confusion of maturation.

Ideological Leakage through Intercultural Transaction

Every society has its own belief systems enveloped in its cultural productions, the import of a foreign media work, especially a popular one directed at an age group engaged in active revision of identity, that will bring ideological beliefs across the border. The border crossing is not a cultural inversion because the importation is voluntary. But since the ideological part of the exchange is often unconscious, and the belief systems do not interact in the form of social discourse, it is also not a fair trade. From the host culture's point of view, the exchange of belief systems is a leakage; it takes place when a seemingly self-contained superstructure meets its alien other. Such leakage is inevitable in the postmodern, international context.

Once I showed an episode of *Sailor Moon S* to Hannah, a ten-year-old girl.[10] She was a houseguest, and she watched the video with my own daughters (aged five and seven at the time). Hannah was a very tall, muscular black child, definitely one of those tweens who begin puberty early. Adopted into a well-educated Christian family that believes in a simple living style, she was not raised to be a 'girly girl' and was discouraged from pursuing fads and trends. Her parents did not subscribe to specialty TV channels, so even though *Sailor Moon* was then on Teletoon and YTV several times a

day, she had not seen it before.[11]   She was not shut out from the media culture, nonetheless. She loved cartoons and had a large collection of Disney
films and *Veggietales*. When my children showed her the exotic foreign cartoon series on video, she delightedly chose one with Sailor Uranus on the
back cover. Not long after the show started, she realized that the Sailor
Scouts were infatuated with a girl. She was physically agitated. She could
not remain seated. Restlessly, she came to me to complain that something
was seriously wrong with the show. Not the most articulate girl, she became
incoherent in her agitation: "This is crazy... she is a girl!" For her, the idea
of girls being in love with girls was mind-blowing. What happened, I believe, is an example of cross-cultural ideological leakage. Although Hannah's soft-spoken parents were not homophobic, the topic never came up in
her cultural environment. Her perception of sexuality was grounded on the
heterosexual fairytale of Prince Charming, direct from Disney, and in an environment semi-protected from mass media.

   Sailor Moon is not in every way radically inventive. It preserves many of
the ideological and aesthetic principles typical of the Japanese cartoon industry. However, its freshness opens new fictional possibilities for the North
American market, essentially due to cultural differences. In North America,
popular culture has embraced the idea of gay and lesbian relations in all sorts
of film and television programs for teens and grown-ups, but the subject remains taboo in children's media culture (even though tweens are absorbing
sexual images flooding music videos and TV movies like the *Travel Around
the World* series of the Olsen sisters). Since the industry's definition of 'children's program' is not yet clearly subdivided into finer sections for various
age groups, it is hard to develop programs that deal with social and sexual
topics for tweens. In North America, there is a tendency to protect children
from infancy to age 13 from the 'ugliness' of the adult world. But this conventional categorization is changing, which is why *Sailor Moon* was imported in the first place. Also, cultural context makes a difference. In this
sense, importing is a way to accelerate cultural transformation because the
different cultural contexts enrich cultural resources for inventing new metaphors and stories. In Japan's own cultural context, for example, the Tarazuka
tradition paves a smooth transition for exposing lesbian sexuality to children;
to an American audience without such a cultural connection, the lesbian
scouts are a shock. The import of Japanese girl fighters was at first intended

to fill the void of an ignored market, but the cultural exchange has given its viewers more than just entertainment.

Nevertheless, *Sailor Moon*'s Japan is not in every way a 'foreign' country. After centuries of communication with the West, European and American mythologies are already part of Japanese culture. For this reason, cultural references and mythological revisions in *Sailor Moon* are multicultural and transcultural. The series may contain Japanese traditions that are little known and sometimes shocking to Western popular culture, but more often, the cultural raw materials in *Sailor Moon* are, to the East or to the West, recognizable. The cultural revision, therefore, builds on the West's fictional resources instead of being an invasion by a foreign culture.

The Promise of the Rose

Although it is a cultural hybrid, nevertheless, *Sailor Moon*'s basic tenets endorse Japan's Zen Buddhist ethos. Encoded in the show's manifest content are certain philosophical motifs that prioritize human connection over domination, acceptance over isolation, friendship over hostility, healing over fighting, multiplicity over dualism, impermanence over stability, and disillusionment over triumph. To provide a glimpse into this ideological content, I would like to focus on a particular *Sailor Moon* movie for closer analysis. There are three *Sailor Moon* movies, each containing an independent plot apart from the rest of the TV series. Without the formulaic repetition of the television episodes, each movie is really a miniature of a season's story development.

The Promise of the Rose (screenplay by Sukenro Tomita and directed by Kunihiko Ikuhara) is the first of the three movies. Produced in 1994, it was condensed into a one-hour English version in 2000. The story centers on Darien's alien friend Fiore. When Darien loses his parents in a car accident, he meets a lonely alien boy in the hospital. Consoling each other's loneliness, they become good friends. Unfortunately, Earth's atmosphere was not suitable for Fiore. At his departure, Darien gives him a rose, and Fiore promises to travel through the galaxy to search for a flower deserving of Darien's friendship. One day, as the Sailor Scouts and Darien are touring a nursery, Fiore returns with his flower.

The rose, East or West, symbolizes romantic love. Throughout the series, Darien turns into Tuxedo Mask. His weapon is a rose that he throws like a dart. When Serena is in danger, he always distracts her enemy by throwing his rose in order for Serena to transform or to retreat. His existence, obviously, fits into the submissive fantasy of male rescue and eternal love. Fiore's return with a flower, therefore, immediately raises sexual tension. Although Sailor Neptune and Sailor Uranus have not been introduced in *Sailor Moon R*, homosexuality is a possibility: in *Sailor Moon*, love is a continuum; the boundary of romance is so ambiguously drawn that love can always surpass friendship and gender.

The flower that Fiore brings back is called Kisenian Blossom. She has a female figure. She plans to suck out all of Earth's positive energy so that she can colonize the planet. By herself, however, she has no physical strength. She requires Fiore's weak mind to transmit her power. The flower is attached to his lapel and its power to his mind. Monsters in *Sailor Moon* are by and large psychic projections instead of physical evil characters. They may be controlled by 'bad guys,' but the 'bad guys' often turn away from their destructive ways because of Sailor Moon's kindness and transformative power. In *Sailor Moon*, 'evil' is a negative form of energy that exists in every being; while the weak-minded submit to negativity (and therefore become evil), healing can take place when negativity is purged or dissolved. Fiore's weak-minded character is conquered by loneliness and jealousy.

The way that the flower attaches itself to Fiore is sensual. The story asserts that the flower feeds on his destructive energy. Psychologically speaking, it is more like a male projection of femininity: it reflects his desires, his negative emotions, his fear, and his dissatisfaction. In a few scenes, when Fiore's hatred is challenged by Sailor Moon's acts of love and friendship, the multiplied flowers surrounding him simply dissolve into nothingness, like an interruption signal that can be filtered. The Kisenian Blossom corresponds to a *femme fatale* figure in the iconography of Western popular culture. On the surface, the flower uses her sexual power to manipulate Fiore to achieve her fearful ambition. Yet, since her existence relies on Fiore's state of mind, she can be understood as his projection. She reflects Fiore's psychological darkness: Fiore is the one failing to mature and give up his infantile, narcissistic projection of love and friendship; his infantile libido—the desire to possess his love object—feeds power to the Kisenian Blossom. In this sense, the Kisenian Blossom represents a male perception of femininity in the patriarchal culture; it is passive, manipulative, and fatal; it is a signifier of the castration fear.[12]

In *Sailor Moon*, the battle against the *femme fatale* is different from that in film noir. In the film noir tradition, the male protagonist is caught between the dichotomy of the innocent, nurturing woman and the deadly temptress. Typified in films like *Double Indemnity*, the man is manipulated to murder for the woman, and then in trying to escape her control, he meets his tragic fate. *Sailor Moon*'s protagonist is female. But Serena is not portrayed as the *femme fatale*'s dichotomized other (the nurturing woman is as much a male projection as the *femme fatale*). Zen Buddhism's philosophy of disillusionment enters at this point: Serena has to learn to change the projector in order to dissolve his projection. Since the projection is a symptom, victory cannot be achieved through violence but through healing. During a battle, in an attempt to save Sailor Moon, Tuxedo Mask is injured and taken to Fiore's meteor. In their effort to find Tuxedo Mask, the Sailor Scouts engage in a battle with Fiore. The first revelation of the true nature of the Kisenian Blossom as Fiore's projection takes place when Fiore tortures the captive Scouts to force Sailor Moon to surrender. As Sailor Moon puts down her scepter and gives up, saying that she cannot see her friends suffer, Fiore is moved. For a brief moment, the images of the Kisenian Blossoms at his back disappear.

Eventually, in the finale, disillusionment (not fighting power) is the key to survival. While Fiore attempts to kill Sailor Moon, Tuxedo Mask breaks out of containment and throws a rose to stop the attack. The rose hits Fiore's heart—it is a gesture of their friendship's termination. In despair, all flowers disappear, except for the one on his lapel. Conquered by hatred, Fiore announces that the meteor is on a collision course towards Earth. Everyone will die, and the flower will suck the energy of the entire planet. At this point, Sailor Moon rises up and tries to use her crystal power to change the trajectory of the meteor. Knowing her intention, Fiore grabs the crystal on her bosom. In response, Sailor Moon takes him by the arm and shares her memory with him, which reveals that the rose that the child Darien gave Fiore was a gift from Serena. Darien had been crying because Fiore had to leave. To console him, Serena gave him a rose. As Fiore recognizes that the rose came from Sailor Moon, he transforms his personal narcissistic interests into gratitude. The positive emotion melts away the Kisenian Blossom.

In *Sailor Moon*, images and stories are mixed with conflicting ideologies—in the conflict, there is no resolution; instead, there is ideological collision as a result of cultural hybridization. While in one moment the narrative is preoccupied with Buddhist disillusionment, Western fairytales and Christian ideas take over in the next. As Sailor Moon holds up her crystal to save her friends and the planet from the falling meteor, she turns into Moon Princess, and Tuxedo Mask into her prince. All the Sailor Scouts join their power behind Moon Princess and her prince. In *Sailor Moon*, royalty is a symbol of status. Only through loving others do they become royalty, exalted for the possession of the most noble human quality. As the Sailor Scouts use their power to support the Moon Princess, fragments of their memories are intercut into the scene to explain why they treasure her friendship: each in her own way is marginal in society, and, one by one, they remember how Serena unconditionally accepts their differences and binds them together with her sincerity. In the story, fighting together as a group for survival is a metaphor for human connectedness.

With all the energy of the Sailor Scouts combined, they shift the trajectory of the meteor. Unfortunately, the mission drains all of Sailor Moon's energy, the crystal shatters, and the superhero blacks out in the arms of Tuxedo Mask. The feminist twist is that Tuxedo Mask does not possess the power to wake up the girl fighter. Fiore, liberated from the grasp of the Kisenian Blossom through Sailor Moon's healing power, gives Tuxedo Mask a friendship flower that contains his positive energy—the flower that he promised, as he explains—and Fiore returns to his innocent child form. Tuxedo Mask is instrumental. He drinks the nectar of the flower and kisses Sailor Moon to revive her. The image recalls the ending of *Sleeping Beauty* and *Snow White*; however, in the context of tween culture, one may argue that the fairytale images open a transition from childhood fantasy to tween revision. The fictional archetype of the West is recalled; its rigidity is, however, softened by the sentiment of the East, as the female defender of love and justice reconnects with the energy of life that she gives away for her friends. The awakening of Sailor Moon is through a return of *karma*.

Every piece of story intersects with our own fictional worlds—our own stories concerning ourselves, our emotions, our social worlds, and our interrelations with others. Culture, in the broad sense of the word, refers to the ideas, customs, or arts of a given people. One can draw the boundaries of a culture by age, sex, class, race, geography, ethnicity, etc. But the boundaries are never clear. Everyone dances through numerous cultural fields. Beneath the 'epidermic' surface of the text, media production is more than an event of cultural negotiations—it is, as Angharad N. Valdivia (1995) argues in *Feminism, Multiculturalism and the Media: Global Diversities*, "a spectrum of possibilities that includes coalitions, collusions, and collisions" (11). In the collisions, we may hope that ideological leakage from one culture to another can enrich the fictional resources crucial to healthy revisions of identity.

Notes

[1] There has been greater investment recently in commercial television and film productions with such programmes as the Olsen twins' *Travel around the World* series. No North American programme, however, has yet achieved the popularity and cultural impact of the Japanese tweentoons. Conversely, for decades, public television networks in Canada have produced programmes suitable for tweens. One successful example was *Delgrassi Junior High*, a tween oriented soap opera in the 80s. *Road to Avonlea* in the 90s can also be regarded as a piece of tween fiction. These public television programmes are produced for cultural and educational purposes instead of for advertising revenue. This topic deserves its own study.

[2] In *Schoolgirl Fictions*, Walkerdine examines all kinds of fictional materials related to girlhood development, which includes cultural products that are not intended for the age group, such as *Rocky II* in the essay "Video Replay." *Sailor Moon*, however, is not only produced for 'schoolgirls'; it also specifically targets tweens.

[3] Anderson's work is only an example of complex systems theory used in the study of language and human development. For further readings, the following books can provide a more comprehensive introduction: Becvar and Becvar (1988), Gold (2002), and Parry and Doan (1994).

[4] An interview with Charles McCarter at Comic Con International, posted in, http://www.ex.org/3.6/13-feature_takeuchi.html.

[5] My summary is based on interviewing a number of *Sailor Moon* fans in my community, as well as monitoring chat rooms on a number of websites devoted to *Sailor Moon*.

[6] P. B. Kaplowitz et al. (1999).

[7] The documentary was aired on 23 April 2003.

[8] *Sailor Moon* had a total of five seasons, 200 episodes, made from 1992 to 1997: *Sailor Moon* (episodes 1–46); *Sailor Moon R* (47–89); *Sailor Moon S* (90–127); *Sailor Moon SuperS* (128–166); *Sailor Stars* (167–200). There are also three *Sailor Moon* movies. The initial North American broadcasts were between 1995 and 2002.

[9] By 'female perversions,' I allude specifically to Louise Kaplan's defining publication, *Female Perversions: The Temptations of Emma Bovary* (1991).

[10] Hannah is not her real name.

[11] *Sailor Moon* was popular on network channels between 1995 and 2002, and then the show retreated to specialty channels as succeeding productions such as *Cartcaptors* replaced the show.

[12] There are many psychoanalytic readings of the *femme fatale*. See, for example, Ann Mary Doane's *Femmes Fatales: Feminism, Film Theory, and Psychoanalysis* (1991).

References

Anderson, H. *Conversation, Language, and Possibilities*. New York: Basic Books, 1997.

Becvar, D., and R. Becvar. *Family Therapy: A Systemic Integration*. Boston: Allyn and Bacon, 1988.

Doane, A. M. *Femmes Fatales: Feminism, Film Theory, and Psychoanalysis*. New York: Routledge, 1991.

Gold, J. *The Story Species: Our Life-Literature Connection*. Markham: Fitzhenry & Whiteside, 2002.

Kaplan, L. *Adolescence: The Farewell to Childhood*. New York: Simon and Schuster, 1984.

———. *Female Perversions: The Temptations of Emma Bovary*. New York: Doubleday, 1991.

Kaplowitz, P. B., S. E. Oberfield, and the Drug and Therapeutics and Executive Committees. "Reexamination of the Age Limit for Defining when Puberty Is Precocious in Girls in the U.S.: Implications for Evaluation and Treatment." *Pediatrics* 10, no. 4 (1999): 936–941.

Parry, A., and R. E. Doan. *Story Re-visions: Narrative Therapy in the Postmodern World*. New York: The Guilford Press, 1994.

Valdivia, A. N. "Feminist Media Studies in a Global Setting: Beyond Binary Contradictions and into Multicultural Spectrums." In *Feminism, Multiculturalism, and the Media: Global Diversities*, edited by V. N. Valdivia, 7–29. London: Sage, 1995.

Walkerdine, V. "Video Replay." In *Formations of Fantasy*, edited by V. Burgin, J. Donald, and C. Kaplan, 167–199. London: Methuen, 1986.

Walkerdine, V. *Schoolgirl Fictions*. London: Verso, 1990.

CHAPTER NINETEEN

Re-imagining Girlhood: Hollywood and the Tween Girl Film Market

Peggy Tally

Introduction: Following the Money Trail,
or Hollywood Goes after the Tween Audience

To understand the relationship of contemporary Hollywood cinema to tween culture, it is first necessary to understand why Hollywood has been searching for audiences for their films more generally since the 1950s. Such diverse scholars of film history as Murray Smith (2000), Richard Maltby (2000), Douglas Gomery (1998), and Peter Kramer (1999) generally agree that one of the central dynamics of the film industry in the post-World War II United States has been the problem of how to stem the tide of loss of viewership for their films. Prior to World War II, Hollywood enjoyed mass film attendance for their fare, as movie-going was an entrenched and enduring part of life in pre-World War II America. Hollywood has been grappling with declining overall viewership for the past forty years, however, caused in large part by such larger social transformations as the advent of suburbanization in the 1950s and the attendant rise in television watching and other leisure activities. Because of these larger-scale trends, ticket sales during the 1950s and 1960s declined to very low levels. Hollywood has been chasing after their elusive audience ever since and has seesawed between creating mass 'tentpole' or 'blockbuster' pictures while at the same time trying to understand where they might customize their films for more specific audiences.

Though producing and marketing blockbuster films generally occupies the largest share of the movie studios' attention, then, there has also been a recent flowering of more 'niche' pictures directed to targeted audiences. Many of these films have done surprisingly well at the box office despite limited budgets and marketing. It is within this slice of the industry that tween girls emerged as a viable niche audience to cultivate and create films for.

While it is now abundantly clear that 'tween' girl films have a place in the Hollywood production lineup, this development was by no means inevitable. In fact, the whole notion of a tween girl, as opposed to a child or teenager, is itself arguably the result of marketing initiatives by the advertising industry, which supposedly 'discovered' this group while tracking patterns of consumption among children and teenagers. These critics argue that the tween category is itself a 'media creation' which was devised by programmers as a new way to package their products.

Whether it is a real phenomenon or one invented by advertisers, the first media executive group to realize the potential spending power of tweens was the music industry. Tween girls were responsible for propelling such stars as Britney Spears, the Backstreet Boys, and 'NSync to superstardom. Television companies also decided that tweens were a sufficiently 'real' group to merit special programming, and the Disney Channel and Nickelodeon have devoted a good portion of their television line-up to them. Movie executives came somewhat later to the bandwagon, and it is only recently that they have produced fare explicitly for tweens. Media critic David Bloom (2002), for example, notes that:

> Meanwhile Hollywood studios have produced a surfeit of tween-minded movies in the past 18 months. *Harry Potter* was the monster tween hit, but last summer the modestly budgeted *Spy Kids* scooped up $113 million and a quick order for a sequel. Tweens also flocked to *Shrek*, *Ice Age*, *Big Fat Liar*, *Snow Dogs*, *Legally Blonde* and *The Princess Diaries*.

Bloom goes on to cite MGM Production President Alex Gartner, who, observing the success of these films, commented that "I think what you're seeing is a further definition of a demographic that got lumped together with the others." Some observers of the film industry believe that this was because film executives did not previously view tween girls as a viable market on their own. Commenting on this earlier received wisdom, film producer Jane Startz (cited in Chautard 2003) notes that:

> The time I was growing up in this industry, the conventional wisdom was girls will watch something that has a boy [as the lead character], but the boys won't watch something that has a girl. That may or may not be true. But I think what people are

realizing is it really doesn't matter that much if the boys are going to come or not because there is such a faithful following for some of these girl projects.

How did Hollywood finally come to realize that there was indeed a 'faithful following' for films for tween girls especially? One indication that there was an audience separate and apart from other groups was the profitable success of 'chick flicks,' whose audiences consisted of a large majority of tween girls. Such recent films as *The Princess Diaries* (2001), *Legally Blonde* (2001), and *Save the Last Dance* (2001) were very large successes in part because they had a huge following of tween girls.

The success of these films is backed up by current numbers on the attendance rates overall for tween girls. Though variously described at different ages, tween girls are thought to be anywhere from 8–14. Generally, the best estimate for this media-driven category is that older tweens are 11- to 12-year-olds, and younger tweens are between 8–10 years old. Hollywood is continually trying to gain more clarity about this age range in order to target more efficiently to the tweens. And recently, it seems, they have hit their target with surprising skill. For example, *Freaky Friday* (2003), with Lindsay Lohan and Jamie Lee Curtis as the daughter and mother who switch bodies, grossed $6 million dollars in its first 24 hours. Uttering lines like "So we're stuck in this suck-fest," the tween girl daughter had an immense appeal to the tween girl audience.

Currently, there is a whole slate of new films aimed specifically at the tween girl audience. Interestingly enough, many of these films draw on books that are also popular with girls, including *Ella Enchanted, Confessions of a Teenage Drama Queen, All-American Girl*, and *Sisterhood of the Traveling Pants*. These films, like their novel counterparts, often center on "Cinderella stories, coming-of-age tales and sassy comic novels" (Chautard 2003).

As a niche audience, tween girls are very attractive for a number of reasons. First, as a consumer group, though the numbers cited vary wildly, tween girls are considered to be very large consumers themselves as well as being highly influential in their parents' purchasing decisions. Their spending dollars have gone towards clothing, music, movie tickets, make-up, etc. Mandy Moore, who starred in the tween girl movie *How to Deal* (2003), believes that Hollywood is rightly catering to this important spending group as when she unself-consciously notes that:

We are the consumers. We are the people who are going to see most of these films
and buy most of the music, magazines, clothes and whatnot. So of course I'm proud
to be part of a movement that's catering to my generation, toward giving people
what they want. (Cited in Stepp 2003)

In addition, in terms of their film habits, market research has also shown
that tweens can be counted on to see the same film several times. They are
repeat filmgoers, in other words, which is always an attractive proposition for
a movie studio. As well, it is relatively inexpensive to market to girls, since
they are already fragmented into different cable channel audiences and Internet sites and can therefore be targeted on these channels and sites. As one
film executive has put it, "You can segment your audience with a laser"
(cited in Dade 2003).

Finally, tweens are a desirable audience because they are particularly
susceptible to word-of-mouth advertising, especially if it stems from older
teens. Interestingly enough, it may be part of girl culture to share information
with one another about their favorite books and movies and to recommend
their favorites to other fans. This, in turn, fuels the kind of word-of-mouth
advertising that Hollywood loves. The fact that the Internet now accelerates
that kind of communication has also served as a boon to the industry, as these
girls go online to spread the word about their favorite films.

From the production end, tween girls also prove to be an attractive
demographic to create films for. Unlike many blockbuster films which are
directed towards teenage boys, younger 'chick flick' movies generally cost a
lot less to make, so the potential for profit is not offset by high production
costs. Rob Reiner, who recently made *Alex and Emma* (2003), has observed,
"Expensive, high-profile action flicks have to do big business to make
money. You can hit a broad audience with a romantic comedy and the profit
margin is huge" (cited in Cruz and Schwartz 2003).

Television executives have also realized the huge profit margin to be
made by catering to tween girls, and Disney and Nickelodeon have been
ahead of the pack in reaching out to this demographic. For example, Teen
Nick is a block of programming that was created by Nickelodeon that
adopted a strategy of playing to the tweens' desire to be perceived as teenagers. In so doing, Nickelodeon was able to realize a 10% jump in their tween
audience for shows like *Caitlin's Way*, *As Told by Ginger,* and *The Brothers
Garcia*. The Disney Channel has also adopted a similar strategy of marketing
heavily to tweens in their creation of the Zoog Disney programming bloc.

The Lizzie McGuire Show is a prime example of this new marketing strategy and has paid off with high rates of audience viewing. Executives for these companies are not only proud to have 'discovered' this group of viewers, but as well, they contend that they can help them ride the rocky path from childhood to adolescence. As Rich Ross (cited in Bloom 2002) of the Disney Channel explained:

> Four years ago, people didn't know what the word tween,' was…. They thought we were insane. But I'd like to think our programming is a decoder ring for kids who are getting ready to go through adolescence.

More generally, the emphasis on 'tween' culture has coincided with other developments in Hollywood, including the push towards 'synergy' between the various divisions within the 'parent' corporation. For example, the success of *The Lizzie McGuire Show* for the Disney Channel has also meant that the other divisions of Disney, which draw on 'Lizzie McGuire,' can also earn high profits. In fact, it could be argued that the success of Lizzie McGuire is fueling the overall profits for Disney in part because, as one analyst observed, "The Disney Channel is probably the best run of all the businesses at Disney" (cited in Boorstin and Wheat 2003). From *The Lizzie McGuire Show*, ancillary products flowed, which increased the overall profits of the Disney Company. Disney Press started to publish Lizzie books and Disney's music group has produced and released a soundtrack from the series, which included some songs sung by Hilary Duff, the actor who plays Lizzie. By September of 2002, *The Lizzie McGuire Show* was airing every day on the Disney Channel. From these initial products and programs, more products flowed. Here is a partial list (Boorstin and Wheat 2003):

> Also in 2002, Disney's consumer products division began marketing everything from Lizzie dolls and sleeping bags to Lizzie pencils and notebooks. Last February it licensed the Lizzie name to retailer Kohl's for a line of apparel that is already a top seller in Kohl's 450 stores. Last May, Walt Disney Pictures released *The Lizzie McGuire Movie* (Duff's reported pay: $1 million), which debuted as the No. 2 film in the country and grossed nearly $50 million at the U.S. box office. Buena Vista released the movie soundtrack, of course; it went platinum too. It's hard to quantify how much the Lizzie franchise has earned Disney altogether, but it's reasonable to assume that the amount is nearing $100 million.

As part of this synergy, tween girls' love of certain fiction, as mentioned earlier, coincides with Hollywood now giving the green light to movies that are based on these books. There is great potential for these successful young adult books to attract loyal fans that will go to see the movie version of the book. These young readers are already a 'captive' audience who has formed an allegiance to the story and want to see it realized on screen. At the same time, Hollywood has also found that they can make a film that has not previously been in book form and then release the book version of the movie— e.g., *Tuck Everlasting* (2002)—as another way to generate profits.

Powerful Girls and Girl Power

In thinking about how tween girls are marketed to, it becomes clear that specific themes emerge in the storylines of these films. One marketing researcher, for example, has noted that stories that include themes such as family and friendships, revenge and rescue fantasies, and transformations are especially appealing to this group and "there's a strong fantasy element of 'I wish that could happen to me'" (cited in Bloom 2002). And, while they aspire to being teenagers, this does not necessarily mean that they are comfortable watching films that feature more sophisticated teen themes involving sex, drugs, or alcohol.

It is possible, for example, that the Britney Spears movie debacle, *Crossroads* (2002), had only a limited success because the plotline, which consists of Spears' good-girl character attempting to lose her virginity, was alienating for her tween girl fans. This would suggest that while this age group is thought to be more worldly than in previous generations, as evidenced by their clothing, for example, this does not mean that there have been fundamental changes in their core sense of self. As consumers, then, tween girls may be making choices for fashion items that are more daring than earlier generations (especially when these items are being heavily marketed to them), but there is no evidence to suggest that they have become miniature adults in all respects. And, judging by the success of such 'childish' films as *Shrek* (2001) and *Harry Potter* (2001) with the tween girl audience, it is clear that these young women can also be enthusiastic filmgoers for all kinds of films as long as there is precisely not an explicitly 'adult' theme such as losing one's virginity.

Thinking about compelling themes for tween girls, one popular motif in many of the new films coming out includes the portrayal of young women as powerful and able to exercise a degree of control over their lives. As Chris McGurk, vice chairperson and COO of MGM, puts it: "The studios have found that there is a very strong market for movies that feature young women in roles that are empowering" (cited in Cruz and Schwartz 2003:). McGurk goes on to note that such films as *Legally Blond* (2001), which appealed primarily to young women, were incredibly successful, bringing in grosses of $96 million dollars. This directly counters earlier thinking in Hollywood that it was necessary to create films that would appeal to the demographic cohort of 14–24-year-old males. Now, there is the realization that young girls constitute their own, very large audience and that the studios can generate large profits by catering specifically to them or as Nancy Utley, Fox Searchlight marketing president, observes, "the success of *Legally Blond* and female titles shows that when girls feel a connection to a movie they come out in droves. It's a very viable audience" (cited in Cruz and Schwartz 2003).

In thinking about this tween girl audience, some critics have noted that because this generation of young girls has in a sense grown up with the concept of 'girl power' in their own lives, at least in comparison with earlier generations, they are looking for images on film which also portray strong female characters such as Elle of *Legally Blonde*. Commenting on her role as Elle in *Legally Blonde*, Reese Witherspoon in fact describes choosing the role in part because it offered a vision of a young woman who doesn't have to choose between "Barbie or brainy": "[*Blonde*] had a modern, feminist attitude. It was about a woman who's girlie and feminine, but is also really ambitious and successful and driven" (cited in Cruz and Schwartz 2003).

For anyone who has sat through *Legally Blonde*, however, Witherspoon's suggestion that her character has a feminist attitude would raise serious questions as to what exactly constitutes feminism in Hollywood today. While many of these movies are ostensibly about girls gaining power in some realm—for Elle, it was first Harvard Law School, and then in *Legally Blonde Two* (2003) the sequel, the Senate—the screen images are filled with another set of powerful, consumerist, and arguably anti-feminist messages, including high-consumption items such as cars, vacations, beautiful clothes, well-crafted, perfect bodies, etc. In addition, in terms of the issue of race, Hollywood still creates universes that are, for the most part, white, suburban and upper middle class. As media critic, Laura Sessions Stepp (2003) has noted:

> Most female films this season may preach empowerment, but with thin plots, one-dimensional characters and unabashed emphasis on good looks and tight-fitting wardrobes, they ignore the myriad challenges that run through girls' lives.

In these films, then, much of what passes for empowerment is in reality the freedom for these young women to use their feminine skills and purchasing power to attain their goals. And, even in those films where feminine wile is not employed—since too much of it would be a turn-off to young girls anyway—there is nevertheless the usual 'payoff' where the girl becomes conventionally beautiful at the end of the film as a result of a 'makeover.' For example, in *Princess Diaries* (2001), the protagonist straightens her hair and puts on contact lenses in order to become the princess she was destined to be. This Cinderella story was so successful that it generated $108 million in the box office. Money and the pursuit of beauty are the real visual substance of these films, no matter how progressive the ostensible message is supposed to be.

In this marriage of marketing and message, then, a seamless fit emerges where advertising for products, freedom to consume, and self-transformation are fused in an overall 'feel good' film. As part of this process of marketing and self-transformation, it becomes crucial for the tween girls to form an identification with the female protagonists in the film, who are themselves undergoing some kind of transformation. For that to happen, these actors must usually be identifiable somehow from other media worlds that the girls have already had some exposure to. That is why there is such a strong incentive to 'recruit' actors from the ranks of television, where the tween viewers have already become familiar with the characters. The thinking is that somehow, through their previous acts of consumption and identification, the tweens will transfer their loyalty to watching these actors on the big screen.

For example, actors such as Hilary Duff, or the Olsen Twins (Mary Kate and Ashley,) or Amanda Byrnes, are already a part of tween girls' media world through the Nickelodeon and Disney channels. In their recent films, each of these young women undergoes a personal trial and thus arrives at a kind of self-knowledge. The feminist 'moment' in the story usually occurs when the girl realizes that it is more important to be who she is than to get 'the guy,' and often the guy is jettisoned in the process. More often, however, is the case where the boy waits passively on the sidelines while the girl enacts her own struggle, which only indirectly involves him. For tween girls, in other words, the drama that unfolds is only indirectly related to the heterosexual romance in the storyline.

Even in terms of the display of conventional beauty, tween girls will not accept this as an explicit goal for women, even if it becomes part of the 'payoff' at the end of the film. In fact, it can become the foil for ironic humor, which accounts for the large success of *Miss Congeniality* (2000). In this film, Sandra Bullock self-consciously mocks the beauty pageant aesthetic, even as she is forced to go underground and become a beauty queen for her FBI job.

Generally speaking, since tween girls are in-between childhood and adolescence, they are drawn to not only young actresses from television but to teen and twenty-something actresses who have also formed part of their earlier media landscape. As long as the storyline is not too graphic in terms of sexuality or other serious, adult themes, tweens will be drawn to watching Jennifer Lopez, Kate Hudson, Sandra Bullock, etc., on screen, since they are already familiar with them from television and magazines. This may explain, in part, why such films as *How to Lose a Guy in Ten Days* (2003), *Just Married* (2003), *Maid in Manhattan* (2002), *Two Weeks Notice* (2002), and *My Best Friend's Wedding* (1997), enjoyed such high box office receipts, derived in large part from the tween girl audience.

Commenting on the popularity of these romantic comedies for the tween girl audience, Peter Adee, president of worldwide marketing for MGM, observes that, "there's no question about it. There are just a lot of movies out there that the tween audience is driving. Teens are the main audience, followed by tweens" (cited in Puig 2003). In his view, teens are the first to go see these films, and they then tell their younger siblings about it, which brings in the tweens through this word-of-mouth network. Though these films are often romantic comedies, tween girls are not necessarily drawn to these films simply to see the romance occurring on screen. This is not to say that they do not generate interest and desire for the 'cute guy' in the film (witness the craze that Leonardo DiCaprio generated in *Titanic* with tween girl filmgoers), but that is not the only narrative they are drawn to. Tween girls enjoy watching the struggle that the female protagonist goes through, whether it is comedic or dramatic.

For example, in the film, *Maid in Manhattan*, film actor Jennifer Lopez's character works as a cleaner in a hotel where a rich politician (Ralph Fiennes) is staying. Through a wardrobe mishap, she is mistaken for a rich woman. In this film, the classic Cinderella fantasy is re-enacted. That she is loved in the end for being who she really is—that is, a working-class girl— also fits in with the themes of tween girl movies, which portray empowerment for girls through self-acceptance. And, while the ultimate feel-good message may be about loving oneself for who one is, once again a good may be about loving oneself for who one is, once again a good portion of the film portrays a fantastic world of wealth and power.

Family Movies and the Tween Girl Audience

While films such as *How to Deal* or *The Princess Diaries* may have been produced specifically with tween girls in mind, it is also true that tween girls are desirable in large part because they can be counted on to attend other kinds of films as well. For example, Hollywood has dealt with their never-ending quest for audience attendance by producing films that can be considered family entertainment as a means of drawing children, tweens, and teens along with their parents. And, while romantic comedies are viewed as an important film genre that tween girls will be drawn to, there is an equally strong pull to market these 'family films' to tween girls, precisely because they enjoy and can be counted on to attend and/or rent or buy a variety of these family films.

When thinking about the relationship of tween girls to family films, it may be useful to review a brief history of the development of this particular genre of film. For example, film scholar Robert C. Allen (1999) has made the argument that these kinds of family films arose in the wake of such larger social transformations as the 'echo boom,' the rise of the VCR, and the post-modern family. In his view, after the baby 'bust' between 1965 to 1980, the birth rate finally began to climb back up, to the point where by 1995, 28 percent of the U.S. population was under the age of 18. In fact, by 1998, fully 70 million Americans were under the age of 18.

In addition to a new and sizable population of young people, during this period the VCR became to the echo bust generation what the television had been to the boomers. Commenting on the impact of the VCR on the American population, Allen writes that:

> It took seventy years for the telephone to reach 50 per cent penetration of US households, cable television thirty-nine years, and television fifteen years. It took the VCR just twelve years, with 80 per cent of that penetration occurring in less than forty-eight months. To put this remarkable rate of adoption into perspective, we should recall that another revolutionary piece of electronic technology, the personal computer, was also introduced in the early 1980s. By the end of 1997, fewer than half of American households owned a computer, while nearly 90 percent owned a VCR. (111–112)

Given the enormous popularity of the VCR in the American home and the large percentage of Americans who are under the age of 18, it makes sense that the 'family' film would become an important genre to develop. And, in fact, Hollywood has attempted since that time to exploit the potential of VCRs, and now DVDS, with as many kinds of films as possible that a family might watch. What the VCR has done, in effect, is to multiply the potential profits of any given film from initial ticket sales in movie theaters, to repeat viewing in the 'home entertainment center.'

In terms of the question of genres, it is not immediately apparent what is considered a family film. Allen contends that the family film arose in the late 1980s and early 90s as a specific category, one that included a variety of other genres, such as realistic comedies, adventure fantasies, animated films and live action/animation hybrids. Thus, films as diverse as *Pirates of the Caribbean* (2003), *Finding Nemo* (2003), *Seabiscuit* (2003), *The Little Mermaid* (1992), *Jurassic Park* (1993), *Lion King* (1994), *Home Alone* (1990), etc., might all be considered family films. Also included may be films which are arguably inappropriate for younger children, but which are heavily marketed to them in an effort to draw their families into the theaters and video rental stores. Such films as *Spider-Man* (2002), which includes violent scenes, as well as Austin Powers in *Goldmember* (2002), which includes very suggestive sexual and scatological humor, are examples of films that had huge market campaigns that were directed in part at younger family members.

Writers such as A.O. Scott have observed that in the early 70s, Hollywood produced films that were far more challenging than the films cited above and that dealt with the social and political turmoil of the times. These films were clearly aimed at adults. Now, because of these changing demographics, 'mainstream' is considered the youth market. And this youth market does not simply include male teenagers but female teens and tweens as well as children and not least the parents who take them to the movies. As Scott (2003) notes:

> The really big blockbusters—from *Shrek* to *Lord of the Rings*, from the *Toy Story* movies to the *Harry Potter* franchise—are engineered for maximum cross-generational appeal. Sometimes this is achieved by playing to the sweetness of the very young, the flippancy and vulgarity of their older siblings and the self-mocking nostalgia of the grownups. *Shrek* is the most successful recent example of such a strategy; it won over adults (and a good many critics) by pandering to their curious

need to feel smarter than the children sitting next to them, conquering the audience by dividing it.

Overall, this strategy of creating films that will have cross-generational appeal has meant that Hollywood now produces more films than ever that are rated PG or PG–13. These films are viewed not only in the movie theaters but are bought for home viewing as well, or as Allen (1999) notes, "the single largest category of video purchases is parents buying videos for children. Videos aimed specifically at kids…represent 37 percent of all video sales." (116)

Though the family film is not exclusively aimed at tween girls, once one takes into consideration that these girls have powerful influences in terms of their parents' purchasing decisions, it is easy to see why, as a member of the family, tween girls would become an important group to market to. In addition, since they are more open-ended in terms of their film preferences, enjoying both children's films as well as teenager and twenty-something films, they represent a group who can be exploited by Hollywood because they are not as fixed in their tastes. Thus, while the tween girl thoroughly enjoys the more targeted tween films such as *The Princess Bride* (1987), she can also be counted on to go to *Cheaper by the Dozen*, (the new Steve Martin film), or *Harry Potter* (2001), or *Titanic* (1997) as well.

Finally, even when a film is specifically targeted to the tween girl audience, there is oftentimes the effort to generate cross-generational appeal for that film. It would be difficult to make the case that *The Lizzie McGuire Movie* (2003) or *Passport to Paris* (1999) (with Mary Kate and Ashley Olsen) have any cross-generational appeal—to parents, for example. However, it is the case that other fare, such as *Josie and the Pussycats* (2001), *Freaky Friday* (2003), *Little Women* (1994), and *The Parent Trap* (1998) do have something for other generations as well. Sometimes the appeal is a kind of wink and a nod to the parents, whereas other times it may be more connected to the plot of the movie; still other times, it may be trying to create a sense of nostalgia for the parents. In fact, in some recent Hollywood films, all three strategies are at work: plots that portray parent-child conflicts as well as the use of irony and nostalgia.

'Freakin' Amazing'[1]: Hollywood Re-Visions Tween Girlhood

In the recent Disney re-make of *Freaky Friday* (2003), these strategies of creating plots that involve a family dynamic, nostalgia, and irony are all in evidence. The film was explicitly targeted to tween girls, or as one critic (Berardinelli 2003) observed, "*Freaky Friday* is aimed squarely at the tween audience, and they will universally enjoy this movie, as will mothers who end up accompanying their offspring to theaters." The commercials for the film on television played up the potential tween appeal of the film, as when we hear the daughter say, upon realizing she has her mother's body and face, "Oh, I'm like the crypt keeper!"

The plot revolves around the mother-daughter dynamic, played by Jamie Lee Curtis and Lindsay Lohan, respectively. As the mother, Tess (Curtis) is the incarnation of the Hollywood version of the 'new' mother as workaholic. Having been widowed in the not-too-distant past, Curtis is portrayed as a harried psychiatrist who is micro-managing every aspect of her family's life while at the same time being disconnected from their 'real' struggles. Once again, the family, despite having a single parent as the primary wage earner, nevertheless has a high earner single parent, so the lifestyle they are shown as leading is upper middle class. Curtis is engaged to marry a new man (Mark Harmon) and in combination with her wedding plans and best-selling book is portrayed as having precious little time for her daughter and son's real needs.

Anna (Lohan), the daughter, is portrayed as rebelling against her mother, in part due to the alienation she feels at being disconnected from her and pain at the fact that she is remarrying so soon after her father's death. Rather than dwell on these potentially real-life struggles that viewers might identify with, that is, with a single mm trying to keep it all together and stay connected to her children, we are instead quickly taken in an escapist or fantastic direction. After they have entered a Chinese restaurant and demonstrated their conflicts openly at the dinner table, a wise and knowing Chinese mother (played by Lucille Soong) who is working at the restaurant gives Anna and Tess a fortune cookie which, when broken, creates the body-switch between mother and daughter. Commenting on the role this other-mother character is meant to play, media scholar Cynthia Fuchs (2003) observes that "And so, once again, well-heeled Caucasians who've lost touch with 'traditional' values are serviced by the inscrutable local Others or, as Anna observes, 'It was some strange Asian voodoo.'"

From this point on, the humorous aspects of the body-switch predominate for the remainder of the film, and at the end of the film there is the requisite message that it is important to understand what the other is going through in order to make peace with them and ultimately oneself. That the realization of this homily in fact leads to the mother and daughter being able to switch back reinforces this upbeat message of the need for acceptance of the other leading to reclaiming oneself. For the substance of the film, however, there are the comical aspects of what it means to be a modern-day teenager or a harried career woman. There is also the wish fulfillment for the mothers in the audience of a younger man being attracted to them as when Anna's would-be suitor ends up falling for Tess.

For tween girls, who may be working out the complications of coming out of latency, there is as well the specter of adult male desire as when the character played by Mark Harmon wants to kiss and hug his fiancée, and the audience watches him trying to kiss Lindsay Lohan. That aspect of the plot is quickly squelched, however, and for the remainder of the film, tween girls can enjoy the more pleasurable aspects of the film. Some of these filmic pleasures include being able to watch the daughter using Mom's credit card to make multiple purchases and watching with triumph as the mother discovers how unfair Anna's English teacher has been to her. And, of course, there is the ultimate fantasy at the end, which includes not only a harmonious resolution with the mom, but acceptance of the new father who will make the family whole again. Add to this the fact that the young suitor falls hard for the daughter again and that she is shown singing in a rock band at her mother's wedding at the end of the film, and it becomes clear why this film was such a success with tween girls.

While it is perhaps true that teen males might not have gone to see the film of their own accord, the film was clever enough and delivered enough jokes that it was able to appeal somewhat to other groups of viewers as well. Commenting on the cross-sex appeal of the film, film critic James Berardinelli (2003) notes that:

> *Freaky Friday* is motion picture cotton candy—sweet while it lasts, easily disposed of, and insubstantial. It will please those who seek it out, and probably won't horrify or disgust anyone who ends up seeing it for other reasons (dragged along, bribed, or otherwise coerced). There are enough clever and/or funny moments to provoke laughter from even a scowling 13-year old boy who wants to be next door watching *Terminator 3* for the third time.

The larger point is that even a tween girl film that is explicitly marketed to tween girls can be even more successful to the degree that it taps into the family film's cross-generational appeal.

What Is Past Is Prologue: Hollywood Re-Makes the Tween Girl

In thinking about the larger questions of how tweens are represented in these contemporary Hollywood films, then, it may be instructive to compare the re-make of *Freaky Friday*, with its original 1976 version, which was itself drawn from the 1972 Mary Rodgers novel. When comparing the two, one interesting question immediately arises: what happened to the father? In the original version of the film, with Jodie Foster and Barbara Harris as the daughter and mother, respectively, the father is not dead but very much alive. In the earlier version, John Astin plays the father, and he is described quite explicitly as a "male chauvinist pig." In 1976, the theme of a sexist father ordering his child and stay-at-home wife around may have resonated with female audiences of that era, and Disney, not known for its proto-feminism, retained this theme which originated from the children's novel.

In the earlier version of the film, furthermore, Jodie Foster's character of Annabel is portrayed as a sloppy and careless and very talented athletically, in short, a 'tomboy.' Her mother, Tess, is portrayed as an alienated, cigarette-smoking bourgeois housewife, who must contend with a myriad of household duties as her family leaves the house for school and work. The tension that ensues once the bodies are switched has to do with Annabel learning how to manage a household, deal with carpet cleaners, drunken housekeepers, nosy neighbors, and so on. Interestingly enough, when Annabel realizes she has her mother's body, though she is horrified not to be herself, the camera nevertheless shows her smiling approvingly as she runs her hands along her newfound (mother's) breasts. Compare this smile to the 2003 re-make, where Jamie Lee Curtis smiles approvingly as she feels the buttocks of her daughter in her newly acquired daughter's body. It is no longer clear, in this sense, how far women have progressed if the mother is now portrayed as wanting the tween daughter's body rather than the other way around as it was in the original.

In all fairness, it is true that as the film was coming out, Jamie Lee Curtis was feted for appearing in a woman's magazine in her 'own' body; that is, she wanted women to see what a middle-aged star's body looks like when it is not re-touched by photography. She was lauded in the media for being so 'brave' as to show 'the truth' about the aging process for women. In this way, the 'supra-text' of the film dealt directly with what it means for a contemporary middle-aged woman to have a 'real' body in an age where young bodies are held out as the norm. At the same time, the text of the film itself precisely played into middle-aged women's anxieties about not having a younger body. Thus, the cultural messages of the film in a sense undercut the seemingly progressive messages of the media publicity surrounding Curtis.

At another level, the portrayal of girlhood in the original film is arguably far more progressive than the vision we are offered in the re-make. For, in the earlier version, the Jodie Foster character is decidedly not a grown woman, and in the 1970s is not yet immersed in all the products and images that would engulf tween girls in later decades. The Foster character may be shown trying on her mother's rouge and false eyelashes, but in this version she ends up looking like a circus clown and is happier being the 'tomboy' she is. Counter this image of tween girlhood with the 2003 version of the film, where the daughter goes on a spending spree in her mother's body and creates a wardrobe for her that is intended to make her look more youthful. In this version, the daughter, far from being a tomboy, is a putative sex kitten, dressing her mother's body in slinky, tight-fitting outfits with high heels, piercing, etc. In this sense, the re-make has re-visioned what the stakes are for tween girls today: no longer tomboys but rather would-be hosts of a Hollywood makeover program. This is where the irony comes in as well. Tween girls can knowingly laugh at the daughter's frustration with her mother's dowdy looks and can enjoy watching the mother become a new, younger self with her daughter's wise guidance.

By the year 2003, then, *Freaky Friday* arguably took on a completely new set of meanings. First, all traces of sexism in the family have disappeared, and we are now instead faced with the specter of a castrating, workaholic mother figure. Part of the tension of the new version precisely consists of how the family will be 'blended' or reconstituted with a mother who is barely at home and with the arrival of a new father to replace the dead father. Whereas the old family, then, was troubled as a result of lingering sexism and the 'male chauvinist pig' behavior of the father, the new family is trying to figure out a way to bring a male back into its fold with a 'liberated' mother. Thus, one could make the argument that in this film—and many other 'family' films—it is precisely the modern fractured family that creates the dramatic tension. As well, it is this dynamic that would arguably appeal to both the tween girls as well as their (guilt-ridden) working mothers viewing the film together. The laugh may be on the mother, but the tensions in the film resonate with both daughters and mothers.

In terms of the specific images of what constitutes tween girlhood today, furthermore, it is clear that the 'tomboy' image is not valorized in the later version of the film. Rather, the new tween girl in the re-make is a beautiful, hair-dyed, would-be rock guitarist, who comes replete with Britney Spears like belly rings, short shifts and perfectly made-up face. The dramatic tension for this girl is that she supposedly cannot fit in at school and has created a garage band as an alternative identity to that displayed by the popular girls in school. That anyone could believe that the beautiful and sharply dressed Lindsay Lohan would ever be ostracized in any school stretches the imagination.

The more important point is that the earlier pre-teen angst for the Jodie Foster character lay in the fact that her identity as a tomboy did not fit in with her mother's image of who she wanted her to be. In the new version of the film, the stakes have shifted, and it is now the fact that the daughter tries to act too grown-up, piercing her belly, playing in a rock band, etc., that agonizes her mother. It could be argued, therefore, that tween girlhood, at least in Hollywood's representations, has thus gone from being the place where girls are negotiating the freedom of their childhood, which allowed them to be tomboys, to a place where they are demonstrating their rebellion through creating self-images that are far more sophisticated and sexual than their earlier counterparts.

Conclusion

In conclusion, in this brief rehearsal of the relationship of contemporary Hollywood to tween girl culture, it is clear that tween girls have become an important group that studios are finally paying attention to. From its initial efforts to create films for a mass audience, to targeting adult audiences, to finally, the teen and then 'youth' market, Hollywood has been in a never-ending search to find the right films that will appeal to diverse audiences. In this search, tween girls were finally 'discovered,' and the studios have been scrambling to meet the increasing demand for films for tween girls ever since.

While these studios have been very successful in targeting this new demographic, a deeper question emerges—what kinds of images of girlhood are ultimately being portrayed on screen in these mainstream films? For, while the messages behind these films are often touted as being progressive and 'empowering,' the mise-en-scene of white, upper-middle-class suburban landscapes in effect undercuts the progressive messages of the texts themselves. Add to this the effect of a steady stream of consumer activities and purchases that the protagonists oftentimes make in these films, and it is easy to criticize these films as one long commercial for a consumer society. Ultimately, the dominant image of tween girlhood that these films offer is one of a subject who is ensconced in a white, primarily suburban America, one where conflicts are raised and a resolution is found, and the girl gets the wardrobe, the intact family, and the guy to boot.

On a final note, though Hollywood has too often gone this conventional route in creating tween girl films, many exceptions might provide a pathway for other filmmakers to follow in the future. For example, the tween girl film *Blue Crush* (2002) is arguably in the group just described, that is, a progressive message film with a pretty white girl who is portrayed in a small bikini for a good portion of the film. However, the film, which is about a working-class girl who wants to be a world-class surfer, is redeemed somewhat by its accurate portrayal of working-class life and by its attempt to show how girls can have the same desires as men (as in *Rocky*) to fight against all odds for their goals. Similarly, films like *Little Women* (1994), with Wynona Ryder and Susan Sarandon, demonstrate that a female-bonding film can be entertaining and meaningful at the same time.

Finally, there are many non-US films, including such recent films as *Whale Rider* (2002) and *Bend It like Beckham* (2002), which do not simply valorize white upper-middle-class suburban life. In these films, women 'of color' are portrayed as struggling to offset the stereotypes and injunctions against females that exist in their worlds. The point is that Hollywood does not have to marry commerce with tween culture in order to create inspiring, popular films that tween girls will flock to. Speaking of the genesis of the 'chick flick' more generally, Paramount executive Lynda Obst (cited in McNary 2003) has observed that, "Chick flicks were originally first and foremost a form of counter programming, so I think it's a tremendous show of confidence that they now have enough muscle and crossover potential to open in the summer." The recent and surprise successes of films like *Whale Rider* and *Bend It Like Beckham* demonstrate that crossover films for tween girls can also be extremely popular and profitable. Ultimately, as more of these kinds of films get the 'green light' for production and are funded appropriately (including marketing campaigns and better distribution), girls will get to see varied and diverse images of empowered young women. Then, tween girls might finally be able to get more than a sugarcoated and consumerist message from Hollywood about what their own empowerment could consist of.

Notes

[1] See Gordon and Smith (2003).

References

Allen, R. C. "Home Alone Together: Hollywood and the 'Family Film.'" In *Identifying Hollywood's Audiences: Cultural Identity and the Movies*, edited by M. Stokes and R. Maltby, 111–116. London: British Film Institute, 1999.

Berardinelli, J. "Freaky Friday." *ReelViews*, 2003. http://movie-reviews.colossus.net/master. html.

Bloom, D. "Targeting those Twicky Tweenagers." *Variety*, April 29, 2002.

Boorstin, J., and A. Wheat. "Disney's Tween Machine." *Fortune*, September 29, 2003.

Chautard, A. "Little Miss Moviegoer; The 8–18 Female Audience not Only Reads a Lot of Books but Also Flocks to Movies Based on Those Books, as Hollywood Is Discovering." *Los Angeles Times*, August 3, 2003, E8.

Cruz, C., and M. Schwartz. "girlPOWER." *Entertainment Weekly*, August 11, 2003, 38.

Dade, H. "Hollywood Revels in Niche Riches." *Variety*, April 29, 2003, 1, 2p, 4c.

Fuchs, C. "That Asian Voodoo." *Pop Matters*, 2003. http://popmatters.com/film reviews/f/ freaky-friday.html.

Gomery, D. "Hollywood Corporate Business Practice and Periodizing Contemporary Film History." In *Contemporary Hollywood Cinema*, edited by S. Neale and M. Smith, 47–57. London: Routledge, 1998.

Gordon, D., and S. Smith. "Freakin' Amazing." *Newsweek*, August 18, 2003.

Kramer, P. "A Powerful Cinema-Going Force? Hollywood and Female Audiences since the 1960s." In *Identifying Hollywood's Audiences: Cultural Identity and the Movies*, edited by M. Stokes and R. Maltby, 93–109. London: British Film Institute, 1999.

Maltby, R. "'Nobody Knows Everything': Post-Classical Historiographies and Consolidated Entertainment." In *Contemporary Hollywood Cinema*, edited by S. Neale and M. Smith, 21–40. London: Routledge, 2000.

McNary, D. "Femme Films Find Their Footing." *Variety,* May 11, 2003.

Puig, C. "Fluff of Romance, Comedy Entices Preteens." *USA Today*, March 13, 2003.

Scott, A. O. "It's a Joyride, and the Kids Are Driving." *The New York Times*, August 11, 2003.

Smith, M. "Theses on the Philosophy of Hollywood History." In *Contemporary Hollywood Cinema*, edited by S. Neale and M. Smith, 3–20. London: Routledge, 2000.

Stepp, L. S. "Hollywood's Material Girls; For Young Moviegoers, Summer Heroines Offer Consuming Life Lessons." *The Washington Post*, August 3, 2003, N.01.

CHAPTER TWENTY

The Consumption Chronicles: Tales from Suburban Canadian Tweens in the 1980s

Natalie Coulter

I grew up in the1980s. I remember rushing home from school to see the latest video on the new Canadian TV show *Video Hits*, and in true Valley Girl fashion, I was perpetually being 'gagged by a spoon.' I cheered for Bo and Luke Duke to cross the county line, listened to Michael Jackson's *Thriller,* and always wore my collar of my pink Polo shirt turned upwards. When I look at pictures of my younger self, I stare in awe and wonder: who was this girl who seemed to awkwardly latch on to every trend as she dealt with the challenges of her developing body? I was a product of the 1980s—well, let's make this clear—I was a product of white, middle-class, suburban Canada in the 1980s. As a young girl, I was similar to the other girls who grew up in the same social space. But who were we? Who were these girls that innocently played with Cabbage Patch Dolls while singing along with Madonna's *Like a Virgin.*

The 1980s were unique times to be a girl. For many of us our mothers had headed off to the workplace in the 1970s only to be disillusioned with incredible pressures of trying to balance working and being a parent. The myth of the 'Super Mom' was dissolving while it was becoming increasingly apparent that the utopia of the feminist movement that was promised to the 'new woman' would not be entirely realized. In this tumultuous space, as young girls, we were the 'latch-key kids' who came home to empty houses after school and watched TV until it was time to start making dinner. But we were also the girls that were 'discovered' by marketers as 'tweens' by the late 1980s. What were we doing that required being discovered? This chapter has two sections; the first will be to place this discovery of the tween within the broader socio-historical frames of twentieth century capitalist consumer culture, particularly the expanding commodification of youth cultures and the gendering of consumption in the post-War era. The second section will give a voice to the tween girls who were 'being discovered' by marketers. This section is based on a series of in-depth, retrospective interviews conducted with women who were tweens in the 1980s. These interviews were designed to explore the lived experiences of the girls with these consumer goods, specifically, looking at how the girls produced and negotiated the social meanings of these commodities and how their interactions with consumer products informed, framed, and defined their gendered selves in the turbulent social space of the 1980s. This chapter is situated at the intersection of ideologies of gender, the self, and the market by exploring how suburban Canadian youth actively negotiated consumer culture in the construction of the gendered self in the everyday.

'Discovering' the Tween

It was in light of the dissolving feminist utopia mentioned earlier that tweens were discovered as a unique life stage. By the 1980s, middle-class family dynamics had significantly shifted away from the traditional post-war model family with the housewife having time to purchase all of the consumer goods necessary to fulfill the family's needs. Many children were now living in two-career households or in households with a single parent who worked. In 1980, 50 percent of married women in the United States (Cross 2000: 230) and 47 percent of Canadian wives were in the workforce (Ram 1990: 92). The percentage of women in the workforce increased during the 1980s. In Canada, the number of married women in the workforce rose to 57 percent by 1986. For these parents in dual-income families the demands of employment were high. The pressure to work late coupled with long commutes from the suburbs on snarled highways to the various industrial and business centers meant that there was little time for parents to complete household chores. In order to withstand these pressures, the children were often left to pick up the slack, undertaking such tasks as grocery shopping, cleaning the house, and making meals. It was the chore of grocery shopping that is of particular importance in the 'discovery' of tweens. Marketers were very interested in the fact that tweens were given more buying power within the family.

By the end of the 1980s, Madison Avenue had clearly detected the rise of young girls in the nation's stores and in true capitalist spirit recognized tweens as a valuable marketing opportunity. By 1989, this 'discovery' was making national press. In an article in *US News and World Report,* journalist Alice Z. Cuneo pointed out that the 25 million "tweens, from 9–15 year olds, [were] no longer viewed as the $2 allowance crowd," instead they bought or influenced over 45 billion dollars (US) worth of merchandise a year. In response to the increasing pressures on working parents' time, tweens were frequenting supermarkets and convenience stores, "making the brand decisions previously made by housewives" (Cuneo 1989: 84). This increasing buying power of the tween consumer was a sentiment echoed two years by Peter Zollo of Teenage Research Unlimited. According to Zollo:

> One-third of 12–15 year olds do the family's grocery shopping on a weekly basis. Parents give them a list that says 'mayonnaise' but they have to pick the brand. People used to say this group wasn't reachable but now they see they just have to know how to catch them. (McLaughlin 1991: 63)

Girls' magazines such as *Seventeen* informed marketers how to catch these young girls by taking out full-page spreads in such publications as *Advertising Age,* informing a wide range of marketers of young women's new purchasing power and, of course, suggesting that *Seventeen* magazine was the vehicle to reach these girls.

Although the 'discovery' of tweens began with young girls having influence over family spending habits, it was the disposable income of the young girls that really solidified their position as a separate marketing niche. By 1991, marketers touted that tween girls shopped at least three times a week and saved 30% of their money for large items, which was more than 'little kids or teenagers' (McLaughlin 1991: 63).

This interest in tweens as a consumer demographic with access to a vast amount of discretionary income has intensified through the 1990s and into the 2000s. By the late 1990s, tweens were considered one of the fastest growing consumer segments. Media Metrix, a New York-based research firm, estimated that the tween demographic was second only to the senior demographic in terms of spending power (Mark 2001: 2).[1] According to the New York-based Institute for International Research, tweens spent nearly $14 billion (US) and influenced over $128 billion in spending in 2001(Mark 2001: 2). In 1998, in Canada, tweens represented almost $1.4 billion (Steinberg 1998: 61). The consumer influence of the tween culture is epitomized by the huge success of the Spice Girls in the mid-1990s and the dramatic increase in popular clothing stores with offshoots specifically targeted to the tween demographic such as La Senza Girl and Le Château Junior Girl.

The 'discovery' of tweens in the late 1980s took place within the realm of consumer culture. The segmentation of tween as a separate age category, distinct from adolescence and childhood, has been constructed within market terms. Marketers discovered tweens as they began to gain influence over the family's purchases and had access to their own disposable incomes. Tweens only became visible as consumers, not as citizens or active members of a society, but as consumers. The entire definition of tweens from their attitudes, values, sense of humor, and level of sophistication has largely been defined in market terms. The problem with this is that in segmenting youth into categories constructed purely in market terms, young people are often reduced to objects where they are "commodified and marketed back to themselves, stripped of any history, individual identity or power" (Giroux, cited in Brooks 2003: 13).

In the twentieth century, there is a long history of organizing the population into consumer categories. This history of a segmented fraction of youth discovered and defined within the narrow confines of consumer culture is not a new phenomenon. In the shifting cultural landscape and rising affluence of the post-World War II era, youth became defined as teenagers. Before the War, the teen had no major amount of spending power, but in the late 1940s and 50s, shifting economic and demographic variables changed this. Teenagers became a large demographic and with the newfound affluence of post-war suburbia, teens could live at home longer with substantial disposable income. In response, consumer and media culture began to tailor themselves to meet the demands of this growing youth culture and exploit it as a new market (Ewen 1976; Cohen 1980; Griffin 1993).

This commercialization of youth culture continued throughout the latter half of the 20th century. The division of tweens into a consumer segment in the 1980s was part of this broader trend of a deepening commercialization of youth culture that also extends to children's culture. For example, the deregulation of television in the United States in 1983 by FCC allowed broadcasters to transform children's programs into advertisements. Cartoons such as He-Man, G.I. Joe, The Care Bears, and Strawberry Shortcake were in effect program-length commercials created entirely to advertise a new toy line. By 1985, these cartoons featured all ten of the top-selling toys, and childhood became an "interconnected industry that encompassed movies, TV shows,

videos and other media forms along with toys, clothing and accessories"
(Cross 2000: 210). It is no surprise that in this vastly commercial space advertisers and marketers started to carve childhood into smaller, narrower
niches in order to optimize marketing opportunities.

The construction of the tween in the late 1980s occurs in the context of
this long history of the commercialization of youth cultures where young
people are targeted as consumers as they are fractured and consolidated into
smaller niches that provide more intense marketing opportunities. Turning
young people into consumer markets has been essential for the continuation
of industrial capitalism (Ewen 1976). Capitalism, as Judith Williamson argues, is constantly searching for "new areas to colonize" (1986: 116). The
colonization of new markets provides an outlet for overproduction. Capitalism's productive capacity is always growing to the extent that it overpro-
duces. To circumvent overproduction it has to look for new markets (Leiss et
al., 1997: 20). In the past 50 years, youth have been one of capitalism's new
markets as every age of youth; the teen, the young child and now the tween,
have been consolidated and produced as lucrative consumer markets.

The Feminization of Consumption

Not only is tween a label that has been constructed within the frames of marketing discourses that have commodified youth cultures, but it is also a category that is clearly gendered in that it is part of a wider misogynistic view
that reifies a link between the feminine and consumption. Over the course of
the past century, the acts of shopping and purchasing have been inscribed as
feminine (Currie 1999: 135; McRobbie 1989: 192; Nava 1992: 190). In the
affluent post-War era, the ideal consumer was the suburban housewife.[2] She
controlled 80% of the family buying (Scott, cited in Nava 1992: 190) and
was perceived as leisurely spending her time grocery shopping while her
male counterpart worked to provide for the family. In such a scenario the
female housewife was the antithesis to the male breadwinner; the female
consumer was dichotomous to the male producer, a dichotomy that has been
played out both in cultural representations such as women's magazines, television shows and movies, and also within academia. In this dichotomy, the
female consumer has been constructed as impulsive, passive, and irrational
(Nava 1992: 191; Hollows 2000: 115) while the male producer was rational
and autonomous with the potential to resist the manipulative powers of consumer culture. Joy Parr argues that the associations of masculinity and the

capacity to resist became so naturalized that male rebellion was treated more as an empirical observation than as dogma by the 1960s (Parr 1999: 7).[3] On the other hand, a wide range of social commentators and cultural theorists such as Betty Friedan, Vance Packard, Theodore Adorno and Herbert Marcuse have argued that capitalism has persuaded people to consume against their wills by creating false needs. Given that women have largely been signified as the consumers, these views become highly gendered.

It is within these ideological frames that naturalize the passive female consumer as easily manipulated or duped by advertisers that notions of 'tweenhood' are constructed. The stereotype of the tween girl is a voracious consumer who latches on to every new trend. This image is further perpetuated as recent moral panics about tween girls center largely around what they consume. One of the main concerns with the Spice Girls, for example, was that young girls were rushing out to the nearest shopping mall to buy the garish makeup and provocative clothes of Ginger Spice.[4] Another example of the naturalization of tween girls as manipulated consumers is the recent Global Television documentary entitled "*Tweens: Too Fast, Too Soon*" shown on Canadian television in the spring of 2003. The documentary used the common stereotypes of tween girls and boys. In the documentary young girls were depicted as spending large amounts of their parents' money at the shopping mall in order to keep up with current trends. In opposition, the concern with tween boys was centered on their media consumption, particularly the amount of time that the boys played video games. The boys were never problematized in terms of how they spent their money or what they bought at the mall. Instead, these boys were problematized in the home, the private sphere, while girls were defined in the public space, a reversal of traditional constructions of boyhood and girlhood. However, this reversal does not offer any emancipatory opportunities. Instead, it continues to reify females as passive and 'dupable.' Young girls face the double burden of having little agency since both female and youth are coded as being manipulated by the consumer culture.

Giving Tweens a Voice

The coding of the girl consumer as having little agency raises the obvious questions: Was this was the actual experience of female consumers? Did the young girls who were discovered by marketers in the 1980s have any agency? And, what were these girls really doing that warranted being discovered? It would be easy to make assumptions about what girls were doing in the 1980s by simply looking at the media the girls would have consumed at the time. But this would deny these women a voice in their own history. In the wide range of critical work conduct on consumer culture and on youth, the voices of both consumers and youth have routinely been undervalued. One of the challenges of consumer culture is gathering data that gives the user of the object a narrative position (Woodward 2001: 130). While writing about youth, there is a tendency to speak on behalf of the subject, denying the subject her or his own voice. To avoid these pitfalls, I conducted intensive, in-depth oral history interviews with women who were girls in the 1980s, asking them questions about their relationships with others, how they conceived of notions of girlhood, their experiences shopping for and using consumer goods and their favorite objects.[5] All of these questions were designed to generate a narrative around consumption, gender, and notions of the self.

The interviewees were born between the years of 1970 and 1975, which means that by 1980, the oldest cohort was 10 and the youngest 5 years old; by 1989 the oldest cohort would have been 19 and the youngest 14. I was particularly interested in exploring their tween years, which I have loosely defined as ages 10 to 13, which translates into grades 6, 7, and 8.[6] The girls in this study, who are now women, grew up in the suburbs surrounding Toronto, Canada's largest city. I decided to narrow my interviews to girls from the suburbs for a number of reasons. In particular, because the key tween demographic marketers were targeting was the middle-class suburban girl with two working parents, who often suffered long commutes to work. The interviewees were solicited by snowballing, i.e., one women interviewee gave the name of another. This allowed for a level of intimacy that would not have been possible by random sampling. The difficulty with such a methodology is that it does not allow one to claim a representative sampling, but this weakness is overpowered by the fact that having a personal connection with the interviewees allowed me to ask intimate questions about their youth that yielded many meaningful insights.

Girls in the 1980s desired, purchased, and used a whole array of consumer products. As marketers had discovered by the late 1980s, some of these goods were purchased for the family. But many goods were bought for the girls themselves. Individual purchases that girls made ranged from grooming products such as deodorant, make-up, and acne cream to the latest fashions, including Ralph Lauren polo shirts and brightly colored stirrup pants. Obviously, these goods played many utilitarian roles from masking body odors to covering the body, but embedded in these goods were a multitude of cultural values including gender, age, sexuality, class, and notions of the body. This means that the act of consuming goods is not a passive process of need satisfaction as one might think; instead, it is an active and dynamic process of the construction of the self.

This, of course, is one of the key doctrines of capitalist consumer culture, that the self and self-identity are formed through a wealth of consumer goods. In western consumer culture, the vast array of consumer goods that is available provides the material and symbolic resources of identity (Fiske 1989; McCracken 1988; Slater 1997). Social identity largely depends on one's ability to construct a coherent narrative of the self through the selection of a distinct set of commodities (Crawford 1992). Of course, consumer culture is not the only site in the Western world where people work out, navigate, and narrate their own identities. Nevertheless, for many of the privileged, it is a prime site. Ultimately, as Celia Lury points out, in such a culture identities have become more than the relationship of people to goods but instead are commodities in and of themselves (1996: 8).

The act of consumption as the prime mode of constructing identities is a message that is constantly reinforced in the discourse of media culture. While this message plays a role in forming the sign-value of goods, to use Baudrillard's terminology, meaning is ultimately located in the act of using the good. The construction, formation, and articulation of identities in consumer culture are located in the use of commodities and not in the commodities themselves. Following such logic, the questions that need to be raised are how girls that came to be called tweens by marketers used the wide array of commodities offered to them and how this use played a role in constituting notions of girlhood and the self.

Consuming Gender and Age

Tweenhood is a life stage separate from childhood. It is framed as a period of transition and represents a shift away from childhood towards being an adult or at least a teenager. Of course tied to this notion of maturation is gender. Being a tween means more than simply growing up; it means that a girl is growing up to become a young woman. Puberty is central to the tween discourse. For many of the women interviewed, activities such as shaving their underarms, buying bras, and menstruating were all milestones in defining their experiences in grades 6, 7, and 8:

> Janet: *What were grades 6, 7, and 8 like? Oh God, for me they were awful. Eve-*
>   *rything changed. It meant getting your period, your body changed and*
>   *you didn't know what to do with it.*

Laurel had similar sentiments:

> *Being that age meant getting your period. That was huge. Realizing that you had to*
> *get your first bra and realizing that playing with boys was now different.*

For the interviewees, the transitions to womanhood were largely marked by bodily changes and having to respond to these changes by engaging in such endeavors as wearing a training bra, shaving body hair, or buying tampons. Catherine Driscoll has noted that for girls the changes that signify the shifts to womanhood are bodily, biological changes as opposed to personal experiences (2002: 90). What is interesting in the interviews is how these bodily changes were not noted empirically in and of themselves by the interviewees. Instead, the response to the changes is remembered as the rite of passage. Puberty was signified not by the awareness of body hair or breasts but by the experience of shaving or buying a bra, experiences that took place within the marketplace. For example, for Victoria, puberty was signaled by finally using the sanitary napkin pads that her mother had bought specifically for her and had tucked away for the time when she would need them:

> *I remember the box of Kotex and the belt already to go in my Mother's bathroom*
> *cupboard for when I would get my period.*

For Laurel, it was the realization that she was beginning to perspire and then having to buy deodorant:

> *Oh God, in grade 8 my older cousin told me I smelt funny, so I had get my Mom to*
> *go and buy me deodorant. That's when I knew things were changing.*

By the 1980s, puberty had become a highly commodified experience as consumer culture provided the markings of the transitions towards adulthood. These markings took place at different sites on the body, i.e., under the arms, on the chest, or in the vagina. The girl body was fractured into multiple sites, with each site providing valuable marketing opportunities (Lury 1996: 134).

Shaving one's armpits, wearing a bra for the first time, or getting one's period were all potential marketing opportunities for companies to exploit. Ultimately, puberty was constructed as a series of bodily changes strung together over a few years of one's youth as opposed to a continual transformation.

The fracturing of the pubescent body is part of a larger phenomenon of turning the body into a project. In the 20th century, the body had become the central project for North American girls and was an important means of self-definition (Brumberg 1997). It was something that needed to be monitored, controlled, shaped, and contained. And consumer culture has been able to provide the accoutrements of this required vigilance. There has been a huge array of goods targeted to the tween in the personal project of the body. Products such as skin cleansers to eliminate acne, special pink plastic razors designed for novice shavers and small, discrete-looking tampons that easily slip into the back pocket of a favorite pair of jeans have all successfully been marketed to girls.

The experience of shopping also signified a sense of maturity for the girls. Shopping was a site in which the girls could articulate and express a certain amount of autonomy. Having the freedom to make consumer decisions about what to buy connoted a sense of adulthood:

> Andrea: *I remember the first tape I bought on my own. I saved up my money and*
> *bought Prince's* Purple Rain *album. I remember it was in the United*
> *States and it was 14 American dollars. That was a big thing. I felt so*
> *adult.*

The freedom to make these types of consumer choices without any parental influence could only come with having one's own money to spend. This indicated a separation and autonomy from parents. Kim, for example, vividly recalls her first babysitting job as "a big deal because I had my own money to spend." Having money signaled a shift for these girls as it meant a certain freedom from parents in being able to make their own decisions as young consumers, often decisions that they knew their parents would not make. This was true for Lorna:

> *I distinctly remember going with my first paycheck to Hazleton Lanes in Toronto*
> *and going right to the Ralph Lauren store and buying my 75-dollar blue and white*
> *striped polo button down shirt and going to Club Monaco and buying 85-dollar*

jeans. I went with my friends and bought exactly what I wanted. My Mom would
never have let me spend that kind of money on a shirt and a pair of jeans.

Susan also indicated such feelings:

It was important to have my own money. I babysat and had a paper route. I didn't
get an allowance so having my own money meant that I could go to the movies, go
skiing or buy the stuff that I wanted.

What is fascinating about these responses is that none of the women suggested that the job itself gave her this sense of autonomy or made her feel more adult. Instead, the pay offered the potential for freedom. It was the freedom that babysitting money, for example, allowed—not the actual act of taking care of children in a household without adults for a few hours—that indicated maturity. Of course the shopping mall was not the only site for autonomy, many of the women indicated that as young girls they were allowed to play freely outside of the home, riding bikes or going to the park, but these freedoms did not warrant the same sense of maturity and autonomy that consumer culture offered. Shopping provided a space for these girls to make their own decisions as consumers, relatively free from parental pressures.

Not only did consumer culture provide the markings of the shift from youth to adulthood, but it also provided tangible reminders that one was still a child. One of the biggest fads in the 1980s was the Cabbage Patch Doll, followed by its various incarnations of Corn Silk Cabbage Patch and Cabbage Patch Preemies. The dolls were incredibly popular and stores had great difficulty keeping them in stock. Many of the women interviewed had a Cabbage Patch Doll, with one interviewee having a number of them. Although the dolls were clearly status symbols, as they were expensive, hard to get, and a huge fad, they did not sit idly on the shelves of these girls' bedrooms as trophies, instead they were brought to school and played with at recess time.

The Cabbage Patch Dolls illustrate the fluidity of the life stage of tweenhood as a struggle to be more mature while at the same time holding onto the vestiges of youth. According to Driscoll, the meaning of girl at this age is unfixed as girlhood is performed as a transitional role of becoming (2002: 59). The Cabbage Patch Dolls provided a transitional space, as they were one of the consumer objects available that allowed girls to oscillate between childhood and adolescence without having to commit to either life stage. The incongruity of trying to purchase the signifiers of adulthood such as make-up and nylons while at the same time buying dolls was clearly noticed by one of the interviewees. In reference to a picture of her at 11 years old, looking very serious while wearing makeup and an olive green dress, she makes this connection:

Andrea: *Look at me here, I was wearing olive green nylons, and I thought I was so grown up. And yet, in the same year I was playing with Cabbage Patch Dolls.*

Natalie: *Did you notice that when you were at the age?*

Andrea: *Oh no, it seemed perfectly normal. Both were cool, playing with Cabbage Patch Dolls and also wearing makeup.*

For the girls of the 1980s, consumer culture played a central role in the performance of age and gender. It provided the markings of puberty and autonomy while also providing the means of holding onto youth. However, this was not the only role that it played in these young women's lives.

Consuming Social Hierarchies

The act of consumption played a vital role in the hierarchy and stratification of tween cultures. Joe Austin and Willard Michael suggest that the peer group has become the major institution of socialization for youth during the 20th century and potentially has a greater influence than any other institution (1998: 6). The influence of peers was constantly reinforced in the interviews. Many of the subjects vividly recalled purchasing something important copied from a peer or sometimes an older sibling who was deemed 'cooler' than they were. In every case, the interviewee recalled the full name of the individual and was able to describe in detail what that person wore and did to warrant the title of 'cool.'

In the social hierarchy of girls, culture status was based partly on clothes and style.[7] Gaining this status was a highly contentious endeavor, and for most girls there was a certain social logic to it. One of the key aspects of style was novelty. Status, signified by the word 'cool,' could be conferred when someone had something first. Lorna illustrates this point quite clearly:

If there was something I knew was cool, I copied it from my sister or the kids at camp and wore it at school. Then I knew I had it first and I was cool.

Janet also iterates the role of novelty:

The goal was to become a trendsetter yourself. To get something that other people saw and wanted.

Having fashionable items before others signified a certain form of knowledge, which Sarah Thornton has defined as subcultural capital. Subcultural capital, as she argues, is the "embodied form" of "being in the know" (1997: 202). Wearing a certain fashionable item indicates to ones' peers that you have access to this knowledge and are 'in the know.' However, as nothing depletes subcultural capital more than 'trying too hard,' this knowledge is supposed to come naturally and be authentic[8] (Thornton 1997: 203). 'Trying too hard' garners the label of being a poser. This distinction is noted in Dick Hebdige's work on punk subcultures. Hebdige distinguishes the differences between the "originals and hangers-on," with the originals being the "self-conscious innovators" of the punk scene (1979: 122). For the girls of the 1980s, being a trendsetter was a means of aligning oneself with being an originator and having subcultural capital.

In suburban Canada, there was a particular geography to being 'in the know' or cool. Subcultural capital was tied to place when the city became the site of knowledge. Where one bought clothes was almost as important as what one bought, an insight articulated by Dorie:

You knew who got to go out of town because they had the Roots and Cotton Ginny clothes, as opposed to stuff that you could only get in town.

Traveling to the city to go shopping gave young consumers an edge in accessing subcultural capital. For Susan, being cool meant having a different style and wearing different clothes:

Clothes that came from outside Newmarket (a Toronto suburb) were cool. They weren't run of the mill, but maybe came from the city.

The wide array of consumer objects available to these young girls played a role in the stratification of these young girls, but socialization is a double-edged sword. It is about belonging, but it is also about not belonging. One of the key problems that virtually all of the interviewees faced at one point during their youth was being alienated or outcast from a group of girlfriends. This was a very traumatic, potentially devastating, experience. Sometimes the girls knew why they were alienated. Either they had stood up for another girl who was being picked on, or maybe they did not participate in the right type of activity, such as a playing on a sports team, or what they wore did not fit into the right image. But many times the girls had no clue as to why they were suddenly on the outside of a group. In these cases many of the women suggested that it was simply because "girls were just mean" (an insight that clearly warrants further study). What is interesting in the context of this chapter is the way that the interviewees dealt with this alienation. For many of the girls it was the vestiges of consumer culture, such as clothes, that would become the means of dealing with this alienation and signifying this to others:

> Amanda: *I remember in grade 8 all of my friends decide to alienate me. So, I had to hang out with a different group of people. I decided to dress differently. I began to wear all black and started to hang out with the Mod crowd at school. Me and my friends, we were the Mod girls.*

This should come as no surprise, considering the idea that consumption can solve problems is a central doctrine of consumer culture. Advertising has been a highly successful discourse as it promises consumers that the solutions to their difficulties can be solved by products—even though many argue that consumer culture can never fully deliver on these promises (Leiss et al. 1997). Yet, in the narratives of these girls, consumer goods do offer potential solutions. For Amanda, clothes were a means of indicating the separation from her former crowd of friends and helped to ease her transition to a new group. The offerings of consumer culture played a central role for these girls in trying to locate themselves within the various social hierarchies of youth. This is what Celia Lury refers to when she describes identities as purchasable commodities (1997: 8). Consumer culture enables girls who have access to the right type of goods to navigate youth culture while hampering those who do not have this access.

Conclusion

The tween, as a specific demographic separate from childhood and adolescence, has been constructed within the socio-historical frames of consumer culture that have segmented and consolidated youth culture into separate niches in order to optimize marketing opportunities. The tween girl was constructed in the late 1980s as girls began to assert themselves as consumers with a healthy amount of power in the marketplace. This power has been recognized in purely economic terms based on how much money tween girls

spend or influence the spending of, and these girls are not credited with having any real agency. Tweens face this interpretation of having a lack of
agency on two fronts. First, young people have been constructed as being
devoid of agency, and second, the female, as the consumer, is perceived as
being passively manipulated by media culture. Since the tween is both young
and often female, she is constructed as not having any real power.

Yet, the young women interviewed for this paper suggest that they did
have a sense of agency, especially as consumers. In their descriptions of their
youth, having money and the power to buy what they wanted was incredibly
freeing and allowed them to separate themselves from parental control. In
addition, consumer purchases—particularly clothes—were an integral means
of negotiating the social hierarchy of youth culture. Consumer culture has
also provided a discourse for tween girls to construct notions of self. Tweenhood is unfixed; instead, it is a life-stage of transformation. To mark this
transformation, rituals that are framed by the marketplace such as shaving
with the pink Daisy razor or shopping without parental monitoring provided
the milestones for young girls in the 1980s. But at the same time, consumer
culture also supplied the vestiges of childhood that allowed young girls to
swing backwards to their youth, briefly postponing the inevitable shift to
maturity.

Although I am still not entirely sure of who I was in the 1980s, I now
have a much clearer understanding. My pink Polo shirt, Cabbage Patch doll,
and Madonna album were not insignificant items. They were tangible artifacts that provided frames for the negotiation of my young female self.

Notes

1   Mark is defining tween as ages 8–13. It should be noted that this is slightly different from
    Cuneo's definition of tweens as aged 9–15 and Zollo's categorization of them as 12–15.

2   The feminization of the consumer has its roots in rise of the department store in the latter
    half of the 19th century. For a discussion on this topic, see such works as Hollows (2000).

3   See, for example, the work that was being done during this time in Britain at the Centre
    for Contemporary Cultural Studies such as Hall and Jefferson (1976).

4   Tied to this fear of girls buying these consumer items is the greater panic around young
    girls' sexuality.

5   Woodward argues that asking about 'epiphanic' or important goods is a means of allowing
    the interviewee to construct a narrative around consumption (2001).

6   I have loosely narrowed my definition of tween to ages 10–13 since this means that the
    women were usually in grades 6–8. Asking questions based on the girls' experiences in
    various grades instead of by age is critical as it is easier for people to remember their ex-

periences in certain grades than at specific ages. Grade 6–8 is a natural division for young girls in Ontario as many students transfer to a Senior Public School for grade 6 to grade 8. By grade 9, students attend a high school, which is a very different social experience.

[7] These were not the only perquisites for status. Some interviewees also mentioned educational and athletic accomplishments or having a unique talent or a specific attitude as other signifiers for being cool, but these were never discussed with the same sense of importance as clothes and style.

[8] Although there has been a critique the artificiality of the notion of authenticity by such authors as David Muggleton (2000) and Angela McRobbie (1989), authenticity is still integral to youth's perceptions of subcultural capital.

References

Austin, J., and W. Michael., Eds. *Generations of Youth: Youth Cultures and History in the Twentieth Century America.* New York: New York UP, 1998.

Brooks, K. "Nothing Sells like Teen Spirit: The Commodification of Youth Culture." In *Youth Culture; Texts, Images and Identities,* edited by K. Mallan and S. Pearce, 1–16. Westport, Connecticut: Praeger, 2003.

Brumberg, J. J. *The Body Project: An Intimate History of American Girls.* New York: Random House, 1997.

Cohen, S. *Folk Devils and Moral Panic.* Oxford: Basil Blackwell, 1980.

Clark, A., "How Teens Got the Power." *Maclean,* March 22 1999, 42–50.

Crawford, M. "The World in a Shopping Mall." In *Variations on a Theme Park,* edited by M. Sorkin, 3–30. New York: Hill and Wang, 1992.

Cross, G. *An All-Consuming Century: Why Commercialism Won in Modern America.* New York: Columbia University Press, 2000.

Cuneo, A. "Curing Kids Who Want It All." *US News and World Report,* March 20, 1989, 83–85.

Currie, D. *Girl Talk: Adolescent Magazines and Their Readers.* Toronto: University of Toronto Press, 1999.

Driscoll, C. *Girls: feminine adolescence in popular culture & cultural theory.* New York: Columbia University Press, 2002.

Ewen, S. *Captains of Consciousness: Advertising and the Social Roots of Consumer Culture.* New York: McGraw-Hill Book Company, 1976.

Fiske, J. *Reading the Popular.* London: Routledge, 1989.

Global TV. "Tweens: Too Fast, Too Soon." Global Television and Pyramid Productions. Global TV: Toronto, April 23, 2003.

Griffin, C. *Representation of Youth. The Study of Youth and Adolescence in Britain and America.* Cambridge: Polity Press, 1993.

Hall, S., and T. Jefferson., eds. *Resistance through Rituals.* London: Routledge, 1976.

Hall, S., J. Clarke, T. Jefferson, and B. Roberts. "Subcultures, Cultures and Class." In *Resistance through Rituals,* edited by S. Hall and T. Jefferson, 100–111. London: Routledge, 1976.

Hebdige, D. *Subculture: The Meaning of Style.* London: Methuen, 1988.

Hollows, J. *Feminism, Femininity and Popular Culture*. Manchester: Manchester University Press, 2000.

Leiss, W., S. Kline, and S. Jhally. *Social Communication in Advertising,* 2nd edition. London: Routledge, 1997.

Lury, C. *Consumer Culture*. Oxford: Polity Press, 1996.

McCraken, G. *Culture and Consumption: New Approaches to the Symbolic Character of Consumer Goods*. Indianapolis: Indiana University Press, 1988.

McLaughlin, L. "Tweens Blossom as Consumer Group." *Ad Age,* October 14 1991, 63.

McRobbie, A. "Second Hand Dresses and the Role of the Rag Market." In *Zoot -Suits and Second Hand Dresses: An Anthology of Fashion and Music*, edited by A. McRobbie, 135–154. London, Macmillan Press: 1989.

McRobbie, A., and J. Garbner. "Girls and Subcultures: An Exploration." *Resistance through Rituals*, edited by S. Hall and T. Jefferson, 209–22. London: Routledge, 1976.

Mark, A. "Niche Markets." *Catalog Age*, February 1 2001.

Muggleton, D. *Inside Subculture: The Postmodern Meaning of Style*. New York. Berg Publishers, 2000.

Nava, M. *Changing Culture: Feminism, Youth and Consumerism*. London: Sage Publications, 1992.

Parr, J. *Domestic Goods: The Material, the Moral and the Economic in the Postwar Years*. Toronto: University of Toronto Press, 1999.

Ram, B. *Current Demographic Analysis: New Trends in the Family*. Ottawa: Minister of Supply and Services Canada, 1990.

Slater, D. *Consumer Culture and Modernity*. Oxford: Polity Press, 1997.

Steinberg, S. "Have Allowance, Will Transform Economy." *Canadian Business* 71.4 (March 13 1998) 58-71.

Thornton, S. "The Social Logic of Subcultural Capital." In *The Subcultures Reader*, edited by K. Gelder and S. Thornton, 200–209. New York: Routledge, 1997.

Valentine, G., T. Skelton, and D. Chambers. "Cool Places: An Introduction to Youth and Youth Culture." In *Cool Places: Geographies of Youth Cultures*, edited by T. Skelton and G. Valentine, 1–32. London: Routledge, 1998.

Williamson, J. "Woman Is an Island: Femininity and Colonization." In *Studies in Entertainment*, edited by T. Modleski, 99–118. Bloomington: Indiana University Press, 1986.

Woodward, I. "Domestic Objects and the Taste Epiphany: A Resource for Consumption Methodology." *Journal of Media Culture* 6, no. 20 (2001): 115–136.

CONTRIBUTORS

The Editors

Claudia Mitchell is a James McGill Professor in the Faculty of Education, at McGill University. She is the co-author of *That's Funny, You Don't Look Like a Teacher: Interrogating Images of Identity in Popular Culture* (with S. Weber, 1995); *Reinventing Ourselves as Teachers: Beyond Nostalgia* (with S. Weber, 1999); *Researching Children's Popular Culture: The Cultural Spaces of Childhood* (with J. Reid-Walsh, 2002); and co-editor of *Not Just Any Dress: Narratives of Memory, Body and Identity* (with S. Weber; Peter Lang, 2004); and *Just who do we think we are? Methodologies for autobiography and self-study in teaching* (with S. Weber and K. O'Reilly-Scanlon, 2005).

Jacqueline Reid-Walsh teaches at Bishop's University. She received her Ph.D. from McGill University in the Department of English in children's literature and in women writers of the late 18th century. In addition to publishing in both areas, she is co-author with C. Mitchell of *Researching Children's Popular Culture: The Cultural Spaces of Childhood* (2002).

Contributors

The Balkishori Team consists of health activists, a doctor, researchers, an educationist, an anthropologist, and media persons. Vacha (meaning speak or articulation in several Indian languages) is a Mumbai-based resource centre for women and girls. The centre offers a number of educational and health-based programs for pre-adolescent girls in the immediate area and in the surrounding region. They also serve as resource for training and development on gender and education.

Deevia Bhana's research deals with gender, sexuality, and young children. Her current research examines the notion of childhood innocence in the age of AIDS. She lectures in the School of Education at the University of Kwa-Zulu-Natal (Durban).

Meredith Cherland taught junior high and high school English for eight years in the United States and Canada before she became a teacher educator. Since 1978, she has served the Faculty of Education at the University of Regina, Saskatchewan, as Professor of Language and Literacy Education. In 1994, she received the University of Regina's Alumni Award for Excellence in Undergraduate Teaching. In 1997, she was awarded a national 3M Teaching Fellowship. She is the author of *Private Practices: Girls Reading Fiction and Constructing Identity* (1994) and of many articles about gender, justice, literature, and teaching.

Hoi F. Cheu teaches film theory and media aesthetics at Laurentian University, Sudbury, Ontario, and will soon publish *Postfeminist Story Re-visions: Metafiction in Women's Cinema.*

Natalie Coulter is currently working on her doctoral dissertation at Simon Fraser University in the area of youth, gender, and consumer culture. She is particularly interested in how both girls and boys used consumer products in the 1980s as a means of constructing their gender identities. She teaches in the Communication Studies department at Wilfred Laurier University. Coulter has co-authored a report for MediaWatch entitled "Watching the Watchers: Gender Justice and Co-Regulation in the New Media Marketplace."

Catherine Driscoll is a Senior Lecturer in Gender and Cultural Studies at the University of Sydney, Australia, where she is also convenor of Graduate Studies. Her research and teaching are strongly interdisciplinary, encompassing media, film and popular culture, philosophy and cultural theory, literature, modernism, and sociological analysis of gender and youth. Recent key publications include essays on Deleuze and Kristeva for *Deleuze and Feminist Theory* (2000), DeCerteau and the everyday for *South Atlantic Quarterly* (2001), and her first book, *Girls: Feminine Adolescence in Popular Culture and Cultural Theory* (2002). Forthcoming publications include books on *Buffy the Vampire Slayer* and modernist cultural studies.

Sonya Corbin Dwyer is an Associate Professor of Educational Psychology at the Faculty of Education, University of Regina. Her current areas of scholarship are women and education, metacognition, assessment and evaluation, experiences of psychiatric labels, teacher wellness, and roles and responsibilities of guidance counselors in local and Chinese settings. Sonya earned her Ph.D. from the University of Calgary.

Marika Flockemann teaches at the University of the Western Cape. Her primary research interest is the comparative study of the aesthetics of transformation. Her publications include comparative studies of writing by women from South Africa and the African and Asian Diasporas, youth literature, teaching methodologies and South African theatre and performance.

Marnina Gonick is the author of *Between Femininities: Ambivalence, Identity and the Education of Girls*, (2003). She is also co-author of *Young Femininity: Girls, Power, and Social Change* (with S. Aapola and A. Harris, 2005). She completed her doctoral work in the Dept of Sociology and Equity Studies at the Ontario Institute of Studies in Education/University of Toronto. She is currently Assistant Professor of Curriculum, Instruction, and Women's Studies at the Pennsylvania State University.

Kristina Hackmann is a sociologist at the Center for Interdisciplinary Research on Women and Gender Studies at the University of Oldenburg, Germany. Her current research project is the status of women in the scientific discipline of mathematics. Her main academic fields are empirical women and gender studies, girlhood and heteronormativity, qualitative methods in social and educational Studies. She completed her Ph.D. at Oldenburg University with an empirical study on female adolescence. She studied Education and Women Studies at Bremen University (Germany) and Middlesex University London (UK).

Anita Harris lectures in Sociology at Monash University, Australia. She is the author of *Future Girl: Young Women in the Twenty First Century,* (2004); co-author of *Young Femininity: Girlhood, Power and Social Change* (with S. Aapola and M. Gonick, 2005); and editor of *All About the Girl: Power, Culture and Identity*, (2004).

Yasmin Jiwani is a faculty member in the Department of Communication Studies at Concordia University. Prior to her move to Montreal, she was the Executive Coordinator and Principal Researcher at the BC/Yukon FREDA Center for Research on Violence Against Women and Children. In that capacity, she conducted numerous participatory action research studies on the impact of violence on diverse communities. Her interest in issues pertaining to violence stems from her advocacy within the wider anti-racism movement and her research background on race and racism. Her doctoral dissertation at Simon Fraser University dealt with race and representation in mainstream Canadian television news.

Jackie Kirk completed her PhD in the Faculty of Education, McGill University in 2003, and has since been working on post-doc research on the topic of gender, education and conflict with the UNESCO Centre at the University of Ulster. She has been collaborating with Vacha since 2002 and has worked with them on a number of publications.

Amy T.Y. Lai earned her B.A. and MPhil. in Comparative Literature from The Chinese University of Hong Kong, before doing her Ph.D. in Postcolonial and Gender Studies at Cambridge. She is now a visiting scholar with the School of Humanities and Social Sciences, The Hong Kong University of Science and Technology. Her publications include essays on Gao Xingjian and other Chinese writers. Forthcoming work includes a monograph on *Golden Chicken*, a Hong Kong film.

Farah Malik has completed her Master's degree in Media and Communications at the London School of Economics. Her interests lie in theories of urban space, fashion, music, and material culture. A major theme in all of her academic, professional, as well as community work has been to instigate and maintain a cross-pollination of ideas between dominant and marginal artistic genres and cultural groups. She is currently writing a book, *The Rise and Fall of Cassette Tape Culture.*

Relebohile Moletsane is Associate Professor in the School of Education at the University of KwaZulu-Natal, Durban. She teaches and researches in the fields of curriculum studies, professional development, human rights education, and youth, race, gender, health, HIV and AIDS education.

Kathleen O'Reilly-Scanlon teaches undergraduate and graduate courses in language arts, literacy, and curriculum at the Faculty of Education, University of Regina, in western Canada. Her research interests are primarily in the area of literacy and teacher education, with an emphasis on memory work, self-study, and Indigenous education and research methodologies. She is a co-editor of *Just who do we think we are? Methodologies for autobiography and self-study in teaching* (with C. Mitchell and S. Weber, 2005). She received her Ph.D. from McGill University.

Elizabeth Seaton is Director of York University's Graduate Program in Communication and Culture and a faculty member of the Communication Studies Program. She is currently completing a book on the historical relationships of biological and social reproduction.

Peggy Tally is an Associate Professor of Sociology at the State University of New York, Empire State College, where she teaches in the area of media studies, gender and family studies, and the sociology of work. Her book, *Television Culture and Women's Lives: Thirtysomething and the Contradictions of Gender* (1995), was an ethnographic study of female viewers of the television show *Thirtysomething*. She has also published in the area of women and work, most recently in the edited volume titled, *The Politics of Selfhood: Bodies and Identities in Global Capitalism* (2003). Her recent work includes research into Eastern European and Western European women's views of U.S. popular films, and she is also currently working on a study of tween girls' reception of *The Lord of the Rings: Return of the King*.

Shannon Walsh is a researcher, filmmaker, and activist working out of McGill University. Walsh recently directed *Fire & Hope*, a film about HIV and AIDS made with youth, for youth, in South Africa and is currently finishing a fiction film and a documentary on youth and youth culture. Her research areas focus on arts-based methodology and activism, independent and community-based film, youth, gender, HIV and AIDS. She has contributed chapters to collected works and has also published a number of articles in journals such as *Feminist Media Studies*, *Agenda,* and *Sex Education*. Walsh received her M.A. from Concordia University's Special Individualized Program.

Rebekah Willett taught primary school for 12 years whilst pursuing her academic interest in children's popular culture. She received her M.A. and Ph.D. from the Institute of Education, University of London, studying children's story writing, identity work, and media cultures. Rebekah now works as a research officer at the Centre for the Study of Children, Youth, and Media at the Institute of Education, conducting research that focuses on the digital practices of children and young people.

AUTHOR INDEX

SUBJECT INDEX

Studies in the Postmodern Theory of Education

General Editors
Joe L. Kincheloe & Shirley R. Steinberg

Counterpoints publishes the most compelling and imaginative books being written in education today. Grounded on the theoretical advances in criticalism, feminism, and postmodernism in the last two decades of the twentieth century, Counterpoints engages the meaning of these innovations in various forms of educational expression. Committed to the proposition that theoretical literature should be accessible to a variety of audiences, the series insists that its authors avoid esoteric and jargonistic languages that transform educational scholarship into an elite discourse for the initiated. Scholarly work matters only to the degree it affects consciousness and practice at multiple sites. Counterpoints' editorial policy is based on these principles and the ability of scholars to break new ground, to open new conversations, to go where educators have never gone before.

For additional information about this series or for the submission of manuscripts, please contact:

> Joe L. Kincheloe & Shirley R. Steinberg
> c/o Peter Lang Publishing, Inc.
> 29 Broadway, 18th floor
> New York, New York 10006

To order other books in this series, please contact our Customer Service Department:
> (800) 770-LANG (within the U.S.)
> (212) 647-7706 (outside the U.S.)
> (212) 647-7707 FAX

Or browse online by series:
> www.peterlang.com